GW00853290

# UK income tax rates (England, Wales and N

| | 2017-18 | 2016-17 | 2015-16 |
|---|---|---|---|
| | % | % | % |
| Basic rate[1] | 20 | 20 | 20 |
| Higher rate[1] | 40 | 40 | 40 |
| Additional rate[1] | 45 | 45 | 45 |
| Starting rate for savings income[2] | 0 | 0 | 0 |
| Savings basic rate[3] | 20 | — | — |
| Savings higher rate[3] | 40 | — | — |
| Savings additional rate[3] | 45 | — | — |
| Dividend ordinary rate [effective rate with tax credit[4]] | 7.5 | 7.5 | 10 [0] |
| Dividend upper rate [effective rate with tax credit[4]] | 32.5 | 32.5 | 32.5 [25] |
| Dividend additional rate [effective rate with tax credit[4]] | 38.1 | 38.1 | 37.5 [30.6] |
| Default basic rate[5] | 20 | — | — |
| Default higher rate[5] | 40 | — | — |
| Default additional rate[5] | 45 | — | — |
| Trust rate | 45 | 45 | 45 |
| Dividend trust rate | 38.1 | 38.1 | 37.5 |
| | £ | £ | £ |
| Starting rate limit (savings income)[3] | 5,000 | 5,000 | 5,000 |
| Basic rate band | 1–33,500 | 1–32,000 | 1–31,785 |
| Maximum at basic rate | 33,500 | 32,000 | 31,785 |
| Higher rate band | 33,501–150,000 | 32,001–150,000 | 31,786–150,000 |
| Maximum at higher rate | 116,500 | 118,000 | 118,215 |

**Notes**

[1] From 2017–18, the main rates are separated into the main rates, the savings rates and the default rates with the main rates continuing to apply to non-savings, non-dividend income only (income to which the main rates apply includes income from employment, property or pensions not subject to the Scottish rate of income tax). Prior to 6 April 2017, main rates applied to all non-dividend income, including income from savings, employment, property or pensions.

[2] The starting rate is available for savings income only. If an individual's taxable non-savings income (i.e. after deduction of their personal allowance) exceeds the starting rate limit, then the starting rate is not available.

[3] From 6 April 2017, savings rates apply to savings income. Prior to 6 April 2017, basic rate, higher rate or additional rate applied.

[4] From April 2016, the dividend tax credit is abolished and replaced with a £5,000 tax-free dividend allowance.

[5] From 6 April 2017, the default rates apply to non-savings and non-dividend income of any taxpayer that is not subject to either the main rates or the Scottish rates of income tax.

## Scottish income tax rates

| | 2017-18 | 2016-17 | 2015-16 |
|---|---|---|---|
| | % | % | % |
| Basic rate[2] | 20 | 20[1] | — |
| Higher rate[2] | 40 | 40[1] | |
| Additional rate[2] | 45 | 45[1] | |
| | £ | £ | £ |
| Basic rate band | 1–31,500 | 1–32,000[3] | — |
| Maximum at basic rate | 31,500 | 32,000[3] | |
| Higher rate band | 31,501–150,000 | 32,001–150,000[3] | |
| Maximum at higher rate | 118,500 | 118,000[3] | |

**Notes**

[1] For the 2016–17 tax year, the Scottish rate of income tax was 10% and was added to the UK basic rate, higher rate or additional rate minus ten percentage points; the rates shown in the table above are the resultant effective rates. See ¶1-100 for full table of rates.

[2] For the tax year 2017–18 and subsequent tax years, separate rates of income tax apply to certain non-savings and non-dividend income of a Scottish taxpayer (ITA 2007, s. 11A).

[3] UK income tax bands applied for the tax year 2016–17.

## Income tax reliefs

| | 2017–18 £ | 2016–17 £ | 2015–16 £ |
|---|---|---|---|
| Personal allowance[1] | 11,500 | 11,000 | — |
| – born after 5 April 1948 | — | — | 10,600 |
| – born after 5 April 1938 but before 6 April 1948 | — | — | 10,600 |
| – born before 6 April 1938 | — | — | 10,660 |
| Income limit for personal allowance | 100,000 | 100,000 | 100,000 |
| Marriage allowance | 1,150 | 1,100 | 1,060 |
| Married couple's allowance | | | |
| – entitlement partner born before 6 April 1935 | 8,445 | 8,355 | 8,355 |
| Minimum amount of allowance | 3,260 | 3,220 | 3,220 |
| Income limit for MCA (reliefs for older taxpayers) | 28,000 | 27,700 | 27,700 |
| Abatement income ceilings | | | |
| Personal allowance (basic) | 123,000 | 122,000 | 121,200 |
| Single (age personal allowance) | | | |
|     – born after 5 April 1938 but before 6 April 1948 | — | — | — |
|     – born before 6 April 1938 | — | — | 27,820 |
| Married couples allowance (only) | 38,370 | 37,970 | 37,970 |
| Married (age personal allowance and MCA) | | | |
|     – born after 5 April 1938 but before 6 April 1948 | — | — | — |
|     – born before 6 April 1938 | — | — | 38,090 |
| Blind person's allowance | 2,320 | 2,290 | 2,290 |
| Dividend allowance | 5,000 | 5,000 | — |
| Personal savings allowance | | | |
| – basic rate taxpayers | 1,000 | 1,000 | — |
| – higher rate taxpayers | 500 | 500 | — |
| 'Rent-a-room' limit | 7,500 | 7,500 | 4,250 |

**Note**

[1] From 2016–17 onwards, all individuals are entitled to the same personal allowance, regardless of the individual's date of birth.

## National Insurance contributions

| Class 1 primary (employee) contributions | 2017–18 | 2016–17 | 2015–16 |
|---|---|---|---|
| Lower earnings limit (LEL) | £113 weekly | £112 weekly | £112 weekly |
| Primary threshold | £157 weekly | £155 weekly | £155 weekly |
| Upper earnings limit (UEL) | £866 weekly | £827 weekly | £815 weekly |
| Upper accrual point (UAP) | — | — | £770 weekly |
| Rate on earnings up to primary threshold | 0% | 0% | 0% |
| Rate above primary threshold | 12% on £157.01 to £866 weekly; 2% above £866 | 12% on £155.01 to £827 weekly; 2% above £827 | — |
| Not contracted-out rate | — | — | 12% on £155.01 to £815 weekly; 2% above £815 weekly |
| Contracted-out rate | — | — | 10.6% on £155.01 to £770 weekly; 12% on £770.01 to £815 weekly; 2% above £815 weekly |
| Reduced rate | 5.85% on £157.01 to £866 weekly; 2% above £866 | 5.85% on £155.01 to £827 weekly; 2% above £827 | 5.85% on £155.01 to £815 weekly; 2% above £815 |

| Class 1 secondary (employer) contributions | 2017–18 | 2016–17 | 2015–16 |
|---|---|---|---|
| Secondary earnings threshold (ST) | £157 weekly £680 monthly £8,164 yearly | £156 weekly £676 monthly £8,112 yearly | £156 weekly £676 monthly £8,112 yearly |
| Upper secondary threshold for U21s (UST) | £866 weekly £3,750 monthly £45,000 yearly | £827 weekly £3,583 monthly £43,000 yearly | £815 weekly £3,532 monthly £42,385 yearly |
| Apprentice upper secondary threshold for U25s (AUST) | £866 weekly £3,750 monthly £45,000 yearly | £827 weekly £3,583 monthly £43,000 yearly | – |
| Rate | 13.8% on earnings above the ST/UST/AUST | 13.8% on earnings above the ST/UST/AUST | – |
| Not contracted-out rate | – | – | 13.8% on earnings above the ST/UST |
| Contracted-out rate | – | – | 10.4% for salary-related (COSR) on earnings from ST to UAP (plus 3.4% rebate on earnings from LEL to ST), then 13.8% above UAP |
| Employment allowance (per year, per employer) | £3,000 | £3,000 | £2,000 |

| Class 2 – Self-employed | 2017–18 | 2016–17 | 2015–16 |
|---|---|---|---|
| | £ | £ | £ |
| Small earnings exemption limit (annual) | 6,025 | 5,965 | 5,965 |
| Weekly rate | 2.85 | 2.80 | 2.80 |
| **Class 3 – Voluntary contributions** | **2017–18** | **2016–17** | **2015–16** |
| | £ | £ | £ |
| Weekly rate | 14.25 | 14.10 | 14.10 |
| **Class 4 – Self-employed** | **2017–18** | **2016–17** | **2015–16** |
| | £ | £ | £ |
| Annual earnings limit – upper | 45,000 | 43,000 | 42,385 |
| – lower | 8,164 | 8,060 | 8,060 |
| Rate | 9% (£8,164–£45,000); 2% above £45,000 | 9% (£8,060–£43,000); 2% above £43,000 | 9% (£8,060–£42,385); 2% above £42,385 |

## Taxation of capital gains

| | Individuals % | Trustees and PRs % |
|---|---|---|
| **2016–17 and 2017–18** | | |
| – Gains eligible for entrepreneurs' relief | 10 | 10 |
| – Standard rate (within income tax basic rate band) | 10 | 28 |
| – Higher rate (above income tax basic rate band) | 20 | |
| – Gains on residential property not eligible for private residence relief and carried interest gains | 18/28 | 28 |
| **2011–12 to 2015–16** | | |
| – Gains eligible for entrepreneurs' relief | 10 | 10 |
| – Standard rate (within income tax basic rate band) | 18 | 28 |
| – Higher rate (above income tax basic rate band) | 28 | |

| Exemptions and reliefs | 2017–18 £ | 2016–17 & 2015–16 £ | 2014–15 £ |
|---|---|---|---|
| Annual exempt amount | 11,300 | 11,100 | 11,000 |
| Chattel exemption (max. sale proceeds) | 6,000 | 6,000 | 6,000 |

## Inheritance tax

| | Gross rate of tax | |
|---|---|---|
| **Gross cumulative transfer (on or after 6 April 2017)** | Transfers on death % | Lifetime transfers % |
| £1–£325,000 | Nil | Nil |
| Above £325,000     Rate | 40 | 20 |
|     Reduced rate for estates leaving 10% or more to charity | 36 | – |

**Note**
Estate on death taxed as top slice of cumulative transfers in the seven years before death. Most lifetime transfers (other than to discretionary trusts) are potentially exempt, only becoming chargeable where death occurs within seven years.

| Residence nil-rate band | | Tapered withdrawal | |
|---|---|---|---|
| Year of death | Additional nil-rate band £ | Net estate value £ | Withdrawal rate |
| 2017–18 | 100,000 | > £2m | £1 for £2 |

| | |
|---|---|
| Annual exemption | £3,000 |
| Small gift exemption (to the same person) | £250 |

## Taxation of companies

| Financial year | 2017 | 2016 | 2015 |
|---|---|---|---|
| Main rate[1] | 19% | 20% | 20% |
| Intellectual property rate | 10% | 10% | 10% |

**Note**
[1] Main rate on ring fence profits (CTA 2010, s. 276) is 30%, small profits rate is 19% and the marginal relief ring fenced fraction is 11/400ths.

## VAT

| Standard rate | |
|---|---|
| From 4 January 2011 | 20% |
| 1 January 2010 – 3 January 2011 | 17.5% |
| 1 December 2008 – 31 December 2009 | 15% |
| 1 April 1991 – 30 November 2008 | 17.5% |
| Annual registration limit – taxable supplies (from 1 April 2017) | 85,000 |
| Deregistration limit – taxable supplies (from 1 April 2017) | 83,000 |
| VAT fraction | |
| For standard rate of 20% | 1/6 |
| For standard rate of 17.5% | 7/47 |
| For standard rate of 15% | 3/23 |

## Bank base rates

| Date effective | | Rate % | Date effective | | Rate % |
|---|---|---|---|---|---|
| 2016 | 4 August | 0.25 | 2006 | 9 November | 5.00 |
| 2009 | 5 March | 0.50 | | 3 August | 4.75 |
| | 5 February | 1.00 | 2005 | 4 August | 4.50 |
| | 8 January | 1.50 | 2004 | 5 August | 4.75 |
| 2008 | 4 December | 2.00 | | 10 June | 4.50 |
| | 6 November | 3.00 | | 6 May | 4.25 |
| | 8 October | 4.50 | | 5 February | 4.00 |
| | 10 April | 5.00 | 2003 | 6 November | 3.75 |
| | 7 February | 5.25 | | 10 July | 3.50 |
| 2007 | 6 December | 5.50 | | 6 February | 3.75 |
| | 5 July | 5.75 | 2001 | 8 November | 4.00 |
| | 10 May | 5.50 | | 4 October | 4.50 |
| | 11 January | 5.25 | | | |

# PREFACE

Now in its 51st edition, *Hardman's Tax Rates & Tables* contains the numerical and factual data in everyday use by the tax practitioner. The material is conveniently arranged in 23 chapters:

- Principles of income tax
- Taxation of business profits
- Taxation of investment income
- Taxation of earnings
- Taxation of capital gains
- Inheritance tax
- Taxation of companies
- Capital allowances
- National Insurance contributions
- Tax credits
- State benefits and statutory payments
- General
- Stamp taxes
- Value added tax
- Insurance premium tax
- Landfill tax
- Aggregates levy
- Climate change levy
- Air passenger duty
- Vehicle excise duty
- Scottish taxes
- Welsh taxes
- Northern Irish taxes

This edition takes full account of Spring Budget 2017.

Cross-references to CCH's *Tax Reporter, Indirect Tax Reporter* and *SDLT Reporter* are included.

The data in this book is maintained by Sarah Arnold of Elucidate Tax Limited and CCH's team of tax writers: Mark Cawthron, Julie Clift, Paul Davies, Stanley Dencher, Stephen Relf and Meg Wilson.

Every effort has been taken to include, within the constraints of available space, th~ information of greatest use to the practitioner. A number of changes have been m~nes the light of suggestions received from users of previous years' editions. CCH ᵥ further suggestions as to material which might be inserted in future edition~aul Robbins

April 2017

**Note:** the late Philip Hardman was the original edit~ CCH gratefully acknowledges the considerable b~

~n's Tax Rates & Tables.
~nce that he provided.

## Disclaimer

This publication is sold with the understanding that neither the publisher nor the authors, with regard to this publication, are engaged in rendering legal or professional services. The material contained in this publication neither purports, nor is intended to be, advice on any particular matter.

Although this publication incorporates a considerable degree of standardisation, subjective judgment by the user, based on individual circumstances, is indispensable. This publication is an 'aid' and cannot be expected to replace such judgment.

Neither the publisher nor the authors can accept any responsibility or liability to any person, whether a purchaser of this publication or not, in respect of anything done or omitted to be done by any such person in reliance, whether sole or partial, upon the whole or any part of the contents of this publication.

## Legislative and other material

While copyright in all statutory and other materials resides in the Crown or other relevant body, copyright in the remaining material in this publication is vested in the publisher.

The publisher advises that any statutory or other materials issued by the Crown or other relevant bodies and reproduced and quoted in this publication are not the authorised official versions of those statutory or other materials. In the preparation, however, the greatest care has been taken to ensure exact conformity with the law as enacted or other material as issued.

Crown copyright legislation is reproduced under the terms of Crown Copyright Policy Guidance issued by HMSO. Other Crown copyright material is reproduced with the permission of the controller of HMSO. European Communities Copyright material is reproduced with permission.

## Telephone Helpline Disclaimer Notice

Where purchasers of this publication also have access to any Telephone Helpline Service operated by Wolters Kluwer (UK), then Wolters Kluwer's total liability to contract, tort (including negligence, or breach of statutory duty) misrepresentation, restitution or otherwise with respect to any claim arising out of its acts or alleged omissions in the provision of the Helpline Service shall be limited to the yearly subscription fee paid by the Claimant.

ISBN: 978-1-78540-387-3
CCH Code: UP/TRT-BI17001

British Library Cataloguing-in-Publication Data.

A catalogue record for this book is available from the British Library.

Typeset by Innodata Inc., India

Printed by Gutenberg Press Ltd, Malta

# About the Publisher

CCH is part of the Wolters Kluwer Group. Wolters Kluwer is the leading international publisher specialising in tax, business and law publishing throughout Europe, the US and the Asia Pacific region. The Group produces a wide range of information services in different media for the accounting and legal professions and for business.

All CCH publications are designed to be practical and authoritative reference works and guides and are written by our own highly qualified and experienced editorial team and specialist outside authors.

CCH publishes information packages including electronic products, loose-leaf reporting services, newsletters and books on UK and European legal topics for distribution world-wide. The UK operation also acts as distributor of the publications of the overseas affiliates.

Wolters Kluwer
145 London Road
Kingston upon Thames
KT2 6SR
Telephone: 0844 561 8166
Facsimile: +44 (0)208 247 2637
E-mail: uk-customer.services@wolterskluwer.com
Website: www.wolterskluwer.com

# Acknowledgements

Certain material in this publication is Crown Copyright and is reproduced with the kind permission of the Controller of Her Majesty's Stationery Office.

CCH acknowledges the endorsement of this publication by the Chartered Institute of Taxation and the Tax Faculty of the Institute of Chartered Accountants in England and Wales.

THE
CHARTERED
INSTITUTE OF
TAXATION

The Association of Taxation Technicians

# PRINCIPLES OF INCOME TAX

## INCOME TAX RATES

**Note**: See also ¶26-100 for rates applicable in Scotland from April 2016.

### [¶1-000]   Structure of income tax rates: 2017–18

(ITA 2007, s. 9A, 10–15; FA 2016, s. 6)

*Finance Act* 2016 includes legislation to separate the income tax rates that apply to savings (the savings rates), from those that apply to non-savings, non-dividends income (the main rates), with effect for the tax year 2017–18 (as the first tax year for which the Scottish Government can set Scottish rates of income tax (SI 2016/1161, reg. 3)) and subsequent tax years, in order to facilitate the devolution of income tax rates to Scotland (for Scottish taxpayers) and, in due course, to Wales (for Welsh taxpayers).

The savings and dividend rates are not being devolved and will apply across the UK whereas the main rates will be devolved to Scotland from April 2017 (for Scottish taxpayers) and, in due course, to Wales (for Welsh taxpayers).

*Finance Act* 2016 also creates a default rate of income tax on non-savings, non-dividends income that will apply to, but is not limited to, trustees and non-residents.

The general effect of ITA 2007, s. 10–15 is outlined in the following table:

| Type of taxpayer | Rates payable on savings income | Rates payable on most dividend income | Rates payable on other income |
|---|---|---|---|
| UK resident individual who is neither a Scottish taxpayer nor a Welsh taxpayer | Savings rates | Dividend rates | Main rates |
| Scottish taxpayer | Savings rates | Dividend rates | Scottish rates |
| Welsh taxpayer | Savings rates | Dividend rates | Main rates while ITA 2007, s. 11B is not in force; Welsh rates once in force |
| Non-UK resident individual | Savings rates | Dividend rates | Default rates |
| Non-individual, except some trustees subject to trust rate or dividend trust rate in certain circumstances | Default basic rate | Dividend ordinary rate | Default basic rate |

**Note**

[1] The table does not address the effect of some exceptions referred to in ITA 2007, s. 10–15.

# [¶1-003]  Income tax rates: 2017–18

(ITA 2007, s. 6–9; FA 2016, s. 6)
(Tax Reporter: ¶148-075ff.)

|  | Rate % | Taxable income band £ | Tax on band £ |
|---|---|---|---|
| **Main rates**[(1)(2)] | | | |
| Basic rate | 20 | 1–33,500[(3)] | 6,700 |
| Higher rate | 40 | 33,501–150,000 | 46,600 |
| Additional rate | 45 | Over 150,000 | |
| **Default rates**[(4)] | | | |
| Default basic rate | 20 | 1–33,500[(3)] | 6,700 |
| Default higher rate | 40 | 33,501–150,000 | 46,600 |
| Default additional rate | 45 | Over 150,000 | |
| **Scottish rates** | | | |
| Scottish basic rate | 20 | 1–31,500 | 6,300 |
| Scottish higher rate | 40 | 31,501–150,000 | 47,400 |
| Scottish additional rate | 45 | Over 150,000 | |

| Other rates | Rate % | Taxable income |
|---|---|---|
| **Savings rates** | | |
| Starting rate for savings[(5)] | 0 | £1–£5,000 |
| Savings nil rate[(6)] | 0 | First £1,000 or £500 |
| Savings basic rate | 20 | Savings income otherwise chargeable at basic rate or default basic rate |
| Savings higher rate | 40 | Savings income otherwise chargeable at higher rate or default higher rate |
| Savings additional rate | 45 | Savings income otherwise chargeable at additional rate or default additional rate |
| **Dividend rates** | | |
| Dividend nil rate[(7)] | 0 | First £5,000 |
| Dividend ordinary rate | 7.5 | Dividend income otherwise chargeable at basic rate or Scottish basic rate |
| Dividend upper rate | 32.5 | Dividend income otherwise chargeable at higher rate or Scottish higher rate |
| Dividend additional rate | 38.1 | Dividend income otherwise chargeable at additional rate or Scottish additional rate |

| Other rates | Rate % | Taxable income |
|---|---|---|
| **Special rates for trustees' income**[8] | | |
| Trust rate | 45 | Trustees accumulated or discretionary income and other amounts under ITA 2007, Pt. 9, Ch. 3–6 |
| Dividend trust rate | 38.1 | |

**Notes**

[1] Income tax lock: F(No. 2)A 2015, s. 1 sets a ceiling for the main rates of income tax at 20%, 40% and 45% respectively for tax years beginning on or after 18 November 2015 (Royal Assent) but before the date of the first parliamentary general election after that day.

[2] From 2017–18, the main rates are separated into the main rates, the savings rates and the default rates. From 6 April 2017, the main rates apply to non-savings, non-dividend income (income to which the main rates apply includes income from employment, property or pensions not subject to the Scottish rate of income tax). Prior to 6 April 2017, the main rates applied to all non-dividend income, including income from savings, employment, property or pensions.

[3] Autumn Statement 2016 confirmed the Government's commitment to raise the income tax personal allowance to £12,500 and the higher rate threshold to £50,000, by the end of this Parliament, on which figures the basic rate limit will increase to £37,500.

[4] Default rates apply from 6 April 2017 to non-savings and non-dividend income of any taxpayer that is not subject to either the main rates or the Scottish rates of income tax.

[5] The 'starting rate for savings' is available for savings income only. If an individual's taxable non-savings income (i.e. after deduction of their personal allowance) exceeds the starting rate, then the starting rate is not available and an individual's savings income is chargeable at the nil rate (to the extent available), the basic, higher or additional rate (as would otherwise apply).

[6] From 6 April 2016, a savings allowance is available to individuals with savings income, 'the savings nil rate'. The savings allowance is £1,000 for basic rate taxpayers, £500 for higher rate taxpayers and nil for additional rate taxpayers. Savings income within the savings allowance is chargeable at the savings nil rate 0% (ITA 2007, s. 12A and 12B). The 'savings nil rate' is available in addition to the 'starting rate for savings' (where this is available) on savings income above the starting rate limit.

[7] From April 2016, the dividend tax credit was abolished and replaced with a £5,000 tax-free dividend allowance. The allowance operates as a 0% tax rate substituted for the dividend ordinary rate, dividend upper rate or dividend additional rate as would otherwise apply on the first £5,000 of an individual's dividend income (ITA 2007, s. 13A). From April 2018, the dividend allowance will be reduced to £2,000 (Spring Budget 2017; Finance Bill 2017).

[8] The special trust rates do not apply to the first £1,000 slice of the 'trust rate income'. Instead, the normal income tax rates (currently the basic rate and dividend ordinary rate) apply as appropriate (ITA 2007, s. 491(1)–(3)).

# [¶1-004]   Income tax rates: 2016–17

(ITA 2007, s. 6–15; FA 2015, s. 4; FA 2016, s. 1)

(Tax Reporter: ¶148-075ff.)

## UK rates (England, Wales and Northern Ireland)

| | Taxable income band £ | Tax rate[1] % | Tax on band £ |
|---|---|---|---|
| Basic rate | 1–32,000 | 20 | 6,400 |
| Higher rate | 32,001–150,000 | 40 | 47,200 |
| Additional rate | Over 150,000 | 45 | |
| Starting rate for savings income | 1–5,000 | 0 | |

## Scottish rates

| UK rate for England, Wales and Northern Ireland | Taxable income band £ | UK rate paid in Scotland % | Scottish rate % | Total rate for Scottish taxpayers % |
|---|---|---|---|---|
| Basic rate 20% | 1–32,000 | 10 | 10 | 20 |
| Higher rate 40% | 32,001–150,000 | 30 | 10 | 40 |
| Additional rate 45% | Over £150,000 | 35 | 10 | 45 |

## Savings, dividends and special trust rates

| | |
|---|---|
| Starting rate for savings income[2] | 0% up to starting rate limit |
| Rate on non-dividend savings income | 0% on savings income charged at the savings nil rate[2]<br>20% up to basic rate limit<br>40% up to higher rate limit<br>45% thereafter |
| Dividend nil rate[4] | 0% on first £5,000 dividends |
| Dividend ordinary rate | 7.5%[4] up to basic rate limit |
| Dividend upper rate | 32.5%[4] up to higher rate limit |
| Dividend additional rate | 38.1%[4] above higher rate limit |
| Trust rate | 45%[3] |
| Dividend trust rate | 38.1%[3] |

**Notes**

[1] Income tax lock: F(No. 2)A 2015, s. 1 sets a ceiling for the main rates of income tax at 20%, 40% and 45% respectively for tax years beginning on or after 18 November 2015 (Royal Assent) but before the date of the first parliamentary general election after that day.

[2] The 'starting rate for savings' is available for savings income only. If an individual's taxable non-savings income (i.e. after deduction of their personal allowance) exceeds the starting rate limit, then the starting rate is not available and an individual's savings income is chargeable at the basic, higher or additional rate (as would otherwise apply). From 6 April 2016, a new savings allowance is available to individuals with savings income, 'the savings nil rate'. The savings allowance is £1,000 for basic rate taxpayers, £500 for higher rate taxpayers and nil for additional rate taxpayers. Savings income within the savings allowance is chargeable at the savings nil rate 0% (ITA 2007, s. 12A and 12B). The 'savings nil rate' is available in addition to the 'starting rate for savings' (where this is available) on savings income above the starting rate limit.

[3] The special trust rates do not apply to the first £1,000 slice of the 'trust rate income'. Instead, the normal income tax rates (currently the basic rate and dividend ordinary rate) apply as appropriate (ITA 2007, s. 491(1)–(3)).

[4] From April 2016, the dividend tax credit was abolished and replaced with a £5,000 tax-free dividend allowance. The allowance operates as a 0% tax rate substituted for the dividend ordinary rate, dividend upper rate or dividend additional rate as would otherwise apply on the first £5,000 of an individual's dividend income (ITA 2007, s. 13A).

## [¶1-005]   Income tax rates: 2015–16

(ITA 2007, s. 6–15; FA 2014, s. 2)

(Tax Reporter: ¶148-075ff.)

**2015–16**

|  | Taxable income band £ | Tax rate % | Tax on band £ |
|---|---|---|---|
| Basic rate | 1–31,785 | 20 | 6,357 |
| Higher rate | 31,786–150,000 | 40 | 47,286 |
| Additional rate | Over 150,000 | 45 |  |

| Rate on non-dividend savings income | 0% up to £5,000[1]<br>20% up to basic rate limit<br>40% up to higher rate limit<br>45% thereafter |
|---|---|
| Dividend ordinary rate<br>(effective rate with tax credit) | 10% up to basic rate limit<br>0% |
| Dividend upper rate<br>(effective rate with tax credit) | 32.5% up to higher rate limit<br>25% |
| Dividend additional rate<br>(effective rate with tax credit) | 37.5% above higher rate limit<br>30.6% |
| Trust rate | 45%[2] |
| Dividend trust rate | 37.5%[2] |

**Notes**

[1] The starting rate is available for savings income only. If an individual's taxable non-savings income (i.e. after deduction of their personal allowance) exceeds the starting rate limit, then the starting rate is not be available.

[2] The special trust rates do not apply to the first £1,000 slice of the 'trust rate income'. Instead, the normal income tax rates (currently the basic rate and dividend ordinary rate) apply as appropriate (ITA 2007, s. 491(1)–(3)).

## [¶1-006]   Income tax rates: 2014–15

(ITA 2007, s. 6–15; FA 2014, s. 1)

(Tax Reporter: ¶148-075ff.)

**2014–15**

|  | Taxable income band £ | Tax rate % | Tax on band £ |
|---|---|---|---|
| Basic rate | 1–31,865 | 20 | 6,373 |
| Higher rate | 31,866–150,000 | 40 | 47,254 |
| Additional rate | Over 150,000 | 45 |  |

| Rate on non-dividend savings income | 10% up to £2,880[1]<br>20% up to basic rate limit<br>40% up to higher rate limit<br>45% thereafter |
|---|---|
| Dividend ordinary rate<br>(effective rate with tax credit) | 10% up to basic rate limit<br>0% |
| Dividend upper rate<br>(effective rate with tax credit) | 32.5% up to higher rate limit<br>25% |
| Dividend additional rate<br>(effective rate with tax credit) | 37.5% above higher rate limit<br>30.6% |
| Trust rate | 45%[2] |
| Dividend trust rate | 37.5%[2] |

**Notes**

[1] A 10% starting rate applies to the first £2,880 of non-dividend savings income. The starting rate does not apply if non-savings income exceeds the personal allowance plus £2,880.

[2] The special trust rates do not apply to the first £1,000 slice of the 'trust rate income'. Instead, the normal income tax rates (currently the basic rate and dividend ordinary rate) apply as appropriate (ITA 2007, s. 491(1)–(3)).

## [¶1-008]   Income tax rates: 2013–14

(ITA 2007, s. 6–15; FA 2013, s. 3)

(Tax Reporter: ¶148-075ff.)

**2013–14**

|  | Taxable income band<br>£ | Tax rate<br>% | Tax on band<br>£ |
|---|---|---|---|
| Basic rate | 1–32,010 | 20 | 6,402 |
| Higher rate | 32,011–150,000 | 40 | 47,196 |
| Additional rate | Over 150,000 | 45 |  |

| Rate on non-dividend savings income | 10% up to £2,790[1]<br>20% up to basic rate limit<br>40% up to higher rate limit<br>45% thereafter |
|---|---|
| Dividend ordinary rate<br>(effective rate with tax credit) | 10% up to basic rate limit<br>0% |
| Dividend upper rate<br>(effective rate with tax credit) | 32.5% up to higher rate limit<br>25% |
| Dividend additional rate<br>(effective rate with tax credit) | 37.5% above higher rate limit<br>30.6% |
| Trust rate | 45%[2] |
| Dividend trust rate | 37.5%[2] |

**Notes**
(1) A 10% starting rate applies to the first £2,790 of non-dividend savings income. The starting rate does not apply if non-savings income exceeds the personal allowance plus £2,790.
(2) The special trust rates do not apply to the first £1,000 slice of the 'trust rate income'. Instead, the normal income tax rates (currently the basic rate and dividend ordinary rate) apply as appropriate (ITA 2007, s. 491(1)–(3)).

## [¶1-009]   Income tax rates: 2012–13

(ITA 2007, s. 6–15)

(Tax Reporter: ¶148-075ff.)

**2012–13**

|  | Taxable income band £ | Tax rate % | Tax on band £ |
|---|---|---|---|
| Basic rate | 1–34,370 | 20 | 6,874 |
| Higher rate | 34,371–150,000 | 40 | 46,252 |
| Additional rate | Over 150,000 | 50 |  |

| | |
|---|---|
| Rate on non-dividend savings income | 10% up to £2,710[1]<br>20% up to basic rate limit<br>40% up to higher rate limit<br>50% thereafter |
| Dividend ordinary rate (effective rate with tax credit) | 10% up to basic rate limit<br>0% |
| Dividend upper rate (effective rate with tax credit) | 32.5% up to higher rate limit<br>25% |
| Dividend additional rate (effective rate with tax credit) | 42.5% above higher rate limit<br>36.1% |
| Trust rate | 50%[2] |
| Dividend trust rate | 42.5%[2] |

**Notes**
(1) A 10% starting rate applies to the first £2,710 of non-dividend savings income. The starting rate does not apply if non-savings income exceeds the personal allowance plus £2,710.
(2) The special trust rates do not apply to the first £1,000 slice of the 'trust rate income'. Instead, the normal income tax rates (currently the basic rate and dividend ordinary rate) apply as appropriate (ITA 2007, s. 491(1)–(3)).

## [¶1-100]   Personal allowances and reliefs

(ITA 2007, s. 35–46)

(Tax Reporter: ¶155-000ff.)

From 2016–17 onwards, there is one income tax personal allowance of £11,500 regardless of an individual's date of birth.

Autumn Statement 2016 confirmed the Government's commitment to raise the personal allowance to £12,500 by the end of this Parliament (first announced at Summer Budget 2015).

For tax years up to 2012–13, higher (age-related) allowances were available for individuals attaining 'age 65–74' or age '75 and over' in the tax year. These allowances were frozen at 2012–13 rates and phased out between 2013–14 and 2015–16 as the basic personal allowance caught up with the frozen amounts of the former allowances.

From 6 April 2016, a personal savings allowance is available for up to £1,000 of a basic rate taxpayer's savings income and up to £500 of a higher rate taxpayer's savings income each year. The personal savings allowance is not available to additional rate taxpayers. Automatic deduction of 20% income tax by banks and building societies on non-ISA savings also ceased from the same date (amendments by FA 2016, s. 39–41 and Sch. 6).

Existing legislation within ITA 2007 requires the Government to increase personal allowances and rate limits (except the £150,000 higher rate limit, £100,000 personal allowance income limit) by the annual percentage increase in the consumer prices index (CPI) for the year to September preceding the new tax year (indexation). Amounts determined by the annual indexation order may be overridden by provision in a Finance Act.

Existing legislation further provides that once the personal allowance has reached £12,500, it will be uprated in line with the national minimum wage (NMW) (and CPI based provisions would no longer apply). However, at Autumn Statement 2016, it was announced that once the personal allowance reaches £12,500, it will continue to be uprated in line with CPI rather than in line with the NMW.

## Transferable tax allowances for married couples

(ITA 2007, Pt. 3, Ch. 3A)

(Tax Reporter: ¶156-725)

From the 2015–16 tax year, a spouse or civil partner who is not liable to income tax because their income is below their personal allowance or who is liable to income tax at the basic rate, dividend ordinary rate or the starting rate for savings has been able to elect to transfer a portion (set at 10%) of their personal allowance to their spouse or civil partner, with a corresponding reduction to the transferring spouse's personal allowance. Only a spouse or civil partner who is liable to income tax at the basic rate, dividend ordinary rate or the starting rate for savings can receive the transferred personal allowance. The transferred allowance is given effect as a reduction to the recipient's income tax liability at the basic rate of tax. Married couples or civil partners entitled to claim the married couple's allowance are not entitled to make a transfer.

## Property and trading income allowances

As announced at Budget 2016, and confirmed at Autumn Statement 2016, the Government will legislate in Finance Bill 2017 to create a £1,000 allowance for property income and a £1,000 allowance for trading income, with effect from the 2017–18 tax year. The new allowances will mean that individuals with property income below £1,000 or trading income below £1,000 will no longer need to declare or pay tax on that income. The trading income allowance will also apply to certain miscellaneous income from providing assets or services. Those with income above the allowance will be able to calculate their taxable profit either by deducting their expenses in the normal way or by simply deducting the relevant allowance from their gross income.

| Type of relief | 2017–18 £ | 2016–17 £ | 2015–16 £ | 2014–15 £ | 2013–14 £ | 2012–13 £ |
|---|---|---|---|---|---|---|
| **Personal allowance**[3] | | | | | | |
| All ages | 11,500 | 11,000 | — | — | — | — |
| – born after 5 April 1948 | — | — | — | 10,000 | 9,440 | 8,105 |
| – born after 5 April 1938 | — | — | 10,600 | — | — | — |
| – born after 5 April 1938 but before 6 April 1948 | — | — | — | 10,500 | 10,500 | 10500[2] |
| – born before 6 April 1938 | — | — | 10,660 | 10,660 | 10,660 | 10660[2] |
| **Marriage allowance** | 1,150 | 1,100 | 1,060 | — | — | — |
| **Married couple's allowance**[4][5] | | | | | | |
| – born before 6 April 1935 and age 75 and over | 8,445 | 8,355 | 8,355 | 8,165 | 7,915 | 7,705 |
| – minimum amount of allowance | 3,260 | 3,220 | 3,220 | 3,140 | 3,040 | 2,960 |
| **Maximum income before abatement of:** | | | | | | |
| – personal allowance[3] | 100,000 | 100,000 | 100,000 | 100,000 | 100,000 | 100,000 |
| – reliefs for older taxpayers | 28,000 | 27,700 | 27,700 | 27,000 | 26,100 | 25,400 |
| **Abatement income ceiling** | | | | | | |
| **Personal allowance** (basic) | 123,000 | 122,000 | 121,200 | 120,000 | 118,880 | 116,210 |
| Single (age personal allowance) | | | | | | |
| – born after 5 April 1938 but before 6 April 1948 | — | — | — | 28,000 | 28,220 | 30,190[2] |
| – born before 6 April 1938 | — | — | 27,820 | 28,320 | 28,540 | 30,510[2] |
| **Married couple's allowance** (only) | 38,370 | 37,970 | 37,970 | 37,050 | 35,850 | 34,890[6] |
| Married (age personal allowance and MCA) | | | | | | |
| – relevant partner born after 5 April 1938 but before 6 April 1948 | — | — | — | 38,050 | 37,970 | 39,680[7] |
| – relevant partner born before 6 April 1938 | — | — | 38,090 | 38,370 | 38,290 | 40,000[8] |
| **Blind person's allowance** | 2,320 | 2,290 | 2,290 | 2,230 | 2,160 | 2,100 |
| **Dividend allowance**[10] | 5,000 | 5,000 | — | — | — | — |
| **Personal savings allowance**[11] | | | | | | |
| Basic rate taxpayers | 1,000 | 1,000 | — | — | — | — |
| Higher rate taxpayers | 500 | 500 | — | — | — | — |
| **Life assurance relief** (policies issued before 14 March 1984)[9] | — | — | —[9] | 12.5% of premiums | 12.5% of premiums | 12.5% of premiums |
| **'Rent-a-room' limit** | 7,500 | 7,500 | 4,250 | 4,250 | 4,250 | 4,250 |

**Notes**

[1] For 2012–13 and earlier years, entitlement to the basic personal allowance was by reference to age under 65 in the tax year, with higher (age-related) allowances being available for individuals attaining 'age 65–74' or '75 and over' in the tax year. These allowances were phased out between 2013–14 and 2015–16. Individuals born after 5 April 1948 were aged under 65 on 5 April 2013 and remained entitled to only the basic allowance from 2013–14 onwards.

[2] For 2012–13 and earlier years, entitlement to higher age related personal allowances was based on attaining age 65–74, or age 75 and over, in the tax year. Individuals born before 6 April 1948 but after 5 April 1938 attained age 65–74 during 2012–13 and individuals born before 6 April 1938 attained age 75 or over during 2012–13. As part of the phasing out of these allowances between 2013–14 and 2015–16, entitlement to either the age 65–74 or 75 and over higher personal allowance continued (but the amounts were frozen) for those individuals so entitled at 5 April 2013.

[3] From April 2010, the personal allowance is gradually withdrawn for income over £100,000 at a rate of £1 of allowance lost for every £2 over £100,000 until it is completely removed (ITA 2007, s. 35).

[4] Relief is given as a tax reduction at a rate of 10%.

(5) The married couple's allowance is available only where at least one partner reached the age of 65 before 6 April 2000, i.e. was born before 6 April 1935. That partner will have become 75 at some point during 2009–10 and, therefore, will be entitled to the higher amount of the allowance for that tax year and subsequent tax years, i.e. for those aged 75 or over.
(6) Relevant partner aged under 65 in the tax year.
(7) Relevant partner aged 65–74 in the tax year.
(8) Relevant partner aged 75 or over in the tax year.
(9) By relief at source. Abolished for payments becoming due and payable on or after 6 April 2015, and payments becoming due and payable before 6 April 2015 but actually paid on or after 6 July 2015 (FA 2012, s. 227 and Sch. 39, para. 23).
(10) From 6 April 2016, a 0% rate of tax (the dividend nil rate) applies to the first £5,000 of dividend income received (ITA 2007, s. 13A). Spring Budget 2017 announced that the dividend allowance will be reduced to £2,000 from April 2018.
(11) From 6 April 2016, a new 0% rate of tax applies to an individual's savings income (the savings nil rate or savings allowance). The savings nil rate applies to the first £1,000 of a basic rate taxpayer's savings income, or the first £500 of a higher rate taxpayer's savings income. The savings nil rate is not available to additional rate taxpayers (ITA 2007, s. 12A and 12B).
Personal allowances and rate limits (except the £150,000 higher rate limit, the £100,000 personal allowance income limit) are indexed by the annual percentage increase in CPI (RPI until 2014–15) for the year to September preceding the new tax year.

## [¶1-110]   High income child benefit charge

(ITEPA 2003, s. 681B–681H)

(Tax Reporter: ¶490-075)

The high income child benefit charge applies from 7 January 2013 to individuals whose income exceeds £50,000 who are themselves, or whose partner is, in receipt of child benefit. The charge is levied on the partner with the highest income, irrespective of which partner claims the child benefit. The charge is calculated as the 'appropriate percentage' of child benefit payments received during the tax year (but for 2012–13 restricted to amounts received after 7 January 2013 only) which equates to 1% of the amount of child benefit received for every £100 of income over £50,000. From 2013–14, coding out of the charge has been possible.

| Adjusted Net Income | Appropriate percentage |
|---|---|
| £60,000 and over | 100% |
| £50,001–£59,999 | $\frac{ANI - L}{X}$ % |
| Up to £50,000 | Nil |

**Where:**

ANI = Adjusted Net Income
L = £50,000
X = £100

**Adjusted Net Income** is calculated as:

- net income (total income charged to income tax less income tax reliefs);
- less grossed up (at basic rate) gift aid donations;

- less gross pension contributions (before deduction of basic rate tax);
- add back any relief for payments to trade unions or police organisations (ITEPA 2003, s. 457 or 458) deducted in calculating net income.

| Child benefit(1) | 2017–18 £/week | 2016–17 £/week | 2015–16 £/week | 2014–15 £/week | 2013–14 £/week | 2012–13 £/week |
|---|---|---|---|---|---|---|
| Eldest qualifying child | 20.70 | 20.70 | 20.70 | 20.50 | 20.30 | 20.30 |
| Each other child | 13.70 | 13.70 | 13.70 | 13.55 | 13.40 | 13.40 |

**Note**
(1) Individuals who elected not to continue to receive child benefit before 7 January 2013 were not liable for the charge for 2012–13 and individuals who opted out by 28 March 2013 were not liable for the charge for 2013–14. From 2014–15 onwards, individuals who opt out and whose payments stopped before the beginning of the tax year will not be liable for the charge and will otherwise be liable only for the period until payments stop.

## [¶1-120]   Cap on income tax relief

(ITA 2007, s. 24A)

(Tax Reporter: ¶148-450)

From 6 April 2013, a limit applies to the amount of certain income tax reliefs that may be deducted from income under the *Income Tax Act* 2007, s. 24. The limit does not apply to charitable reliefs.

| From | Amount of cap |
|---|---|
| 6 April 2013(1) | greater of: <br> – £50,000; or <br> – 25% of adjusted total income |

**Note**
(1) The limit applies for the tax year 2013–14 and subsequent tax years, and additionally, where loss relief is claimed for a tax year before 2013–14 in relation to losses made in 2013–14 or a later year. However, the limit does not apply in relation to property loss relief arising from a loss made in 2012–13 where the loss is claimed for relief against general income in the tax year 2013–14.

| Limited reliefs | Legislation |
|---|---|
| Trade loss relief against general income (excluding relief for losses attributable to overlap relief and business premises renovation allowances (BPRA)) [and excluding deductions so far as made from profits of the trade or business to which the relief relates – see next table] | ITA 2007, s. 64 |
| Early trade loss relief (first four years of trade, profession or vocation; excluding relief for losses attributable to overlap relief and BPRA) [and excluding deductions so far as made from profits of the trade or business to which the relief relates – see table below] | ITA 2007, s. 72 |
| Post-cessation trade relief (qualifying payments or qualifying events within seven years of the permanent cessation of the trade) [and excluding deductions so far as made from profits of the trade or business to which the relief relates – see table below] | ITA 2007, s. 96 |

| Limited reliefs | Legislation |
|---|---|
| Property loss relief against general income (property business losses arising from capital allowances or agricultural expenses; excluding relief for losses attributable to BPRA)<br>[and excluding deductions so far as made from profits of the trade or business to which the relief relates – see table below] | ITA 2007, s. 120 |
| Post-cessation property relief (qualifying payments or qualifying events within seven years of the permanent cessation of the UK property business)<br>[and excluding deductions so far as made from profits of the trade or business to which the relief relates – see table below] | ITA 2007, s. 125 |
| Employment loss relief against general income (certain circumstances where losses or liabilities arise from employment) | ITA 2007, s. 128 |
| Former employees' deductions for liabilities (payment made by former employees for which they are entitled to claim a deduction from their general income in the year in which the payment is made) | ITEPA 2003, s. 555 |
| Share loss relief on non-EIS/SEIS/SI shares (capital losses on the disposal, or deemed disposal, of certain qualifying shares) | ITA 2007, Pt. 4, Ch. 6 |
| Losses on deeply discounted securities (losses on gilt strips and on listed securities held since at least 26 March 2003) | ITTOIA 2005, s. 446, 454(4) |
| Qualifying loan interest (interest paid on certain loans including loans to buy an interest in certain types of company or to invest in a partnership) | ITA 2007, Pt. 8, Ch. 1 |

| Excluded reliefs | Legislation |
|---|---|
| Deductions attributable to business premises renovation allowances | CAA 2001, Pt. 3A |
| Deductions so far as made from profits of the trade or business to which the relief relates in respect of:<br><br>• trade loss relief;<br>• early trade loss relief;<br>• post-cessation trade relief;<br>• property loss relief;<br>• post-cessation property relief. | ITA 2007, s. 64, 72, 96, 120 and 125 |
| Deductions so far as attributable to a deduction for overlap relief profit in final tax year or on change of accounting date (allowed under ITTOIA 2005, s. 205 or 220) in respect of:<br><br>• trade loss relief;<br>• early trade loss relief. | ITA 2007, s. 64 and 72 |
| Deductions for amounts of relief for share losses:<br><br>• where the shares in question are qualifying shares to which EIS relief is attributable;<br>• where SEIS relief is attributable to the shares in question;<br>• where SI tax relief is attributable to the shares in question. | ITA 2007, Pt. 4, Ch. 6<br>ITA 2007, s. 131(2)(a)<br>ITA 2007, Pt. 5A<br>ITA 2007, Pt. 5B |

## [¶1-150]    Gifts of assets

| Nature of asset | Legislation | Effect of relief |
|---|---|---|
| Stock manufactured or sold by trader that is given to charity, etc. (Tax Reporter: ¶226-650) | CTA 2009, s. 105; ITTOIA 2005, s. 108 | No amount is brought into account as trading receipt as result of the donation |
| Plant and machinery used by trader given to a charity, etc. (Tax Reporter: ¶238-235) | CAA 2001, s. 63 | Disposal value is nil for capital allowances purposes |
| Stock manufactured or sold by trader that is given to a designated educational establishment and qualifies as plant or machinery in the donee's hands (Tax Reporter: ¶226-650) | CTA 2009, s. 105; ITTOIA 2005, s. 108 | No amount is brought into account as a trading receipt as result of the donation |
| Plant or machinery used by trader that is given to a designated educational establishment and qualifies as plant and machinery in the donee's hands (Tax Reporter: ¶238-235) | CAA 2001, s. 63 | Disposal value is nil for capital allowances purposes |
| Listed shares and securities and securities dealt with on a recognised stock exchange, units in unit trusts, etc. interests in land, that are given to a charity (Tax Reporter: ¶115-575; ¶716-640) | CTA 2010, s. 203; ITA 2007, s. 431 | Full value of gift is deductible in calculating profits for IT or CT purposes |
| Property settled by gift on a UK trust which has a charity as a beneficiary and the settlor retains an interest (Tax Reporter: ¶356-450) | ITTOIA 2005, s. 628 | The trust income allocated to the settlor is reduced by an amount equal to the income paid to the charity in the year |

## [¶1-200]    Gifts to the nation

(FA 2012, Sch. 14)

For the tax year 2012–13 and subsequent tax years, a reduction in income tax and/or capital gains tax is available where an individual makes a gift of pre-eminent property to be held for the benefit of the public or the nation. The tax reduction is 30% of the value of the gift. A gift offer must be made and registered in accordance with the scheme and relief is available against the individual's liability for the year in which the gift offer is registered and/or any of the succeeding four tax years.

Pre-eminent property includes any picture, print, book, manuscript, work of art, scientific object or other thing that is pre-eminent for its national, scientific, historic or artistic interest, collections of such items and any object kept in a significant building where it is desirable that it remain associated with the building.

# ADMINISTRATION

## [¶1-250] Submission dates for 2017–18 personal tax returns

(TMA 1970, s. 8)

(Tax Reporter: ¶180-125)

The *Taxes Management Act* 1970, s. 8 contains provisions concerning submission dates for returns issued on or after 6 April 2018 which relate to 2017–18, as follows:

- paper returns (whether or not HMRC are to calculate the tax liability) must be filed by 31 October 2018; and
- online returns must be filed by 31 January 2019.

There are the following exceptions:

| Circumstances | Filing date[1] |
| --- | --- |
| Return issued after 31 July 2018 but before 31 October 2018 | Three months from the date of issue (paper returns); 31 January 2019 (online returns) |
| Return issued after 31 October 2018 | Three months from date of issue |
| Taxpayer wishes underpayment (below £3,000) to be coded out under PAYE in a subsequent year (paper returns) | 31 October 2018 |
| Taxpayer wishes underpayment (below £3,000) to be coded out under PAYE in a subsequent year (online returns) | 30 December 2018 |

**Note**

[1] The time allowed for making a self-assessment when HMRC have served a notice to file a return is four years after the end of the tax year to which it relates (TMA 1970, s. 34A, as inserted by FA 2016, s. 168, with effect from 15 September 2016).

### Withdrawing a notice to file a self-assessment return

(TMA 1970, s. 8B and 12AAA)

With effect in respect of returns for the tax year 2012–13 and subsequent tax years, HMRC will withdraw a notice to file a return, on request or otherwise, where they agree a self-assessment return is not required and cancel any late filing penalty already issued in respect of the outstanding return. A notice may only be withdrawn within the period of two years beginning with the end of the relevant year of assessment or period in respect of which the return is required or, in exceptional circumstances, such extended period as HMRC may agree.

### Simple assessment

*Finance Act* 2016 provides a new power to allow HMRC to make an assessment of an individual's income tax or capital gains tax liability without them first being required to complete a self-assessment return where it has sufficient information about that individual to make the assessment. This measure will have effect in relation to the 2016–17 tax year and subsequent years (TMA 1970, s. 28H–28J and 59BA, as inserted by FA 2016, s. 167 and Sch. 23).

## [¶1-260]   Making tax digital

(Finance Bill 2017)

At Budget 2015, the Government set out the vision for a transformed tax system, and in December 2015 it published the Making Tax Digital roadmap. This set out the Government's plans to make fundamental changes to the tax system, transforming tax administration by 2020 through the use of online digital tax accounts and quarterly digital reporting.

Businesses (including self-employed and landlords) will be able to keep records of their income and expenditure digitally, and send summary updates quarterly to HMRC from their software (or app). Businesses, self-employed people and landlords with turnovers under £10,000 are exempt from the requirements. Employees with secondary income of more than £10,000 will be required to use the digital service.

| Business, self-employed and landlords with: | Start date |
|---|---|
| Profits chargeable to income tax and Class 4 National Insurance contributions with turnover in excess of the VAT threshold | April 2018 |
| Profits chargeable to income tax and Class 4 National Insurance contributions with turnover below the VAT threshold | April 2019 |
| Registered for and pay VAT | April 2019 |
| Liable for corporation tax | April 2020 |

## [¶1-300]   Payment dates 2017–18

(TMA 1970, s. 59A, 59B)

(Tax Reporter: ¶182-725ff.)

Tax is paid on 31 January next following the year of assessment as a single sum covering capital gains tax[3] and income tax on all sources. Interim payments on account may be required. No interim payments are required if:

- the tax paid by assessment was less than £1,000; or
- more than 80% of the tax due the previous year was collected at source.

A payment on account can never exceed 50% of the net tax for the preceding year, even though it may already be clear, at the time the payments are made, that the actual liability for the year will exceed that for the preceding year. Net tax is the excess of assessed tax over tax deducted at source (incl. tax credits on dividends before 6 April 2016). For 2017–18, the following due dates apply:

| | |
|---|---|
| First interim payment | 31 January 2018 |
| Second interim payment | 31 July 2018 |
| Final balancing payment | 31 January 2019 |
| Simple assessment[4] | 31 January 2019 |

**Notes**

[1] If a return is not issued until after 31 October 2018 and the taxpayer has notified chargeability by 5 October 2018, the due date for the final payment becomes three months from the issue of the return (TMA 1970, s. 59B).

[2] In line with the announcement that digital tax accounts will be introduced to replace self-assessment tax returns, March Budget 2015 announced a new payment process to enable tax and NICs to be collected through digital accounts, instead of self-assessment (March Budget 2015).

⁽³⁾ Autumn Statement 2015 announced that from April 2019, a payment on account of any CGT due on the disposal of residential property will be required to be made within 30 days of the completion of the disposal. This will not affect gains on properties which are not liable for CGT due to private residence relief (PRR). The Government will publish draft legislation for consultation in 2016 (Finance Bill 2017).

⁽⁴⁾ The due date for income tax and capital gains tax payable under a 'simple assessment' (from 2016–17) is three months after the day on which the simple assessment notice was given if given after 31 October following the year of assessment and otherwise on 31 January next following the year of assessment (TMA 1970, s. 59BA).

## [¶1-325]  Direct recovery of debts
(F(No. 2)A 2015, s. 51 and Sch. 8)

*Finance (No. 2) Act* 2015 introduced a new power, with effect from 18 November 2015 (Royal Assent), to allow HMRC to recover debts due to it (including tax and tax credit debts) directly from the bank and building society accounts (including individual savings accounts) of debtors. This is also known as the direct recovery of debts (DRD). The power can only be used to recover debts of more than £1,000, and is subject to a number of statutory safeguards, including a 30-day right of objection and a limit of £5,000 as the minimum amount HMRC must always leave across a debtor's accounts above the amount that has been held.

## [¶1-350]  Main penalty provisions 2017–18

| Offence⁽⁹⁾⁽¹⁰⁾ | Penalty⁽¹⁾⁽²⁾ | | |
|---|---|---|---|
| **Late return for 2010–11 and later years** (FA 2009, Sch. 55; Tax Reporter: ¶181-500)⁽³⁾ | | | |
| Failure to submit by the filing date (by 31 October 2017 for 2016–17 paper return; by 31 January 2018 for 2016–17 online return) | £100 | | |
| Failure continues three months after the filing date (1 February 2018 for 2016–17 paper returns; 1 May 2018 for 2016–17 online returns) by HMRC notice | £10 per day for a period up to 90 days beginning with the date specified in the notice (maximum £900) | | |
| Failure still continues six months after the filing date (1 May 2018 for 2016–17 paper return; 1 August 2018 for 2016–17 online return) | The greater of £300 or 5% of the liability to tax shown by the return | | |
| Failure still continues after 12 months (1 November 2018 for 2016–17 paper return; 1 February 2019 for 2016–17 online return): | The greater of relevant percentage of liability shown by the return and £300 | | |
| | **Relevant percentage** | | |
| | Category 1⁽⁷⁾ | Category 2 | Category 3 |
| • withholding information deliberate and concealed | 100% | 150% | 200% |
| • withholding information deliberate but not concealed | 70% | 105% | 140% |
| • any other case | 5% | 5% | 5% |

| Offence[9][10] | Penalty[1][2] | | |
|---|---|---|---|
| Reductions for disclosure: maximum reduction weighted according to quality of disclosure determined as: | **Tax years commencing on or after 6 April 2016** | | |
| | **Domestic matters** | | |
| *Disclosure of relevant information relating to domestic matter* | **Standard penalty** | **Prompted disclosure minimum** | **Unprompted disclosure minimum** |
| • 30% for telling HMRC | 70% | 35% | 20% |
| • 40% for helping to quantify | 100% | 50% | 30% |
| • 30% for giving access to records | | | |
| *Discloses relevant information that relates to an offshore matter or offshore transfer* | **Offshore matters and offshore transfers** | | |
| | **Standard penalty** | **Prompted disclosure minimum** | **Unprompted disclosure minimum** |
| • telling HMRC | 70% | 45% | 30% |
| • helping to quantify | 87.50% | 53.75% | 35% |
| • giving access to records | 100% | 60% | 40% |
| • providing additional information | 105% | 62.50% | 40% |
| | 125% | 72.50% | 50% |
| | 140% | 80% | 50% |
| | 150% | 85% | 55% |
| | 200% | 110% | 70% |
| | No reduction below £300 | | |
| | **Tax years prior to 6 April 2016** | | |
| | **Standard penalty** | **Prompted disclosure minimum** | **Unprompted disclosure minimum** |
| | 70% | 35% | 20% |
| | 105% | 52.5% | 30% |
| | 140% | 70% | 40% |
| | 100% | 50% | 30% |
| | 150% | 75% | 45% |
| | 200% | 100% | 60% |
| **Late return for years up to and including 2009–10** (TMA 1970, s. 93)[3][4]: | | | |
| • if paper return not filed by the deadline | £100 | | |
| • if paper return still not filed six months after the deadline | £100 | | |
| • for continuing delay | Up to £60 per day (not restricted to the liability shown by the return) | | |
| • failure continues beyond the anniversary of the filing date | Tax geared | | |
| **Failure to notify chargeability** For failures after 1 April 2010 (FA 2008, Sch. 41; Tax Reporter: ¶181-350): | **Percentage of potential lost revenue** | | |
| | **Category 1[7]** | **Category 2** | **Category 3** |
| • failure deliberate and concealed | 100% | 150% | 200% |
| • failure deliberate but not concealed | 70% | 105% | 140% |
| • any other case | 30% | 45% | 60% |

| Offence[9][10] | Penalty[1][2] |
|---|---|
| Reductions for disclosure: maximum reduction weighted according to quality of disclosure determined as:<br><br>*Failures involving domestic matters and non-deliberate failures involving offshore matters*<br>• 30% for telling HMRC<br>• 40% for helping to quantify<br>• 30% for giving access to records<br><br>*Deliberate failures involving offshore matters and failures involving offshore transfers*<br>• telling HMRC<br>• helping to quantify<br>• giving access to records<br>• providing additional information | (see penalty tables below) |

**Tax years commencing on or after 6 April 2016**

**Domestic matters**

| Standard penalty | Prompted disclosure minimum | | Unprompted disclosure minimum | |
|---|---|---|---|---|
| | Case A | Case B | Case A | Case B |
| 30% | 10% | 20% | 0% | 10% |
| 70% | 35% | | 20% | |
| 100% | 50% | | 30% | |

**Offshore matters and offshore transfers**

| Standard penalty | Prompted disclosure minimum | | Unprompted disclosure minimum | |
|---|---|---|---|---|
| | Case A | Case B | Case A | Case B |
| 30% | 10% | 20% | 0% | 10% |
| 37.5% | 12.5% | 25% | 0% | 12.5% |
| 45% | 15% | 30% | 0% | 15% |
| 60% | 20% | 40% | 0% | 20% |
| 70% | 45% | | 30% | |
| 87.5% | 53.75% | | 35% | |
| 100% | 60% | | 40% | |
| 105% | 62.5% | | 40% | |
| 125% | 72.5% | | 50% | |
| 140% | 80% | | 50% | |
| 150% | 85% | | 55% | |
| 200% | 110% | | 70% | |

**Tax years prior to 6 April 2016**

| Standard penalty | Prompted disclosure minimum[5] | | Unprompted disclosure minimum[5] | |
|---|---|---|---|---|
| | Case A | Case B | Case A | Case B |
| 30% | 10% | 20% | 0% | 10% |
| 45% | 15% | 30% | 0% | 15% |
| 60% | 20% | 40% | 0% | 20% |
| 70% | 35% | | 20% | |
| 105% | 52.5% | | 30% | |
| 140% | 70% | | 40% | |
| 100% | 50% | | 30% | |
| 150% | 75% | | 45% | |
| 200% | 100% | | 60% | |

| Offence | Penalty |
|---|---|
| **Failure to notify chargeablility**<br>For failures before 1 April 2010 (TMA 1970, s. 7; Tax Reporter: ¶181-525) | Tax geared up to 100% of the tax, subject to mitigation |
| **Failure to keep and retain tax records** (TMA 1970, s. 12B; Tax Reporter: ¶181-900) | Up to £3,000 per year of assessment |
| **False statements to reduce interim payments** (TMA 1970, s. 59A(6); Tax Reporter: ¶182-725) | Up to the difference between the amount correctly due and the amount paid |
| **Failure to comply with an information notice** (FA 2008, Sch. 36, para. 39 and 40; Tax Reporter: ¶186-550ff.)<br>• standard amount<br>• continued failure | <br><br>£300<br>Daily penalty of £60 |
| Tax-related penalty where significant tax is at risk (FA 2008, Sch. 36, para. 50) | Tax geared amount decided by Upper Tribunal |

| Offence[9][10] | Penalty[1][2] | | |
|---|---|---|---|
| **Inaccurate information/documents in complying with an information notice** (FA 2008, Sch. 36) Inaccuracy careless or deliberate | Up to £3,000 for each inaccuracy | | |
| **Errors in returns** Errors in returns for periods starting 1 April 2008 where return is filed on or after 1 April 2009 (FA 2007, Sch. 24; Tax Reporter: ¶184-850)[6] | **Percentage of potential lost revenue** | | |
| | Category 1[7] | Category 2 | Category 2 |
| • careless action | 30% | 45% | 60% |
| • deliberate but not concealed action | 70% | 105% | 140% |
| • deliberate and concealed action | 100% | 150% | 200% |
| Reductions for disclosure: maximum reduction weighted according to quality of disclosure determined as: | **Tax years commencing on or after 6 April 2016** | | |
| | **Domestic matters** | | |
| *Domestic matters and careless inaccuracies involving offshore matters* | Standard penalty | Prompted disclosure minimum | Unprompted disclosure minimum |
| • 30% for telling HMRC | 30% | 15% | 0% |
| • 40% for helping to quantify | 70% | 35% | 20% |
| • 30% for giving access to records | 100% | 50% | 30% |
| *Deliberate inaccuracies involving offshore matters and inaccuracies involving offshore transfers* | **Offshore matters and offshore transfers** | | |
| • telling HMRC | Standard penalty | Prompted disclosure minimum | Unprompted disclosure minimum |
| • helping to quantify | | | |
| • allowing access to records | 30% | 15% | 0% |
| • providing additional information | 37.5% | 18.75% | 0% |
| | 45% | 22.5% | 0% |
| | 60% | 30% | 0% |
| | 70% | 45% | 30% |
| | 87.5% | 53.75% | 35% |
| | 100% | 60% | 40% |
| | 105% | 62.5% | 40% |
| | 125% | 72.5% | 50% |
| | 140% | 80% | 50% |
| | 150% | 85% | 55% |
| | 200% | 110% | 70% |
| | **Tax years prior to 6 April 2016** | | |
| | **Percentage of potential lost revenue** | | |
| | Standard penalty | Prompted disclosure minimum | Unprompted disclosure minimum |
| | 30% | 15% | 0% |
| | 45% | 22.5% | 0% |
| | 60% | 30% | 0% |
| | 70% | 35% | 20% |
| | 105% | 52.5% | 30% |
| | 140% | 70% | 40% |
| | 100% | 50% | 30% |
| | 150% | 75% | 45% |
| | 200% | 100% | 60% |

| Offence[9][10] | Penalty[1][2] |
|---|---|
| **Incorrect return or accounts** (fraudulently or negligently); periods starting before 1 April 2008 where return is filed before 1 April 2009 (TMA 1970, s. 95, 95A; Tax Reporter: ¶184-875) | Tax geared up to 100% of the tax, subject to mitigation |
| **Offshore asset moves** (FA 2015, Sch. 21) Additional penalty for offshore asset moves from specified territory[8] to non-specified territory on or after 26 March 2015 following an original deliberate failure penalty under: FA 2007, Sch. 24, para. 1; FA 2008, Sch. 41, para. 1; or FA 2009, Sch. 55, para. 6. | 50% of original penalty |
| **General anti-abuse rule penalty** (FA 2013, s. 212A and Sch. 43C) from 15 September 2016 Penalty where counteraction notice given under FA 2013, Sch. 43, para. 12, Sch. 43A, para. 8 or 9, or Sch. 43B, para. 8 | 60% of the value of the counteracted advantage |
| **Enabling offshore tax evasion or non-compliance** (FA 2016, Sch. 20) from 1 January 2017 Penalty for engaging in offshore tax evasion or non-compliance where the tax at stake is income tax, capital gains tax or inheritance tax. Standard penalty: <br><br> Where a penalty under FA 2015, Sch. 21, para. 1 arises: | <br><br><br><br><br> The higher of: 100% of the potential lost revenue; or £3,000 <br> The higher of: 50% of the potential lost revenue; or £3,000 |

**Asset based penalty for offshore inaccuracies and failures**
(FA 2016, Sch. 22) for tax years commencing on or after 6 April 2016
Additional penalty where one or more standard offshore penalties and the offshore potential lost revenue in relation to a tax year exceeds £25,000.
Standard offshore penalties means penalties under:
FA 2007, Sch. 24, para. 1;
FA 2008, Sch. 41, para. 1; or
FA 2009, Sch. 55, para. 6
imposed involving offshore matters or offshore transfers and deliberate behaviour.

Lower of 10% of value of asset and offshore PLR x 10.

Reductions for:
- disclosing to HMRC
- providing a reasonable value
- providing information or access to records to assist HMRC value the asset
- special circumstances

| | Reduction factors | |
|---|---|---|
| | Unprompted disclosure | Prompted disclosure |
| | 50% | 20% |

**Notes**

[1] Interest is charged on penalties not paid when due. The due date is 30 days after the notice of determination of the penalty is issued.

[2] Defences of 'reasonable excuse' or 'special circumstances' may be available.

[3] Late return penalties are cumulative, e.g. for a return six months late there are two penalties.

[4] The two fixed £100 penalties are reduced if the total tax payable by assessment is less than the penalty which would otherwise be chargeable.

[5] The case A minimum applies if HMRC become aware of the failure less than 12 months after the time when the tax first becomes unpaid by reason of the failure, otherwise the case B minimum applies.

[6] No penalty for inaccuracies that occur despite taking reasonable care.

[7] FA 2015, s. 120 and Sch. 20 introduce a new category of penalty, category 0 from a date to be appointed. The new category of penalty will carry the lowest level of penalty equivalent to those currently in category 1 (i.e. 30%, 70% and 100%) and the penalty percentages for category 1 penalties will be increased to 37.5%, 87.5% and 125% respectively. New tables as follows:

| Late return | Relevant percentage | | | |
|---|---|---|---|---|
| | Category 0 | Category 1 | Category 2 | Category 3 |
| • withholding information deliberate and concealed | 100% | 125% | 150% | 200% |
| • withholding information deliberate but not concealed | 70% | 87.5% | 105% | 140% |
| • any other case | 5% | 5% | 5% | 5% |

| Failure to notify chargeability | Percentage of potential lost revenue | | | |
|---|---|---|---|---|
| | Category 0 | Category 1 | Category 2 | Category 3 |
| • failure deliberate and concealed | 100% | 125% | 150% | 200% |
| • failure deliberate but not concealed | 70% | 87.5% | 105% | 140% |
| • any other case | 30% | 37.5% | 45% | 60% |

| Errors in returns | Percentage of potential lost revenue | | | |
|---|---|---|---|---|
| | Category 0 | Category 1 | Category 2 | Category 3 |
| • careless action | 30% | 37.50% | 45% | 60% |
| • deliberate but not concealed action | 70.0% | 87.50% | 105% | 140% |
| • deliberate and concealed action | 100% | 125% | 150% | 200% |

[8] See ¶1-370 for table of specified territories.

[9] *Finance Act* 2016 contains the following changes:
- a new criminal offence that removes the need to prove intent for the most serious cases of failing to declare offshore income and gains (TMA 1970, s. 106B–106H, as inserted by FA 2016, s. 166, with effect from a date to be appointed by Treasury Order);
- increased public naming of tax evaders (FA 2009, s. 94, as amended by FA 2016, s. 164, with effect from 1 April 2017 (SI 2017/261)); and
- a new regime of warnings and escalating sanctions for those who persistently engage in tax avoidance schemes which HMRC defeats. Following the first defeat of a tax avoidance scheme, HMRC will place the taxpayer on a warning for five years. If the taxpayer uses any further schemes while under warning which HMRC defeats, the rate of penalty will be 20% for the first defeat, 40% for the second defeat and 60% for the third defeat. If HMRC defeat three tax avoidance schemes while the taxpayer is on warning, the taxpayer's details can be published. If three avoidance schemes which exploit reliefs are used while under warning and HMRC defeat them, the taxpayer will be denied further benefit of reliefs until the warning period expires. The regime comes into effect on 6 April 2017 (FA 2016, s. 159 and Sch. 18).

[10] Autumn Statement 2016 announced a new penalty for any person who has enabled another person or business to use a tax avoidance arrangement that is later defeated by HMRC (following consultation).

## [¶1-360] Offshore penalties – territory categories

The table below shows which territories are classified in 'category 1' and 'category 3' for the purposes of penalties for offshore non-compliance. Territories not listed here (other than the UK) are in 'category 2'. Penalties for domestic (UK) matters fall into category 1.

Territories are allocated into one of the categories depending upon the level of information exchange arrangements with the UK, with category 1 territories having the highest level of information sharing arrangements so penalties are the same as for penalties involving domestic matters, whereas territories in categories 2 and 3 have correspondingly poorer information exchange arrangements.

A new category of territory, category 0, is prospectively introduced by FA 2015, s. 120 and Sch. 20, with effect from a date to be appointed. The new category of penalty will apply to overseas territories making information exchange arrangements with the UK that meet the new Common Reporting Standard. It is envisaged that most or all territories currently in category 1 will, over time, make arrangements so as to fall within category 0 (FA 2015, Sch. 20).

| Category 1 | Category 3[1] |
|---|---|
| Anguilla | Albania |
| Aruba | Algeria |
| Australia | Andorra |
| Belgium | Bonaire, Sint Eustatius and Saba |
| Bulgaria | Brazil |
| Canada | Cameroon |
| Cayman Islands | Cape Verde |
| Cyprus | Colombia |
| Czech Republic | Congo, Republic of the |
| Denmark (not including Faroe Islands and Greenland which are in category 2) | Cook Islands |
| | Costa Rica |
| Estonia | Curacao |
| Finland | Cuba |
| France | Democratic People's Republic of Korea |
| Germany | Dominican Republic |
| Greece | Ecuador |
| Guernsey (includes Alderney and Sark) | El Salvador |
| Hungary | Gabon |
| Ireland | Guatemala |
| Isle of Man | Honduras |
| Italy | Iran |
| Japan | Iraq |
| Korea, South | Jamaica |
| Latvia | Kyrgyzstan |
| Lithuania | Lebanon |
| Malta | Macau (China and Hong Kong are in category 2) |
| Montserrat | Marshall Islands |
| Netherlands (not including Bonaire, Sint Eustatius and Saba) | Micronesia, Federated States of |
| New Zealand (not including Tokelau) | Monaco |
| Norway | Nauru |
| Poland | Nicaragua |
| Portugal (includes Madeira and the Azores) | Niue |
| Romania | Palau |
| Slovakia | Panama |
| Slovenia | Paraguay |
| Spain (includes the Canary Islands and other overseas territories of Spain) | Peru |
| Sweden | Seychelles |
| Switzerland (from 24 July 2013) | Sint Maarten |
| United States of America (not including overseas territories and possessions of the United States of America which are in category 2) | Suriname |
| | Syria |
| | Tokelau |
| | Tonga |
| | Trinidad and Tobago |
| | United Arab Emiratess |
| | Uruguay |

**Note**
(1) Before 24 July 2013, category 3 territories included additionally:
* Antigua and Barbuda;
* Armenia;
* Bahrain;
* Barbados;
* Belize;
* Dominica;
* Grenada;
* Mauritius;
* Saint Kitts and Nevis;
* Saint Lucia;
* Saint Vincent and the Grenadines;
* San Marino.

# [¶1-370]   Offshore asset moves penalties: specified territories
(SI 2015/866)

| | | | |
|---|---|---|---|
| Albania | Andorra | Anguilla | Antigua and Barbuda |
| Argentina | Aruba | Australia | Austria |
| The Bahamas | Barbados | Belgium | Belize |
| Bermuda | Brazil | British Virgin Islands | Brunei Darussalam |
| Bulgaria | Canada | Cayman Islands | Chile |
| China | Colombia | Costa Rica | Croatia |
| Curaçao | Cyprus | Czech Republic | Denmark |
| Dominica | Estonia | Faroe Islands | Finland |
| France | Germany | Gibraltar | Greece |
| Greenland | Grenada | Guernsey | Hong Kong |
| Hungary | Iceland | India | Indonesia |
| Ireland | Isle of Man | Israel | Italy |
| Japan | Jersey | Korea (South) | Latvia |
| Liechtenstein | Lithuania | Luxembourg | Macau |
| Malaysia | Malta | Marshall Islands | Mauritius |
| Mexico | Monaco | Montserrat | Netherlands (including Bonaire, Sint Eustatius and Saba) |
| New Zealand (not including Tokelau) | Niue | Norway | Poland |
| Portugal | Qatar | Romania | Russia |
| Saint Kitts and Nevis | Saint Lucia | Saint Vincent and the Grenadines | Samoa |
| San Marino | Saudi Arabia | Seychelles | Singapore |
| Sint Maarten | Slovak Republic | Slovenia | South Africa |
| Spain | Sweden | Switzerland | Trinidad and Tobago |
| Turkey | Turks and Caicos Islands | United Arab Emirates | United States of America (not including overseas territories and possessions) |
| Uruguay | | | |

## [¶1-400]   Penalties for late payment of tax 2017–18

(FA 2009, Sch. 56)

(Tax Reporter: ¶182-875)

The current penalty regime for late payments under income tax self-assessment was introduced by FA 2009, Sch. 56 and applies from 6 April 2011 to payments for the tax year 2010–11 and later years.

| Tax overdue | Penalty |
|---|---|
| 30 days | 5% of tax overdue |
| 6 months | further 5% of tax overdue |
| 12 months | further 5% of tax overdue |

These penalties will be issued automatically and are in addition to the interest that will be charges on all outstanding amounts, including unpaid penalties, until payment is received.

Penalties apply to:

- final tax payments on self-assessments (this includes any amounts due as interim payments which remain unpaid);
- tax on inspector's amendments to a self-assessment made during or as a result of an audit; and
- discovery assessments.

## [¶1-450]   Interest 2017–18

(FA 2009, s. 101–105 and Sch. 53 and 54)

(Tax Reporter: ¶182-925; ¶182-975)

The current regime for interest on overdue and overpaid tax was introduced by FA 2009, s. 101–105 and Sch. 53 and 54, with effect in relation to any self-assessment amount payable or repayable on or after 31 October 2011.

**Late payment interest:** is payable from the 'late payment interest start date':

| Payment | Late payment interest start date |
|---|---|
| First interim payment[1] | 31 January 2018 |
| Second interim payment | 31 July 2018 |
| Final payment[2] | 31 January 2019 |
| Tax due on an amendment to a return | 31 January 2019 |
| Tax due on determination of appeal | 31 January 2019 |

**Notes**

[1] Where the taxpayer has provided HMRC in good time with the information required to issue a statement of account ahead of the payment date of 31 January, but no statement is received before 1 January, interest on the tax to be paid will run from 30 days after the taxpayer is actually notified rather than from 31 January.

[2] Where notice to make a return is issued after 31 October following the end of the tax year, provided there has been no failure to notify chargeability under TMA 1970, s. 7, the date from which interest is payable becomes the last day in the period of three months beginning with the day notice to make a return was given.

Repayment interest: runs from the date of payment (deemed to be 31 January following the tax year in respect of tax deducted at source) to the date on which the order for the repayment is issued.

## [¶1-500]   Rates of interest

(FA 2009, s. 101–102; SI 2011/2446)

(Tax Reporter: ¶182-925; ¶182-975)

The following table gives the rates of interest applicable in recent years.

| From | Late payment % | Repayment % |
|---|---|---|
| 23 August 2016 | 2.75 | 0.50 |
| 29 September 2009 to 22 August 2016 | 3.00 | 0.50 |

**Notes**

SI 2011/2446 sets the interest rates for the purposes of s. 101 and 102 at the Bank of England base rate plus 2.5% and minus 1% respectively. Changes in interest rates announced in Bank of England Monetary Policy Committee meetings take effect from the 13th working day following the meeting and apply in respect of interest running from before that date as well as interest running from on or after that date.

(1) Tax-related judgment debts: the Government will set the rate of interest which applies on taxation-related debts payable under a court judgment or order by HMRC to a rate equal to the Bank of England base rate plus 2%. The Government will also apply the late payment interest rate to taxation-related debts owed to HMRC under a court judgment or order. These changes will apply to new and pre-existing judgments and orders in respect of interest accruing on and after 8 July 2015 (F(No. 2)A 2015, s. 52).

## [¶1-600]   Interest rates on certificates of tax deposit (CTD)

CTDs can be purchased to settle most tax liabilities, except PAYE, VAT and corporation tax falling due under Pay and File, or for subsequent encashment. (No CTDs are available for purchase for use against corporation tax liabilities since the start of the Pay and File regime.) A higher rate of interest is paid if the CTD is used in payment of tax. Interest is allowed/paid gross and is taxable.

Rates of interest vary according to the period for which the deposit is held. The rates in force at issue apply for one year; thereafter, the rate applicable is that on the most recent anniversary of the date of issue.

Details of how to purchase a CTD and use it in payment of tax can be found on the HMRC website at www.gov.uk/guidance/certificate-of-tax-deposit-scheme.

Rates applicable over recent years have been as follows:

Principles of Income Tax

| Deposits on or after | Deposits under £100,000 | | Deposits of £100,000 or more | | | | | | | | | |
|---|---|---|---|---|---|---|---|---|---|---|---|---|
| | | | Deposits held for under 1 month | | Deposits held for 1 to under 3 months | | Deposits held for 3 to under 6 months | | Deposits held for 6 to under 9 months | | Deposits held for 9–12 months | |
| | Applied in payment of tax % | Cash value % | Applied in payment of tax % | Cash value % | Applied in payment of tax % | Cash value % | Applied in payment of tax % | Cash value % | Applied in payment of tax % | Cash value % | Applied in payment of tax % | Cash value % |
| 7 May 1997 | 2.75 | 1.50 | 2.75 | 1.50 | 5.50 | 2.75 | 5.25 | 2.75 | 5.50 | 2.75 | 5.25 | 2.75 |
| 9 June 1997 | 3.00 | 1.50 | 3.00 | 1.50 | 5.50 | 2.75 | 5.50 | 2.75 | 5.50 | 2.75 | 5.50 | 2.75 |
| 11 July 1997 | 3.25 | 1.75 | 3.25 | 1.75 | 6.00 | 3.00 | 5.75 | 3.00 | 5.75 | 3.00 | 6.00 | 3.00 |
| 8 Aug. 1997 | 4.50 | 2.25 | 4.50 | 2.25 | 6.00 | 3.00 | 6.00 | 3.00 | 6.00 | 3.00 | 5.75 | 3.00 |
| 7 Nov. 1997 | 4.00 | 2.00 | 4.00 | 2.00 | 6.50 | 3.25 | 6.50 | 3.25 | 6.25 | 3.25 | 6.25 | 3.25 |
| 5 June 1998 | 4.00 | 2.00 | 4.00 | 2.00 | 6.50 | 3.25 | 6.25 | 3.25 | 6.25 | 3.25 | 6.00 | 3.00 |
| 9 Oct. 1998 | 3.75 | 2.00 | 3.75 | 2.00 | 6.25 | 3.25 | 5.75 | 3.00 | 5.50 | 2.75 | 5.25 | 2.75 |
| 6 Nov. 1998 | 3.25 | 1.75 | 3.25 | 1.75 | 5.75 | 3.00 | 5.25 | 2.75 | 5.00 | 2.50 | 4.75 | 2.50 |
| 11 Dec. 1998 | 3.00 | 1.50 | 3.00 | 1.50 | 5.25 | 2.75 | 4.75 | 2.50 | 4.50 | 2.25 | 4.25 | 2.25 |
| 8 Jan. 1999 | 2.50 | 1.25 | 2.50 | 1.25 | 5.00 | 2.50 | 4.50 | 2.25 | 4.00 | 2.00 | 4.00 | 2.00 |
| 5 Feb. 1999 | 1.75 | 1.00 | 1.75 | 1.00 | 4.50 | 2.25 | 4.00 | 2.00 | 3.75 | 2.00 | 3.75 | 2.00 |
| 9 Apr. 1999 | 1.75 | 1.00 | 1.50 | 0.75 | 4.25 | 2.25 | 4.00 | 2.00 | 3.75 | 2.00 | 4.00 | 2.00 |
| 11 June 1999 | 1.50 | 0.75 | 1.75 | 1.00 | 4.00 | 2.00 | 4.00 | 2.00 | 4.00 | 2.00 | 4.50 | 2.25 |
| 9 Sept. 1999 | 1.75 | 1.00 | 2.00 | 1.00 | 4.50 | 2.25 | 4.50 | 2.25 | 4.50 | 2.25 | 4.75 | 2.50 |
| 4 Nov. 1999 | 2.00 | 1.00 | 2.25 | 1.25 | 5.00 | 2.50 | 4.75 | 2.50 | 4.75 | 2.50 | 5.25 | 2.75 |
| 14 Jan. 2000 | 2.25 | 1.25 | 2.50 | 1.25 | 5.00 | 2.50 | 5.00 | 2.50 | 5.00 | 2.50 | 5.25 | 2.75 |
| 11 Feb. 2000 | 2.50 | 1.25 | 2.25 | 1.25 | 5.25 | 2.75 | 5.00 | 2.50 | 5.25 | 2.75 | 4.00 | 2.00 |
| 9 Feb. 2001 | 2.25 | 1.25 | 2.00 | 1.00 | 4.75 | 2.50 | 4.25 | 2.25 | 4.25 | 2.25 | 3.50 | 1.75 |
| 6 Apr. 2001 | 2.00 | 1.00 | 2.00 | 1.00 | 4.25 | 2.25 | 4.00 | 2.00 | 3.75 | 2.00 | 3.75 | 2.00 |
| 11 May 2001 | 2.00 | 1.00 | 1.50 | 0.75 | 4.00 | 2.00 | 4.00 | 2.00 | 3.75 | 2.00 | 3.75 | 2.00 |
| 3 Aug. 2001 | 1.50 | 0.75 | 1.25 | 0.50 | 4.00 | 2.00 | 3.75 | 2.00 | 3.75 | 2.00 | 3.00 | 1.50 |
| 19 Sept. 2001 | 1.25 | 0.75 | 1.00 | 0.50 | 3.50 | 1.75 | 3.25 | 1.75 | 3.25 | 1.75 | 3.00 | 1.50 |
| 5 Oct. 2001 | 1.00 | 0.50 | 0.50 | 0.25 | 3.25 | 1.75 | 3.00 | 1.50 | 3.00 | 1.50 | 2.25 | 1.25 |
| 9 Nov. 2001 | 0.50 | 0.25 | 0.25 | Nil | 2.75 | 1.50 | 2.50 | 1.25 | 2.25 | 1.25 | 2.00 | 1.00 |
| 7 Feb. 2003 | Nil | Nil | Nil | Nil | 2.75 | 1.25 | 2.25 | 1.00 | 2.25 | 1.00 | 2.00 | 1.00 |
| 11 July 2003 | Nil | Nil | Nil | Nil | 2.50 | 1.25 | 2.25 | 1.00 | 2.00 | 1.00 | 2.00 | 1.00 |
| 7 Nov. 2003 | 0.25 | Nil | 0.25 | Nil | 3.00 | 1.50 | 3.00 | 1.50 | 3.00 | 1.50 | 3.00 | 1.50 |
| 6 Feb. 2004 | 0.50 | 0.25 | 0.50 | 0.25 | 3.00 | 1.50 | 3.00 | 1.50 | 3.00 | 1.50 | 3.00 | 1.50 |

| Deposits on or after | Deposits of £100,000 or more | | | | | | | | | | | |
| --- | --- | --- | --- | --- | --- | --- | --- | --- | --- | --- | --- | --- |
| | Deposits under £100,000 | | Deposits held for under 1 month | | Deposits held for 1 to under 3 months | | Deposits held for 3 to under six months | | Deposits held for 6 to under 9 months | | Deposits held for 9–12 months | |
| | Applied in payment of tax % | Cash value % | Applied in payment of tax % | Cash value % | Applied in payment of tax % | Cash value % | Applied in payment of tax % | Cash value % | Applied in payment of tax % | Cash value % | Applied in payment of tax % | Cash value % |
| 7 May 2004 | 0.75 | 0.25 | 0.75 | 0.25 | 3.25 | 1.50 | 3.25 | 1.50 | 3.25 | 1.50 | 3.25 | 1.50 |
| 11 June 2004 | 1.00 | 0.50 | 1.00 | 0.50 | 3.75 | 1.75 | 3.50 | 1.75 | 3.75 | 1.75 | 3.75 | 1.75 |
| 6 Aug. 2004 | 1.25 | 0.50 | 1.25 | 0.50 | 3.75 | 1.75 | 3.75 | 1.75 | 3.75 | 1.75 | 3.75 | 1.75 |
| 5 Aug. 2005 | 1.00 | 0.50 | 1.00 | 0.50 | 3.50 | 1.75 | 3.25 | 1.50 | 3.00 | 1.50 | 3.00 | 1.50 |
| 4 Aug. 2006 | 1.75 | 0.75 | 1.75 | 0.75 | 4.25 | 2.00 | 4.25 | 2.00 | 4.00 | 2.00 | 4.00 | 2.00 |
| 10 Nov. 2006 | 1.50 | 0.75 | 1.50 | 0.75 | 4.00 | 2.00 | 4.00 | 2.00 | 3.75 | 1.75 | 3.75 | 1.75 |
| 12 Jan. 2007 | 1.50 | 0.75 | 1.50 | 0.75 | 4.25 | 2.00 | 4.00 | 2.00 | 4.00 | 2.00 | 4.00 | 2.00 |
| 11 May 2007 | 2.00 | 1.00 | 2.00 | 1.00 | 4.75 | 2.25 | 4.50 | 2.25 | 4.50 | 2.25 | 4.50 | 2.25 |
| 6 July 2007 | 2.25 | 1.10 | 2.25 | 1.10 | 5.00 | 2.50 | 4.75 | 2.25 | 4.75 | 2.25 | 4.75 | 2.25 |
| 7 Dec. 2007 | 3.00 | 1.50 | 3.00 | 1.50 | 5.50 | 2.75 | 5.00 | 2.50 | 4.75 | 2.25 | 4.50 | 2.25 |
| 8 Feb. 2008 | 2.00 | 1.00 | 2.00 | 1.00 | 4.50 | 2.25 | 4.25 | 2.25 | 4.00 | 2.00 | 3.75 | 1.50 |
| 11 Apr. 2008 | 2.00 | 1.00 | 2.00 | 1.00 | 4.75 | 2.25 | 4.50 | 2.25 | 4.25 | 2.00 | 4.25 | 2.00 |
| 9 Oct. 2008 | 2.50 | 1.25 | 2.50 | 1.25 | 5.25 | 2.50 | 5.00 | 2.50 | 5.00 | 2.50 | 4.75 | 2.25 |
| 7 Nov. 2008 | 1.75 | 0.75 | 1.75 | 0.75 | 4.50 | 2.25 | 4.25 | 2.00 | 4.25 | 2.00 | 4.00 | 2.00 |
| 5 Dec. 2008 | 0.00 | 0.00 | 0.00 | 0.00 | 2.50 | 1.25 | 2.50 | 1.25 | 2.50 | 1.25 | 2.25 | 1.00 |
| 9 Jan. 2009 | 0.00 | 0.00 | 0.00 | 0.00 | 1.50 | 0.75 | 1.25 | 0.50 | 1.25 | 0.50 | 1.25 | 0.50 |
| 6 Feb. 2009 | 0.00 | 0.00 | 0.00 | 0.00 | 1.00 | 0.50 | 1.00 | 0.50 | 1.00 | 0.50 | 0.75 | 0.25 |
| 6 Mar. 2009 | 0.00 | 0.00 | 0.00 | 0.00 | 0.75 | 0.25 | 0.75 | 0.25 | 0.75 | 0.25 | 0.75 | 0.25 |

# [¶1-650]   Remission of tax for official error
(ESC A19)

Arrears of income tax and capital gains tax may be given up if they result from HMRC's failure to make proper and timely use of information supplied by the taxpayer, or in certain circumstances by the taxpayer's employer or the Department for Work and Pensions.

The taxpayer must have reasonably believed that his or her affairs were in order. Tax will normally only be given up where there was a gap of 12 months or more between HMRC receiving the information that tax was due, and notifying the taxpayer of the arrears.

# TAXATION OF BUSINESS PROFITS

## [¶2-000]  Relief for fluctuating profits (farming and market gardening; creative artists): from 2016–17

(ITTOIA 2005, s. 221ff.)

(Tax Reporter: ¶272-300ff.; ¶268-300)

**Two-year averaging**

From 2016–17, marginal relief is removed and full two-year averaging relief will be availabe where the profits of one year are 75% or less of the profits of the other year (FA 2016, s. 25).

**Five-year averaging**

For 2016–17 and subsequent years, individuals will be able to claim to average trading profits for income tax purposes over five consecutive tax years where the 'volatility' condition is met.

The volatility condition is that:

(a)   one of the following is less than 75% of the other:

    (i)   the average of the relevant profits of the first four tax years to which the claim relates;

    (ii)  the relevant profits of the last of the tax years to which the claim relates; or

(b)   the relevant profits of one or more (but not all) of the five tax years to which the claim relates are nil.

(ITTOIA 2005, s. 222A, as inserted by *Finance Act* 2016, with effect from the tax year 2016–17 (meaning that a five-year averaging claim with 2016–17 as the final year would involve averaging the profits of the years 2012–13 to 2016–17).)

## [¶2-005]  Relief for fluctuating profits (farming and market gardening; creative artists): up to 2015–16

(ITTOIA 2005, s. 221ff.)

(Tax Reporter: ¶272-300ff.; ¶268-300)

**Full averaging**

Full averaging applies where profits of one of the tax years are less than 70% of profits for the other year or where profits of one (but not both) of the tax years are nil.

**Marginal averaging**

The amount of the adjustment to the profits of each relevant tax year, where lower profits are between 70% and 75% of higher profits, is computed as follows:

$$(D \times 3) - (P \times 0.75)$$

Where:

D   is the difference between the relevant profits of the two years; and

P   is the relevant profits of the tax year of which those profits are higher.

Marginal relief is removed by FA 2016, s. 25, with effect where the latest year is 2016–17 (and subsequent tax years).

## [¶2-010]   Cash basis for small businesses

(ITTOIA 2005, Pt. 2, Ch. 3A)

(Tax Reporter: ¶206-481ff.)

From April 2013 (with effect for the tax year 2013–14 and subsequent tax years), eligible businesses may elect to calculate their profits on the cash basis instead of in accordance with generally accepted accountancy principles. The cash basis is optional but circumstances under which a business can leave the scheme are limited (businesses must continue to use the scheme until their circumstances change so that the cash basis is no longer suitable for them). Under the scheme, businesses calculate their taxable income by taking business income received in a year and deducting business expenses paid in a year. This means they do not need to adjust for debtors, creditors and stock, and generally do not have to distinguish between revenue and capital expenditure. Capital allowances remain available for expenditure on cars only. Businesses using the cash basis do not have to use the simplified flat rate expenses for their cars.

Eligible barristers are able to choose either to use the cash basis and simplified expenses or the accruals basis. The existing cash basis arrangement for barristers is withdrawn except for barristers already using it, for the remainder of their qualifying period.

| | Relevant max. Joining[2] £ | Leaving Threshold[2] £ |
|---|---|---|
| **From 6 April 2017** | | |
| Standard | 150,000 | 300,000 |
| Recipients of universal credit[1] | 300,000 | |
| **2016–17** | | |
| Standard | 83,000 | 166,000 |
| Recipients of universal credit[1] | 166,000 | |
| **2015–16** | | |
| Standard | 82,000 | 164,000 |
| Recipients of universal credit[1] | 164,000 | |
| **2014–15** | | |
| Standard | 81,000 | 162,000 |
| Recipients of universal credit[1] | 162,000 | |
| **2013–14** | | |
| Standard | 79,000 | 158,000 |
| Recipients of universal credit[1] | 158,000 | |

**Notes**

[1] Recipients of universal credit must use the cash basis for income assessment for UC purposes.

[2] Joining and leaving thresholds are prescribed by ITTOIA 2005, s. 31B (as amended by SI 2017/293, for tax the tax year 2017–18 and subsequent tax years).

**Excluded businesses:**

- companies;
- limited liability partnerships;
- partnerships with a non-individual partner during the basis period;
- lloyds underwriters;
- farming businesses with a herd basis election in effect for the tax year;
- farming and creative businesses with a profits averaging election in effect for the tax year;
- businesses that have claimed business premises renovation allowances within the previous seven years (ending immediately before the basis period);
- businesses that carry on a mineral extraction trade during the basis period for the tax year;
- businesses that still own an asset in respect of which research and development allowances have been claimed (at any time).

### Simplified cash basis for unincorporated businesses

(Finance Bill 2017)

As announced in January 2017, the Government will legislate in Finance Bill 2017 to provide a simple list of disallowed expenditure in order to simplify the rules for allowable deductions within the cash basis. These changes will have effect from April 2017, though for the 2017–18 tax year trading profits can be calculated using either the new rules or the existing rules.

Also from 6 April 2017, legislation in Finance Bill 2017 will allow most unincorporated property businesses (other than limited liability partnerships, trusts, partnerships with corporate partners or those with receipts of more than £150,000) to calculate their taxable profits using a cash basis of accounting. Landlords will continue to be able to opt to use generally accepted accounting principles (GAAP) to prepare their profits for tax purposes.

To align the treatment with those who opt to use GAAP, the initial cost of items used in a dwelling-house will also not be an allowable expense under the cash basis. The existing 'replacement of domestic items relief' will continue to be available for the replacement of these items when the expenditure is paid. Interest expense will be treated consistently between those using the cash basis and those using GAAP.

## [¶2-020]  Trade profits: deductions allowable at a fixed rate

(ITTOIA 2005, Pt. 2, Ch. 5A)

(Tax Reporter: ¶208-380)

From April 2013 (with effect for the tax year 2013–14 and subsequent tax years), unincorporated businesses are entitled to use flat rates to calculate certain types of expenses rather than having to calculate actual amounts.

*Taxation of Business Profits*

| Expense | From 6 April 2013 |
|---|---|
| **Expenditure on vehicles** Car or goods vehicle – first 10,000 miles – above 10,000 miles Motorcycle | £0.45/mile £0.25/mile £0.24/mile |
| | **Rate per Month** £ |
| **Use of home for business**[1][3] 25–50 hours per month 51–100 hours per month 101 hours or more per month Or claim allowable portion of actual costs | 10.00 18.00 26.00 |
| **Premises used both as home and business premises**[2][3] Disallowance (for personal element of expenses) one occupant using premises as a home two occupants using premises as a home three or more occupants using premises as a home Or identify allowable portion of actual costs | 350.00 500.00 650.00 |

**Notes**
[1] Deduction is given for each month or part of a month in relation to the number of hours spent wholly and exclusively on work done by the person in their home wholly and exclusively for the purposes of the trade (ITTOIA 2005, s. 94H).
[2] Available for premises which are mainly used for the purposes of carrying on the trade but also used by the person as a home. Instead of apportioning expenses between business and personal use, a deduction may be claimed for the full expense minus the relevant flat rate non-business use amount (ITTOIA 2005, s. 94I).
[3] *Finance Act* 2016 amends the simplified expenses regime, with effect for the tax year 2016–17 and subsequent tax years, to ensure that partnerships can fully access the provisions in respect of the use of a home and where business premises are also a home.

## [¶2-030]  Limited liability partnerships: salaried members

(ITTOIA 2005, s. 863A–863G)

(Tax Reporter: ¶292-650)

From 6 April 2014, an individual member (M) of an LLP is treated as an employee for tax purposes (subject to PAYE and to tax on any benefits in kind) if all of the three conditions set out below are met. The rules apply only to LLPs formed under the *Limited Liability Partnership Act* 2000, not to general partnerships or limited partnerships that are formed under the *Partnership Act* 1890 and the *Limited Partnership Act* 1907, respectively.

| Condition | Requirements for condition to be satisfied |
|---|---|
| **Condition A: Disguised salary** | Arrangements are in place under which: • M is to perform services for the LLP; and • it is reasonable to expect that at least 80% of the total amount payable by the LLP in respect of M's performance of those services will be 'disguised salary' (i.e. fixed, or variable but without reference to the overall amount of the profits or losses of the LLP; or not in practice affected by the overall profits or losses of the LLP). |

| Condition | Requirements for condition to be satisfied |
|---|---|
| **Condition B: Significant influence** | If the mutual rights and duties of the members and the LLP do not give M significant influence over the affairs of the partnership. |
| **Condition C: Capital contribution** | M's contribution to the LLP is less than 25% of the disguised salary which it is reasonable to expect will be payable in a relevant tax year in respect of M's performance of services for the partnership. |

## [¶2-050]  Car hire: leases starting from 6 April 2009

(ITTOIA 2005, s. 48ff.)

(Tax Reporter: ¶212-025)

Leased cars, where the lease begins from 6 April 2009 (for income tax purposes), suffer a 15% disallowance of relevant payments if $CO_2$ emissions exceed the limits set out below, otherwise no disallowance. This applies to all cars (not just those costing more than £12,000).

| | $CO_2$ emissions |
|---|---|
| From 6 April 2013 | Over 130g/km |
| 6 April 2009 to 5 April 2013 | Over 160g/km |

## [¶2-060]  Car hire: leases starting before 6 April 2009

(ITTOIA 2005, s. 48ff.)

(Tax Reporter: ¶212-050)

For leased cars where the lease began before 6 April 2009, the restricted deduction for hire charges of motor cars with a retail price greater than £12,000 is calculated as follows:

$$\text{Allowable amount} = \frac{£12{,}000 + \frac{1}{2}\,(\text{retail price} - £12{,}000)}{\text{retail price}} \times \text{hire charge}$$

# [¶2-100]   Time limits for elections and claims

(TMA 1970, s. 43(1))

(Tax Reporter: ¶191-635)

In the absence of any provision to the contrary, under self-assessment for the purposes of income tax, the normal rule is that claims are to be made within four years from the end of the tax year to which they relate. Before 1 April 2010, the time limit was generally five years from 31 January following the end of the tax year.

Other specific income tax provisions are as below.

| Provision | Time limit | Statutory reference |
|---|---|---|
| Averaging of profits of farmers or creative artists | first anniversary of the normal self-assessment filing date for the second tax year | ITTOIA 2005, s. 222 |
| Stock transferred to a connected party on cessation of trade (or, from April 2009, profession or vocation) to be valued at higher of cost or sale price | first anniversary of the normal self-assessment filing date for the tax year of cessation | ITTOIA 2005, s. 178 |
| Post-cessation expenses relieved against income and chargeable gains | first anniversary of the normal self-assessment filing date for the tax year | ITTOIA 2005, s. 257(4); ITA 2007, s. 96 |
| Current and preceding year set-off of trading losses | first anniversary of the normal self-assessment filing date for the loss-making year | ITA 2007, s. 64 |
| Three-year carry-back of trading losses in first four years of trade | first anniversary of the normal self-assessment filing date for the tax year in which the loss is made | ITA 2007, s. 72 |
| Carry-forward of trading losses | normal rules apply (see above) | ITA 2007, s. 83ff. |
| Carry-back of terminal losses | normal rules apply (see above) | ITA 2007, s. 89 |

# TAXATION OF INVESTMENT INCOME

## [¶3-000]   Registered pension schemes

(FA 2004, Pt. 4, Ch. 1–7 and Sch. 28–36; SI 2014/1843)

From 6 April 2006, ('A' day) a revised set of rules applies to all forms of pension provision.

### Age restrictions

Normal minimum pension age is 55 from 6 April 2010 (previously 50) except for retirement on ill-health grounds and some preserved lower retirement ages – see below.

From 2010–11 onwards, there is no minimum benefit age. Previously, benefits had to be taken by the age of 77 at the latest (age 75 before 22 June 2010).

### Recent and forthcoming changes

- From April 2017 (as announced at Autumn Statement 2016 and confirmed at Spring Budget 2017):
  - the Money Purchase Annual Allowance is reduced to £4,000 from April 2017;
  - legislation in Finance Bill 2017 will more closely align the treatment of foreign pensions with the UK's domestic pension regime. Following consultation, the legislation has been revised to set out the position for defined benefit specialist pension schemes for those employed abroad (s. 615 schemes) and clarify that all lump sums paid out of funds built up before 6 April 2017 will be subject to existing tax treatment. These changes will have effect from 6 April 2017;
  - legislation in Finance Bill 2017 will apply a 25% tax charge to pension transfers made to QROPS (see ¶3-100);
  - legislation in Finance Bill 2017 will apply UK tax rules to payments from funds that have had UK tax relief and have been transferred, on or after 6 April 2017, to a qualifying recognised overseas pension scheme. UK tax rules will apply to any payments made in the first five full tax years following the transfer, regardless of whether the individual is or has been UK resident in that period.
- *Finance Act* 2016 legislated for a number of minor changes to the pensions tax rules to ensure that they operate as intended following the introduction of pension flexibility in April 2015, with effect from 15 September 2016, that:
  - remove the requirement that a serious ill-health lump sum can only be paid from an arrangement that has never been accessed;
  - replace the 45% tax charge on serious ill-health lump sums paid to individuals who have reached age 75 with tax at the individual's marginal rate;
  - enable dependants with drawdown or flexi-access drawdown pension who would currently have to use all of this fund before age 23 or pay tax charges of up to 70% on any lump sum payment, to continue to access their funds as they wish after their 23rd birthday;

- remove the rule on paying a charity lump sum death benefit out of drawdown pension funds and flexi-access drawdown funds where the member dies under the age of 75 because the equivalent tax-free payment may be made as another type of lump sum death benefit;
- enable money purchase pensions in payment to be paid as a trivial commutation lump sum;
- enable the full amount of dependants benefits to be paid as authorised payments where there are insufficient funds in a cash balance arrangement when the member dies.

## Tax relief on contributions

(ITEPA 2003, s. 308; FA 2004, Pt. 4, Ch. 4)

(Tax Reporter: ¶376-000ff.; ¶376-500ff.)

| Type of contribution | Tax relief |
|---|---|
| Individual | Up to 100% of individual's earned income or £3,600 if higher per annum |
| Employer | No income tax for employee (not a taxable BIK)<br>No NIC liability<br>Tax deductible for employer[1] |

Where contributions in a chargeable period exceed 210% of the contributions made in the immediately preceding chargeable period, relief for the excess of the current period contributions over 110% of the previous period's contributions (where that excess amounts to £500,000 or more) is to be spread forward into future chargeable periods. A fraction of the excess is to be treated as being paid in the current and subsequent periods (as below) with any remainder of the excess being relieved in the current period:

- excess £500,000 or more but less than £1m: one-half of excess allowed in current period and the next succeeding periods;
- excess £1m or more but less than £2m: one-third of excess allowed in the current period and the two following periods;
- excess £2m or more: one quarter of excess allowed in current period and the three following periods (FA 2004, s. 197).

## [¶3-050]   Authorised payments limits

(ITEPA 2003, s. 636A; FA 2004, s. 164ff., Sch. 28 and 29)

(Tax Reporter: ¶378-000ff.)

| Payments | Limits |
|---|---|
| Pension commencement[1] | 25% tax free lump sum (75% as pension income at marginal rate) |
| Capped drawdown[2] | 150% maximum on or after 27 March 2014 (previously 120%) |
| Flexible drawdown[3] | No limit from 6 April 2015 (£12,000 minimum income requirement on or after 27 March 2014; previously £20,000) |
| Trivial commutation lump sum[4] | £30,000 on or after 27 March 2014 (previously £18,000) |
| Small pension pot[4][5] | £10,000; three lump sums on or after 27 March 2014 (previously £2,000; two lump sums) |
| Dependants' trivial commutation lump sum death benefit[6] | £30,000 from 6 April 2015 (previously, £18,000) all at dependant's marginal rate |
| Uncrystallised funds pension lump sum[7] | 25% tax free 75% at marginal rate |

**Notes**

[1] From 6 April 2015, the *Taxation of Pensions Act* 2014 amends the anti-recycling rules in FA 2004, Sch. 29, para. 3A which prevent the exploitation of the pensions tax rules to generate artificially high amounts of tax relief by using the pension commencement lump sum to make a further tax-relieved contribution into a registered pension scheme. The amendment reduces to £7,500 (from 1% of the standard lifetime allowance) the minimum aggregate value of pension commencement lump sums paid to an individual in a 12-month period that triggers the recycling rule.

[2] Under capped drawdown, the maximum amount of drawdown pension that can be paid is 150% of the amount of an equivalent single life annuity that the member's drawdown pension fund could buy (the basis amount) for drawdown years beginning on or after 27 March 2014. Previously, the maximum was 120% (FA 2004, s. 165). The *Taxation of Pensions Act* 2014 amended FA 2004, s. 165(1) to provide that the cap on the amount that can be taken each year applies only to a member's drawdown pension fund as defined in FA 2004, Sch. 28, para. 8. Where funds are withdrawn from flexi-access drawdown funds (as defined in FA 2004, Sch. 28, para. 8A–8D), there is accordingly no cap on the amount that can be withdrawn each year.

[3] From 6 April 2015, there is no limit on how much can be taken from a flexi-access drawdown fund, but when benefits are first accessed from that fund, the money purchase annual allowance rules described in Pt. 4 are triggered in respect of that member. Prior to 6 April 2015, certain conditions had to be met to take flexible drawdown (i.e. as much of their member's drawdown pension fund as they wish in any year), including that an individual had to have a guaranteed pension income of at least £12,000 a year (for flexible drawdown declarations made on or after 27 March 2014, previously, the limit was £20,000) (FA 2004, Sch. 28, para. 14A).

[4] Apart from flexible drawdown, the only circumstances where an individual can normally take all of their pension pot as a single one-off payment is where their total pension savings in all funds are less than £30,000 (the trivial commutation limit for commutation periods beginning on or after 27 March 2014, previously, the limit was £18,000) or in certain circumstances where the value of a small pension pot is less than £10,000 (for payments made on or after 27 March 2014, previously the limit was £2,000). From 6 April 2015, a trivial commutation lump sum can be paid only

in respect of a defined benefits arrangement. Those with relatively small amounts of money purchase savings will be able to take an UFPLS from this date, so there is no longer a need for trivial commutation lump sum rules for money purchase arrangements. To qualify for these payments, the individual must have reached normal minimum pension age (normally age 55) or satisfy the ill-health condition in FA 2004, Sch. 28, para. 1 (from 6 April 2015; previously, individuals had to have reached age 60). From 15 September 2016, a trivial commutation lump sum may be paid out of a money purchase scheme pension that is already in payment (FA 2004, Sch. 29, para. 7 and ITEPA 2003, s. 636B, as amended by FA 2016, s. 22 and Sch. 5).

[5] The maximum number of small lump sums payable increased from two to three for payments made on or after 27 March 2014 (SI 2009/1171).

[6] A trivial commutation lump sum death benefit can be paid to a dependant and, from 6 April 2015, to an individual in respect of any entitlement they had to receive any guaranteed pension payments of a lifetime annuity or scheme pension payable after the member's death. The whole lump sum will be taxable at the dependant's marginal rate. The limit is also increased to £30,000, for payments made on or after 6 April 2015, to bring the maximum in line with a trivial commutation lump sum.

[7] A new type of authorised lump sum payment (UFPLS) can be paid on or after 6 April 2015 directly from pension savings under a money purchase arrangement to certain individuals aged 55 or over. Individuals who meet the conditions to have an UFPLS can, therefore, if they wish, access as much of their money purchase pension savings as they want, without having first to designate the funds as available for drawdown. Where an UFPLS is paid, then this is flexible access and the money purchase annual allowance rules are triggered in respect of that member (FA 2004, s. 166(1) and Sch. 29, para. 4A).

## [¶3-075]   Annual and lifetime allowances

(FA 2004, s. 214ff. and 227ff.)

(Tax Reporter: ¶386-000 and ¶384-000)

Since A-day, there have been no limits on the amount of pension savings an individual can have, but there are limits on the amount of tax relief that is available. These are the lifetime allowance and the annual allowance.

| Year | Annual allowance limit[1][2][3] | Annual allowance income limit[4] | Money purchase annual allowance[5] | Lifetime allowance[6][8][9][10] | Lifetime allowance charge[7] |
|---|---|---|---|---|---|
| 2017–18 | £40,000 | £150,000 | £4,000 | £1m | 25% as pension; 55% as lump sum |
| 2016–17 | £40,000 | £150,000 | £10,000 | £1m | 25% as pension; 55% as lump sum |

| Year | Annual allowance limit[1][2][3] | Annual allowance income limit[4] | Money purchase annual allowance[5] | Lifetime allowance[6][8][9][10] | Li... a... cha... [7] |
|---|---|---|---|---|---|
| **2015–16**[3] 9 July 2015 – 5 April 2016 ('post-alignment tax year') | £40,000 | — | | | 25% as pension; 55% as lump sum |
| **2015–16**[3] 6 April 2015 – 8 July 2015 ('pre-alignment tax year') | £80,000 | — | £10,000 | £1.25m | |
| 2014–15 | £40,000 | — | — | £1.25m | 25% as pension; 55% as lump sum |
| 2013–14 and 2012–13 | £50,000 | — | — | £1.5m | 25% as pension; 55% as lump sum |
| 2011–12 | £50,000 | — | — | £1.80m | 25% as pension; 55% as lump sum |

**Notes**

*Annual allowance*

[1] An individual's annual allowance (AA) applies to all of that individual's pension arrangements for a year. It measures the 'pension input amount' for a tax year. That is the increase in the pension savings in that tax year (including contributions made by the individual and employer); and/or the increase in the value of the individual's pension rights (depending on the type of scheme, i.e. money purchase, defined benefit, etc.). If the 'pension input amount' for a year exceeds the AA for that year, the excess is subject to the charge. For future years the AA will be fixed by Treasury Order. Where for 2011–12 onwards, an annual allowance charge arises the annual allowance for that year may be increased by the unused annual allowance of the three immediately preceding years, except where the charge arises in 2015–16 or later and in a preceding year, the member or a dependant elected for flexible drawdown (in which case, no carry forward of unused annual allowance from that preceding year is possible) (FA 2004, s. 228A). From 6 April 2016, pension input periods are aligned with the tax year. See note (3) below.

[2] An AA charge is the liability of the individual member of the scheme (or schemes where an individual is a member of more than one scheme), but provisions introduced from 6 April 2011 enable the member to transfer that liability onto the scheme administrator in certain circumstances (Tax Reporter: ¶386-010; FA 2004, s. 227–238). From 2011–12 onwards, the rate of tax to be charged on the excess is to be the 'appropriate rate'; that is, the rate or rates which would be charged on the excess if it was to be added to the individual's 'reduced net income' for the tax year concerned. That figure is the sum calculated at Step 3 of the prescribed method of calculating income tax liabilities. Any increase in the basic rate or higher rate bands due to pension contributions made under deduction of tax or gift aid payments is also taken into account for this purpose.

(3) From 6 April 2016, pension input periods are aligned with the tax year. The 2015–16 tax year is split into two parts for the purposes of the annual allowance, the 'pre-alignment tax year' which ends on 8 July 2015 and the 'post-alignment tax year' which starts on 9 July 2015 and ends on 5 April 2016. Every member of a registered pension scheme has an annual allowance of £80,000 for the 2015–16 tax year, subject to an allowance of £40,000 for the period from 9 July 2015 to 5 April 2016, in addition to any existing unused annual allowance carried forward from the three previous tax years.

- For members of registered pension schemes in the pre-alignment tax year, this is achieved by doubling the normal annual allowance for the pre-alignment tax year to £80,000 or £20,000 for those who have flexibly accessed their pension savings (the money purchase annual allowance) and setting the annual allowance and the alternative annual allowance (normally AA minus £10,000 (FA 2004, s. 227B)) for the post-alignment tax year as nil. The money purchase annual allowance for this period will be £10,000 less any amount that their money purchase savings for the pre-alignment tax year exceeded £10,000. Up to £40,000 of unused annual allowance from the pre-alignment tax year may be carried forward and added to the nil annual allowance for the post-alignment tax year, however, where an individual exceeded the money purchase annual allowance in the pre-alignment tax year, this carry forward is limited to £30,000.
- For individuals who are not members of a registered pension scheme in the pre-alignment tax year, their annual allowance will be £40,000 for the post-alignment tax year.

Only one annual allowance charge can arise in 2015–16 which is the sum of any charge arising under the pre-alignment and post-alignment tax years (FA 2004, s. 228C, 237ZA, 238, 238ZA–238ZB).

(4) From 6 April 2016, the existing £40,000 annual allowance is gradually reduced to £10,000 for those with incomes, including the amount of any pension savings, above £150,000. For each £2 of income above £150,000, an individual's annual allowance will reduce by £1 until the individual's income reaches £210,000 or over, when their annual allowance will be £10,000 (FA 2004, s. 228ZA and 228ZB).

(5) Where an individual has flexibly accessed their pension savings on or after 6 April 2015, an annual allowance will immediately apply to their future money purchase pension savings: the money purchase annual allowance rules. However, those individuals will retain an annual allowance for defined benefits pension savings, depending on the value of new money purchase pension savings. Unused annual allowance brought forward from earlier tax years will not be available to increase the money purchase annual allowance (FA 2004, s. 227ZA–227G).

*Lifetime allowance*

(6) An individual's lifetime allowance (LTA) is a measure of the total value of an individual's pension savings at the time that pension benefits begin to be taken. For future years the LTA will be fixed by Treasury Order.

(7) An LTA charge (55% on any excess over the LTA constituting a lump sum payment; and 25% on any excess over the LTA not used to pay a lump sum but to fund pension payments) is the joint and several liability of the individual and the pension scheme administrator (Tax Reporter: ¶384-050; FA 2004, s. 214–226).

(8) *Finance Act* 2013, Sch. 22 provided a transitional protection regime (fixed protection 2014) for individuals with UK tax relieved pension rights (or anticipated rights) of more than £1.25m who notified HMRC by 5 April 2014.

(9) *Finance Act* 2014 introduced a further transitional protection regime, individual protection 2014 (IP14) which entitled individuals with pension savings on 5 April 2014 of greater than £1.25m but who did not have primary protection to a lifetime allowance equal to the value of those savings, subject to an overall limit of £1.5m. SI 2014/1842 sets out relevant notice requirements.

(10) *Finance Act* 2016 reduced the lifetime allowance for pension contributions to £1m for the tax years 2016–17 and 2017–18. *Finance Act* 2016 also provides a requirement for the Treasury to make regulations before the start of tax year 2018–19 and each subsequent tax year, specifying the amount of the standard lifetime allowance for the year. The allowance will be increased by CPI (rounded up to the nearest £100) where the CPI for the year to the previous September is higher than it was 12 months earlier, otherwise, the allowance will remain the same as for the previous tax year (FA 2004, s. 218, as amended by FA 2016, s. 19). Transitional protection for pension rights already over £1m was introduced by way of two new transitional protections 'fixed protection 2016' and 'individual protection 2016', also from 6 April 2016 (FA 2016, Sch. 4).

## [¶3-100]   Pension schemes: tax charges

### Authorised payment charges

(FA 2004, s. 204–207)

(Tax Reporter: ¶383-000ff.)

| Tax charges | Pre-6 April 2015 | From 6 April 2015 |
|---|---|---|
| Short service refund lump sum charge[1] (FA 2004, s. 205; Tax Reporter: ¶383-100) | 20% up to £20,000; 50% on excess | 20% up to £20,000; 50% on excess |
| Serious ill health lump sum charge[2][7] (FA 2004, s. 205A; Tax Reporter: ¶383-120) | 55% | 45% |
| Special lump sum death benefits charge[3][4][5][6] (FA 2004, s. 206; Tax Reporter: ¶383-150) | 55% | 45% |
| Authorised surplus payments charge (FA 2004, s. 207; Tax Reporter: ¶383-200) | 35% | 35% |

**Notes**

[1] A tax charge arises where a registered pension scheme repays tax-relieved pension contributions to a member who has completed less than two years service ('short service refund lump sums'). The rate is 20% on the first £20,000 and 50% thereafter.

[2] A charge also arises where a serious ill-health lump sum is paid on or after 6 April 2011 to a member over the age of 75. Tax is charged at the rate of 55%. Tax is also chargeable under this heading in respect of a lump sum paid to a 'relieved member' or a 'transfer member' of a 'relevant non-UK scheme'.

[3] A special lump sum death benefits charge arises where a pension protection lump sum death benefit, an annuity protection lump sum death benefit or a drawdown (previously, unsecured) pension fund lump sum death benefit is paid by a registered pension scheme. Tax is also chargeable under this heading in respect of a lump sum paid to a relieved member or a transfer member of a 'relevant non-UK scheme'. For lump sums paid on or after 6 April 2015, this charge only applies where the member had reached age 75 at their death.

[4] From 6 April 2011, the charge also applies to a defined benefits lump sum death benefit or an uncrystallised funds lump sum death benefit paid in respect of a member who dies having reached the age of 75.

[5] From 6 April 2015, the charge also applies if a member dies before age 75, and a drawdown pension fund lump sum death benefit, a flexi-access drawdown fund lump sum death benefit or an uncrystallised funds lump sum death benefit is paid outside a two-year period; and also if a beneficiary dies before age 75, and prescribed lump sum death benefits are paid outside the two-year period (FA 2004, s. 206(1B)(1C)).

[6] From 2016–17, the 45% tax rate that applies on lump sums paid from the pension of someone who dies aged 75 and over is reduced to the marginal rate of the recipient (ITEPA 2003, s. 636A, 636AA).

[7] From 15 September 2016, where an individual would meet the requirements to take a serious ill-health lump sum but for the fact that they have accessed their pension, they will be able to take the remaining funds that have not been accessed as a serious ill-health lump sum. Where a serious ill-health lump sum is paid to an individual who has reached the age of 75, it will be taxable at that individual's marginal rate rather than at a flat rate of 45% (amendments by FA 2016, Sch. 5).

Taxation of Investment Income

## Other charges

(FA 2004, s. 208–213, 242)

(Tax Reporter: ¶383-500ff.; ¶388-500)

| Charge | Rate |
|---|---|
| Unauthorised payments charge[1]<br>(FA 2004, s. 208; Tax Reporter: ¶383-550) | 40% |
| Unauthorised payments surcharge[2]<br>(FA 2004, s. 209; Tax Reporter: ¶383-600) | 15% |
| Scheme sanction charge[3]<br>(FA 2004, s. 239; Tax Reporter: ¶383-700) | 40% |
| Deregistration charge[4]<br>(FA 2004, s. 242; Tax Reporter: ¶388-500) | 40% |
| Overseas transfer charge (from 9 March 2017 on certain transfers to and from a QROPS) (Finance Bill 2017) | 25% |

**Notes**

[1] If unauthorised payments are made out of a registered pension scheme, the person receiving the payment(s) (i.e. the member, the employer or the recipient of any death benefit) is liable to a tax charge equal to 40% of the payment(s).

[2] A surcharge may be added to the unauthorised payment charge if a scheme pays out more than 25% of the scheme's fund in unauthorised payments.

[3] The scheme sanction charge is imposed at the rate of 40% of the aggregate of the 'scheme chargeable payments' (as defined by FA 2004, s. 241). The person liable to the scheme sanction charge is the scheme administrator. Where the scheme chargeable payment is also an unauthorised payment which has given rise to an unauthorised payments charge, the tax due under the scheme sanction charge is effectively reduced by the amount of tax actually paid (rather than charged) under the unauthorised payments charge.

[4] Where a registered scheme loses its registered status, a 'deregistration charge' of 40% of the aggregate value of the pension scheme's assets is levied on an payable by the scheme administrator.

[5] Spring Budget 2017 announced that the Government will legislate in Finance Bill 2017 to apply a 25% tax charge to pension transfers made to QROPS. Exceptions will be made to the charge, allowing transfers to be made tax free where people have a genuine need to transfer their pension, where:

- both the individual and the pension scheme are in countries within the European Economic Area (EEA);
- if outside the EEA, both the individual and the pension scheme are in the same country; or
- the QROPS is an occupational pension scheme provided by the individual's employer.

If the individual's circumstances change within five tax years of the transfer, the tax treatment of the transfer will be reconsidered. The changes will take effect for transfers requested on or after 9 March 2017.

## [¶3-150]   Early retirement ages: retirement annuity contracts and personal pension schemes

### From 6 April 2006

(FA 2004, Sch. 36, para. 23)

(Tax Reporter: ¶390-450)

Under the simplified pensions' rules applying from 6 April 2006 onwards, early retirement ages (apart from on ill-health grounds) are eliminated for all new schemes. The 'normal minimum pension age' is 55. Where arrangements for pre-6 April 2006 schemes permit retirement earlier than 55 the 'normal minimum pension age' will be 50, with effect from 6 April 2006; rising to 55, with effect from 6 April 2010.

It is possible for members of pre-6 April 2006 schemes that permit retirement earlier than the 'normal minimum pension age' to preserve their rights to early retirement in some circumstances. Members of retirement annuity contracts or personal pension schemes will be able to protect their right to take pension and lump sum benefits before the 'normal minimum pension age' (i.e. before 50 until 6 April 2010) by establishing their 'unqualified right', as at 6 April 2006, to a protected pension age that is lower than the 'normal minimum pension age'.

In order to exercise the right to a lower than normal pension age, the member must:

- be or have been in one of the occupations prescribed in the list at the *Registered Pension Schemes (Prescribed Schemes and Occupations) Regulations* 2005 (SI 2005/3451), Sch. 2, prior to 6 April 2006; and

- have had an 'unqualified right' to take a pension before the age of 50, prior to 6 April 2006 (an 'unqualified right' is when the individual needs no other party to consent to their request to take an early pension before it becomes binding upon the scheme or contract holder).

The list below will continue to apply to retirement annuity contract holders and personal pension scheme members who are able to meet the conditions for a protected pension age lower than 50, as at 6 April 2006. All of the professions noted in the list below that have a retirement age of less than 50 are included in the list at SI 2005/3451, Sch. 2.

| Profession or occupation | Retirement age[1] | |
|---|---|---|
| | Retirement annuity contracts | Personal pension schemes |
| Athletes (appearance and prize money) | 35 | 35 |
| Badminton players | 35 | 35 |
| Boxers | 35 | 35 |
| Cricketers | 40 | 40 |
| Cyclists | 35 | 35 |
| Dancers | 35 | 35 |
| Divers (saturation, deep sea and free swimming) | 40 | 40 |
| Footballers | 35 | 35 |
| Golfers (tournament earnings) | 40 | 40 |
| Ice hockey players | 35 | 35 |
| Jockeys – flat racing | 45 | 45 |
| – national hunt | 35 | 35 |
| Members of the reserve forces | 45 | 45 |
| Models | 35 | 35 |
| Motorcycle riders (motorcross or road racing) | 40 | 40 |
| Motor racing drivers | 40 | 40 |
| Rugby league players | 35 | 35 |

Taxation of Investment Income

| Profession or occupation | Retirement age[1] | |
| | Retirement annuity contracts | Personal pension schemes |
| --- | --- | --- |
| Rugby union players | 35 | 35 |
| Skiers (downhill) | — | 30 |
| Snooker or billiards players | 40 | 40 |
| Speedway riders | 40 | 40 |
| Squash players | 35 | 35 |
| Table tennis players | 35 | 35 |
| Tennis players (including real tennis) | 35 | 35 |
| Trapeze artistes | 40 | 40 |
| Wrestlers | 35 | 35 |

**Note**

[1] The pension age shown applies only to pension arrangements funded by contributions paid in respect of the relevant earnings from the occupation or profession carrying that age.

If an individual wishes to make pension provisions in respect of another source of relevant earnings to which the pension age shown above does not apply then a separate arrangement, with a pension age within the normal range, must be made.

In particular, the ages shown above for professional sportsmen apply only to arrangements made in respect of relevant earnings from activities as professional sportsmen, e.g. tournament earnings, appearance and prize money. They do not apply to relevant earnings from sponsorship or coaching.

## [¶3-175]   Equalisation of and increase in pensionable ages for both men and women

For the purposes of social security legislation, an individual's pensionable age is determined by the following rules and tables. These gradually increase the pensionable age for women from the traditional age of 60 to bring it into line with that for men, while also increasing the ages for both sexes. Dates in the table below are grouped in one-month periods. A person born towards the end of one of these periods would have a slightly younger pension age than someone born at the beginning.

A man born before 6 December 1953 still attains pensionable age at age 65, while a woman born before 6 April 1950 attained pensionable age at age 60. The date the pensionable age is attained by individuals born after those dates is set out in the tables below. Table 1 relates to women born before 6 December 1953, while Table 2 relates to someone of either sex born on or after that date.

Autumn Statement 2013 announced that state pension age will increase to age 68 in the mid 2030s and to age 69 in the late 2040s.

**Table 1: Women**

| Date of birth (by month) | State pension age y.m | Pensionable age attained |
| --- | --- | --- |
| 06/04/50 to 05/05/50 | 60.1–60.0 | 06/05/2010 |
| 06/05/50 to 05/06/50 | 60.2–60.1 | 06/07/2010 |

| Date of birth (by month) | State pension age y.m | Pensionable age attained |
|---|---|---|
| 06/06/50 to 05/07/50 | 60.3–60.2 | 06/09/2010 |
| 06/07/50 to 05/08/50 | 60.4–60.3 | 06/11/2010 |
| 06/08/50 to 05/09/50 | 60.5–60.4 | 06/01/2011 |
| 06/09/50 to 05/10/50 | 60.6–60.5 | 06/03/2011 |
| 06/10/50 to 05/11/50 | 60.7–60.6 | 06/05/2011 |
| 06/11/50 to 05/12/50 | 60.8–60.7 | 06/07/2011 |
| 06/12/50 to 05/01/51 | 60.9–60.8 | 06/09/2011 |
| 06/01/51 to 05/02/51 | 60.10–60.9 | 06/11/2011 |
| 06/02/51 to 05/03/51 | 60.11–60.10 | 06/01/2012 |
| 06/03/51 to 05/04/51 | 61.0–60.11 | 06/03/2012 |
| 06/04/51 to 05/05/51 | 61.1–61.0 | 06/05/2012 |
| 06/05/51 to 05/06/51 | 61.2–61.1 | 06/07/2012 |
| 06/06/51 to 05/07/51 | 61.3–61.2 | 06/09/2012 |
| 06/07/51 to 05/08/51 | 61.4–61.3 | 06/11/2012 |
| 06/08/51 to 05/09/51 | 61.5–61.4 | 06/01/2013 |
| 06/09/51 to 05/10/51 | 61.6–61.5 | 06/03/2013 |
| 06/10/51 to 05/11/51 | 61.7–61.6 | 06/05/2013 |
| 06/11/51 to 05/12/51 | 61.8–61.7 | 06/07/2013 |
| 06/12/51 to 05/01/52 | 61.9–61.8 | 06/09/2013 |
| 06/01/52 to 05/02/52 | 61.10–61.9 | 06/11/2013 |
| 06/02/52 to 05/03/52 | 61.11–61.10 | 06/01/2014 |
| 06/03/52 to 05/04/52 | 62.0–61.11 | 06/03/2014 |
| 06/04/52 to 05/05/52 | 62.1–62.0 | 06/05/2014 |
| 06/05/52 to 05/06/52 | 62.2–62.1 | 06/07/2014 |
| 06/06/52 to 05/07/52 | 62.3–62.2 | 06/09/2014 |
| 06/07/52 to 05/08/52 | 62.4–62.3 | 06/11/2014 |
| 06/08/52 to 05/09/52 | 62.5–62.4 | 06/01/2015 |
| 06/09/52 to 05/10/52 | 62.6–62.5 | 06/03/2015 |
| 06/10/52 to 05/11/52 | 62.7–62.6 | 06/05/2015 |
| 06/11/52 to 05/12/52 | 62.8–62.7 | 06/07/2015 |
| 06/12/52 to 05/01/53 | 62.9–62.8 | 06/09/2015 |
| 06/01/53 to 05/02/53 | 62.10–62.9 | 06/11/2015 |
| 06/02/53 to 05/03/53 | 62.11–62.10 | 06/01/2016 |
| 06/03/53 to 05/04/53 | 63.0–62.11 | 06/03/2016 |
| 06/04/53 to 05/05/53 | 63.3–63.2 | 06/07/2016 |
| 06/05/53 to 05/06/53 | 63.6–63.5 | 06/11/2016 |
| 06/06/53 to 05/07/53 | 63.9–63.8 | 06/03/2017 |
| 06/07/53 to 05/08/53 | 64.0–63.11 | 06/07/2017 |
| 06/08/53 to 05/09/53 | 64.3–64.2 | 06/11/2017 |
| 06/09/53 to 05/10/53 | 64.6–64.5 | 06/03/2018 |
| 06/10/53 to 05/11/53 | 64.9–64.8 | 06/07/2018 |
| 06/11/53 to 05/12/53 | 65.0–64.11 | 06/11/2018 |

Taxation of Investment Income

Table 2: Men and Women

| Date of birth (by month) | State pension age[1] y.m | Pensionable age attained[1] |
|---|---|---|
| 06/12/53 to 05/01/54 | 65.3–65.2 | 06/03/2019 |
| 06/01/54 to 05/02/54 | 65.4–65.3 | 06/05/2019 |
| 06/02/54 to 05/03/54 | 65.5–65.4 | 06/07/2019 |
| 06/03/54 to 05/04/54 | 65.6–65.5 | 06/09/2019 |
| 06/04/54 to 05/05/54 | 65.7–65.6 | 06/11/2019 |
| 06/05/54 to 05/06/54 | 65.8–65.7 | 06/01/2020 |
| 06/06/54 to 05/07/54 | 65.9–65.8 | 06/03/2020 |
| 06/07/54 to 05/08/54 | 65.10–65.9 | 06/05/2020 |
| 06/08/54 to 05/09/54 | 65.11–65.10 | 06/07/2020 |
| 06/09/54 to 05/10/54 | 66.0–65.11 | 06/09/2020 |
| 06/10/54 to 05/04/60 | Age 66 | [06/10/2020–05/04/2026] |
| 06/04/60 to 05/05/60 | Age 66 years and 1 month | [06/05/2026–05/06/2026] |
| 06/05/60 to 05/06/60 | Age 66 years and 2 months | [06/07/2026–05/08/2026] |
| 06/06/60 to 05/07/60 | Age 66 years and 3 months | [06/09/2026–05/10/2026] |
| 06/07/60[2] to 05/08/60 | Age 66 years and 4 months | [06/11/2026–05/12/2026] |
| 06/08/60 to 05/09/60 | Age 66 years and 5 months | [06/01/2027–05/02/2027] |
| 06/09/60 to 05/10/60 | Age 66 years and 6 months | [06/03/2027–05/04/2027] |
| 06/10/60 to 05/11/60 | Age 66 years and 7 months | [06/05/2027–05/06/2027] |
| 06/11/60 to 05/12/60 | Age 66 years and 8 months | [06/07/2027–05/08/2027] |
| 06/12/60[3] to 05/01/61 | Age 66 years and 9 months | [06/09/2027–05/10/2027] |
| 06/01/61[4] to 05/02/61 | Age 66 years and 10 months | [06/11/2027–05/12/2027] |
| 06/02/61 to 05/03/61 | Age 66 years and 11 months | [06/01/2028–05/02/2028] |
| 06/03/61 to 06/04/77 | Age 67 | [06/03/2028–06/04/2044] |
| 06/04/77 to 05/05/77 | 67.1–67.0 | 06/05/2044 |
| 06/05/77 to 05/06/77 | 67.2–67.1 | 06/07/2044 |
| 06/06/77 to 05/07/77 | 67.3–67.2 | 06/09/2044 |
| 06/07/77 to 05/08/77 | 67.4–67.3 | 06/11/2044 |
| 06/08/77 to 05/09/77 | 67.5–67.4 | 06/01/2045 |
| 06/09/77 to 05/10/77 | 67.6–67.5 | 06/03/2045 |
| 06/10/77 to 05/11/77 | 67.7–67.6 | 06/05/2045 |
| 06/11/77 to 05/12/77 | 67.8–67.7 | 06/07/2045 |
| 06/12/77 to 05/01/78 | 67.9–67.8 | 06/09/2045 |
| 06/01/78 to 05/02/78 | 67.10–67.9 | 06/11/2045 |
| 06/02/78 to 05/03/78 | 67.11–67.10 | 06/01/2046 |
| 06/03/78 to 05/04/78 | 68.00–67.11 | 06/03/2046 |
| On or after 06/04/78 | Age 68 | [On or after 06/04/2046] |

**Notes**

[1] Individuals born between 06/04/54 and 06/04/77 and those born on or after 06/04/78 attain state pension age at the age shown in column 2 (with figures in square brackets in column 3 being calculated date ranges). Otherwise, individuals attain state pension age at the date shown in column 3.

⁽²⁾ A person born on 31 July 1960 is to be taken to attain the age of 66 years and four months at the commencement of 30 November 2026.
⁽³⁾ A person born on 31 December 1960 is to be taken to attain the age of 66 years and nine months at the commencement of 30 September 2027.
⁽⁴⁾ A person born on 31 January 1961 is to be taken to attain the age of 66 years and ten months at the commencement of 30 November 2027.

## [¶3-200]  State retirement pensions

| | Weekly rates | | | |
|---|---|---|---|---|
| | Full rate of state pension⁽¹⁾ £ | Single person £ | Married couple wife not a contributor £ | Age addition (over 80) each £ |
| From 6 April 2017 | 159.55 | 122.30 | 195.60 | 0.25 |
| 6/4/16 to 5/4/17 | 155.65 | 119.30 | 190.80 | 0.25 |
| 6/4/15 to 5/4/16 | — | 115.95 | 185.45 | 0.25 |
| 7/4/14 to 5/4/15 | — | 113.10 | 180.90 | 0.25 |
| 8/4/13 to 6/4/14 | — | 110.15 | 176.15 | 0.25 |
| 9/4/12 to 7/4/13 | — | 107.45 | 171.85 | 0.25 |
| 11/4/11 to 8/4/12 | — | 102.15 | 163.35 | 0.25 |

**Note**
⁽¹⁾ The *Pensions Act* 2014 introduced a new single tier pension from 6 April 2016. Individuals reaching pensionable age after that date are no longer entitled to the two-component state pension (the basic state pension and additional state pension based on amounts of National Insurance contributions (NICs) paid) but are instead entitled to a single-component flat-rate pension. Basic conditions of entitlement at the full rate include having attained pensionable age and having 35 or more 'qualifying years' of NICs (based on the individuals earnings factor reaching the qualifying amount for the tax year). Entitlement is subject to a minimum number of qualifying years (no more than ten) and pro-rated for individuals with fewer than 35 years. Transitional provisions apply for individuals who have paid, or are treated as having paid, NICs in respect of tax years before the introduction of the new state pension; for inheriting entitlement from a late spouse or civil partner who had made contributions prior to the introduction of the new state pension; for women who before 1977 elected to pay a reduced rate of NICs, and for sharing a pension with a former spouse or civil partner upon divorce.

## [¶3-300]  Gilt-edged securities held by non-residents
(ITTOIA 2005, s. 713; ITA 2007, s. 893–897, 1024)

(Tax Reporter: ¶120-800)

Interest on all gilt-edged securities is payable gross. Interest may be paid net, if the holder wishes, by notice to the Registrar of Government Stock. Payment gross does not of itself imply that the interest is exempt from tax.

All gilt-edged securities are automatically given FOTRA status (Free Of Tax for Residents Abroad), thereby guaranteeing exemption from tax for holders not resident in the UK. Where income tax has been deducted from such gilts, a repayment claim (on form R43) may be submitted to HM Revenue & Customs, Saxon House, 1 Causeway Lane, Leicester, England, LE1 4AA.

Taxation of Investment Income

# [¶3-350]   Individual savings accounts (ISAs)

(ITTOIA 2005, s. 694–701; SI 1998/1870; SI 2004/1450)
(Tax Reporter: ¶315-000)

| | 2017–18 | 2016–17[10] | 2015–16 | 2014–15[7] | | 2013–14 | 2012–13 |
|---|---|---|---|---|---|---|---|
| | | | | 1 July 2014 – 5 April 2015 | 6 April 2014 – 30 June 2014 | | |
| | £ | £ | £ | £ | £ | £ | £ |
| **'Adult' ISAs** | | | | | | | |
| Maximum subscription limit | 20,000 | 15,240 | 15,240 | 15,000 | 11,880 | 11,520 | 11,280 |
| Cash limit | —[4] | —[4] | —[4] | —[4] | 5,940 | 5,760 | 5,640 |
| **Junior ISAs/Child Trust Funds[5][6]** | | | | | | | |
| Maximum subscription limit | 4,128 | 4,080 | 4,080 | 4,000 | 3,840 | 3,720 | 3,600 |
| **Lifetime ISA[11]** | | | | | | | |
| Maximum subscription limit | 4,000 | — | — | — | — | — | — |
| Government contribution | 25% | — | — | — | — | — | — |
| **Help to buy ISA[9]** | | | | | | | |
| Maximum savings per month | 200 | 200 | 200 | — | — | — | — |
| Government contribution | 25% | 25% | 25% | — | — | — | — |

**Notes**

[1] To open an ISA, an individual has to be aged 18 or over (or over the age of 16 for cash ISAs) and resident in the UK for tax purposes.

[2] All income and gains derived from investments within the account are tax free and withdrawals from the account will not attract any tax charge.

[3] From 6 April 2011, the ISA subscription limits have been increased in line with inflation. From 2012–13 onwards, the index used is the consumer prices index (CPI) (previously RPI).

[4] From 1 July 2014, the restriction that only 50% of the overall subscription limit may be invested in a cash ISA was removed. SI 1998/1870 was also amended to allow transfers to be made from a stocks and shares account to a cash account (SI 2014/1450).

[5] Children born between 1 September 2002 and 2 January 2011, living in the UK and in receipt of child benefit were eligible for a Child Trust Fund account. Child Trust Funds are now closed to new accounts but subscriptions can still be paid into existing accounts. Withdrawals are not permitted until the child has reached the age of 18, except in cases of terminal illness. The Child Trust Fund subscription limit for 2011–12 was £1,200 to 30 October 2011 and increased to equal the Junior ISA subscription limit with effect from 1 November 2011.

[6] Junior ISAs became available form 1 November 2011 to any child under 18, living in the UK, who is not eligible for a Child Trust Fund account. Withdrawals are not permitted until the child has reached the age of 18, except in cases of terminal illness.

[7] From 3 December 2014, if an ISA saver in a marriage or civil partnership dies, their spouse or civil partner will inherit their ISA tax advantages. From 6 April 2015, surviving spouses will be able to invest as much into their own ISA as their spouse used to have, on top of their usual allowance.

(8) From 6 April 2016, ISA savers can withdraw and replace money from their cash ISA without it counting towards their annual ISA subscription limit for that year (SI 1998/1870, as amended by SI 2016/16).

(9) From 1 December 2015, the 'Help to buy ISA' was launched for individuals saving for their first home. Individuals are able to save up to £200 per month with the Government topping up the account with £50 for every £200 saved (with a maximum of £3,000 for £12,000 savings). The accounts are only available for first time buyers and can be opened with an additional one off deposit of £1,000 (see www.helptobuy.gov.uk/help-to-buy-isa/how-does-it-work/).

(10) *Finance Act* 2016 introduces legislation to allow the ISA savings of a deceased person to continue to benefit from tax advantages during the administration of their estate (ITTOIA 2005, s. 694A, as inserted by FA 2016, s. 27).

(11) The Lifetime ISA is available from 6 April 2017, allowing adults under the age of 40 to save up to £4,000 each year and receive a government bonus of 25% (up to £1,000 a year), which can be withdrawn tax-free to buy a first home or when the individual turns 60.

## [¶3-400]   Enterprise investment scheme (EIS)

(ITA 2007, Pt. 5)

(Tax Reporter: ¶323-000ff.; ¶565-400ff.)

EIS relief is available for qualifying individuals who subscribe cash for the issue of qualifying shares issued by non-quoted trading companies (except those carrying on prohibited trades).

| Qualifying EIS shares issued:[5][6][7][8] | Maximum individual investment[3] | Rate of IT relief on investment | Disposal of qualifying EIS shares | Carry back of EIS relief to previous tax year[2] |
|---|---|---|---|---|
| On or after 6 April 2012 but before 6 April 2025 | £1,000,000 per annum | 30% | Capital gains not chargeable, losses allowable[1] | Entire investment (subject to not exceeding £1,000,000 for the earlier year). |
| 2011–12 | £500,000 per annum | 30% | Capital gains not chargeable, losses allowable[1] | Entire investment (subject to not exceeding £500,000 for the earlier year). |

**Notes**

(1) The exemption from capital gains applies where EIS shares are held for more than three years from their issue. Losses are eligible for relief in the normal way but the base cost is treated as reduced by any EIS income tax relief which has been given and not withdrawn. A CGT deferral relief permits the postponement of a capital gain to be claimed where an investor subscribes for EIS shares within the period of one year prior to and three years after the gain accrues.

(2) Carry back of EIS relief was permitted for years to 2008–09, subject to the limits, where qualifying shares are subscribed for between 6 April and 5 October in a tax year. Those limits were removed for 2009–10 onwards.

(3) For an investment to qualify under EIS, the company must have raised no more than £5m (from 6 April 2012) under any or all EIS, VCT, SEIS (from 6 April 2012) or CVS (pre-1 April 2010) schemes in the 12 months ending on the date of the relevant investment. Between 17 July 2007 and 5 April 2012, the limit was £2m and prior to 17 July 2007 there was no limit. From 18 November 2015, investments under the SITR will also count towards the company's annual maximum amount as will any 'relevant investments' the company's subsidiaries have received or used in the year and investments in any trade transferred from another company.

(4) From 6 April 2015, companies benefiting substantially from subsidies for the generation of renewable energy will be excluded from also benefiting from EIS, SEIS and VCTs (ITA 2007, s. 198A–198B).

(5) EIS will cease to apply to new investments from 6 April 2025, unless the legislation is renewed. The date may be changed by Treasury Order and is set to be no later than ten years after the date of the European Commission's letter approving the EIS as compatible with state aids rules, following the formal notification of the scheme in June 2015 (ITA 2007, s. 157(1)(aa)).

Taxation of Investment Income

(6) Further changes to the EIS rules, with effect from 18 November 2015 (except where stated otherwise), subject to state aid approval, include:

- introducing a requirement that all investors are 'independent' from the company at the time of the first share issue (excluding any connection by virtue of holding 'founder shares' or shares subscribed for under the EIS, the SEIS or the SITR rules);
- introducing a cap on the total amount of investment a company may receive through the EIS and VCT of £20m for knowledge intensive companies and £12m for other qualifying companies;
- with effect in relation to shares issued on or after 6 April 2015, removing the requirement that the company must have to have spent 70% of any SEIS funds already raised;
- introducing a requirement that all investments are made with the intention to grow and develop a business;
- introducing new rules to prevent EIS funds being used to acquire existing businesses regardless of whether it is through share purchase or asset purchase;
- introducing new qualifying criteria to limit relief to investment in companies that meet certain conditions demonstrating that they are 'knowledge intensive' companies within ten years of their first commercial sale, and other qualifying companies within seven years of their first commercial sale (except where the investment represents more than 50% of turnover averaged over the preceding five years); and
- increasing the employee limit for knowledge intensive companies to 500 employees.

(7) From 6 April 2016, all remaining energy generation activities are excluded from the venture capital schemes, as well as from the enlarged SITR (amendments by FA 2016, s. 28). Autumn Statement 2015 also announced the introduction of increased flexibility for replacement capital within EIS and VCT, subject to state aids approval.

(8) Spring Budget 2017 confirmed amendments announced at Autumn Statement 2016 providing clarification of the EIS and SEIS rules for share conversion rights, with effect for shares issued on or after 5 December 2016 (Finance Bill 2017).

## [¶3-420]  Seed enterprise investment scheme (SEIS)

(TCGA 1992, Sch. 5BB; ITA 2007, Pt. 5A)

(Tax Reporter: ¶319-000ff.; ¶568-500ff.)

SEIS relief is available to qualifying individuals who subscribe cash for the issue of qualifying shares in unquoted trading companies with fewer than 25 employees and assets of up to £200,000, carrying on or preparing to carry on new business.

| Qualifying SEIS shares issued:[4][5][6][7][8] | Maximum individual investment[2] | Rate of IT relief on investment | Disposal of qualifying SEIS shares[1] | Carry back of SEIS relief to previous year | Capital gains reinvestment limit[3] |
|---|---|---|---|---|---|
| 2017–18 (from 2013–14) | £100,000 per annum | 50% | Capital gains not chargeable, losses allowable | Entire investment (subject to not exceeding £100,000 for the earlier year) | 50% of qualifying SEIS expenditure |
| 2012–13 | £100,000 per annum | 50% | Capital gains not chargeable, losses allowable | N/A | 100% of qualifying SEIS expenditure |

**Notes**

(1) The exemption from capital gains applies where SEIS shares are held for more than three years from their issue. Losses are eligible for relief in the normal way but the base cost is treated as reduced by any SEIS income tax relief which has been given and not withdrawn.

(2) For an investment to qualify under SEIS, the company must have raised no more than £150,000 and must not have raised any capital under EIS or VCT.

(3) The reinvestment exemption is available in respect of a gain arising on the disposal of any asset with so much of the gain that is matched with the relevant percentage of qualifying SEIS investment expenditure being exempt from CGT (subject to the £100,000 investment limit). The investment exemption was introduced initially for 2012–13 only, but extended by FA 2013 to 2013–14 and was made permanent by FA 2014.

(4) *Finance Act* 2013 amended the control and independence requirement so as to prevent a company from being disqualified from SEIS where it is established by a corporate formation agent before sale to its ultimate owners, with effect in relation to shares issued on or after 6 April 2013.

(5) Initially due to end on 5 April 2017, FA 2014 made the relief permanent.

(6) From 6 April 2015, companies benefiting substantially from subsidies for the generation of renewable energy will be excluded from also benefiting from EIS, SEIS and VCTs (ITA 2007, s. 198A–198B).

(7) From 6 April 2016, all remaining energy generation activities are excluded from the venture capital schemes, as well as from the enlarged SITR (amendments by FA 2016, s. 28).

(8) Spring Budget 2017 confirmed amendments announced at Autumn Statement 2016 providing clarification of the EIS and SEIS rules for share conversion rights, with effect for shares issued on or after 5 December 2016 (Finance Bill 2017).

# [¶3-430]   Social investment tax relief (SITR)

(TCGA 1992, s. 255A–255E, Sch. 8B; ITA 2007, Pt. 5B)

(Tax Reporter: ¶322-000ff.; ¶569-300ff.)

SITR is available to individual investors who invest in cash in new shares or new qualifying debt investments in qualifying social enterprises (an unquoted community interest company, community benefit society or charity with fewer than 250[6] full-time equivalent employees).

Relief is not available on any investment in respect of which the investor has obtained relief under the EIS, the SEIS or the CITRS.

| Qualifying investment made[5] | Maximum individual investment[3] | Rate of IT on investment | Disposal of qualifying investment[1] | Carry back of SI relief to previous tax year |
|---|---|---|---|---|
| On or after 6 April 2015 and before 6 April 2019 | £1m[4] per annum | 30% | Capital gains not chargeable, losses allowable | From 2015–16, entire investment (subject to not exceeding £1m for the earlier year) |
| On or after 6 April 2014 | £1m per annum | 30% | Capital gains not chargeable, losses allowable[2] | — |

**Notes**

(1) The exemption from capital gains applies where an investment on which income tax relief has been received (and not subsequently withdrawn) is disposed of after it has been held for at least three years. If no claim to income tax relief is made, the investment will not qualify for exemption from capital gains tax. Losses are eligible for relief in the normal way but the base cost is treated as reduced by the amount of the SI relief attributable to the asset.

(2) A capital gains tax deferral relief enables a capital gain arising from the disposal of any asset in the period from 6 April 2014 to 5 April 2019 to be deferred where the gain is reinvested (within the period one year before to three years after the gain arising) in shares or debt investments which also qualify for SITR income tax relief. It is not, however, necessary for the investor to have made a claim for SITR income tax relief.

(3) For an investment to qualify under SI, the social enterprise must (including its subsidiaries if a parent company) have no more than £15m in gross assets immediately before the investment and £16m immediately after the

investment. Additionally, the social enterprise is restricted as to the amount of money it may raise under SITR, as determined by the formula:

$$\left( \frac{€200,000 - M}{RCG + RSI} \right) - T$$

Where:  T is the total of any earlier SITR investments made in the previous three years;
M is the total of any other de minimis aid received in the previous three years by the social enterprise, or by a qualifying subsidiary;
RCG is the highest rate of capital gains tax in the previous three years; and
RSI is the highest rate of SITR income tax relief in the previous three years.

(4) At Autumn Statement 2014, it was announced that the annual investment limit would be increased to £5m per annum up to a total of £15m per organisation and relief to be extended to small scale community farms and horticultural activities, however, these changes have not yet been legislated. At Spring Budget 2017, it was confirmed that, as announced at Autumn Statement 2016, the amount of investment social enterprises aged up to seven years old can raise through SITR will increase to £1.5m, with effect for investments made on or after 6 April 2017. However, the current limit will continue to apply to older social enterprises.

(5) From 6 April 2016, all remaining energy generation activities are excluded from the venture capital schemes, as well as from the enlarged SITR (amendments by FA 2016, s. 28).

(6) Limit on number of full-time equivalent employees reduced to below 250 employees (previously 500 employees) with effect for investments made on or after 6 April 2017 (Spring Budget 2017). Spring Budget 2017 also announced further amendments to the requirements for the SITR, with effect for investments made on or after 6 April 2017, including the exclusion of certain activities, excluding use of the monies raised to pay off loans, ensuring only individuals who are independent of the social enterprise will qualify for the relief and excluding investments which deliver benefits to persons connected with the social enterprise.

## [¶3-450]   Venture capital trusts (VCTs)

(TCGA 1992, s. 151A, 151B; ITTOIA 2005, s. 709; ITA 2007, Pt. 6)

(Tax Reporter: ¶326-000ff.)

A VCT is a specialised form of investment trust, which has been approved by the Board of HMRC on or since 6 April 1995. Certain tax advantages are obtained by individuals who subscribe for eligible shares issued by a qualifying VCT for the purposes of raising money.

| Qualifying VCT Shares issued:[1][2][3][4][5][6][7][8][9] | Maximum individual investment | Rate of IT relief on investment | Dividends paid by VCT | Disposal of shares in VCT | Minimum holding period |
|---|---|---|---|---|---|
| On or after 6 April 2006 but before 6 April 2025 | £200,000 per annum | 30% | Exempt from IT in hands of investor | Exempt from CGT | 5 years |
| 2005–06 and 2004–05 | £200,000 per annum | 40% | Exempt from IT in hands of investor | Exempt from CGT | 3 years |
| 2000–01 to 2003–04 | £100,000 per annum | 20% | Exempt from IT in hands of investor | Exempt from CGT | 3 years |

**Notes**

(1) An investment in qualifying VCT shares, issued prior to 6 April 2004, was eligible for a CGT deferral relief that enabled an investor to postpone the incidence of a capital gain arising on the disposal of a chargeable asset.

(2) To obtain and retain HMRC's approval, a VCT must satisfy a number of detailed conditions. The main ones are as follows: it must be a non-close company whose shares are quoted on the stock exchange; its income must be wholly or mainly derived from investments in shares or securities; at least 70% (by value) of its total investments must comprise of 'qualifying holdings' (broadly, shares and securities in unquoted trading companies except those carrying on prohibited trades; from 6 April 2007, cash held will be treated as an 'investment' for the purposes of the percentage limits); no holding in any company (other than a VCT or a company that would qualify as a VCT but for

the listing condition) can represent more than 15% of the value of the VCT's investments; the gross assets of the companies in which the VCT has invested may not exceed £15m immediately before the issue of shares to the VCT and £16m immediately afterwards (from 19 July 2012, previously these limits were £7m and £8m respectively).

(3) For an investment to qualify under VCT, the company must have raised no more than £5m (from 6 April 2012) under any or all EIS, VCT, SEIS (from 6 April 2012) or CVS (pre-1 April 2010) schemes in the 12 months ending on the date of the relevant investment (ITA 2007, s. 292A). Between 6 April 2007 and 5 April 2012, the limit was £2m (other than in respect of 'protected money' (as defined by FA 2007, Sch. 16, para. 6)) and prior to 6 April 2007, there was no limit. From 18 November 2015, investments under the SITR will also count towards the company's annual maximum amount as will any 'relevant investments' the company or group has received or used in the year and imported investments (in any trade transferred from another company).

(4) From April 2014, investments that are conditionally linked in any way to a VCT share buy-back, or that have been made within six months of a disposal of shares in the same VCT, will not qualify for new tax relief (ITA 2007, s. 264A). *Finance Act* 2014 also includes legislation to enable investors to subscribe for shares in a VCT via a nominee (with effect from 17 July 2014) (ITA 2007, s. 330A) and to prevent VCTs returning capital subscribed by investors within three years from the end of the accounting period in which the shares were issued (from 6 April 2014) (ITA 2007, s. 281).

(5) From 6 April 2015, companies benefiting substantially from subsidies for the generation of renewable energy will be excluded from also benefiting from EIS, SEIS and VCTs (ITA 2007, s. 309A–309B).

(6) VCTs will no longer qualify for relief from 6 April 2025, unless the legislation is renewed. The date may be changed by Treasury Order and is set to be no later than ten years after the date of the European Commission's letter approving the VCT rules as compatible with state aids rules, following the formal notification of the scheme in June 2015.

(7) Further changes to the VCT rules, with effect from 18 November 2015 (except where stated otherwise), subject to state aid approval, include:

- introducing two extra conditions a company must meet in order to be approved as, and retain its status as, a VCT: 'the permitted maximum age condition' and 'the no business acquisition condition';
- introducing two extra limits an investee company must meet if a VCT is to make an investment in that company. As well as meeting the total annual investment limit of £5m, the relevant company must also meet a total (lifetime) investment limit of £20m for knowledge-intensive companies and £12m for other companies as at the date the VCT invests in it and, in certain circumstances, that limit must not be breached for the following five years;
- introducing new qualifying criteria to limit relief to investment in companies that meet certain conditions demonstrating that they are 'knowledge intensive' companies within ten years of their first commercial sale, and other qualifying companies within seven years of their first commercial sale (except where the investment represents more than 50% of turnover averaged over the preceding five years);
- introducing a requirement that all investments are made with the intention to grow and develop a business;
- introduce new rules to prevent VCT funds being used to acquire existing businesses, including extending the prohibition on management buyouts and share acquisitions to VCT non-qualifying holdings and VCT funds raised pre-2012, and preventing money raised through VCT from being used to make acquisitions of existing business regardless of whether it is through share purchase or asset purchase;
- with effect in relation to shares issued on or after 6 April 2015, removing the requirement that the company must have to have spent 70% of any SEIS funds already raised; and
- increasing the employee limit for knowledge intensive companies to 500 employees.

(8) From 6 April 2015, all remaining energy generation activities are excluded from the venture capital schemes, as well as from the enlarged SITR (amendments by FA 2016, s. 28). Autumn Statement 2015 also announced the introduction of increased flexibility for replacement capital within EIS and VCT, subject to state aids approval.

(9) Spring Budget 2017 confirmed amendments announced at Autumn Statement 2016 to provide additional flexibility for follow-on investments made by VCTs in companies with certain group structures to align with EIS provisions, for investments made on or after 6 April 2017 and the introduction of a power to enable VCT regulations to be made in relation to certain shares for share exchanges to provide greater certainty to VCTs, with effect from Royal Assent of Finance Bill 2017.

## Social venture capital trusts

At Autumn Statement 2014, the Government announced the introduction of a new social venture capital trust scheme.

At March Budget 2015, it was announced that the scheme will be based on the existing VCT scheme, the rate of income tax relief for investment in a social VCT will be 30% (subject to state aid clearance) and investors will pay no tax on dividends received from a social VCT or capital gains tax on disposals of shares in Social VCTs (March Budget 2015; future Finance Bill).

## [¶3-465]   Community investment tax relief

(ITA 2007, Pt. 7; CTA 2010, Pt. 7)

(Tax Reporter: ¶325-000ff.)

Tax relief is claimed on an annual basis at the rate of 5% of the 'invested amount' for the tax year (or accounting period for a corporate investor) in which the investment date falls and the four subsequent tax years (or accounting periods). If the investment is by way of a loan, the 'invested amount' is not necessarily the amount of the loan made available at the beginning of the five-year investment period. The tax relief cannot reduce the taxpayer's tax liability below zero for any single tax year (or accounting period).

## [¶3-500]   Lease premiums

(ITOIA 2005, s. 277; CTA 2009, s. 217)

(Tax Reporter: ¶300-110; ¶711-375)

Where a short-term lease (i.e. one not exceeding 50 years in duration) is granted, a proportion of any premium charged on the grant is assessable as property business profits. The amount of the premium to be treated as rental income, received at the time of the grant, is given by a formula:

$$P \times \frac{50 - Y}{50} = TP$$

Where:

- 'P' is total premium paid;
- 'Y' is duration of lease in complete years (ignoring the first year). Only whole years are counted, part years are ignored; and
- 'TP' is the amount of the premium taxed on the landlord as if it were rent.

Amount taken into account in calculating a chargeable gain will be the balance of the premium (TCGA 1992, s. 240 and Sch. 8, para. 5 and 7) for which the restriction of allowable expenditure is applicable:

| Length of lease in complete years | Premium % chargeable as gain | Premium % chargeable as rent |
|---|---|---|
| Over 50 | 100 | 0 |
| 50 | 98 | 2 |
| 49 | 96 | 4 |
| 48 | 94 | 6 |
| 47 | 92 | 8 |
| 46 | 90 | 10 |
| 45 | 88 | 12 |
| 44 | 86 | 14 |
| 43 | 84 | 16 |
| 42 | 82 | 18 |
| 41 | 80 | 20 |
| 40 | 78 | 22 |
| 39 | 76 | 24 |

| Length of lease in complete years | Premium % chargeable as gain | Premium % chargeable as rent |
|---|---|---|
| 38 | 74 | 26 |
| 37 | 72 | 28 |
| 36 | 70 | 30 |
| 35 | 68 | 32 |
| 34 | 66 | 34 |
| 33 | 64 | 36 |
| 32 | 62 | 38 |
| 31 | 60 | 40 |
| 30 | 58 | 42 |
| 29 | 56 | 44 |
| 28 | 54 | 46 |
| 27 | 52 | 48 |
| 26 | 50 | 50 |
| 25 | 48 | 52 |
| 24 | 46 | 54 |
| 23 | 44 | 56 |
| 22 | 42 | 58 |
| 21 | 40 | 60 |
| 20 | 38 | 62 |
| 19 | 36 | 64 |
| 18 | 34 | 66 |
| 17 | 32 | 68 |
| 16 | 30 | 70 |
| 15 | 28 | 72 |
| 14 | 26 | 74 |
| 13 | 24 | 76 |
| 12 | 22 | 78 |
| 11 | 20 | 80 |
| 10 | 18 | 82 |
| 9 | 16 | 84 |
| 8 | 14 | 86 |
| 7 | 12 | 88 |
| 6 | 10 | 90 |
| 5 | 8 | 92 |
| 4 | 6 | 94 |
| 3 | 4 | 96 |
| 2 | 2 | 98 |
| 1 or less | 0 | 100 |

The following arrangements relating to short leases may also cause amounts to be treated as rent paid to the landlord:

- the tenant carrying out work on the rented premises;
- the commutation of rent for some other type of payment;
- the payment of a lump sum from the surrender of a lease;
- the payment of a lump sum for the variation or waiver of a lease's terms; and
- the assignment of a lease which has been previously granted at undervalue.

Taxation of Investment Income

*Premiums paid by instalment*

Where an amount of a premium is received by instalments any income tax or corporation tax due on the amount may be paid by instalments, at the taxpayer's request and by agreement with HMRC. The tax instalment period may not exceed eight years and must end on or before the time that the final instalment of the premium is due (ITTOIA 2005, s. 299 for income tax; and CTA 2009, s. 236(1)–(3) for corporation tax).

*Relief for premiums paid*

Where a tenant occupies land, under a short lease, for the purposes of a trade, profession or vocation and has paid a premium in respect of the lease; an amount of lease premium paid is allowed as a deduction in computing the business profits (ITTOIA 2005, s. 60 for income tax; and CTA 2009, s. 62 for corporation tax). The amount of the premium taxed as rent in the hands of the landlord (see above) is treated as if it were daily rent paid by the tenant over the course of the lease. The effective deduction for an accounting or basis period is therefore:

$$\frac{TP}{\text{Lease duration in days}} \times \text{No. of days in accounting or basis period} = DRP$$

Where:

- 'TP' is the amount of the premium taxed on the landlord as if it were rent; and
- 'DRP' is the amount of the deemed rent paid by the tenant.

Relief is also available, in respect of premiums paid, for the computation of property business profits where an intermediate landlord has paid a premium to the superior landlord for premises that are in turn sub-let to a tenant.

## [¶3-525]   Restricted deductions for finance costs related to residential property

(ITTOIA 2005, s. 272A–272B, 274A–274B; ITA 2007, s. 399A–399B)

(Tax Reporter: ¶300-350)

| Year | Restricted deduction[1] |
|------|------------------------|
| 2017–18 | 75% |
| 2018–19 | 50% |
| 2019–20 | 25% |
| 2020–21 | 0% |

**Note**

[1] In calculating for income tax purposes the profits of a property business, the deduction allowed for finance costs of a dwelling-related loan is restricted to the percentage shown of the amount that would be allowed apart from the restriction. A tax reduction for such costs is available instead and calculated by reference to the basic rate of income tax. The restriction and tax reduction will have effect for costs incurred on or after 6 April 2017.

## [¶3-550]   Settlements on children

(ITTOIA 2005, s. 629(3))

(Tax Reporter: ¶356-300)

Income paid to or for the benefit of a minor child arising from capital provided by a parent is not treated as parents' income if it does not exceed £100 per tax year.

## [¶3-700]   Time limits for elections and claims

In the absence of any provision to the contrary, for the purposes of income tax, the normal rule is that claims are to be made within four years from the end of the tax year to which they relate. Before 1 April 2010, the time limit was generally five years from 31 January next following the end of the tax year (TMA 1970, s. 43(1)).

In certain cases, HMRC *may* permit an extension of the strict time limit in relation to certain elections and claims.

| Provision | Time limit | Statutory reference |
| --- | --- | --- |
| Averaging election for furnished holiday accommodation | 12 months from 31 January following year to which claim applies | ITTOIA 2005, s. 326 (Tax Reporter: ¶303-170) |
| Set-off of property business loss against income of current or next year | 12 months from 31 January following year of set-off | ITA 2007, s. 124 (Tax Reporter: ¶303-220) |
| Property business post-cessation relief | 12 months from 31 January following year in which deduction to be made | ITA 2007, s. 125 (Tax Reporter: ¶303-230) |
| Set-off of loss on disposal of shares in unquoted trading company against income | 12 months from 31 January following year in which loss arose | ITA 2007, s. 132 (Tax Reporter: ¶330-000ff.) |
| EIS, SEIS and SI relief | Five years from 31 January following tax year in which shares are issued (or previous tax year in relation to carry back claims) | ITA 2007, s. 202, 257EA and 257P (Tax Reporter: ¶323-120; ¶319-120) |

# TAXATION OF EARNINGS

## Company cars

### [¶4-000]  Car benefits 2017–18
(ITEPA 2003, s. 139)

(Tax Reporter: ¶415-050ff.)

The benefit is calculated as a percentage of the list price of the car appropriate to the level of the car's $CO_2$ emissions. The 'appropriate percentage' depends upon whether the car was first registered on or after 1 January 1998 and whether it has a $CO_2$ emissions figure or is a diesel car. Relevant percentages are set out below.

**For cars registered on or after 1 January 1998 (with $CO_2$ emissions figures)**

| $CO_2$ emissions[6] | 2013–14 & 2012–13 | 2014–15 | 2015–16 | 2016–17 | 2017–18 | 2018–19[3] | 2019–20[4] |
|---|---|---|---|---|---|---|---|
| 50g/km or below[2] | 5%[2] | 5%[2] | 5% | 7% | 9% | 13% | 16% |
| 51–75g/km | | | 9% | 11% | 13% | 16% | 19% |
| Above 75g/km up to relevant threshold | 10% | 11% | 13% | 15% | 17% | 19% | 22% |
| Equal to relevant threshold[1] | 11% | 12% | 14% | 16% | 18% | 20% | 23% |
| Above relevant threshold: Increase per 5g/km[1] | 1% | 1% | 1% | 1% | 1% | 1% | 1% |
| Up to maximum | 35% | 35% | 37% | 37% | 37% | 37% | 37% |
| Diesel supplement[5] | 3% | 3% | 3% | 3% | 3% | 3% | 3% |

**Notes**

[1] Where $CO_2$ emissions are not a multiple of five, round down to the nearest multiple of five.

[2] If a car cannot emit $CO_2$ by being driven, the appropriate percentage is 0% until 5 April 2015 (when the five-year exemption for zero-carbon cars ends).

[3] In 2018–19, the appropriate percentage of list price subject to tax will increase by two percentage points for cars emitting more than 75g/km $CO_2$, to a maximum of 37%. In 2018–19, there will be a three percentage point differential between the 0–50 and 51–75g/km $CO_2$ bands and between the 51–75 and 76–94g/km $CO_2$ bands (FA 2015, s. 8).

(4) In 2019–20, the appropriate percentage of list price subject to tax will increase by three percentage points for cars emitting more than 75g/km $CO_2$, to a maximum of 37%. There will be a three-percentage point differential between the 0–50 and 51–75g/km $CO_2$ bands (FA 2016, s. 8).
(5) All diesel cars are currently subject to a 3% addition (but subject to the absolute cap). The 3% diesel supplement was due to be abolished from 2016–17 (FA 2014, s. 24), however, FA 2016, s. 10 retains the diesel supplement in company car tax. Further provisions to remove the diesel supplement are expected to be made in a future Finance Bill, with effect from 6 April 2021.
(6) Autumn Statement 2016 announced that for 2020–21, lower bands will be introduced for the lowest emitting cars and the appropriate percentage for cars emitting greater than 90g/km $CO_2$ will rise by one percentage point. Rates were published at Spring Budget 2017, see ¶4-002.

The relevant threshold is as follows:

| Year | Relevant threshold |
|---|---|
| 2017–18 | 95g/km |
| 2013–14 to 2016–17 | 95g/km |
| 2012–13 | 100g/km |

## Cars registered on or after 1 January 1998 without $CO_2$ emissions, or cars first registered before 1 January 1998

| | 2014–15 Registered | | 2015–16 Registered | | 2016–17 | 2017–18 | 2018–19(3) | 2019–20(4) |
|---|---|---|---|---|---|---|---|---|
| | on or after 01/01/1998 | before 01/01/1998 | on or after 01/01/1998 | before 01/01/1998 | | | | |
| *Cylinder capacity of car with internal combustion engine in cubic centimetres* | | | | | | | | |
| • 1,400 or less | 15% | 15% | 15% | 15% | 16% | 18% | 20% | 23% |
| • more than 1,400 but not more than 2,000 | 25% | 22% | 25% | 22% | 27% | 29% | 31% | 34% |
| • more than 2,000 | 35% | 32% | 37% | 32% | 37% | 37% | 37% | 37% |
| *Cars without an internal combustion engine* | | | | | | | | |
| • zero-emission cars registered on or after 1 January 1998 | 0%(1) | — | 5% | — | 7% | 9% | 13% | 16% |
| • any other case | 35% | 32% | 37% | 32% | 37% | 37% | 37% | 37% |
| Diesel supplement(2) | 3% | N/A | 3% | N/A | 3% | 3% | 3% | 3% |

**Notes**
(1) If emissions are zero when driven, the appropriate percentage is zero until 5 April 2015.
(2) All diesel cars registered on or after 1 January 1998 are currently subject to a 3% addition (but subject to the absolute cap). The 3% diesel supplement was due to be abolished from 2016–17 (FA 2014, s. 24), however, FA 2016, s. 10 retains the diesel supplement in company car tax. Further provisions to remove the diesel supplement are expected to be made in a future Finance Bill, with effect from 6 April 2021.
(3) Rates per FA 2015, s. 8 (amending ITEPA 2003, s. 140 and 142).
(4) Rates per FA 2016, s. 8 (amending ITEPA 2003, s. 140 and 142).

# [¶4-002]  Car benefits: table of percentages 2012–13 to 2019–20

**Table of taxable percentages**

(ITEPA 2003, s. 139)

(Tax Reporter: ¶415-720)

| $CO_2$ emissions | Appropriate percentage | | | | | | | |
|---|---|---|---|---|---|---|---|---|
| | 2012–13[1] | 2013–14[1] | 2014–15[1] | 2015–16[1] | 2016–17[1] | 2017–18[1] | 2018–19[1,2] | 2019–20[1,3] |
| 0 | 0 | 0 | 0 | 5 | 7 | 9 | 13 | 16 |
| 1–50 | 5 | 5 | 5 | | | | | |
| 51–75 | | | | 9 | 11 | 13 | 16 | 19 |
| 76–94 | 10 | 10 | 11 | 13 | 15 | 17 | 19 | 22 |
| 95–99 | | 11 | 12 | 14 | 16 | 18 | 20 | 23 |
| 100–104 | 11 | 12 | 13 | 15 | 17 | 19 | 21 | 24 |
| 105–109 | 12 | 13 | 14 | 16 | 18 | 20 | 22 | 25 |
| 110–114 | 13 | 14 | 15 | 17 | 19 | 21 | 23 | 26 |
| 115–119 | 14 | 15 | 16 | 18 | 20 | 22 | 24 | 27 |
| 120–124 | 15 | 16 | 17 | 19 | 21 | 23 | 25 | 28 |
| 125–129 | 16 | 17 | 18 | 20 | 22 | 24 | 26 | 29 |
| 130–134 | 17 | 18 | 19 | 21 | 23 | 25 | 27 | 30 |
| 135–139 | 18 | 19 | 20 | 22 | 24 | 26 | 28 | 31 |
| 140–144 | 19 | 20 | 21 | 23 | 25 | 27 | 29 | 32 |
| 145–149 | 20 | 21 | 22 | 24 | 26 | 28 | 30 | 33 |
| 150–154 | 21 | 22 | 23 | 25 | 27 | 29 | 31 | 34 |
| 155–159 | 22 | 23 | 24 | 26 | 28 | 30 | 32 | 35 |
| 160–164 | 23 | 24 | 25 | 27 | 29 | 31 | 33 | 36 |
| 165–169 | 24 | 25 | 26 | 28 | 30 | 32 | 34 | 37 |
| 170–174 | 25 | 26 | 27 | 29 | 31 | 33 | 35 | |
| 175–179 | 26 | 27 | 28 | 30 | 32 | 34 | 36 | |
| 180–184 | 27 | 28 | 29 | 31 | 33 | 35 | 37 | |
| 185–189 | 28 | 29 | 30 | 32 | 34 | 36 | | |
| 190–194 | 29 | 30 | 31 | 33 | 35 | 37 | | |
| 195–199 | 30 | 31 | 32 | 34 | 36 | | | |
| 200–204 | 31 | 32 | 33 | 35 | 37 | | | |
| 205–209 | 32 | 33 | 34 | 36 | | | | |
| 210–214 | 33 | 34 | 35 | 37 | | | | |
| 215–219 | 34 | 35 | | | | | | |
| 220+ | 35 | | | | | | | |

ation of Earnings

**Notes**
(1) All diesel cars are subject to a 3% loading, but not to take the maximum figure above 37% (from 2015–16, previously, 35%). This addition was due to be abolished from 2016–17 (FA 2014, s. 24), however, FA 2016, s. 10 retains the diesel supplement in company car tax. Further provisions to remove the diesel supplement are expected to be made in a future Finance Bill, with effect from 6 April 2021.
(2) In 2018–19, the appropriate percentage of list price subject to tax will increase by two percentage points for cars emitting more than 75g/km $CO_2$, to a maximum of 37%. In 2018–19, there will be a three percentage point differential between the 0–50 and 51–75g/km $CO_2$ bands and between the 51–75 and 76–94g/km $CO_2$ bands (FA 2015, s. 8).
(3) In 2019–20, the appropriate percentage of list price subject to tax will increase by three percentage points for cars emitting more than 75g/km $CO_2$ to a maximum of 37%. There will be a three percentage point differential between the 0–50 and 51–75g/km $CO_2$ bands (FA 2016, s. 8).
(4) Rates for 2020–21 as published at Spring Budget 2017 and reflected in draft Finance Bill 2017 published on 20 March 2017 are as follows:

| 2020–21 | | | | | | |
|---|---|---|---|---|---|---|
| $CO_2$ emissions | Electric range figure | Appropriate percentage | $CO_2$ emissions | Appropriate percentage | $CO_2$ emissions | Appropriate percentage |
| 0 | | 2 | 70–74 | 19 | 120–124 | 29 |
| 1–50 (split by zero emission miles) | 130 or more | 2 | 75–79 | 20 | 125–129 | 30 |
| | 70–129 | 5 | 80–84 | 21 | 130–134 | 31 |
| | 40–69 | 8 | 85–89 | 22 | 135–139 | 32 |
| | 30–39 | 12 | 90–94 | 23 | 140–144 | 33 |
| | less than 30 | 14 | 95–99 | 24 | 145–149 | 34 |
| 51–54 | | 15 | 100–104 | 25 | 150–154 | 35 |
| 55–59 | | 16 | 105–109 | 26 | 155–159 | 36 |
| 60–64 | | 17 | 110–114 | 27 | 160+ | 37 |
| 65–69 | | 18 | 115–119 | 28 | | |

## [¶4-015]   Diesel cars: loading of appropriate percentage

(ITEPA 2003, s. 141)

(Tax Reporter: ¶415-740)

Most diesel cars have an appropriate percentage that is three points higher than an equivalent petrol car (but still subject to a 37% overall cap). See ¶4-000ff. for details of the petrol figures.

The 3% diesel supplement was due to be abolished from 6 April 2016 (FA 2014, s. 24), however, FA 2016, s. 10 retains the diesel supplement in company car tax. Further provisions to remove the diesel supplement are expected to be made in a future Finance Bill, with effect from 6 April 2021.

### Cars that do not meet the Euro IV emissions standard

These cars are subject to the three-point loading in all cases.

### Cars that do meet the Euro IV emissions standard

The following table shows whether or not a 3% loading is needed for diesel cars meeting the Euro IV emissions standard:

| Tax year | Car first registered by 31 December 2005 | Car first registered from 1 January 2006 |
|---|---|---|
| From 2011–12 | 3% loading applies | 3% loading applies |
| 2006–07 to 2010–11 | No loading | 3% loading applies |

### [¶4-025]  Ultra-low emission cars
(ITEPA 2003, s. 139)

(Tax Reporter: ¶415-750)

A reduced appropriate percentage of 5% applied, from 6 April 2010 for five years, for company cars with an approved $CO_2$ emissions figure not exceeding 75g/km. Diesel cars were subject to the appropriate 3% loading: see ¶4-015.

From April 2015, the first-year exemption for ultra-low emission cars ended with two new bands introduced for cars emitting 0–50g/km and 51–75g/km: see ¶4-000.

### [¶4-030]  Zero emission cars
(ITEPA 2003, s. 140)

(Tax Reporter: ¶415-760ff.)

From 6 April 2010 to 5 April 2015, there was a zero tax charge for cars producing no emissions when driven (e.g. electric cars).

For rates from 6 April 2015, see ¶4-000.

Battery electric cars had an appropriate percentage of 9% from 6 April 2006 to 5 April 2010.

# Fuel for company cars

### [¶4-140]  Fuel benefit charges
(ITEPA 2003, s. 150)

(Tax Reporter: ¶416-000ff.)

The additional taxable benefit of free fuel provided for a company car is calculated using the same $CO_2$ percentages as are used for calculating the company car charge.

The fuel benefit is reduced to nil if the employee is required to make good the full cost of all fuel provided for private use, and does so.

A proportionate reduction is made where the company car is only available for part of the year, where car fuel ceases to be provided part-way through the year, or where the benefit of the company car is shared.

The $CO_2$ percentage figure is applied to a fixed amount in accordance with the following table:

| Tax year | £ |
|----------|--------|
| 2017–18  | 22,600 |
| 2016–17  | 22,200 |
| 2015–16  | 22,100 |
| 2014–15  | 21,700 |
| 2013–14  | 21,100 |
| 2012–13  | 20,200 |
| 2011–12  | 18,800 |

## [¶4-160]  Fuel types from 6 April 2011

Employers must notify HMRC of the type of fuel (or other power) used by an employer provided car by entering the appropriate 'key letter' on the forms P11D and P46(Car). The key letters in use for P11D reporting and form P46(Car) in respect of periods post 6 April 2011 are as follows:

| Key letter | Fuel or power type description |
|------------|-------------------------------|
| A | All other cars |
| D | Diesel (all Euro standards) |
| E | Zero emission cars (including electric cars) |

## [¶4-180]  Advisory fuel rates for company cars: recent rates

(Tax Reporter: ¶416-040)

HMRC publish rates that can be used by employers wishing to pay their employees the cost of fuel for business journeys in company cars (or, where the employer initially pays for all fuel, for reimbursement of private mileage by company car drivers to their employers). Passenger payments may be made for company cars as for private cars (see ¶4-220). Petrol hybrid cars are treated as petrol cars for this purpose.

In a change of policy announced in May 2011, HMRC now review the rates four times a year – on 1 March, 1 June, 1 September and 1 December. For one month from the date of change, employers may use either the previous or new current rates, as they choose.

| Engine size | Cost per mile | | |
|-------------|--------|--------|-----|
|             | Petrol | Diesel | LPG |
| **Rates applying from 1 March 2017** | | | |
| 1400cc or less   | 11p | —   | 7p  |
| 1600cc or less   | —   | 9p  | —   |
| 1401cc to 2000cc | 14p | —   | 9p  |
| 1601cc to 2000cc | —   | 11p | —   |
| Over 2000cc      | 22p | 13p | 14p |

| Engine size | Cost per mile | | |
|---|---|---|---|
| | Petrol | Diesel | LPG |
| **Rates applying from 1 December 2016** | | | |
| 1400cc or less | 11p | — | 7p |
| 1600cc or less | — | 9p | — |
| 1401cc to 2000cc | 14p | — | 9p |
| 1601cc to 2000cc | — | 11p | — |
| Over 2000cc | 21p | 13p | 13p |
| **Rates applying from 1 September 2016** | | | |
| 1400cc or less | 11p | — | 7p |
| 1600cc or less | — | 9p | — |
| 1401cc to 2000cc | 13p | — | 9p |
| 1601cc to 2000cc | — | 11p | — |
| Over 2000cc | 20p | 13p | 13p |
| **Rates applying from 1 June 2016** | | | |
| 1400cc or less | 10p | — | 7p |
| 1600cc or less | — | 9p | — |
| 1401cc to 2000cc | 13p | — | 9p |
| 1601cc to 2000cc | — | 10p | — |
| Over 2000cc | 20p | 12p | 13p |
| **Rates applying from 1 March 2016** | | | |
| 1400cc or less | 10p | — | 7p |
| 1600cc or less | — | 8p | — |
| 1401cc to 2000cc | 12p | — | 8p |
| 1601cc to 2000cc | — | 10p | — |
| Over 2000cc | 19p | 11p | 13p |
| **Rates applying from 1 December 2015** | | | |
| 1400cc or less | 11p | — | 7p |
| 1600cc or less | — | 9p | — |
| 1401cc to 2000cc | 13p | — | 9p |
| 1601cc to 2000cc | — | 11p | — |
| Over 2000cc | 20p | 13p | 13p |
| **Rates applying from 1 September 2015** | | | |
| 1400cc or less | 11p | — | 7p |
| 1600cc or less | — | 9p | — |
| 1401cc to 2000cc | 14p | — | 9p |
| 1601cc to 2000cc | — | 11p | — |
| Over 2000cc | 21p | 13p | 14p |

Taxation of Earnings

| Engine size | Cost per mile | | |
|---|---|---|---|
| | Petrol | Diesel | LPG |
| **Rates applying from 1 June 2015** | | | |
| 1400cc or less | 12p | — | 8p |
| 1600cc or less | — | 10p | — |
| 1401cc to 2000cc | 14p | — | 9p |
| 1601cc to 2000cc | — | 12p | — |
| Over 2000cc | 21p | 14p | 14p |
| **Rates applying from 1 March 2015** | | | |
| 1400cc or less | 11p | — | 8p |
| 1600cc or less | — | 9p | — |
| 1401cc to 2000cc | 13p | — | 10p |
| 1601cc to 2000cc | — | 11p | — |
| Over 2000cc | 20p | 14p | 14p |
| **Rates applying from 1 September 2014** | | | |
| 1400cc or less | 14p | — | 9p |
| 1600cc or less | — | 11p | — |
| 1401cc to 2000cc | 16p | — | 11p |
| 1601cc to 2000cc | — | 13p | — |
| Over 2000cc | 24p | 17p | 16p |
| **Rates applying from 1 June 2014** | | | |
| 1400cc or less | 14p | — | 9p |
| 1600cc or less | — | 12p | — |
| 1401cc to 2000cc | 16p | — | 11p |
| 1601cc to 2000cc | — | 14p | — |
| Over 2000cc | 24p | 17p | 16p |
| **Rates applying from 1 March 2014** | | | |
| 1400cc or less | 14p | — | 9p |
| 1600cc or less | — | 12p | — |
| 1401cc to 2000cc | 16p | — | 11p |
| 1601cc to 2000cc | — | 14p | — |
| Over 2000cc | 24p | 17p | 17p |
| **Rates applying from 1 December 2013** | | | |
| 1400cc or less | 14p | — | 9p |
| 1600cc or less | — | 12p | — |
| 1401cc to 2000cc | 16p | — | 11p |
| 1601cc to 2000cc | — | 14p | — |
| Over 2000cc | 24p | 17p | 16p |

| Engine size | Cost per mile | | |
|---|---|---|---|
| | Petrol | Diesel | LPG |
| **Rates applying from 1 September 2013** | | | |
| 1400cc or less | 15p | — | 10p |
| 1600cc or less | — | 12p | — |
| 1401cc to 2000cc | 18p | — | 11p |
| 1601cc to 2000cc | — | 15p | — |
| Over 2000cc | 26p | 18p | 16p |
| **Rates applying from 1 June 2013** | | | |
| 1400cc or less | 15p | — | 10p |
| 1600cc or less | — | 12p | — |
| 1401cc to 2000cc | 17p | — | 12p |
| 1601cc to 2000cc | — | 14p | — |
| Over 2000cc | 25p | 18p | 18p |
| **Rates applying from 1 March 2013** | | | |
| 1400cc or less | 15p | — | 10p |
| 1600cc or less | — | 13p | — |
| 1401cc to 2000cc | 18p | — | 12p |
| 1601cc to 2000cc | — | 15p | — |
| Over 2000cc | 26p | 18p | 18p |
| **Rates applying from 1 December 2012** | | | |
| 1400cc or less | 15p | — | 11p |
| 1600cc or less | — | 12p | — |
| 1401cc to 2000cc | 18p | — | 13p |
| 1601cc to 2000cc | — | 15p | — |
| Over 2000cc | 26p | 18p | 18p |
| **Rates applying from 1 September 2012** | | | |
| 1400cc or less | 15p | — | 10p |
| 1600cc or less | — | 12p | — |
| 1401cc to 2000cc | 18p | — | 13p |
| 1601cc to 2000cc | — | 15p | — |
| Over 2000cc | 26p | 18p | 17p |

Taxation of Earnings

# Private vehicles

## [¶4-200]   Mileage allowance payments
(ITEPA 2003, s. 230)

(Tax Reporter: ¶432-100ff.)

Statutory rates are set for mileage allowance payments. An employer may, of course, reimburse business mileage driven in a privately-owned car at more or less than the statutory rates but any excess is taxable. Any shortfall is tax deductible and the employee may claim relief accordingly. The rates were last amended from 6 April 2011.

| Kind of vehicle | Rate per mile from 6 April 2011 |
|---|---|
| Car or van | 45p for the first 10,000 miles 25p after that |
| Motorcycle | 24p |
| Cycle | 20p |

## [¶4-220]   Passenger payments
(ITEPA 2003, s. 233)

(Tax Reporter: ¶432-150)

No liability to income tax arises in respect of an approved passenger payment made to an employee for a car or a van, whether the vehicle is privately owned or provided by the employer. The approved amount is 5p per passenger mile.

# Company vans

## [¶4-300]   Taxable benefit
(ITEPA 2003, s. 114, 154–164)

(Tax Reporter: ¶416-200ff.)

| | £ |
|---|---|
| 2017–18 | 3,230 |
| 2016–17 | 3,170 |
| 2015–16 | 3,150 |
| 2014–15 | 3,090 |
| 2013–14 (from April 2007) | 3,000 |

But nil if:

(1)   the restricted private use conditions are met (available and used only for ordinary commuting and business travel);

(2)   private use in the tax year is insignificant.

### Zero-emission vans

For tax years 2010–11 to 2014–15, the cash equivalent of the benefit of a van was nil if the van could not produce any $CO_2$ emissions under any circumstances by being driven (e.g. an electric van). From 2015–16, the charge for zero-emission vans is calculated as the 'relevant percentage' per the table below of the main rate as per the table above.

|         | Appropriate percentage |
|---------|------------------------|
| 2015–16 | 20%                    |
| 2016–17 | 20%[1]                 |
| 2017–18 | 20%[1]                 |
| 2018–19 | 40%[1]                 |
| 2019–20 | 60%[1]                 |
| 2020–21 | 80%[1]                 |
| 2021–22 | 90%[1]                 |

**Note**
[1] *Finance Act* 2016 extends the van benefit charge support for zero-emission vans so that from 6 April 2016, the charge is 20% of the main rate in 2016–17 and 2017–18 and will then increase on a tapered basis to 5 April 2022. Previously announced rates were due to increase to 40%, 60%, 80% and 90% in each of tax years 2016–17 to 2019–20 respectively (ITEPA 2003, s. 155).

## [¶4-345]   Fuel for company vans

(ITEPA 2003, s. 160ff.)

(Tax Reporter: ¶416-200ff.)

| Tax Year | £   |
|----------|-----|
| 2017–18  | 610 |
| 2016–17  | 598 |
| 2015–16  | 594 |
| 2014–15  | 581 |
| 2013–14  | 564 |
| 2012–13  | 550 |
| 2011–12  | 550 |

But nil if:

(1)   the restricted private use conditions are met (available and used only for ordinary commuting and business travel);

(2)   private use in the tax year is insignificant; or

(3)   (from 6 April 2010 to 5 April 2015) the van cannot produce any $CO_2$ emissions by being driven.

# Buses

## [¶4-360]   Bus services

(ITEPA 2003, s. 242 and 243)

(Tax Reporter: ¶432-600ff.)

An exemption applies to:

(1)   works transport services, which must be a bus or minibus:

    (a)   available to employees generally;

    (b)   used mainly for qualifying journeys; and

    (c)   used substantially by employees or their children;

(2)   support for public bus services:

    (a)   available to employees generally;

    (b)   used for qualifying journeys by employees of one or more employers; and

    (c)   either:

        (i)   a local bus service; or

        (ii)   the bus must be provided to other passengers on terms that are as favourable as the terms on which the bus is provided to employees.

# Used cycles

## [¶4-380]   Used cycles: valuation table

(Tax Reporter: ¶419-090)

HMRC allow used cycles to be transferred to employees using disposal values as follows:

| Age of cycle | Original price less than £500 | Original price £500+ |
|---|---|---|
| 1 year | 18% | 25% |
| 18 months | 16% | 21% |
| 2 years | 13% | 17% |
| 3 years | 8% | 12% |
| 4 years | 3% | 7% |
| 5 years | Negligible | 2% |
| 6 years & over | Negligible | Negligible |

# Beneficial loans

## [¶4-390]   Beneficial loans threshold

(ITEPA 2003, Pt. 3, Ch. 7; s. 180)

(Tax Reporter: ¶417-000ff.)

A taxable benefit may arise where an employee (or a relative of an employee) is provided with a loan either interest-free or at a favourable rate of interest. A tax charge does not arise where the amount outstanding on the loan does not exceed the threshold at all times during the year. Threshold is as follows:

| Period | Threshold £ |
|---|---|
| 2014–15 and subsequent years | 10,000 |
| 2013–14 and earlier years (post-6 April 1994) | 5,000 |

# Official rates of interest

## [¶4-400]   Official rate of interest

(ITEPA 2003, s. 181)

(Tax Reporter: ¶417-100)

The official rate of interest is used to calculate the cash equivalent of the benefit of an employment-related loan which is a taxable cheap loan. HMRC review the level of the official rate of interest on a quarterly basis but normally set a single rate in advance for the whole tax year in line with a commitment given in January 2000, that (following announcement of the rate for any given tax year) the official rate may be reduced but will not be increased in the light of interest rate changes generally.

| Date | Rate % | SI No. |
|---|---|---|
| From 6 April 2017 | 2.50 | SI 2017/305 |
| 6 April 2016 to 5 April 2017 | 3.00 | —[1] |
| 6 April 2015 to 5 April 2016 | 3.00 | SI 2015/411 |
| 6 April 2014 to 5 April 2015 | 3.25 | SI 2014/496 |
| 6 April 2010 to 5 April 2014 | 4.00 | SI 2010/415 |

**Note**
[1] On 9 February 2016, HMRC announced that the official rate of interest would remain at 3% from 6 April 2016.

The average official rates of interest are given at ¶4-405.

Taxation of Earnings

## [¶4-405] Official rate of interest: average rates

(ITEPA 2003, s. 181)

(Tax Reporter: ¶417-100)

Official rates of interest are given at ¶4-400. Average official rates of interest, given below, should be used if the loan was outstanding throughout the tax year and the normal averaging method of calculation is being used.

| Year | Average official rate % |
|---|---|
| 2016–17 | 3.00 |
| 2015–16 | 3.00 |
| 2014–15 | 3.25 |
| 2013–14 | 4.00 |
| 2012–13 | 4.00 |
| 2011–12 | 4.00 |

## [¶4-420] Official rate of interest: foreign currency loans

(ITEPA 2003, s. 181)

(Tax Reporter: ¶418-100)

| | Swiss Francs % | Japanese Yen % |
|---|---|---|
| From 6 July 1994 | 5.5 | 3.9 |

# Travel and subsistence

## [¶4-500] Day subsistence rates

(Tax Reporter: ¶457-560)

The following 'day subsistence' rates may be used when applying for a dispensation for payments to employees away from home for work purposes:

| Rate | Detail | £ |
|---|---|---|
| Breakfast rate | Irregular early starters | 5 |
| One-meal rate | Away for at least five hours | 5 |
| Two-meal rate | Away for at least ten hours | 10 |
| Late evening meal rate | Irregular late finishers | 15 |

## [¶4-520]   Accommodation and subsistence – overseas rates

(Tax Reporter: ¶457-570)

In March 2008, HMRC published for the first time benchmark scale rates that employers were to be allowed to use when paying for accommodation and subsistence costs for employees working abroad. Payments up to these rates did not require receipts and did not need to be shown on form P11D.

Recent rates (as at the dates shown) are available as follows:

From October 2014[1]: www.gov.uk/government/uploads/system/uploads/ attachment_data/file/359797/2014_Worldwide_subsistence_ rates.pdf;

From October 2013:   www.gov.uk/government/uploads/system/uploads/ attachment_data/file/348024/wwsr-bench-2013.pdf.

**Note**
[1] The rates published in October 2014 will continue to apply for the year commencing October 2016.

## [¶4-540]   Incidental overnight expenses and benefits

(ITEPA 2003, s. 240)

(Tax Reporter: ¶432-900)

Benefits, reimbursements and expenses provided by an employer for employees' minor, personal expenditure whilst on business-related activities requiring overnight accommodation away from home are not taxable provided that the total amount reimbursed, etc. does not exceed the relevant maximum amount(s) per night, multiplied by the number of nights' absence. If the limit is exceeded, the whole amount provided remains taxable.

|  | Authorised maximum per night | |
| --- | --- | --- |
|  | **In UK** | **Overseas** |
| **From** | **£** | **£** |
| 6 April 1995 | 5 | 10 |

## [¶4-550]   Lorry drivers subsistence allowances

(ITEPA 2003, s. 337 and 338)

(Tax Reporter: ¶455-020; ¶455-040)

A subsistence allowance paid to long distance lorry drivers will not be taxed provided the following two conditions are satisfied.

(1)    There is documentary evidence available to show that the employee has spent the night away from home and away from his or her permanent workplace (if any) as a necessary result of a business journey and has incurred expenses in so doing.

(2)    The amounts paid are no more than a reasonable reimbursement to cover the cost of accommodation and subsistence incurred as a result of the business journey.

HMRC accept the following amounts as reasonable for nights in the UK.

Taxation of Earnings

| Year ended | Payment per night | |
| | Drivers with non-sleeper cabs £ | Drivers with sleeper cabs[1] £ |
| --- | --- | --- |
| 31 December 2016 | 34.90 | 26.20 |
| 31 December 2013, 2014 and 2015 | 34.90 | 26.20 |

**Note**
[1] The mere fact that a lorry has a sleeper cab does not prevent the employer paying an amount tax free up to the limit shown for drivers with non-sleeper cabs (or locally agreed limits) provided that the employer is satisfied that the driver did incur expenses on overnight accommodation (for example by staying in a hotel) and meals. HMRC accept that a payment of 75% of the figure shown for drivers with non-sleeper cabs does no more than reimburse the expense incurred when the driver uses the sleeper cab overnight.

# Shares and share incentives

## [¶4-600]   Share incentive plans
(TCGA 1992, s. 236A, 238A, Sch. 7C, 7D, Pt. 1; ITEPA 2003, s. 488ff., Sch. 2)
(Tax Reporter: ¶468-000ff.)

| | Free shares | Partnership shares | Matching shares | Dividend shares |
| --- | --- | --- | --- | --- |
| Employment before eligibility[1] | Up to 18 months employment | Up to 18 months employment[4] where no accumulation period, up to six months with accumulation period | Only awarded to employees who buy partnership shares | Must be acquired with dividends from plan shares |
| Limits | Up to £3,600 per tax year from 6 April 2014 (previously £3,000 per tax year) | Up to £1,800 per tax year from 6 April 2014 (previously £1,500 per tax year) or 10% of salary, if less | Up to two matching shares for each partnership share bought | Dividends from shares in the plan reinvested: – no limit from 2013–14 (previously £1,500 per tax year) |
| Minimum amount if stated[1] | — | £10 per month | — | — |
| Performance measures[1] | Yes | No | No | No |
| Holding period | At least three years from award[2] | None | At least three years from award[2] | Three years from acquisition |

| | Free shares | Partnership shares | Matching shares | Dividend shares |
|---|---|---|---|---|
| Forfeiture on cessation of employment[1] | Yes[5] | No | Yes[5] | No |
| Tax on award | None | None – tax relief for salary used to buy shares | None | None |
| Tax on removal of shares from plan within three years of award[3] | On market value when taken out | On market value when taken out | On market value when taken out | Original dividend taxable but in year when shares taken out of plan |
| Tax on removal between three and five years of award[2] | On lower of: – value at award – value on removal | On lower of: – salary used to buy shares – value on removal | On lower of: – value at award – value on removal | None |
| Tax on removal after five years | None | None | None | None |
| CGT on removal – any time | None | None | None | None |

**Notes**

[1] These conditions can be included at the option of the company.

[2] The holding period may be up to five years at the option of the company.

[3] PAYE and NICs will be operated in relation to any income tax charge where the shares are readily convertible assets.

[4] Maximum accumulation period for partnership shares is 12 months.

[5] Restrictions apply to provisions for forfeiture that may be applied including a maximum forfeiture period of up to three years from award, that forfeiture provisions cannot relate to cesation of employment through injury, disability, redundancy, TUPE transfers, changes of control, retirement (at normal age), death, or be linked to the performance of any person.

[6] From 6 April 2014, SIPs are self-certified by employers rather than approved by HMRC (FA 2014).

[7] From 15 September 2016, rules for share incentive plans previously repealed will be reinstated to enforce the principle that shares with preferential rights cannot be issued to selected employees only (amendments by FA 2016, Sch. 3).

## [¶4-610]　Company share option plan

(TCGA 1992, s. 238A, Sch. 7D, Pt. 3; ITEPA 2003, s. 521–526, Sch. 4)

(Tax Reporter: ¶467-000ff.)

| Maximum options[1][2] | £30,000 |
|---|---|

**Notes**

[1] This includes options granted under the scheme, or under any other approved CSOP scheme established by the scheme organiser or an associated company of the scheme organiser.

[2] The 'market value' of shares is calculated at the date of grant, or of each relevant option grant (if more than one grant); or if any agreement relating to any such shares has been made under ITEPA 2003, Sch. 4, para. 22, the earlier time or times stated in the agreement.

[3] From 6 April 2014, CSOP schemes are self-certified by the scheme organiser rather than approved by HMRC (FA 2014).

## [¶4-620]   Enterprise management incentives (EMI)

(TCGA 1992, s. 238A, Sch. 7D, Pt. 4; ITEPA 2003, s. 527–541, Sch. 5)

(Tax Reporter: ¶466-000ff.)

| | |
|---|---|
| Qualifying company | • Gross assets not exceeding £30m<br>• Fewer than 250 employees (full-time or equivalent),<br>  in relation to options granted from 21 July 2008 |
| Maximum options | £250,000 from 16 June 2012<br>(£120,000 between 6 April 2008 and 15 June 2012 and<br>£100,000 prior to 6 April 2008) |

**Notes**

(1) The above rule is qualified as follows:

(a)   options held by the employee under a (HMRC-approved) Company Share Ownership Plan (CSOP), that are unexercised at the date of grant of an EMI option, are taken into account in applying the maximum figure above;

(b)   by the 'three-year restriction period' rule; the grant of an option to an employee within three years from the most recent EMI option grant to him, cannot itself qualify as an EMI option if the value of the shares which were the subject of all previous EMI option grants, down to and including the most recent grant, amounted to £250,000 (or other applicable threshold figure in earlier periods). This applies whether or not any of such previously granted options have been exercised; and

(c)   there is an overriding company limit; the total value (as defined) of shares in the company that are the subject of unexercised EMI options cannot exceed £3,000,000.

For purposes of (a) and (b) above, one takes into account all options granted by reason of the same employment, or employment by any member of the same group of companies.

(2) *Finance Act* 2016 amends capital gains tax legislation so that a rights issue that takes place on or after 6 April 2016, in respect of shares received on exercise of an enterprise management incentive option, will be treated in the same way for share identification purposes as other rights issues (amendments by FA 2016, Sch. 3).

## [¶4-635]   SAYE

(TCGA 1992, s. 238A, Sch. 7D, Pt. 2; ITEPA 2003, s. 516–520, Sch. 3)

(Tax Reporter: ¶470-000ff.)

| Limits | Savings periods | Monthly contributions |
|---|---|---|
| Minimum | 36 months | £5–£10[1] |
| Maximum[2] | 60 months | £500[3] |

**Notes**

(1) Company may impose a minimum monthly payment of up to £10 per month; otherwise the minimum is £5 per month.

(2) Seven-year savings feature abolished with effect from 23 July 2013.

(3) Limit on contributions increased from £250 to £500 with effect from 6 April 2014 (ITEPA 2003, Sch. 3, para. 25).

(4) From 6 April 2014, SAYE schemes are self-certified by the scheme organiser rather than approved by HMRC (FA 2014).

## [¶4-640]   SAYE bonus rates: multiple of monthly payments

(ITEPA 2003, Sch. 3)

(Tax Reporter: ¶470-000ff.)

The bonus rate applicable to a scheme is set at the time the savings contract is entered into and is unaffected by any subsequent change to the rates. Current and historical rates are shown below. See ¶4-660 for details of the 'early leaver rate' applying for those who withdraw their funds after 12 monthly contributions, but before the three-year anniversary.

| From | 3-year | 5-year | 7-year[1] |
|---|---|---|---|
| 27 December 2014 | 0.0 | 0.0 | — |
| 28 July 2014 | 0.0 | 0.6 | — |
| 1 August 2012 | 0.0 | 0.0 | 0.0 |
| 23 September 2011 | 0.0 | 0.0 | 1.6 |
| 12 August 2011 | 0.0 | 0.9 | 3.5 |
| 27 February 2011 | 0.1 | 1.7 | 4.8 |

**Note**
[1] The seven-year savings period of Save As You Earn (SAYE) Share Option Schemes was withdrawn with effect from 23 July 2013. Employees already saving under existing SAYE contracts before that date were not affected by the change.

## [¶4-660] SAYE 'early leaver rates'

(ITEPA 2003, Sch. 3)

(Tax Reporter: ¶470-000ff.)

The following 'early leaver rates' have applied for employees whose SAYE contracts are cancelled after 12 monthly contributions but before the maturity date:

| Dates | Rates % |
|---|---|
| 27 December 2014 | 0.00 |
| 28 July 2014 | 0.00 |
| 1 August 2012 | 0.00 |
| 23 September 2011 | 0.00 |
| 12 August 2011 | 0.00 |
| 27 February 2011 | 0.12 |

**Note**
The relevant date is that on which the employee starts saving under the contract, not the date on which the contract is cancelled.

## [¶4-680] SAYE effective interest rates

(ITEPA 2003, Sch. 3)

(Tax Reporter: ¶470-000ff.)

| From | 3-year | 5-year | 7-year[1] |
|---|---|---|---|
| 27 December 2014 | 0.00 | 0.00 | — |
| 28 July 2014 | 0.00 | 0.39 | — |
| 1 August 2012 | 0.00 | 0.00 | 0.00 |
| 23 September 2011 | 0.00 | 0.00 | 0.58 |
| 12 August 2011 | 0.00 | 0.59 | 1.25 |
| 27 February 2011 | 0.18 | 1.10 | 1.70 |

**Note**
[1] The seven-year savings period of Save As You Earn (SAYE) Share Option Schemes was withdrawn with effect from 23 July 2013. Employees already saving under existing SAYE contracts before that date were not affected by the change.

## [¶4-690]   Employee shareholder status

(ITEPA 2003, s. 226A–226D)

(Tax Reporter: ¶471-500ff.)

Employee shareholder status (ESS) was introduced from 1 September 2013 to new hire or existing employees. Autumn Statement 2016 announced that the tax advantages linked to shares awarded under ESS will be abolished for arrangements entered into on or after 1 December 2016 and the status itself will be closed to new arrangements at the next legislative opportunity.

Under existing legislation, employees accepting a position under an employee shareholder employment contract must be awarded at least £2,000 (market value) of fully paid up shares in their employer or parent company, at no cost to the employee. Employee shareholders retain the majority of employment rights (such as SSP, SMP, SPP, SAP, certain automatic unfair dismissal rights, TUPE rights, time off rights, NMW entitlement, etc.) but will give up unfair dismissal rights (apart from the exception), rights to statutory redundancy pay, the statutory right to request flexible working except in the two-week period after a return from parental leave and certain statutory rights to request time off to train. Additionally, an employee shareholder will have to give 16 weeks' notice to their employer if they intend to return early from maternity, additional paternity or adoption leave. The employer can, however, choose to offer contractual rights that are more generous than those provided for in statute.

See ¶5-050 for capital gains tax exemption on employee shareholder shares.

|  | From 1 September 2013 £ |
|---|---|
| Minimum value of share award (market value on acquisition) | 2,000 |
| Income tax and NIC exemption[1] (market value on acquisition) | 2,000 |

**Note**
[1] Employee is treated as having made a payment of £2,000 for the acquisition of shares and accordingly; any excess (of market value) over £2,000 is treated as earnings from the employment subject to income tax (and NIC as applicable).

## [¶4-695]   Employee ownership trusts

(ITEPA 2003, s. 312A–312I)

*Finance Act* 2014 introduced provisions that provide an exemption from income tax for any relevant bonus payment made in a tax year to an employee by a qualifying indirectly employee-owned company that meets the relevant conditions (a trading company in which a controlling interest is held by an employee-ownership settlement). A relevant bonus will be a cash award other than regular salary or wages that is paid to all employees on equal terms, although bonuses can be set by an employer by reference to a percentage of salary or length of service or hours worked. The exemption is available from 1 October 2014 and subject to an annual cap per employee for each qualifying company as set out below.

| Period | £ |
|---|---|
| From 1 October 2014 | 3,600 |

# National minimum wage

## [¶4-700]   National minimum wage: from 1 October 2010

(SI 2016/953)

| Period[1] | Workers aged 25 plus[2] £ | Workers aged at least 21 but under 25 £ | Workers aged at least 18 but under 21 £ | Workers aged under 18 £ | Apprentices aged under 19 or in the first year of apprenticeship £ |
|---|---|---|---|---|---|
| From 6 April 2017 | 7.50 | 7.05 | 5.60 | 4.05 | 3.50 |
| 1/10/16–05/04/16 | 7.20 | 6.95 | 5.55 | 4.00 | 3.40 |
| 1/04/16–30/09/16 | 7.20 | 6.70 | 5.30 | 3.87 | 3.30 |
| 1/10/15–31/03/16 | – | 6.70 | 5.30 | 3.87 | 3.30 |
| 1/10/14–30/09/15 | – | 6.50 | 5.13 | 3.79 | 2.73 |
| 1/10/13–30/09/14 | – | 6.31 | 5.03 | 3.72 | 2.68 |
| 1/10/12–30/09/13 | – | 6.19 | 4.98 | 3.68 | 2.65 |
| 1/10/11–30/09/12 | – | 6.08 | 4.98 | 3.68 | 2.60 |
| 1/10/10–30/09/11 | – | 5.93 | 4.92 | 3.64 | 2.50 |

**Notes**
[1] At Summer Budget 2015, the Government announced a review of the NMW timetable to align it to the tax year.
[2] National living wage introduced from 1 April 2016.

## [¶4-720]   National minimum wage: accommodation offset

The maximum permitted daily and weekly rates of accommodation offset in relation to the national minimum wage are as follows:

| Period | Daily offset £ | Weekly offset £ |
|---|---|---|
| From 6/4/2017 | 6.40 | 44.80 |
| 1/10/16–5/4/17 | 6.00 | 42.00 |
| 1/10/15–30/09/16 | 5.35 | 37.45 |
| 1/10/14–30/09/15 | 5.08 | 35.56 |
| 1/10/13–30/09/14 | 4.91 | 34.37 |
| 1/10/12–30/09/13 | 4.82 | 33.74 |
| 1/10/11–30/09/12 | 4.73 | 33.11 |
| 1/10/10–30/09/11 | 4.61 | 32.27 |

# Flat-rate expenses

## [¶4-750] Fixed sum deductions for repairing and maintaining equipment

(ITEPA 2003, s. 367)

(Tax Reporter: ¶457-500)

A tax deduction is given for certain amounts 'representing the average annual expenses incurred by employees of the class to which the employee belongs in respect of the repair and maintenance of work equipment'. The term 'flat-rate expenses' is often used for these figures. The following table is from EIM32712.

**Manual and certain other employees: flat-rate expenses deduction for tools and special clothing**

| Industry | Occupation | | Deduction for 2008–09 onwards £ | Deduction for 2004–05 to 2007–08 £ |
|---|---|---|---|---|
| Agriculture | All workers | | 100 | 70 |
| Aluminium | a. | Continual casting operators, process operators, de-dimplers, driers, drill punchers, dross unloaders, firemen, furnace operators and their helpers, leaders, mouldmen, pourers, remelt department labourers, roll flatteners | 140 | 130 |
| | b. | Cable hands, case makers, labourers, mates, truck drivers and measurers, storekeepers | 80 | 60 |
| | c. | Apprentices | 60 | 45 |
| | d. | All other workers | 120 | 100 |
| Banks and building societies | Uniformed doormen and messengers | | 60 | 45 |
| Brass and copper | Braziers, coppersmiths, finishers, fitters, moulders, turners and all other workers. | | 120 | 100 |
| Building | a. | Joiners and carpenters | 140 | 105 |
| | b. | Cement works, roofing felt and asphalt labourers | 80 | 55 |
| | c. | Labourers and navvies | 60 | 45 |
| | d. | All other workers | 120 | 85 |
| Building materials | a. | Stone-masons | 120 | 85 |
| | b. | Tilemakers and labourers | 60 | 45 |
| | c. | All other workers | 80 | 55 |

| Industry | | Occupation | Deduction for 2008–09 onwards £ | Deduction for 2004–05 to 2007–08 £ |
|---|---|---|---|---|
| Clothing | a. | Lacemakers, hosiery bleachers, dyers, scourers and knitters, knitwear bleachers and dyers | 60 | 45 |
| | b. | All other workers | 60 | 45 |
| Constructional engineering | a. | Blacksmiths and their strikers, burners, caulkers, chippers, drillers, erectors, fitters, holders up, markers off, platers, riggers, riveters, rivet heaters, scaffolders, sheeters, template workers, turners, welders | 140 | 115 |
| | b. | Banksmen labourers, shop-helpers, slewers, straighteners | 80 | 60 |
| | c. | Apprentices and storekeepers | 60 | 45 |
| | d. | All other workers | 100 | 75 |
| Electrical and electricity supply | a. | Those workers incurring laundry costs only (generally CEGB employees) | 60 | 45 |
| | b. | All other workers | 120 | 90 |
| Engineering | a. | Pattern makers | 140 | 120 |
| | b. | Labourers, supervisory and unskilled workers | 80 | 60 |
| | c. | Apprentices and storekeepers | 60 | 45 |
| | d. | Motor mechanics in garage repair shops | 120 | 100 |
| | e. | All other workers | 120 | 100 |
| Fire service | | Uniformed fire fighters and fire officers | 80 | 60 |
| Food | | All workers | 60 | 45 |
| Forestry | | All workers | 100 | 70 |
| Glass | | All workers | 80 | 60 |
| Healthcare staff in the National Health Service, private hospitals and nursing homes | a. | Ambulance staff on active service (i.e. excluding staff who take telephone calls or provide clerical support) | 140 | 110 |
| | b. | Nurses, midwives, chiropodists, dental nurses, occupational, speech, physiotherapists and other therapists, healthcare assistants, phlebotomists and radiographers | 100 | 70 |

Taxation of Earnings

| Industry | | Occupation | Deduction for 2008–09 onwards £ | Deduction for 2004–05 to 2007–08 £ |
|---|---|---|---|---|
| | c. | Plaster room orderlies, hospital porters, ward clerks, sterile supply workers, hospital domestics, hospital catering staff | 100 | 60 |
| | d. | Laboratory staff, pharmacists, pharmacy assistants | 60 | 45 |
| | e. | Uniformed ancillary staff – maintenance workers, grounds staff, drivers, parking attendants and security guards, receptionists and other uniformed staff | 60 | 45 |
| Heating | a. | Pipe fitters and plumbers | 120 | 100 |
| | b. | Coverers, laggers, domestic glaziers, heating engineers and their mates | 120 | 90 |
| | c. | All gas workers, all other workers | 100 | 70 |
| Iron mining | a. | Fillers, miners and underground workers | 120 | 100 |
| | b. | All other workers | 100 | 75 |
| Iron and steel | a. | Day labourers, general labourers, stockmen, time-keepers, warehouse staff and weighmen | 80 | 60 |
| | b. | Apprentices | 60 | 45 |
| | c. | All other workers | 140 | 120 |
| Leather | a. | Curriers (wet workers), fellmongering workers, tanning operatives (wet) | 80 | 55 |
| | b. | All other workers | 60 | 45 |
| Particular engineering | a. | Pattern makers | 140 | 120 |
| | b. | All chainmakers; cleaners, galvanisers, tinners and wire drawers in the wire drawing industry; tool-makers in the lock making industry | 120 | 100 |
| | c. | Apprentices and storekeepers | 60 | 45 |
| | d. | All other workers | 80 | 60 |
| Police force | | Police officers (ranks up to and including Chief Inspector) | 140 | 55 (but £110 for 2007–08) |
| Precious metals | | All workers | 100 | 70 |

Taxation of Earnings

| Industry | Occupation | Deduction for 2008–09 onwards £ | Deduction for 2004–05 to 2007–08 £ |
|---|---|---|---|
| Printing | a. *Letterpress Section*: Electrical engineers (rotary presses), electrotypers, ink and roller makers, machine minders (rotary), maintenance engineers (rotary presses) and stereotypers | 140 | 105 |
| | b. Bench hands (periodical and bookbinding section), compositors (letterpress section), readers (letterpress section) telecommunications and electronic section wire room operators, warehousemen (paper box making section) | 60 | 45 |
| | c. All other workers | 100 | 70 |
| Prisons | Uniformed prison officers | 80 | 55 |
| Public service | a. *Dock and inland waterways*<br>– Dockers, dredger drivers, hopper steerers | 80 | 55 |
| | – All other workers | 60 | 45 |
| | b. *Public transport*<br>– Garage hands (including cleaners) | 80 | 55 |
| | – Conductors and drivers | 60 | 45 |
| Quarrying | All workers | 100 | 70 |
| Railways | (See the appropriate category for craftsmen, e.g. engineers, vehicle, etc.) | | |
| | All other workers | 100 | 70 |
| Seamen | a. Carpenters (Seamen) Passenger liners | 165 | 165 |
| | b. Carpenters (Seamen) Cargo vessels, tankers, coasters and ferries | 140 | 130 |
| Shipyards | a. Blacksmiths and their strikers, boilermakers, burners, carpenters, caulkers, drillers, furnacemen (platers), holders up, fitters, platers, plumbers, riveters, sheet iron workers, shipwrights, tubers, welders | 140 | 115 |
| | b. Labourers | 80 | 60 |
| | c. Apprentices and storekeepers | 60 | 45 |
| | d. All other workers | 100 | 75 |

| Industry | | Occupation | Deduction for 2008–09 onwards £ | Deduction for 2004–05 to 2007–08 £ |
|---|---|---|---|---|
| Textiles and textile printing | a. | Carders, carding engineers, overlookers and technicians in spinning mills | 120 | 85 |
| | b. | All other workers | 80 | 60 |
| Vehicles | a. | Builders, railway vehicle repairers and railway wagon lifters | 140 | 105 |
| | b. | Railway vehicle painters, letterers, and builders' and repairers' assistants | 80 | 60 |
| | c. | All other workers | 60 | 45 |
| Wood and furniture (formerly Wood) | a. | Carpenters, cabinet makers, joiners, wood carvers and woodcutting machinists | 140 | 115 |
| | b. | Artificial limb makers (other than in wood), organ builders and packaging case makers | 120 | 90 |
| | c. | Coopers not providing own tools, labourers, polishers and upholsterers | 60 | 45 |
| | d. | All other workers | 100 | 75 |

**Notes**
'Workers' and 'all other workers' are references to manual workers or to workers who have to pay for the upkeep of tools and special clothing.
'Firemen' means persons engaged to light and maintain furnaces.
'Constructional engineering' means engineering undertaken on a construction site, including buildings, shipyards, bridges, roads and other similar operations.
'Particular engineering' means engineering undertaken on a commercial basis in a factory or workshop for the purposes of producing components such as wire, springs, nails and locks.

# Miscellaneous

## [¶4-800]   Mobile phones

(ITEPA 2003, s. 319)

(Tax Reporter: ¶437-700)

No tax charge on employer-provided mobile phones but exemption restricted to one phone per employee, with no exemption for phones provided for family members. Limited exemption for vouchers supplied for mobile phone use. The right of the employee to surrender the phone for additional pay does not trigger a tax charge.

## [¶4-805]  Recommended medical treatment
(ITEPA 2003, s. 320C)

(Tax Reporter: ¶437-900)

No liability to income tax arises in respect of the provision to an employee of recommended medical treatment, or the payment or reimbursement, to or in respect of an employee of the cost of such treatment, if the provision, payment or reimbursement is not pursuant to relevant salary sacrifice arrangements or relevant flexible remuneration arrangements. The exemption does not apply if, and to the extent that, the value in the tax year exceeds the limit shown in the table below.

| Period | Annual limit |
|---|---|
| From 1 January 2015 | £500 |

## [¶4-810]  Employer-provided childcare (workplace nurseries)
(ITEPA 2003, s. 318)

(Tax Reporter: ¶434-600)

No liability to income tax arises in respect of employer-provided childcare (workplace nurseries) provided certain conditions are met; including that the premises are made available by the employer alone, or that the care is provided under partnership arrangements by persons including the employer, one or more of whom makes the premises available, and under which arrangements the employer is wholly or partly responsible for financing and managing the provision of the care.

## [¶4-815]  Employer-supported childcare
(ITEPA 2003, s. 270A, 318A)

(Tax Reporter: ¶434-800ff.)

A limited exemption is available for childcare vouchers and directly contracted childcare. Where the cash equivalent of the benefit falls above the limits set out in the table below, liability to income tax arises only in respect of so much as exceeds the exempt amount.

The *Childcare Payments Act* 2014 prospectively amends s. 270A and 318A to restrict the availability of the existing tax exemptions for employer-supported childcare where the employee has given their employer a 'chilcare account notice' to say that they no longer want to receive employer-supported childcare so that they or their partner can open a childcare account under the new scheme to be introduced in early 2017 (by gradual roll out) (see ¶10-560). The amendments will take effect in accordance with provision contained in regulations, however, as part of the transition to tax-free childcare, employer-supported childcare will remain open to new entrants until April 2018 (Budget 2016).

| | Basic rate[1] £ | Higher rate £ | Additional rate £ |
|---|---|---|---|
| **From 6 April 2013** | | | |
| Weekly | 55 | 28 | 25 |
| Monthly | 243 | 124 | 111 |
| Annual | 2,915 | 1,484 | 1,325 |
| **From 6 April 2011** | | | |
| Weekly | 55 | 28 | 22 |
| Monthly | 243 | 124 | 97 |
| Annual | 2,915 | 1,484 | 1,166 |

**Note**
[1] The restriction on the amount of the exemption available for higher rate and additional rate taxpayers from 6 April 2011 does not apply where an employee joined the scheme before 6 April 2011, has not ceased to be employed by the employer since that date and there has not been a continuous period of 52 weeks since that date throughout which vouchers were not, or care was not, being provided under the scheme and such employees continue to be entitled to relief at the rates that are otherwise available for basic rate earners only (FA 2011, Sch. 8, para. 8).

## [¶4-830]   Relocation allowance
(ITEPA 2003, s. 271–289)

(Tax Reporter: ¶433-850)

Tax exemption for the provision by employers of removal benefits, or payment or reimbursement of removal expenses in connection with an employee's change of residence where the employee's job or place of work is changed is generally subject to a statutory maximum of £8,000. No tax relief is available for the employee where expenses are not reimbursed by the employer.

## [¶4-840]   Payments and benefits on termination of employment
(ITEPA 2003, s. 401–416)

(Tax Reporter: ¶437-000ff.)

| Period | Relief |
|---|---|
| From 1998–99 | £30,000 exempt |

**Note**
The exemption is not available for any payment or other benefit chargeable to income tax under other legislation (ITEPA 2003, s. 401(3)).
There is therefore no exemption for any amounts already taxable as earnings (e.g. payments made under a contract of employment).
Spring Budget re-confirmed (as announced at Budget 2016 and confirmed at Autumn Statement 2016) that, from April 2018 termination payments over £30,000, which are subject to income tax, will also be subject to employer NICs. Following a technical consultation, tax will only be applied to the equivalent of an employee's basic pay if their notice is not worked, making it simpler to apply the new rules. The first £30,000 of a termination payment will remain exempt from income tax and NIC (Finance Bill 2017).

## [¶4-850]  Scholarships and sandwich courses

(SP 4/86)

(Tax Reporter: ¶419-200)

Subject to conditions, employers may make tax-free payments up to a specified figure to employees who are attending certain educational courses. The specified amount for recent years has been as follows:

| Period | Specified amount |
|---|---|
| From 1/9/07 | £15,480 |

## [¶4-860]  Trivial benefits

(ITEPA 2003, s. 323A)

| From | Annual exempt amount £ |
|---|---|
| 6 April 2016 | 300 |

Finance Act 2016 introduces a statutory exemption for trivial benefits in kind. This measure was originally due to be introduced from April 2015 but did not proceed as part of Finance Act 2015.

## [¶4-870]  Sporting testimonials

(ITEPA 2003, s. 306B)

From 6 April 2017, a one-off exemption of £100,000 from income tax and National Insurance contributions (NICs) will be introduced for income arising from a non-contractual or non-customary sporting testimonial or benefit for an employed sportsperson. The exemption is introduced by Finance Act 2016 (and corresponding legislation for NICs) and will apply to income from a non-contractual or non-customary testimonial being paid to or on behalf of an employed sportsperson. The exemption will apply to income arising from relevant events held in a maximum period of 12 calendar months only, beginning with the date the first event is held in a 'testimonial year', even if that year straddles more than one tax year. If the level of the income arising from the testimonial or testimonial year falls below the value of the exemption, the amount of the unused exemption will not be available to carry forward to a future sporting testimonial or benefit match for the sportsperson, or against any other testimonial events held after the end of that 12-month period. Any non-contractual or non-customary testimonial events held on or after 6 April 2017 from a testimonial that is awarded or arranged for a sportsperson prior to 25 November 2015 will fall within guidance currently published by HMRC on the tax treatment of sporting testimonials and benefits for employed sportspersons which affords a concessionary exemption. Testimonials granted or awarded under contract or custom are already subject to income tax and will not be affected by the new legislation.

# PAYE

## [¶4-900] PAYE thresholds

(SI 2003/2682)

(Tax Reporter: ¶493-240ff.)

| | Amount | |
|---|---|---|
| | **Weekly** | **Monthly** |
| **Tax year** | **£** | **£** |
| 2017–18 | 221.00 | 958.00 |
| 2016–17 | 212.00 | 917.00 |
| 2015–16 | 204.00 | 883.00 |
| 2014–15 | 192.00 | 833.00 |
| 2013–14 | 182.00 | 787.00 |
| 2012–13 | 156.00 | 675.00 |
| 2011–12 | 144.00 | 623.00 |

**Note**

Under normal circumstances, employers need not deduct tax from employees who earn less than the above amounts. The PAYE monthly and weekly thresholds are calculated arithmetically as 1/52 and 1/12 respectively of the personal allowance, rounded to the nearest pound (SI 2003/2682, reg. 9(8)).

## [¶4-920] PAYE codes

The PAYE code enables an employer or payer of pension to give the employee or pensioner the approved amount of tax-free pay.

| | |
|---|---|
| L | Entitled to the basic tax-free personal allowance – 1150L for the 2017–18 tax year. Also used for 'emergency' codes |
| M | Marriage allowance: people who have received a transfer of 10% of their partner's personal allowance |
| N | Marriage allowance: people who have transferred 10% of their personal allowance to their partner |
| S | Income or pension taxed at Scottish rate of income tax |
| T | Tax code includes other calculations to work out the personal allowance (i.e. income-related reduction to the personal allowance) |
| 0T | Allowances fully used up or reduced to nil and income is taxed at the relevant rates, may also be used for a new job where the employee does not have a P45 or has not completed a P46 before the first pay day |
| BR | All income is taxed at the basic rate, currently 20%, most commonly used for a second job or pension |
| SBR | Scottish taxpayer; all income taxed at the basic rate, currently 20% |
| D0 | All income taxed at the higher rate, currently 40%, most commonly used for a second job or pension |
| SD0 | Scottish taxpayer; all income taxed at the higher rate, currently 40% |
| D1 | All income taxed at the additional rate, currently 45%, most commonly used for a second job or pension |
| SD1 | Scottish taxpayer; all income taxed at the additional rate, currently 45% |

NT          No tax to be deducted from income or pension
K           Untaxed income exceeds tax-free allowances (e.g. tax due for previous tax
            year, taxable state benefits or taxable employment benefits)

**Other codes**

Code FT is used for certain farmers employed under a hiring contract.

W1, M1, X are emergency tax code indicators and denote the tax code is operating on
a non-cumulative basis. Also issued where the tax code is adjusted during the tax year
and the adjustment is to reduce net allowances/increase taxable benefits (so that the new
collects on a non-cumulative basis for the remainder of the year). Emergency tax codes
for the 2017–18 tax year are 1150L M1, 1150L W1, 1150L X.

P codes were used until 2014–15 for individuals born between 6 April 1938 and 5 April
1948 entitled to the full personal allowance. That category of personal allowance was
removed from statute from 2015–16 and subsequent tax years.

V codes have been obsolete since 6 April 2009 (as all individuals born before 6 April 1935
and qualifying for married couple's allowance (MCA) will be aged 75 and over during the
tax year ended 5 April 2010. MCA will then be due at the higher rate.)

# [¶4-925]   PAYE coding out limits

**Debts**

(ITEPA 2003, s. 684; SI 2003/2682, reg. 14A–14C)

(Tax Reporter: ¶493-340)

HMRC may collect specified relevant debts up to the permitted limit through the PAYE
system. The table below sets out the maximum amount that may be collected in this way
(but see also the 'overall limit' and the 'overriding limit' below):

| Tax year in which deduction made | Maximum deduction £ |
|---|---|
| From 2015–16 | 17,000 |
| 2012–13 to 2014–15[1] | 3,000 |

**Note**
[1] SI 2003/2682, reg. 14A which provides for determination of a tax code to recover a 'relevant debt' within the
meaning of ITEPA 2003, s. 684 was introduced with effect from 6 April 2012.

To the extent that the payee does not object, HMRC may also determine a code to collect
or repay income tax payable or overpaid in respect of the high income child benefit
charge and, from 2015–16, to collect child or working tax credit debt.

**Self-assessment balancing payments**

(SI 2003/2682, reg.186)

(Tax Reporter: ¶493-330)

| Payments due on or after | Maximum deduction £ |
|---|---|
| 6 April 2012[1] | 3,000 |

**Note**
[1] Prior to 6 April 2012, in relation to amounts due under self-assessment and coded out under SI 2003/2682,
reg. 186, the maximum deductible amount was £2,000.

**Overall limit**

(SI 2003/2682, reg. 14D)

With effect for tax codes issued for the tax year 2015–16 onwards, and to coincide with the increase in the coding out limit above from £3,000 to £17,000, an overall limit on the total amount of 'relevant debt' (under SI 2003/2682, reg. 14A) and 'tax credit debt' (under SI 2003/2682, reg. 14C) that may be recovered from an employee in a tax year via their tax code will be introduced, based on the expected amount of the individual's PAYE income for the tax year and as set out in the table below (subject to the 'overriding limit' below):

| Expected amount of PAYE income in the tax year for which the code is determined | Total amount of debt recoverable in that tax year |
|---|---|
| Less than £30,000 | No more than £3,000 |
| £30,000 or more but less than £40,000 | No more than £5,000 |
| £40,000 or more but less than £50,000 | No more than £7,000 |
| £50,000 or more but less than £60,000 | No more than £9,000 |
| £60,000 or more but less than £70,000 | No more than £11,000 |
| £70,000 or more but less than £80,000 | No more than £13,000 |
| £80,000 or more but less than £90,000 | No more than £15,000 |
| £90,000 or more | No more than £17,000 |

**Overriding limit**

(SI 2003/2682, reg. 2)

The 'overriding limit' is the limit on the amount of tax that may be deducted from a relevant payment and is an amount equal to 50% of the amount of the relevant payment. A relevant payment is defined as a payment of net PAYE income, except PAYE social security income, UK social security pensions, excluded relocation expenses, excluded business expenses, excluded pecuniary liabilities, and excluded notional payments (SI 2003/2682, reg. 4).

Additionally, HMRC will further not code out debts which result in the individual's liability for the year doubling, even though the debt might otherwise fall within the limits set out above (i.e. only debts that equate to less than the individual's expected liability for the tax year will be coded out) (see HMRC manuals, PAYE12070).

## [¶4-930]   PAYE real time information returns

(SI 2012/822; SI 2003/2682)

(Tax Reporter: ¶493-015)

Since 6 April 2013 (or 5 April 2014 for businesses with 50 or less employees), reporting PAYE information in real time has been mandatory, unless HMRC have notified otherwise. Key RTI requirements are as follows:

Taxation of Earnings

| Submissions | Deadlines | Details |
|---|---|---|
| Full Payment Submission (FPS) | On or before the day employees are paid<br><br>Final submission by 19 April (cannot file an FPS after this date) | • include all employees that are paid (including those earning below the NIC lower earnings limit (e.g. students))<br>• information to be submitted includes: amounts paid, deductions (tax and National Insurance), starter and leaver dates (if applicable) |
| Employer Payment Submission (EPS) | 19 April following tax year (by 19 May following tax year to avoid a penalty) | • to report a reduction in the amount you pay to HMRC or if you have not paid any employees in a pay period |
| Earlier Year Update (EYU) | Up to six years after original FPS or EPS filed (by 19 May following tax year to avoid a penalty) | • to correct, after 19 April, any of the year to date totals submitted in your final FPS for the previous tax year. This only applies to years after you started to send information in real time |
| National Insurance verification request (NVR) | — | • to verify or obtain an National Insurance number for new employees |
| Employer Alignment Submission (EAS) | Notified by HMRC | • to align employee records with HMRC records before submission of other information<br>• only required for larger PAYE schemes with over 250 employees, or payroll administered by two or more payroll systems, including those operated by different payroll providers |

## [¶4-932]   PAYE RTI: forms no longer needed

| Reporting PAYE pre-RTI | Reporting in real time |
|---|---|
| Forms P14 and P35 end of year returns – do not use after you have submitted your 2012–13 return | FPS each time you pay employees<br>EPS each month for any adjustments to what you owe<br>Earlier Year Update (EYU) to amend details for earlier years |

| Reporting PAYE pre-RTI | Reporting in real time |
|---|---|
| P45 – do not send any parts to HMRC – only use for the employees own records after 6 April 2013 | Include starters and leavers information on your FPS |
| P46, P46(Pen) or P46(Expat) – do not use these forms after 6 April 2013 | Include starters and leavers on your FPS. |
| Form CA6855 to trace or check a National Insurance number – do not use after 6 April 2013 | Use payroll software to issue a National Insurance number verification request (NVR) to trace or check a National Insurance number |
| Form P38(S) – do not use after 6 April 2013 | Include on your payroll and in your FPS |

## [¶4-935]  PAYE RTI: procedures unchanged

- **PAYE** – remains the same, only reporting that changes;
- **Coding notices** – employers still choose how they receive coding notices as previously;
- **Reporting a change to HMRC**, e.g. updating employee's new name or address for HMRC records – a real time submission will not update HMRC records. It remains the responsibility of the individual employee to notify HMRC of changes to name, address, etc.;
- **HMRC messages to employers** – HMRC continue to use the Data Provisioning Services (DPS) and EDI outbound message services;
- **Payment dates** – remain unchanged;
- **Forms P60** – P60s remain the same;
- **Expenses and benefits** – real time reporting has not changed how expenses and benefits are reported. Employers continue to complete and file any forms P9D, P11D and P11D(b) due under existing arrangements;
- **The Construction Industry Scheme (CIS) payment and reporting process** – real time reporting has not changed the CIS process. Employers continue to complete and file monthly returns (CIS300) due under the existing CIS arrangements. But where a limited company acting as a subcontractor has suffered CIS deductions, amounts should be reported to HMRC on an EPS and, as existing practice, subtract these from the amounts of PAYE due to be paid to HMRC.

## [¶4-938]  PAYE RTI: correcting errors

### Error in a Full Payment Submission (FPS) or EPS in the current tax year

Submit an additional FPS or EPS in the week or month of discovery or include correction in the next FPS or EPS for the next payroll run.

**Error in FPS or EPS for previous tax year**

Errors can be corrected before 20 April by submitting an additional FPS or EPS.

After 20 April, it is not possible to submit an additional FPS and instead the correction must be made on an EYU, however, errors on an EPS may be corrected by submitting an additional EPS for the tax year even after 20 April.

## [¶4-939] PAYE RTI: collection of tax on benefits in kind and expenses

(ITEPA 2003, s. 289Aff. and 684(1ZA); FA 2015, s. 13; SI 2003/2682, Pt. 3, Ch. 3A; SI 2015/1948)

*Finance Act* 2015 included amending legislation to enable the voluntary payrolling of benefits in kind from the 2016–17 tax year. Where an employer opts to payroll benefits in kind for cars, car fuel, medical insurance and gym membership, they will no longer be obliged to make a return (form P11D) and employers will instead report the value of these benefits in kind through Real Time Information (SI 2003/2682, Pt. 3, Ch. 3A).

Payrolling benefits in kind is extended by *Finance Act* 2016 to allow for the payrolling of non-cash vouchers and credit tokens from 2017–18 (amendments to SI 2003/2682, Pt. 3, Ch. 3A by SI 2016/1137).

From April 2016, the £8,500 a year threshold for the taxation of benefits in kind was abolished (FA 2015, s. 13) (meaning all benefits in kind are liable to income tax and National Insurance contributions, whatever the level of the employee's earnings and benefits in kind); and, also with effect from 6 April 2016, the dispensation regime for expenses was also replaced with an exemption for paid and reimbursed expenses (ITEPA 2003, s. 289Aff. and SI 2015/1948).

## [¶4-940] PAYE deadlines

(Tax Reporter: ¶494-700)

**Reporting deadlines**

| Forms | Date | Provision | Penalty provisions |
|---|---|---|---|
| P14, P35, P38 and P38A (non-real time employers only) | 19 May following tax year | *Income Tax (Pay As You Earn) Regulations 2003 (SI 2003/2682),* reg. 73 and 74 | TMA 1970, s. 98A |
| P60 (to employee) | 31 May following tax year | *Income Tax (Pay As You Earn) Regulations 2003 (SI 2003/2682),* reg. 67 | TMA 1970, s. 98A |

| Forms | Date | Provision | Penalty provisions |
|---|---|---|---|
| P11D | 6 July following tax year | *Income Tax (Pay As You Earn) Regulations 2003 (SI 2003/2682), reg. 85* | TMA 1970, s. 98 |
| P46(Car) | 3 May, 2 August, 2 November, 2 February | *Income Tax (Pay As You Earn) Regulations 2003 (SI 2003/2682), reg. 90* | TMA 1970, s. 98 |

| Other deadlines | Date |
|---|---|
| Employee payments in return for benefits in kind (making good) for 2017–18 and subsequent tax years[(1)] | 6 July following tax year |

**Note**
[(1)] Spring Budget 2017 confirmed legislation in Finance Bill 2017 will set the date for an employee to make good on benefits in kind which are not accounted for in real time through PAYE (benefits in kind which are not payrolled) so the taxable value of the benefit in kind will be reduced or removed if making good takes place by that date. The change will affect making good on a tax liability arising in the tax year 2017–18, and subsequent years.

## [¶4-942]   PAYE Late filing penalties

(FA 2009, Sch. 55)

### RTI: From 2014–15

Late filing penalties apply to returns due from employers for the tax year 2014–15 onwards but starting from 6 October 2014 (rather than 6 April 2014) for large employers (with 50 or more employees) and from 6 March 2015 for small employers (with no more than 49 employees at 6 October 2014) and new employers (who become employers after 6 October 2014). Where payment information is not received as expected on an FPS, or HMRC have not been notified that no employees have been paid in a tax period by submission of an EPS, late filing penalties will apply. The rules apply to each PAYE scheme, rather than each employer.

Late filing penalties will apply on a monthly basis, however, no penalty will apply for the first month in each tax year that returns are filed late.

New employers will not be penalised if their first FPS is received within 30 days of making their first payment to an employee.

On 17 February 2015, HMRC announced that employers will not incur penalties for delays of up to three days in filing PAYE information.

## Initial penalties

| Number of employees[1] | Monthly Penalty[2] £ |
|---|---|
| 1–9 | 100 |
| 10–49 | 200 |
| 50–249 | 300 |
| 250 or more | 400 |

**Notes**
[1] HMRC will use the latest information available to determine the number of employees, and the size of the filing penalty for each period where a return is late.
[2] Filing penalty notices will be issued quarterly in July, October, January and April, if appropriate, showing the amount of the filing penalty for each tax month identified in that quarter.

## Additional penalties for returns over three months late

| | Penalty |
|---|---|
| 3 months late | 5%[1] |

**Note**
[1] Calculated as a percentage of the tax/NICs that should have been shown on the late return.

### RTI: 2012–13 and 2013–14

There was no change to the penalties for late filing of returns for the tax years 2012–13 and 2013–14. The penalty regime below applied at the year-end.

HMRC confirmed that employers would not be charged penalties for sending FPS late unless it was the final one for the tax year. This was to ensure that for these two tax years, employers operating PAYE in real time were in a similar position to employers who were still operating traditional PAYE.

| Key deadlines | Penalty |
|---|---|
| Final FPS submitted by 19 April (last date for submission of an FPS) | None |
| EYU submitted after 19 April but by 19 May | None |
| Final payments unreported at 19 May | £100 per 50 employees for each month return outstanding[1] |

**Note**
[1] Penalty notices issued after 19 September (once return outstanding for four months) and again, the following January and May.

### Penalties (fixed, but see ESC B46) imposed for delays (TMA 1970, s. 98A)

| Forms | First 12 months | Thereafter |
|---|---|---|
| P14, P35, P38 and P38A | £100 per 50 employees per month | Additional penalty not exceeding 100% of the tax and NIC payable for the year but remaining unpaid by 19 April following end of tax year |

Taxation of Earnings

**Penalties (mitigable) that may be imposed for delays (TMA 1970, s. 98)**

| Forms | Initial | Continuing |
|-------|---------|------------|
| P11D | £300 per return | £60 per day |

## [¶4-945]   PAYE penalties for incorrect returns

(FA 2007, Sch. 24)

(Tax Reporter: ¶184-850)

HMRC use a risk-based approach to identify employers they think may be submitting incorrect returns. Where HMRC discover careless or deliberate errors, the penalties that could apply will be based on the behaviour that led to the error and the amount of potential lost revenue for that return. Errors that arise despite taking reasonable care attract no penalty at all and penalties for errors due to failure to take reasonable care can be reduced to zero with full and unprompted disclosure to HMRC.

### RTI: 2013–14

HMRC confirmed that for the tax year 2013–14, an inaccuracy in any FPS submitted could attract a penalty based on the potential lost revenue for the FPS which contained the inaccuracy. HMRC could issue one penalty notice for inaccuracy penalties for multiple tax periods in a year.

### RTI: 2012–13

HMRC confirmed that employers who operated PAYE in real time in 2012–13 would not be charged a penalty in-year for inaccuracies on FPS returns submitted each payday, but penalties could be charged after the end of the tax year if there was an error on the final FPS for the year, or a failure to correct earlier errors by the year-end. This was to ensure employers who joined the RTI pilot were treated in line with employers who did not start sending real time information until April 2013.

### Penalties from 1 April 2009

(FA 2007, Sch. 24, para. 1 and 4)

The maximum penalty for an incorrect return is 100% of the potential lost revenue (deliberate and concealed action), 70% (deliberate but not concealed) or 30% (careless action).

## [¶4-946]   PAYE: late payment penalties

(FA 2009, s. 107 and Sch. 56)

(Tax Reporter: ¶184-975)

From April 2015, late payment penalties will be charged in-year on a late payment for the tax year 2015–16 onwards. Late payment penalty notices will be issued quarterly in July, October, January and April showing the amount of the penalty due for each tax month. The total penalty charged can be made up of:

- a default penalty, for failure to pay monthly/quarterly payments on time and in full; and
- penalties for amounts still unpaid after six and 12 months.

From April 2014, HMRC continued to issue late payment penalties on a risk-assessed basis for 2014–15 as in previous years. Penalties would only be charged in respect of the most serious and persistent failures.

### Penalties for late monthly or quarterly PAYE payments

No penalty if only one PAYE amount is late in a tax year, unless that payment is over six months late.

| No. defaults in a tax year | Penalty percentage | Amount to which penalty percentages apply |
|---|---|---|
| 1–3[(1)] | 1% | The total amount that is late in the relevant tax month (ignoring the first late payment in the tax year) |
| 4–6 | 2% | |
| 7–9 | 3% | |
| 10 or more | 4% | |

**Note**
[(1)] The first failure to pay on time does not count as a default.

| Additional penalties | Amount |
|---|---|
| 6 months late | 5% |
| 12 months late | Further 5% |

### Amounts due annually or occasionally (Class 1A and 1B NIC)

| Penalty date | 5% |
|---|---|
| 5 months after initial penalty date | further 5% |
| 11 months after initial penalty date | further 5% |

### Penalty dates

The penalty date varies according to the type of payment. For payments such as Class 1A and Class 1B NICs, HMRC determinations, assessments and amendments, or corrections to returns the 'penalty date' is 30 days after the due date. In most other cases, the penalty date is the day after the due date.

## [¶4-948]   Interest on certain PAYE paid late

(FA 2009, s. 101 and 102)

(Tax Reporter: ¶494-900; ¶494-910)

### From 2014–15

For the tax year 2014–15 onwards, HMRC charge in-year, rather than annual, interest on all unpaid:

- PAYE tax, Class 1 National Insurance contributions (NICs) and student loan deductions, including specified charges (estimates HMRC make in the absence of a PAYE submission);
- Construction Industry Scheme charges;
- In-year late filing penalties (which start from October 2014); and
- In-year late payment penalties (which will be charged automatically from April 2015).

Interest will also be charged on underpayments that arise because of adjustments reported on Earlier Year Updates submitted in respect of tax year 2014–15 onwards.

For annual payments such as Class 1A and Class 1B NICs, HMRC will continue to charge interest on any amount which remains unpaid after the due date.

Interest is charged daily, from the date a payment is due and payable to the date it is paid in full.

Repayment interest will apply where a payment is made and the charge is then reduced resulting in an overpayment which is either reallocated to a later charge or repaid.

**Years to 2013–14**

(SI 2003/2682, former reg. 82, 83)

Where an employer has not paid the net tax deductible by him under PAYE to the collector within 14 days of the end of the tax year, the unpaid tax carries interest at the prescribed rate from the reckonable date until the date of payment. Certain repayments of tax also attract interest.

## [¶4-962]   PAYE electronic communications penalty: form P45 (Part 1 or Part 3), P46 or P46(Pen)

(SI 2003/2682, reg. 210B, 210BA)

(Tax Reporter: ¶498-745; ¶498-750)

| 2013–14 and subsequent years Table 9AA | | 2011–12 and 2012–13 Table 9A | |
|---|---|---|---|
| Number of items | Penalty | Number of items | Penalty |
| | | 1–2 | nil |
| 1–49 | £100 | 3–49 | £100 |
| 50–149 | £300 | 50–149 | £300 |
| 150–299 | £600 | 150–299 | £600 |
| 300–399 | £900 | 300–399 | £900 |
| 400–499 | £1,200 | 400–499 | £1,200 |
| 500–599 | £1,500 | 500–599 | £1,500 |
| 600–699 | £1,800 | 600–699 | £1,800 |

Taxation of Earnings

| 2013–14 and subsequent years Table 9AA | | 2011–12 and 2012–13 Table 9A | |
|---|---|---|---|
| Number of items | Penalty | Number of items | Penalty |
| 700–799 | £2,100 | 700–799 | £2,100 |
| 800–899 | £2,400 | 800–899 | £2,400 |
| 900–999 | £2,700 | 900–999 | £2,700 |
| 1,000+ | £3,000 | 1,000+ | £3,000 |

**Note**
(1)  Number of items of specified information the employer has failed to deliver in the tax year. (Each item mentioned in reg. 207(1), para. (a)–(d) counts as a separate item of specified information.) An item of specified information counts even if it relates to the same employee as one or more other items.

## [¶4-965]   PAYE electronic communications penalty: forms P35 and P14

(SI 2003/2682, reg. 210AA, former 210A)

(Tax Reporter: ¶498-755; ¶498-760; ¶498-765)

| 2010–11 and subsequent years Table 9ZA | |
|---|---|
| Number of employees | Penalty |
| 1–5 | £100 |
| 6–49 | £300 |
| 50–249 | £600 |
| 250–399 | £900 |
| 400–499 | £1,200 |
| 500–599 | £1,500 |
| 600–699 | £1,800 |
| 700–799 | £2,100 |
| 800–899 | £2,400 |
| 900–999 | £2,700 |
| 1,000+ | £3,000 |

**Notes**
(1)  Number of employees for whom particulars should have been included with the specified information.
(2)  But nil for tax year 2004–05 only (50–249 employees).

## [¶4-975] PAYE monthly accounting periods

(SI 2003/2682, reg. 69)

(Tax Reporter: ¶494-510)

| Period | Month no. | Payment due (electronic) | Payment due (other) |
|---|---|---|---|
| 6 Apr to 5 May | 1 | 22 May | 19 May |
| 6 May to 5 June | 2 | 22 June | 19 June |
| 6 June to 5 July | 3 | 22 July | 19 July |
| 6 July to 5 Aug | 4 | 22 August | 19 August |
| 6 Aug to 5 Sept | 5 | 22 September | 19 September |
| 6 Sept to 5 Oct | 6 | 22 October | 19 October |
| 6 Oct to 5 Nov | 7 | 22 November | 19 November |
| 6 Nov to 5 Dec | 8 | 22 December | 19 December |
| 6 Dec to 5 Jan | 9 | 22 January | 19 January |
| 6 Jan to 5 Feb | 10 | 22 February | 19 February |
| 6 Feb to 5 Mar | 11 | 22 March | 19 March |
| 6 Mar to 5 Apr | 12 | 22 April | 19 April |

## [¶4-976] PAYE quarterly accounting periods

(SI 2003/2682, reg. 70)

(Tax Reporter: ¶494-570)

| Period | Month no. | Payment due (electronic) | Payment due (other) |
|---|---|---|---|
| 6 Apr to 5 July | 1–3 | 22 July | 19 July |
| 6 July to 5 Oct | 4–6 | 22 October | 19 October |
| 6 Oct to 5 Jan | 7–9 | 22 January | 19 January |
| 6 Jan to 5 Apr | 10–12 | 22 April | 19 April |

## [¶4-980] Payroll giving scheme

(ITEPA 2003, s. 713)

(Tax Reporter: ¶457-500)

Employees whose remuneration is subject to deduction of tax at source under PAYE can make unlimited tax-deductible donations to charity by requesting that their employers deduct the donations from their pay.

## [¶4-985]   Student loan deductions

(SI 2009/470, reg. 29; SI 2016/606)

There are now three categories of student loans: Plan 1 loans (pre-2012 loans); Plan 2 loans (post-2012 loans) and Postgraduate Master's Degree loans. Each type of loan carries different repayment terms.

### Postgraduate Master's Degree Loans[1]

| Year | Percentage | Threshold |
|------|------------|-----------|
| From 6 April 2019 | 6% | £21,000 |

**Note**
[1] Postgraduate Master's Degree loans are available to eligible students for postgraduate master's degree courses which begin on or after 01 August 2016. No repayment of a postgraduate master's degree loan is required until on or after 6 April 2019.

### Plan 2 (post-2012[1]) student loans

| Year | Percentage | Threshold[2] |
|------|------------|--------------|
| 2017–18 | 9% | £21,000 |
| 2016–17 | 9% | £21,000 |

**Notes**
[1] Plan 2 loans are loans taken out by new students starting courses on or after 1 September 2012 (and as defined by SI 2009/470, reg. 3(2)). Repayment of post-2012 loans commenced from 6 April 2016.
[2] Autumn Statement 2015 announced that the Government the student loan repayment threshold for Plan 2 graduates will be frozen for five years from April 2016.

### Plan 1 (pre-2012) student loans

| Year | Percentage | Threshold[1] |
|------|------------|--------------|
| 2017–18 | 9% | £17,775 |
| 2016–17 | 9% | £17,495 |
| 2015–16 | 9% | £17,335 |
| 2014–15 | 9% | £16,910 |
| 2013–14 | 9% | £16,365 |
| 2012–13 | 9% | £15,795 |
| 2011–12 | 9% | £15,000 |

**Note**
[1] Repayment threshold uprated by RPI for tax years ending after 6 April 2012 (SI 2009/470, reg. 29(7)).

## [¶4-990]   Apprenticeship levy

(FA 2016, Pt. 6)

Autumn Statement 2015 announced that the Government will introduce the apprenticeship levy in April 2017.

Apprenticeship levy is charged where:

*   a person has a pay bill for a tax year; and
*   the relevant percentage of the pay bill exceeds the person's levy allowance (if any) for that tax year.

## Amount of charge

The amount of the charge is equal to–

N – A

where–

N is the relevant percentage of the pay bill for the tax year; and

A is the amount of the levy allowance (if any) to which the person is entitled for the tax year.

| From | Levy allowance[1] £ | Relevant percentage % | Pay bill threshold[2] £ |
|---|---|---|---|
| 6 April 2017 | 15,000 | 0.5 | 3,000,000 |

**Notes**
[1] Two or more companies which form a 'company unit' share a single levy allowance.
[2] Paybill threshold is calculated as the amount by which the employer's pay bill must exceed in order for a positive charge to arise after deducting the levy allowance (i.e. equals the levy allowance divided by the relevant percentage).

# TAXATION OF CAPITAL GAINS

## [¶5-000]   Rates
(TCGA 1992, s. 4)

(Tax Reporter: ¶500-220)

| | Gains eligible for: | | Individuals | | Trustees and PRs | |
|---|---|---|---|---|---|---|
| Tax year | Entrepreneurs' relief | Investors' relief[3] | Main rates[1] | Residential property/ carried interest[2] | Main rate | Residential property/ carried interest[2] |
| 2017–18 | 10 | [10] | 10/20 | 18/28 | 20 | 28 |
| 2016–17 | 10 | [10] | 10/20 | 18/28 | 20 | 28 |
| 2015–16 | 10 | — | 18/28 | 18/28 | 28 | 28 |
| 2014–15 | 10 | — | 18/28 | 18/28 | 28 | 28 |
| 2013–14 | 10 | — | 18/28 | 18/28 | 28 | 28 |
| 2012–13 | 10 | — | 18/28 | 18/28 | 28 | 28 |

**Notes**

[1] For disposals on or after 6 April 2016, the chargeable gains arising from those disposals are aggregated with the individual's taxable income and to the extent that the aggregate falls above the threshold of the income tax basic rate, capital gains tax is charged at 20% (previously 28%) (taking the chargeable gains as being the highest part of that aggregate). If the aggregate falls below the threshold, the capital gains tax rate is 10% (previously 18%) (TCGA 1992, s. 4, as amended by FA 2016, s. 83).

[2] Gains accruing on the disposal of interests in residential properties that do not qualify for private residence relief and carried interest remain chargeable at the 18% and 28% rates as applicable for disposals before 6 April 2016 (TCGA 1992, s. 4, as amended by FA 2016, s. 83).

[3] *Finance Act* 2016 introduces a new relief for investors in unlisted trading companies. The relief applies a lower (10%) rate of capital gains tax on disposals of qualifying holdings (of newly issued shares purchased on or after 17 March 2016), providing they are held for a minimum of three years from 6 April 2016 (meaning that effectively, the relief will not be available until 2019–20) (TCGA 1992, Pt. 5, Ch. 5).

## [¶5-010]   Exemptions
(TCGA 1992, s. 3 and 262)

(Tax Reporter: ¶509-050; ¶535-100)

| | Annual exempt amount[1] | | |
|---|---|---|---|
| Tax year | Individuals, PRs[2], trusts for mentally disabled £ | Other trusts[3] £ | Chattel exemption (max sale proceeds)[4] £ |
| 2017–18 | 11,300 | 5,650 | 6,000 |
| 2016–17 | 11,100 | 5,550 | 6,000 |
| 2015–16 | 11,100 | 5,550 | 6,000 |
| 2014–15 | 11,000 | 5,500 | 6,000 |

Taxation of Capital Gains

| Tax year | Annual exempt amount[1] | | |
| :---: | :---: | :---: | :---: |
| | Individuals, PRs[2], trusts for mentally disabled £ | Other trusts[3] £ | Chattel exemption (max sale proceeds)[4] £ |
| 2013–14 | 10,900 | 5,450 | 6,000 |
| 2012–13 | 10,600 | 5,300 | 6,000 |
| 2011–12 | 10,600 | 5,300 | 6,000 |

**Notes**

[1] The annual exempt amount is increased annually, unless Parliament determines otherwise, by reference to the increase in CPI (from 2013–14, previously by reference to RPI).

[2] For year of death and next two years in the case of personal representatives (PRs) of deceased persons.

[3] Multiple trusts created by the same settlor; each attracts relief equal to the annual amount divided by the number of such trusts (subject to a minimum of 10% of the full amount).

[4] Where disposal proceeds exceed the exemption limit, marginal relief restricts any chargeable gain to $5/3$ of the excess. Where there is a loss and the proceeds are less than £6,000, the proceeds are deemed to be £6,000.

## [¶5-020] ATED-related capital gains on high value residential property

(TCGA 1992, s. 2B, Sch. 4ZZA)

(Tax Reporter: ¶808-015)

From 6 April 2013, capital gains tax applies to companies and other corporate bodies on disposals of UK residential property valued at over the 'threshold amount'. If a residential property which has been subject to annual tax on enveloped dwellings (ATED) is disposed of some or all of the gains or losses will be 'ATED-related' and charged to capital gains tax.

| Tax year | Threshold amount | Rate |
| :--- | :---: | :---: |
| 2017–18 and 2016–17 | £500,000 | 28% |
| 2015–16 | £1,000,000 | 28% |
| 2014–15 and 2013–14 | £2,000,000 | 28% |

The charge applies to any of the following that own an interest in residential property that is subject to ATED:

- companies that are resident in the UK for tax purposes;
- companies that are not UK resident;
- companies (both UK resident and non-UK resident) which are a partner in a partnership; and
- some collective investment schemes, depending on the terms and nature of the scheme.

The charge arises in respect of ATED-related gains only, which, normally, will be gains attributable to periods after 5 April 2013. However, it is possible to elect out of the rules of apportionment between pre- and post-April 2013 periods, and calculate the ATED-related gain by reference to the entire period of ownership. In most cases, such an election will only be beneficial where the market value at 5 April 2013 is greater than the value at the time of disposal.

Gains and losses that are ATED-related are ring-fenced from non-ATED-related gains and losses, and a general computational feature of the rules is that indexation allowance is available only against non-ATED-related gains.

## [¶5-030]   Disposals of UK residential property by non-residents, etc.

(TCGA 1992, s. 14B–14H)

(Tax Reporter: ¶510-750ff.)

The charge to capital gains tax is extended, with effect in relation to disposals made on or after 6 April 2015, to chargeable gains accruing to non-UK resident persons on the disposal of an interest in UK residential property.

| Tax year | Rate | | |
|---|---|---|---|
| | Individuals | Trustees and PRs | Companies |
| From 2015–16 | 18%/28% | 28% | 20% |

Non-UK resident persons include:

- non-UK resident individuals;
- non-UK resident trusts;
- personal representatives of a deceased person who was non-UK resident; and
- non-UK resident companies controlled by five or fewer persons, except where the company itself, or at least one of the controlling persons, is a 'qualifying institutional investor'.

'UK residential property' is broadly, an interest in UK land that has consisted of or included a dwelling at any time during the relevant ownership period, being the period from acquisition or 6 April 2015 (whichever is later) to the day before the date of disposal.

The charge only applies to the portion of any gain that relates to the post-6 April 2015 ownership period calculated by rebasing the property at its 5 April 2015 market value to calculate a notional pre- and post-5 April 2015 gain or loss. An election for straight-line time apportionment will also be possible.

NRCGT losses accruing by a person on chargeable non-resident disposals of UK residential property interests when non-UK resident will be general allowable losses for use against chargeable gains when UK resident but are otherwise ring-fenced and can only be relieved against gains from other UK residential property in the same or a subsequent tax year and cannot be carried back.

## [¶5-040]   Entrepreneurs' relief and investors' relief

(TCGA 1992, s. 169H–169S; and Pt. 5, Ch. 5 (as inserted by FA 2016, s. 87 and Sch. 14)

(Tax Reporter: ¶572-500ff.)

Chargeable gains arising on disposals of qualifying business assets on or after 23 June 2010 are charged to tax at a rate of 10%.

| Period | Lifetime limit for entrepreneurs[1] £ | Lifetime limit for investors[2] £ |
|---|---|---|
| From 2019–20 | – | 10,000,000 |
| From 06.04.11 | 10,000,000 | – |

**Notes**
[1] The limit is a lifetime limit applying to disposals on or after 6 April 2008. Transitional provisions allow relief to be claimed in certain circumstances where gains deferred from disposals made on or before 5 April 2008 subsequently become chargeable (FA 2008, Sch. 3, para. 7 and 8).
[2] *Finance Act* 2016 introduces a new relief for investors in unlisted trading companies. The relief applies a lower (10%) rate of capital gains tax on disposals of qualifying holdings (of newly issued shares purchased on or after 17 March 2016), providing they are held for a minimum of three years from 6 April 2016 (meaning that effectively, the relief will not be available until 2019-20). The relief is subject to a separate lifetime limit of £10m of gains (TCGA 1992, Pt. 5, Ch. 5).

## Restrictions

- **Goodwill on incorporation:** with effect for transfers on or after 3 December 2014, individuals are prevented from claiming entrepreneurs' relief on disposals of the reputation and customer relationships associated with a business ('goodwill') when they transfer the business to a related close company. The restriction does not extend to partners in a firm who do not hold or acquire any stake in the successor company (TCGA 1992, s. 169LA, as inserted by FA 2015, s. 42). However, at Budget 2016, the Government announced that it will allow entrepreneurs' relief to be claimed, subject to certain conditions, on gains on the goodwill of a business when that business is transferred to a company controlled by five or fewer persons or by its directors. The principal condition is that the claimant must hold less than 5% of the acquiring company's shares. There are special rules to allow relief where the acquiring company is then sold to a third party. These changes take effect retrospectively for disposals made on or after 3 December 2014 (amendments by FA 2016, s. 85).

- **Associated disposals:** with effect for disposals on or after 18 March 2015, individuals are prevented from claiming entrepreneurs' relief in respect of gains on disposals of privately held assets used in a business, unless they are associated with a significant material disposal, that is to say a disposal of at least a 5% shareholding in the company or of at least a 5% share in the assets of the partnership carrying on the business (TCGA 1992, s. 169K, as amended by FA 2015, s. 41). However, at Budget 2016, the Government announced that it will allow entrepreneurs' relief to be claimed on a disposal of a privately-held asset when the accompanying disposal of business assets is to a family member. These changes take effect retrospectively for disposals made on or after 18 March 2015 (amendments by FA 2016, s. 84).

- **Joint ventures and partnerships:** with effect for disposals on or after 18 March 2015, individuals are prevented from claiming entrepreneurs' relief in respect of gains on shares in certain companies which invest in joint venture companies, or which are members of partnerships. The new rule will deny relief where the investing company has no trade (or no relevant trade) of its own (TCGA 1992, s. 169S, as amended by FA 2015, s. 43). However, at Budget 2016, the Government announced that it will allow entrepreneurs' relief to be claimed in some cases involving joint ventures and partnerships where the disposal of business assets does not meet the existing 5% minimum holding conditions. The definitions of a trading company and trading group which apply for entrepreneurs' relief purposes will be amended. This will allow a percentage of the activities of a joint venture company to be treated as carried on by a company which holds shares in that company. Where the new definitions apply, trading activities of a company in its capacity as a partner in a firm may be taken into account as such rather than treated as being non-trading. These changes take effect retrospectively for disposals made on or after 18 March 2015 (TCGA 1992, s. 169SA and Sch. 7ZA).

# [¶5-050]   Other exemptions and reliefs

## EMI shares

(TCGA 1992, s. 169I(7A)–(7R))

(Tax Reporter: ¶572-950)

With effect in relation to disposals on or after 6 April 2013 of shares acquired pursuant to the exercise of a qualifying EMI option, entrepreneurs' relief will be available in respect of the disposal notwithstanding that the 'personal company' requirement (5% holding) may not be satisfied. To qualify, the shares must be:

- acquired since 6 April 2012;

- disposed of at least one year after the grant of the option; and

- the individual must have been an employee of the company, or a company in the same trading group, throughout the one year period ending with the disposal.

## Employee shareholder status

(TCGA 1992, s. 236B–236G)

(Tax Reporter: ¶565-050)

Autumn Statement 2016 announced that the tax advantages linked to shares awarded under employee shareholder status will be abolished for arrangements entered into on, or after, 1 December 2016. The status itself will be closed to new arrangements at the next legislative opportunity.

| Period | Gains exemption[1] £ | Lifetime limit[2] £ |
|---|---|---|
| From 17 March 2016 | 50,000 | 100,000 |
| From 1 September 2013 | 50,000 | — |

**Notes**
[1] Gains on the disposal of up to £50,000 worth of shares (based on acquisition value) are exempt from capital gains tax. Where a particular acquisition of shares causes the £50,000 limit to be breached, the remainder of the £50,000 limit is applied against the total value of the particular share acquisition and only that portion of the total number of shares acquired by the particular acquisition will be exempt from capital gains tax. The capital gains tax exemption is not available if the shareholder or connected person has a material interest (25% or more) in the company or parent undertaking. Normal share pooling and share identification rules do not apply to exempt employee shareholder shares.
[2] *Finance Act* 2016 introduces a lifetime limit of £100,000 in respect of capital gains tax exempt gains arising on employee shareholder shares. The limit will apply to employee shareholder shares issued as consideration for entering into employee shareholder agreements from midnight at the end of 16 March 2016. Any past or future gains, realised or unrealised, on employee shareholder shares that were issued in respect of employee shareholder agreements made before midnight at the end of 16 March 2016 will not count towards the limit (TCGA 1992, s. 236B).

See ¶4-690 for further details on employee shareholder status and income tax reliefs.

## Employee-ownership trusts

(TCGA 1992, s. 236H–236U)

(Tax Reporter: ¶361-400ff.)

From 6 April 2014, disposals of shares to a trust with specific characteristics which benefits all employees of a company (or a group) may be wholly relieved from capital gains tax if certain criteria are met. The relief requirements are:

- the trading requirement: the company whose shares are disposed of must be a trading company, or the parent company of a trading group;

- the all-employee benefit requirement: the trust which acquires the shares must operate for the benefit of all employees;

- the controlling interest requirement: the trust must have a controlling interest in the company at the end of the tax year, which it did not have at the start of that year;
- the limited participation requirement: certain participators must be excluded from being beneficiaries of the trust; and
- neither the claimant (nor anyone connected with him) has previously received relief on the same company's (or any group company's) shares.

The relief operates by disapplying TCGA 1992, s. 17(1) (market value disposals) and treats the disposal (and acquisition by the trustees) as a no gain, no loss disposal. The relief is available on disposals which take place in a single tax year; disposals may be made by more than one person and can be of any number of shares. Where a disqualifying event (broadly, the relief requirements cease to be met) occurs in the following tax year, any relief given is withdrawn and where a disqualifying event occurs in any later tax year, this triggers a deemed disposal and reacquisition at market value by the trustees.

### Indexation allowance

(TCGA 1992, s. 53 and 54)

(Tax Reporter: ¶523-250)

Indexation allowance in respect of changes shown by the retail prices indices for months after April 1998 is allowed only for the purposes of corporation tax. For disposals made by individuals, trustees and personal representatives after April 1998 and before 6 April 2008, indexation allowance up to 5 April 1998 and taper relief could be obtained.

The table at ¶11-020 sets out the figure that is determined by the formula of (RD – RI)/RI where RD is the retail prices index for April 1998 and RI is the retail prices index for the later of March 1982 and the date that the item of relevant allowable expenditure was incurred. The indexation allowance is the aggregate of the indexed rise in each item of relevant allowable expenditure. In relation to each item of expenditure, the indexed rise is a sum produced by multiplying the amount of that item of expenditure by the appropriate figure in that table (for a fuller table applying for corporation tax purposes, see ¶11-000ff.).

### er relief

GA 1992, s. 152)

(Tax Reporter: ¶570-100)

To qualify for rollover relief, an asset must fall within one of the 'relevant classes of assets' and the reinvestment must generally take place within the period from 12 months before to three years after the disposal of the old asset. Classes of assets qualifying for relief are as follows, but see TCGA 1992, s. 156ZB for the interaction of this section with the corporation tax rules for gains and losses on intangible fixed assets:

- land and buildings occupied and used exclusively for the purposes of a trade;
- fixed plant or machinery (not forming part of a building);
- ships, aircraft, hovercraft;
- satellites, space stations and spacecraft (including launch vehicles);
- goodwill;
- milk quotas and potato quotas, ewe and suckler cow premium quotas, fish quotas;
- entitlements under the single farm payments scheme;
- entitlements under the basic payment scheme (with effect in relation to disposals of old assets or acquisitions of new assets on or after 20 December 2013); and
- Lloyd's members' syndicate rights and assets treated as acquired by members.

## Private residence relief

(TCGA 1992, s. 222)

(Tax Reporter: ¶540-000)

Relief is given on gains arising on the disposal of a dwelling house and on land enjoyed with the residence as its garden or grounds (up to the permitted area of half a hectare, or more if required for the reasonable enjoyment of the property).

Gains are apportioned across the period of ownership between periods of occupation (including deemed occupation) and other periods, with relief available for the portion of the gain attributable to periods of occupation. The final period of ownership is always eligible for relief provided the property was at some time the only or main residence. For disposals on or after 6 April 2014, the final period exemption applies to the last 18 months of ownership (previously, 36 months) except for individuals who are disabled or in a care home and with no other property who continue to get a 36-month final period exemption.

Where a residence is let during a period of non-occupation, relief is available on the portion of the gain attributable to the let period up to £40,000.

## Enterprise investment scheme

(TCGA 1992, s. 150A; Pt. 5, Ch. 4 and Sch. 5B)

(Tax Reporter: ¶564-400ff.; ¶568-000)

A disposal of shares on which income tax relief has not been withdrawn is exempt from capital gains tax; losses arising are eligible for relief in the normal way, but the base cost is treated as reduced by any EIS income tax relief which has been given and not withdrawn.

Reinvestment relief is available for gains on assets where the disposal proceeds are reinvested in new EIS shares.

See ¶3-400 for EIS income tax relief.

Gains that are eligible for entrepreneurs' relief and deferred into investment under the enterprise investment scheme on or after 3 December 2014 will benefit from entrepreneurs' relief when the gain is realised.

## Seed enterprise investment scheme

(TCGA 1992, Sch. 5BB)

(Tax Reporter: ¶568-500)

*Disposal relief*

The exemption from capital gains applies where SEIS shares are held for more than three years from their issue. Losses are eligible for relief in the normal way but the base cost is treated as reduced by any SEIS income tax relief which has been given and not withdrawn.

*Reinvestment relief*

For 2012–13 initially, a reinvestment exemption is available in respect of a gain arising on the disposal of any asset to the extent that the individual makes a qualifying investment under SEIS in the same tax year. *Finance Act* 2013 extended the relief and *Finance Act* 2014 made it permanent. Capital gains reinvestment relief is subject to the £100,000 annual investment limit which applies for income tax relief.

Taxation of Capital Gains

| Relevant year[1] | Relevant percentage[2] |
|---|---|
| 2017–18 | 50% |
| 2013–14 to 2016–17 | 50% |
| 2012–13 | 100% |

**Notes**
[1] The relevant year is year in which the investor is eligible for and makes a claim for SEIS income tax relief in respect of an amount subscribed for an issue of shares which must be the same tax year as the disposal of the asset and year in which the chargeable gain accrues.
[2] The relevant percentage of the 'available SEIS expenditure' is to be set against a corresponding amount of the original gain. The 'available SEIS expenditure' is the amount specified in the claim (provided that the amount has not been previously set against a gain) but cannot exceed the amount of the gain which remains unmatched after any previous claims or claims under the EIS deferral relief. To the extent that the gain is matched with the relevant percentage of the amount subscribed, it is not a chargeable gain.

## Investment in social enterprises

(TCGA 1992, s. 255A–255E; Pt. 5, Ch. 4 and Sch. 8B)

(Tax Reporter: ¶569-300ff.)

*Disposal relief*

The disposal relief provides an exemption from capital gains tax in respect of the disposal of an investment where the investor has received income tax relief (which has not subsequently been withdrawn) on the cost of the investment, and the investment is disposed of after it has been held for at least three years. However, if no claim to income tax relief is made, then any subsequent disposal of the investment will not qualify for exemption from capital gains tax.

*Deferral relief*

The deferral relief enables the payment of tax on a capital gain to be deferred where the gain is reinvested in shares or debt investments which also qualify for SITR income tax relief. It is not, however, necessary for the investor to have made a claim for SITR income tax relief. The gain can arise from the disposal of any kind of asset, but must arise in the period from 6 April 2014 to 5 April 2019. The SITR qualifying investment must be made in the period one year before or three years after the gain arose. There is no minimum period for which the investment must be held; the deferred capital gain is brought back into charge whenever the investment is disposed of or the social enterprise ceases to meet the requirements of the scheme, but if an amount equal to the gain is once more invested in shares or debt investments which also qualify for SITR income tax relief then the gain may be held over again.

Gains that are eligible for entrepreneurs' relief and deferred into investment under the enterprise investment scheme on or after 3 December 2014 will benefit from entrepreneurs' relief when the gain is realised.

## Charities

(TCGA 1992, s. 256, 257; ITA 2007, s. 518ff.; CTA 2010, s. 466ff.)

(Tax Reporter: ¶815-440)

The gains of charities are not taxable provided they are applicable, and applied, for charitable purposes only. The legislation is designed to charge charities to tax on the amount of their income and gains that has not been invested, lent or spent in an approved way.

A charge to capital gains tax arises if a charity ceases to be a charity, when there is a deemed sale and reacquisition of the trust property by the trustees at market value.

### Gifts to the nation

(TCGA 1992, s. 258; FA 2012, Sch. 14)

(Tax Reporter: ¶535-620)

Gains arising on gifts of pre-eminent property to be held for the benefit of the public or the nation are not chargeable to capital gains tax.

For the tax year 2012–13 and subsequent tax years, a reduction in income tax and/or capital gains tax is available where an individual makes a gift of pre-eminent property to be held for the benefit of the public or the nation. The tax reduction is 30% of the value of the gift. A gift offer must be made and registered in accordance with the scheme and relief is available against the individual's liability for the year in which the gift offer is registered and/or any of the succeeding four tax years.

Pre-eminent property includes any picture, print, book, manuscript, work of art, scientific object or other thing that is pre-eminent for its national, scientific, historic or artistic interest, collections of such items and any object kept in a significant building where it is desirable that it remain associated with the building.

### Disincorporation relief

(TCGA 1992, s. 162B and 162C; CTA 2009, s. 849A; FA 2013, s. 58–60)

Disincorporation relief is a form of rollover or deferral relief which allows a company to transfer certain assets to its shareholders who continue the business in an unincorporated form. The assets are deemed to be transferred at below market value so that no corporation tax charge arises to the company, although shareholders may still be liable to income tax or capital gains tax on the transfer of assets to them by the company. Shareholders will be liable to capital gains tax, as usual, on a future sale of the assets, for which purpose the assets are treated as having been acquired at the reduced transfer value.

The relief applies in relation to a 'qualifying transfer' of a business with a disposal date falling within the period of five years beginning 1 April 2013. A qualifying transfer is one which meets the following conditions:

- the business must be transferred as a going concern;
- the business must be transferred together with all the assets of the business or together with all the assets of the business apart from cash;
- the total market value of the 'qualifying assets' at the time of the transfer must not be more than £100,000;
- the shareholders that the business is transferred to must be individuals; and
- those shareholders must have held shares in the company throughout the 12 months before the transfer.

Qualifying assets are interests in land (other than land held as trading stock) and goodwill. Special rules apply to determine the transfer value of any post-FA 2002 goodwill.

A claim for disincorporation relief must be made jointly by the company and all the shareholders to whom the business is transferred. The claim must be made within two years of the business transfer date.

Taxation of Capital Gains

# [¶5-100]   Leases which are wasting assets

### Restrictions of allowable expenditure

(TCGA 1992, s. 240 and Sch. 8, para. 1)

(Tax Reporter: ¶509-600ff.)

Fraction equal to $\dfrac{P(1) - P(3)}{P(1)}$ excluded from expenditure under TCGA 1992, s. 38(1)(a),

and fraction equal to $\dfrac{P(2) - P(3)}{P(2)}$ excluded from expenditure under TCGA 1992, s. 38(1)(b),

where:

P(1) = table percentage for duration of lease at time of acquisition (or 31 March 1982 where applicable);

P(2) = table percentage for duration of lease at time expenditure incurred; and

P(3) = table percentage for duration of lease at time of disposal.

| Years | % | Monthly[1] increment |
|---|---|---|
| 50 or more | 100 | — |
| 49 | 99.657 | 0.029 |
| 48 | 99.289 | 0.031 |
| 47 | 98.902 | 0.032 |
| 46 | 98.490 | 0.034 |
| 45 | 98.059 | 0.036 |
| 44 | 97.595 | 0.039 |
| 43 | 97.107 | 0.041 |
| 42 | 96.593 | 0.043 |
| 41 | 96.041 | 0.046 |
| 40 | 95.457 | 0.049 |
| 39 | 94.842 | 0.051 |
| 38 | 94.189 | 0.054 |
| 37 | 93.497 | 0.058 |
| 36 | 92.761 | 0.061 |
| 35 | 91.981 | 0.065 |
| 34 | 91.156 | 0.069 |
| 33 | 90.280 | 0.073 |
| 32 | 89.354 | 0.077 |
| 31 | 88.371 | 0.082 |
| 30 | 87.330 | 0.087 |
| 29 | 86.226 | 0.092 |

| Years | % | Monthly[1] increment |
|---|---|---|
| 28 | 85.053 | 0.098 |
| 27 | 83.816 | 0.103 |
| 26 | 82.496 | 0.110 |
| 25 | 81.100 | 0.116 |
| 24 | 79.622 | 0.123 |
| 23 | 78.055 | 0.131 |
| 22 | 76.399 | 0.138 |
| 21 | 74.635 | 0.147 |
| 20 | 72.770 | 0.155 |
| 19 | 70.791 | 0.165 |
| 18 | 68.697 | 0.175 |
| 17 | 66.470 | 0.186 |
| 16 | 64.116 | 0.196 |
| 15 | 61.617 | 0.208 |
| 14 | 58.971 | 0.221 |
| 13 | 56.167 | 0.234 |
| 12 | 53.191 | 0.248 |
| 11 | 50.038 | 0.263 |
| 10 | 46.695 | 0.279 |
| 9 | 43.154 | 0.295 |
| 8 | 39.399 | 0.313 |
| 7 | 35.414 | 0.332 |
| 6 | 31.195 | 0.352 |
| 5 | 26.722 | 0.373 |
| 4 | 21.983 | 0.395 |
| 3 | 16.959 | 0.419 |
| 2 | 11.629 | 0.444 |
| 1 | 5.983 | 0.470 |
| 0 | 0 | 0.499 |

**Note**

[1] Where duration is *not* an *exact* number of years, the table percentage for the whole number of years is increased by 1/12 of the difference between that and the next highest percentage for each odd month. Fourteen odd days or more are rounded up and treated as a month; less than 14 odd days are ignored.

## [¶5-150]   Premiums for short leases: CGT/IT charge

(ITTOIA 2005, s. 277)

(Tax Reporter: ¶509-950)

The chart at ¶3-500 shows the proportion of any premium received in respect of a lease of less than 50 years which is chargeable to capital gains tax and that which is chargeable to income tax as property business profits.

## [¶5-200]   CGT exempt gilt-edged securities

(TCGA 1992, s. 16(2), 115(1) and Sch. 9)

(Tax Reporter: ¶559-000)

Gains on the following securities are not chargeable gains and any losses are not allowable losses.

| Stocks and bonds charged on the National Loans Funds | |
|---|---|
| 2½% | Annuities 1905 or after |
| 2¾% | Annuities 1905 or after |
| 2½% | Consolidated Stock 1923 or after |
| 3½% | War Loan 1952 or after |
| 4% | Consolidated Loan 1957 or after |
| 3½% | Conversion Loan 1961 or after |
| 3% | Treasury Stock 1966 or after |
| 2½% | Treasury Stock 1975 or after |
| 12¾% | Treasury Loan 1992 |
| 8% | Treasury Loan 1992 |
| 10% | Treasury Stock 1992 |
| 3% | Treasury Stock 1992 |
| 12¼% | Exchequer Stock 1992 |
| 13½% | Exchequer Stock 1992 |
| 10½% | Treasury Convertible Stock 1992 |
| 2% | Index-Linked Treasury Stock 1992 |
| 12½% | Treasury Loan 1993 |
| 6% | Funding Loan 1993 |
| 13¾% | Treasury Loan 1993 |
| 10% | Treasury Loan 1993 |
| 8¼% | Treasury Stock 1993 |
| 14½% | Treasury Loan 1994 |
| 12½% | Exchequer Stock 1994 |
| 9% | Treasury Loan 1994 |
| 10% | Treasury Loan 1994 |
| 13½% | Exchequer Stock 1994 |
| 8½% | Treasury Stock 1994 |
| 8½% | Treasury Stock 1994 'A' |
| 2% | Index-Linked Treasury Stock 1994 |
| 3% | Exchequer Gas Stock 1990–95 |
| 12% | Treasury Stock 1995 |
| 10¼% | Exchequer Stock 1995 |
| 12¾% | Treasury Loan 1995 |
| 9% | Treasury Loan 1992–96 |

| Stocks and bonds charged on the National Loans Funds – cont'd | |
|---|---|
| 15¼% | Treasury Loan 1996 |
| 13¼% | Exchequer Loan 1996 |
| 14% | Treasury Stock 1996 |
| 2% | Index-Linked Treasury Stock 1996 |
| 10% | Conversion Stock 1996 |
| 10% | Conversion Stock 1996 'A' |
| 10% | Conversion Stock 1996 'B' |
| 13¼% | Treasury Loan 1997 |
| 10½% | Exchequer Stock 1997 |
| 8¾% | Treasury Loan 1997 |
| 8¾% | Treasury Loan 1997 'B' |
| 8¾% | Treasury Loan 1997 'C' |
| 8¾% | Treasury Loan 1997 'D' |
| 8¾% | Treasury Loan 1997 'E' |
| 15% | Exchequer Stock 1997 |
| 7% | Treasury Convertible Stock 1997 |
| 6¾% | Treasury Loan 1995–98 |
| 15½% | Treasury Loan 1998 |
| 12% | Exchequer Stock 1998 |
| 12% | Exchequer Stock 1998 'A' |
| 9¾% | Exchequer Stock 1998 |
| 9¾% | Exchequer Stock 1998 'A' |
| 7¼% | Treasury Stock 1998 'A' |
| 7¼% | Treasury Stock 1998 'B' |
| 12% | Exchequer Stock 1998 'B' |
| 4⅝% | Index-Linked Treasury Stock 1998 |
| 7¼% | Treasury Stock 1998 |
| 9½% | Treasury Loan 1999 |
| 10½% | Treasury Stock 1999 |
| 12¼% | Exchequer Stock 1999 |
| 12¼% | Exchequer Stock 1999 'A' |
| 12¼% | Exchequer Stock 1999 'B' |
| 2½% | Index-Linked Treasury Convertible Stock 1999 |
| 10¼% | Conversion Stock 1999 |
| 6% | Treasury Stock 1999 |
|  | Floating Rate Treasury Stock 1999 |
| 9% | Conversion Stock 2000 |
| 9% | Conversion Stock 2000 'A' |
| 9% | Conversion Stock 2000 'B' |

| Stocks and bonds charged on the National Loans Funds – cont'd | |
|---|---|
| 9% | Conversion Stock 2000 'C' |
| 8½% | Treasury Loan 2000 |
| 8% | Treasury Stock 2000 |
| 8% | Treasury Stock 2000 'A' |
| 13% | Treasury Stock 2000 |
| 13% | Treasury Stock 2000 'A' |
| 7% | Treasury Stock 2001 |
| 7% | Treasury Stock 2001 'A' |
| 14% | Treasury Stock 1998–2001 |
| 2½% | Index-Linked Treasury Stock 2001 |
| 9¾% | Conversion Stock 2001 |
| 10% | Treasury Stock 2001 |
| 9½% | Conversion Loan 2001 |
| 10% | Treasury Stock 2001 'A' |
| 10% | Treasury Stock 2001 'B' |
| | Floating Rate Treasury Stock 2001 |
| 12% | Exchequer Stock 1999–2002 |
| 12% | Exchequer Stock 1999–2002 'A' |
| 9½% | Conversion Stock 2002 |
| 10% | Conversion Stock 2002 |
| 9% | Exchequer Stock 2002 |
| 7% | Treasury Stock 2002 |
| 9¾% | Treasury Stock 2002 |
| 9¾% | Treasury Stock 2002 'A' |
| 9¾% | Treasury Stock 2002 'B' |
| 9¾% | Treasury Stock 2002 'C' |
| 13¾% | Treasury Stock 2000–2003 |
| 13¾% | Treasury Stock 2000–2003 'A' |
| 2½% | Index-Linked Treasury Stock 2003 |
| 9¾% | Conversion Loan 2003 |
| 6½% | Treasury Stock 2003 |
| 8% | Treasury Stock 2003 |
| 8% | Treasury Stock 2003 'A' |
| 10% | Treasury Stock 2003 |
| 10% | Treasury Stock 2003 'A' |
| 10% | Treasury Stock 2003 'B' |
| 3½% | Funding Stock 1999–2004 |
| 11½% | Treasury Stock 2001–2004 |

| Stocks and bonds charged on the National Loans Funds – cont'd | |
|---|---|
| 9½% | Conversion Stock 2004 |
| 10% | Treasury Stock 2004 |
| 6¾% | Treasury Stock 2004 |
| 5% | Treasury Stock 2004 |
| 6¾% | Treasury Stock 2004 'A' |
| 4⅜% | Index-Linked Treasury Stock 2004 |
| 9½% | Conversion Stock 2004 'A' |
| 12½% | Treasury Stock 2003–2005 |
| 12½% | Treasury Stock 2003–2005 'A' |
| 10½% | Exchequer Stock 2005 |
| 9½% | Conversion Stock 2005 |
| 9½% | Conversion Stock 2005 'A' |
| 8½% | Treasury Stock 2005 |
| 8% | Treasury Loan 2002–2006 |
| 8% | Treasury Loan 2002–2006 'A' |
| 2% | Index-Linked Treasury Stock 2006 |
| 9¾% | Conversion Stock 2006 |
| 7½% | Treasury Stock 2006 |
| 7¾% | Treasury Stock 2006 |
| 11¾% | Treasury Stock 2003–2007 |
| 11¾% | Treasury Stock 2003–2007 'A' |
| 7¼% | Treasury Stock 2007 |
| 4½% | Treasury Stock 2007 |
| 8½% | Treasury Loan 2007 |
| 8½% | Treasury Loan 2007 'A' |
| 8½% | Treasury Loan 2007 'B' |
| 8½% | Treasury Loan 2007 'C' |
| 13½% | Treasury Stock 2004–2008 |
| 9% | Treasury Loan 2008 |
| 9% | Treasury Loan 2008 'A' |
| 9% | Treasury Loan 2008 'B' |
| 9% | Treasury Loan 2008 'C' |
| 9% | Treasury Loan 2008 'D' |
| 5% | Treasury Stock 2008 |
| 2½% | Index-Linked Treasury Stock 2009 |
| 5¾% | Treasury Stock 2009 |
| 8% | Treasury Stock 2009 |
| 4% | Treasury Stock 2009 |

Taxation of Capital Gains

| Stocks and bonds charged on the National Loans Funds – cont'd ||
|---------|----------------------------------------------|
| 8% | Treasury Stock 2009 'A' |
| 6¼% | Treasury Stock 2010 |
| 4¾% | Treasury Stock 2010 |
| 4¼% | Treasury Gilt 2011 |
| 3¼% | Treasury Gilt 2011 |
| 2½% | Index-Linked Treasury Stock 2011 |
| 9% | Conversion Loan 2011 |
| 9% | Conversion Loan 2011 'A' |
| 9% | Conversion Loan 2011 'B' |
| 9% | Conversion Loan 2011 'C' |
| 9% | Conversion Loan 2011 'D' |
| 5½% | Treasury Stock 2008–2012 |
| 9% | Treasury Stock 2012 |
| 9% | Treasury Stock 2012 'A' |
| 5% | Treasury Stock 2012 |
| 5¼% | Treasury Gilt 2012 |
| 2½% | Index-Linked Treasury Stock 2013 |
| 8% | Treasury Stock 2013 |
| 4½% | Treasury Gilt 2013 |
| 5% | Treasury Stock 2014 |
| 2¼% | Treasury Gilt 2014 |
| 7¾% | Treasury Loan 2012–2015 |
| 4¾% | Treasury Stock 2015 |
| 2¾% | Treasury Gilt 2015 |
| 8% | Treasury Stock 2015 |
| 8% | Treasury Stock 2015 'A' |
| 2½% | Treasury Stock 1986–2016 |
| 2½% | Index-Linked Treasury Stock 2016 |
| 2½% | Index-Linked Treasury Stock 2016 'A' |
| 4% | Treasury Gilt 2016 |
| 2% | Treasury Gilt 2016 |
| 12% | Exchequer Stock 2013–2017 |
| 1% | Treasury Gilt 2017 |
| 1¼% | Index-Linked Treasury Gilt 2017 |
| 1¾% | Treasury Gilt 2017 |
| 8¾% | Treasury Stock 2017 |
| 8¾% | Treasury Stock 2017 'A' |
| 1¼% | Treasury Gilt 2018 |
| 5% | Treasury Gilt 2018 |

| Stocks and bonds charged on the National Loans Funds – cont'd | |
|---|---|
| 0⅛% | Index-Linked Treasury Gilt 2019 |
| 1¾% | Treasury Gilt 2019 |
| 4½% | Treasury Gilt 2019 |
| 3¾% | Treasury Gilt 2019 |
| 2½% | Index-Linked Treasury Stock 2020 |
| 2% | Treasury Gilt 2020 |
| 3¾% | Treasury Gilt 2020 |
| 4¾% | Treasury Stock 2020 |
| 1½% | Treasury Gilt 2021 |
| 3¾% | Treasury Gilt 2021 |
| 8% | Treasury Stock 2021 |
| 0½% | Treasury Gilt 2022 |
| 1¾% | Treasury Gilt 2022 |
| 4% | Treasury Gilt 2022 |
| 1⅞% | Index-Linked Treasury Gilt 2022 |
| 2¼% | Treasury Gilt 2023 |
| 0⅛% | Index-Linked Treasury Gilt 2024 |
| 2½% | Index-Linked Treasury Stock 2024 |
| 2¾% | Treasury Gilt 2024 |
| 2% | Treasury Gilt 2025 |
| 5% | Treasury Stock 2025 |
| 0⅛% | Index-Linked Treasury Gilt 2026 |
| 1½% | Treasury Gilt 2026 |
| 1¼% | Index-Linked Treasury Gilt 2027 |
| 4¼% | Treasury Gilt 2027 |
| 6% | Treasury Stock 2028 |
| 0⅛% | Index-Linked Treasury Gilt 2029 |
| 4⅛% | Index-Linked Treasury Stock 2030 |
| 4¾% | Treasury Gilt 2030 |
| 4¼% | Treasury Stock 2032 |
| 1¼% | Index-Linked Treasury Gilt 2032 |
| 0¾% | Index-Linked Treasury Gilt 2034 |
| 4½% | Treasury Gilt 2034 |
| 2% | Index-Linked Treasury Stock 2035 |
| 0⅛% | Index-Linked Treasury Gilt 2036 |
| 4¼% | Treasury Stock 2036 |
| 1⅛% | Index-Linked Treasury Gilt 2037 |
| 1¾% | Treasury Gilt 2037 |
| 4¾% | Treasury Stock 2038 |

Taxation of Capital Gains

| Stocks and bonds charged on the National Loans Funds – cont'd | |
|---|---|
| 4¼% | Treasury Gilt 2039 |
| 0⅝% | Index-Linked Treasury Gilt 2040 |
| 4¼% | Treasury Gilt 2040 |
| 4½% | Treasury Gilt 2042 |
| 0⅝% | Index-Linked Treasury Gilt 2042 |
| 0⅛% | Index-Linked Treasury Gilt 2044 |
| 3¼% | Treasury Gilt 2044 |
| 3½% | Treasury Gilt 2045 |
| 0⅛% | Index-Linked Treasury Gilt 2046 |
| 4¼% | Treasury Gilt 2046 |
| 0¾% | Index-Linked Treasury Gilt 2047 |
| 1½% | Treasury Gilt 2047 |
| 4¼% | Treasury Gilt 2049 |
| 0½% | Index-Linked Treasury Gilt 2050 |
| 0¼% | Index-Linked Treasury Gilt 2052 |
| 3¾% | Treasury Gilt 2052 |
| 1¼% | Indexed-Linked Treasury Gilt 2055 |
| 4¼% | Treasury Gilt 2055 |
| 0⅛% | Index-Linked Treasury Gilt 2058 |
| 4% | Treasury Gilt 2060 |
| 0½% | Index-Linked Treasury Gilt 2060 |
| 0⅜% | Index-Linked Treasury Gilt 2062 |
| 0⅛% | Index-Linked Treasury Gilt 2065 |
| 2½% | Treasury Gilt 2065 |
| 0⅛% | Index-Linked Treasury Gilt 2068 |
| 3½% | Treasury Gilt 2068 |

| Securities issued by certain public corporations and guaranteed by the Treasury | |
|---|---|
| 3% | North of Scotland Electricity Stock 1989–92 |

## [¶5-250]   Securities of negligible value

(TCGA 1992, s. 24(2))

(Tax Reporter: ¶515-150)

The HMRC website contains a list, constantly updated, of shares or securities formerly quoted (largely) on the London Stock Exchange which have been officially declared of negligible value for the purposes of a claim under s. 24(2). A summary of principles, together with a link to the current list (last updated 24 June 2016) may be found at www.gov.uk/guidance/negligible-value-agreements-to-30-june-2014.

The time limit for a claim is two years from the end of the tax year (or accounting period of a company) in which the deemed disposal and reacquisition take place.

# [¶5-300]   Identification of securities

(TCGA 1992, s. 104–109)

(Tax Reporter: ¶556-525ff.)

### Disposals by individuals and trustees: 2008–09 onwards

Disposals on or after 6 April 2008 are to be identified with acquisitions in the following order:

(1)   same-day acquisitions, but subject to an election under s. 105A (see below);

(2)   acquisitions within the following 30 days on the basis of earlier acquisitions in that period, rather than later ones (a FIFO basis); and

(3)   securities within the expanded s. 104 holding, which specifically does not include acquisitions under (1) and (2) above.

Where the number of securities which comprise the disposal exceed those identified under the above rules, that excess is identified with subsequent acquisitions beyond the 30-day period referred to above.

Where an individual acquires shares of the same class on the same day and some of those shares are acquired pursuant to the exercise of approved scheme share options, a s. 105A election may be made. The election treats the option scheme shares as a separate holding from the other shares acquired and as being disposed of after the remainder of the other shares.

### Disposals by companies

The order of identification is:

(1)   any acquisition on the same day;

(2)   acquisitions within the previous nine days;

(3)   acquisitions since 1 April 1982, 'the s. 104 holding', previously termed 'the new holding';

(4)   acquisitions in the period 6 April 1965 to 31 March 1982, 'the 1982 holding'; and

(5)   those held on 6 April 1965, in respect of which no election has been made to include them in the pre-1982 pool; these will be identified on a last-in, first-out (LIFO) basis.

In respect of disposals before 5 December 2005, where a company or group of companies held at least 2% of the shares or securities of that class, acquisitions and disposals within one month (for most quoted shares or securities) or six months (for most other shares or securities) could be matched.

# [¶5-350]   Expenses incurred by personal representatives

(SP 2/04)

(Tax Reporter: ¶367-575)

In respect of deaths after 5 April 2004, the scale of expenses allowable in computing the gains or losses of personal representatives on the sale of assets in a deceased person's estate is as follows:

Taxation of Capital Gains

| Gross value of estate | Allowable expenditure |
|---|---|
| Up to £50,000 | 1.8% of probate value of assets sold by personal representatives |
| £50,001–£90,000 | £900, divided among all assets in the estate in proportion to their probate values and allowed in those proportions on assets sold by personal representatives |
| £90,001–£400,000 | 1% of probate value of assets sold |
| £400,001–£500,000 | £4,000, divided as above |
| £500,001–£1,000,000 | 0.8% of probate value of assets sold |
| £1,000,001–£5,000,000 | £8,000, divided as above |
| Over £5,000,000 | 0.16% of the probate value of the assets sold, subject to a maximum of £10,000 |

**Note**
Computations based either on the above scale or on actual expenditure incurred are accepted.

## [¶5-500]   Compliance and administration

(TMA 1970, s. 8ff.)

(Tax Reporter: ¶180-000ff.)

For summary of the main provisions which relate both to capital gains tax and income tax, see ¶1-250ff.

Capital gains can be reported straightaway using HMRC's capital gains tax online service (www.gov.uk/capital-gains-tax/report-and-pay-capital-gains-tax) or are otherwise reported annually in a self-assessment tax return.

**Submission dates for 2017–18 capital gains tax returns**

| Gain | Filing date | References |
|---|---|---|
| Gains within self-assessment (UK resident individuals, trustees, personal representatives) | 31 January following tax year of disposal | See ¶1-250ff. |
| ATED-related gains | 31 January following tax year or 5 October where tax return not issued | See www.gov.uk/guidance/pay-annual-tax-on-enveloped-dwellings |
| Non-resident capital gains tax returns (NRCGT returns) | Within 30 days of the completion date of the disposal | TCGA 1992, s. 222A; TMA 1970, s. 12ZB (Tax Reporter: ¶545-975) |

## [¶5-950]   Time limits for elections and claims

In the absence of any specific provision to the contrary, under self-assessment the normal rule is that claims by individuals, trustees and companies are to be made within four years from the end of the tax year or chargeable period to which they relate. Before 1 April 2010, these limits were five years from 31 January next following the end of the tax year for individuals and six years from the end of the relevant chargeable period for companies (TMA 1970, s. 43(1) and FA 1998, Sch. 18, para. 55).

In certain cases, HMRC *may* permit an extension of the strict time limit in relation to certain elections and claims.

| Provision | Time limit | References |
|---|---|---|
| Post-cessation expenses relieved against gains | 12 months from 31 January next following the tax year in which expenses paid | TCGA 1992, s. 261D(6) (Tax Reporter: ¶524-125) |
| Trading losses relieved against gains | 12 months from 31 January next following the tax year loss arose | TCGA 1992, s. 261B(8) (Tax Reporter: ¶524-100) |
| Value of asset negligible | Two years from end of tax year (or accounting period if a company) in which deemed disposal/ reacquisition takes place | TCGA 1992, s. 24(2) (Tax Reporter: ¶515-150) |
| Re-basing of all assets to 31 March 1982 values (companies only from 06/04/08) | Two years from end of accounting period of disposal for company | TCGA 1992, s. 35(6) (Tax Reporter: ¶520-350) |
| 50% relief if deferred charge on gains before 31 March 1982 (companies only from 06/04/08) | Two years from end of accounting period of disposal for company | TCGA 1992, s. 36 and Sch. 4, para. 9(1) (Tax Reporter: ¶520-600) |
| Variation within two years of death not to have CGT effect | Six months from date of variation (election not necessary for variations on or after 1 August 2002) | TCGA 1992, s. 62 (Tax Reporter: ¶367-825) |
| Specifying which 'same day' share acquisitions (through employee share schemes) should be treated as disposed of first | Within 12 months from 31 January next following the tax year of disposal | TCGA 1992, s. 105A (Tax Reporter: ¶556-650) |
| Replacement of business assets (rollover relief) | Four years from the end of the tax year/accounting period (before 1 April 2010, five years from 31 January next following the tax year for individuals or six years from the end of the accounting period for companies) Replacement asset to be purchased between 12 months before and three years after disposal of old asset | TCGA 1992, s. 152(1) (Tax Reporter: ¶570-250) |
| Disapplication of incorporation relief under TCGA 1992, s. 162 | Two years from 31 January following the end of the year of assessment in which the business is transferred | TCGA 1992, s. 162A (Tax Reporter: ¶574-125) |
| Holdover of gain on gift of business asset | Four years from the end of the tax year (before 1 April 2010, five years from 31 January next following the tax year) | TCGA 1992, s. 165(1) (Tax Reporter: ¶574-550) |
| Determination of main residence | Two years from acquisition of second property (see ESC D21) | TCGA 1992, s. 222(5) (Tax Reporter: ¶545-950) |
| Determination of main residence: non-resident CGT disposals | Notice must be given in NRCGT return in respect of the disposal which must be filed within 30 days following the completion date for the disposal | TCGA 1992, s. 222A; TMA 1970, s. 12ZB (Tax Reporter: ¶545-975) |

Taxation of Capital Gains

| Provision | Time limit | References |
|---|---|---|
| Irrecoverable loan to a trader | Four years from the end of the tax year/accounting period (before 1 April 2010, five years from 31 January next following the tax year for individuals or six years from the end of the accounting period for companies) | TCGA 1992, s. 253(4A) (Tax Reporter: ¶511-150) |
| Deemed disposal/reacquisition on expiry of mineral lease | Four years from the date of the relevant event (before 1 April 2010, six years) | TCGA 1992, s. 203(2) (Tax Reporter: ¶799-475) |
| Delayed remittances of foreign gains | Four years from the end of the tax year/accounting period (before 1 April 2010, five years from 31 January next following the tax year for individuals or six years from the end of the accounting period for companies) | TCGA 1992, s. 279(5) (Tax Reporter: ¶591-150) |
| Deferred unascertainable consideration: election for treatment of loss | 12 months from 31 January next following the tax year loss arose | TCGA 1992, s. 279A and 279D (Tax Reporter: ¶524-250) |
| Earn out right treated as a security | Within 12 months from 31 January next following the tax year in which the right is received for individuals or two years from the end of the accounting period for companies | TCGA 1992, s. 138A (Tax Reporter: ¶561-600) |
| Appropriations of assets to trading stock; no deemed disposal at market value on transfer to stock but subsequent trading profits adjusted by gain or loss that would have arisen | Within 12 months from 31 January next following tax year of assessment for the period of account in which the appropriation is made for capital gains tax purposes, or within two years from the end of the accounting period in which the appropriation is made for corporation tax | TCGA 1992, s. 161 (Tax Reporter: ¶573-800) |
| Entrepreneurs' relief | Within 12 months from 31 January next following tax year in which qualifying disposal is made | TCGA 1992, s. 169M (Tax Reporter: ¶572-550) |
| Small part disposals of land; no disposal but base cost on subsequent disposal reduce by consideration received | Within 12 months from 31 January next following tax year in which part disposal is made for individuals, or two years from end of accounting period in which part disposal is made for companies | TCGA 1992, s. 242 (Tax Reporter: ¶510-350) |
| Holdover relief on gifts chargeable to inheritance tax | Four years from end of the tax year of gift (before 1 April 2010, five years from 31 January next following the tax year) | TCGA 1992, s. 260 (Tax Reporter: ¶548-700) |
| Disincorporation relief | Within two years beginning with the business transfer date | FA 2013, s. 60 |
| EIS/SEIS/SI deferral relief | Five years from 31 January following tax year in which shares are issued/investment is made | TCGA 1992, Sch. 5B, para. 6; Sch. 5BB, para. 3; Sch. 8B, para. 8 (Tax Reporter: ¶565-600; ¶569-200; ¶569-800) |

# INHERITANCE TAX

## [¶6-000]   Rates of tax

(IHTA 1984, s. 7 and Sch. 1)

(Tax Reporter: ¶607-000; ¶624-000)

**From 15 March 1988**

|  | Gross rate of tax |
|---|---|
| **Lifetime transfers** | |
| Gross transfers up to cumulative limit | Nil |
| Gross transfers over cumulative limit | 20% |
| Grossing-up fraction | $1/_4$ |
| **Death transfers** | |
| Gross transfers up to cumulative limit | Nil |
| Gross transfers over cumulative limit | 40% |
| Grossing-up fraction | $2/_3$ |
| Reduced rate[1] | 36% |

**Note**

[1] For deaths occurring on or after 6 April 2012, a reduced rate of inheritance tax of 36% applies where 10% or more of a deceased person's net estate (after deducting IHT exemptions, reliefs and the nil-rate band) is left to charity. To determine whether the lower rate will apply, the estate is broken down into three components (with the nil-rate band apportioned): the survivorship component (property passing automatically to the survivor), the settled property component (settled property in which the deceased held an interest in possession) and the general component (all other property excluding gifts with reservation of benefit to which the lower rate cannot apply). The 10% test is applied to each component separately and the lower rate applied to those components which satisfy the 10% test. An election to merge components of the estate and apply the 10% test in aggregate is possible, as is an election to opt out of the lower rate for one or more components of the estate. Both elections must be made within two years of the date of death and may be withdrawn within two years and one month of the date of death.

## [¶6-050]   Cumulative chargeable transfers limit

(IHTA 1984, s. 7 and Sch. 1)

**Transfers from 15 March 1988**

| Period | Cumulative chargeable transfers limit[1] £ |
|---|---|
| 2017–18[2] | 325,000 |
| 2009–10 to 2016–17 | 325,000 |
| 2008–09 | 312,000 |

**Notes**

[1] *Finance Act* 2008, s. 10 and Sch. 4 allow a claim to be made to transfer any unused nil-rate band of the first deceased spouse or civil partner to the estate of their surviving spouse or civil partner who dies on or after 9 October 2007.

[2] *Finance Act* 2010, s. 8 froze the inheritance tax nil-rate band at £325,000 for tax years 2012–13 to 2014–15. *Finance Act* 2014, Sch. 25, para. 2 extended the freeze for a further three years from 2015–16 until 2017–18 and F(No. 2)A 2015, s. 10 further extends the freeze until April 2021.

Inheritance Tax

## [¶6-075]   Residence nil-rate band

(IHTA 1984, s. 8D–8M)

| Year | Residential enhancement £ |
|---|---|
| 2017–18 | 100,000 |
| 2018–19 | 125,000 |
| 2019–20 | 150,000 |
| 2020–21 | 175,000 |

**Note**

[1] For deaths on or after 6 April 2017, an additional nil-rate band is available when a residence is passed on death to direct descendants. Amounts are set for years 2017–18 to 2020–21 as per the table above and the amount will then increase in line with CPI from 2021–22 onwards. Any unused nil-rate band will be transferred to a surviving spouse or civil partner. It will also be available when a person downsizes or ceases to own a home on or after 8 July 2015 and assets of an equivalent value, up to the value of the additional nil-rate band, are passed on death to direct descendants. There will also be a tapered withdrawal of the additional nil-rate band for estates with a net value of more than £2m. This will be at a withdrawal rate of £1 for every £2 over this threshold (IHTA 1984, s. 8D–8M, as amended by FA 2016, s. 93 and Sch. 15).

## [¶6-200]   Annual and small gift exemption

(IHTA 1984, s. 19 and 20)

(Tax Reporter: ¶643-200; ¶643-700)

| | On or after 6 April 1981 £ |
|---|---|
| Annual | 3,000 |
| Small gift (to the same person) | 250 |

## [¶6-250]   Gifts in consideration of marriage/civil partnership

(IHTA 1984, s. 22)

(Tax Reporter: ¶644-450)

| Donor | Exemption limit £ |
|---|---|
| Parent of party to the marriage/civil partnership | 5,000 |
| Remote ancestor of party to the marriage/civil partnership | 2,500 |
| Party to the marriage/civil partnership | 2,500 |
| Any other person | 1,000 |

## [¶6-300]   Transfers by UK-domiciled spouse/civil partner to non-UK domiciled spouse/civil partner

(IHTA 1984, s. 18)

(Tax Reporter: ¶644-900)

| Transfer on or after | Exemption limit £ |
|---|---|
| 6 April 2013 | 325,000[1] |
| 9 March 1982 | 55,000 |

**Note**

[1] *Finance Act* 2013 increased the lifetime limit on the amount that can be transferred exempt from IHT to a spouse or civil partner domiciled outside the UK to the exemption limit at the time of the transfer per IHTA 1984, Sch. 1 (the nil-rate band).

## [¶6-325]   Election to be treated as domiciled in UK

(IHTA 1984, s. 267ZA–267ZB)

(Tax Reporter: ¶684-575)

A person who is not domiciled in the UK but who is, or has been married to, or in a civil partnership with, someone who is domiciled in the UK can elect to be treated as domiciled in the UK for the purposes of inheritance tax. There are two types of elections:

(1)   A lifetime election by the non-domiciled individual who is at any time on or after 6 April 2013 and during the period of seven years ending with the date of the election married to or in a civil partnership with a UK-domiciled individual.

(2)   A death election by the personal representatives of a deceased person who was at any time on or after 6 April 2013, and during the period of seven years ending with the date of death themselves domiciled in the UK and married to or in a civil partnership with a non-domiciled person who is, by virtue of the election, to be treated as domiciled in the UK.

The election is irrevocable but ceases to have effect if the individual is not resident in the UK for income tax purposes for four successive tax years. The election must be in writing and in the case of a death election made within two years of the date of death. The election cannot relate back to before 6 April 2013, or more than seven years before either the election is made or the date of death and any date the election relates back to must be a date when the individual was married, or in a civil partnership, and either the individual or their spouse (as the case may be) was UK domiciled on that date.

Inheritance Tax

## [¶6-335]   Non-domiciles

(Tax Reporter: ¶684-300)

### Deemed domicile

Non-domiciled individuals pay inheritance tax only in respect of their UK assets. However, an individual who is not domiciled in the UK can become deemed UK-domiciled for inheritance tax purposes in certain circumstances. Then, they pay UK inheritance tax on their worldwide assets.

Draft Finance Bill 2017 amends the inheritance tax legislation relating to individuals who will be treated as domiciled in the UK. The amendments provide that an individual will be treated as domiciled for IHT purposes if they have been resident in the UK for at least 15 out of the previous 20 tax years, rather than 17 out of the 20 tax years ending with the tax year in question. The changes will take effect from the start of the 2017–18 tax year on 6 April 2017.

Those who become deemed domicile in April 2017, excepting those who were born in the UK with a UK domicile of origin, will be able to treat the cost base of their non-UK based assets as the market value of that asset on 5 April 2017.

### The returning UK dom

Draft Finance Bill 2017 also introduces a separate rule to provide that an individual born in the UK with a UK domicile of origin who has acquired a domicile of choice elsewhere will be treated as domiciled for inheritance tax purposes if at any time they are resident in the UK and have been resident in the UK in at least one out of the two previous tax years. The new rule takes effect from the start of the 2017–18 tax year on 6 April 2017.

### Residential property of non-domiciles

Under IHTA 1984, an individual who is domiciled outside the UK is not liable to tax on any property they own which is situated overseas, unlike UK domiciled individuals who are liable to inheritance tax on their worldwide property. This difference in treatment has been used by some non-doms as a means of avoiding inheritance tax by holding UK residential properties indirectly through overseas structures such as companies, trusts and partnerships. At Summer Budget 2015, the Government announced its intention of extending inheritance tax to UK residential property held by a non-domiciled individual through an overseas structure. Draft Finance Bill 2017 extends the scope of inheritance tax to include residential properties situated in the UK where they are held through overseas structures by amending the definition of excluded property in IHTA 1984 which has the effect of excluding any property of such individuals from inheritance tax where it is situated outside the UK. Minor interests in UK residential property (less than 5%) are disregarded. The extended charge will be effective from 5 April 2017.

## [¶6-350]   Gifts to the nation

(IHTA 1984, s. 25; FA 2012, Sch. 14)

(Tax Reporter: ¶646-050)

Gifts of pre-eminent property to be held for the benefit of the public or the nation are exempt from inheritance tax. Pre-eminent property includes any picture, print, book, manuscript, work of art, scientific object or other thing that is pre-eminent for its national, scientific, historic or artistic interest, collections of such items and any object kept in a significant building where it is desirable that it remain associated with the building.

## [¶6-360]   Employee ownership trusts

(IHTA 1984, s. 13A, 28A, 72(3A), 75A, 86)

(Tax Reporter: ¶646-750; ¶363-770; ¶364-750)

*Finance Act* 2014 introduces an exemption from inheritance tax for transfers on or after 6 April 2014 by individuals of shares in a company to an employee ownership trust and for transfers of cash and other assets by a close company to the employee ownership trust (such transfers are not transfers of value for IHT purposes). Employee ownership trusts are also excluded from the definition of 'relevant property' and, therefore, not subject to the ten-year charge or the exit charge under the relevant property regime (from 6 April 2014).

## [¶6-400]   Agricultural and business property relief

(IHTA 1984, s. 103ff. and 115ff.)

(Tax Reporter: ¶664-000; ¶658-000)

| Type of relief | Rate of relief for disposals on or after 6/4/96 % |
|---|---|
| **Agricultural property**[1][2] | |
| Vacant possession or right to obtain it within 12 months | |
| | 100 |
| Tenanted land with vacant a possession value | 100 |
| Entitled to 50% relief at 9 March 1981 and not since able to obtain vacant possession | 100 |
| Agricultural land let on or after 1 September 1995 | 100 |
| Other circumstances | 50 |
| **Business property** | |
| *Nature of property* | |
| Business or interest in business | 100 |
| Controlling shareholding in quoted company | 50 |
| Controlling shareholding in unquoted[3]company | 100 |
| Settled property used in life tenant's business | 100/50[4] |
| Shareholding in unquoted[3] company: more than 25% interest | 100 |
| Minority shareholding in unquoted[3]company: 25% or less | 100 |
| Land, buildings, machinery or plant used by transferor's company or partnership | 50 |

**Notes**

[1] FA 2009, s. 122 extends agricultural property relief to property in the European Economic Area. IHT due or paid on or after 23 April 2003 in relation to agricultural property located in a qualifying EEA state at the time of the chargeable event will become eligible for relief.

[2] From 6 April 1995, short rotation coppice is regarded as agricultural property.

[3] With effect from 10 March 1992, 'unquoted' means shares not quoted on a recognised stock exchange and therefore includes shares dealt in on the Unlisted Securities Market (USM) or Alternative Investment Market (AIM).

[4] The higher rate applies if the settled property is transferred along with business itself.

Inheritance Tax

## [¶6-450]   Quick succession relief

(IHTA 1984, s. 141)

(Tax Reporter: ¶627-400)

| Years between transfers | | Percentage applied to |
| More than | Not more than | formula below |
|---|---|---|
| 0 | 1 | 100 |
| 1 | 2 | 80 |
| 2 | 3 | 60 |
| 3 | 4 | 40 |
| 4 | 5 | 20 |

**Formula**

$$\text{Tax charge on earlier transfer} \times \frac{\text{Increase in transferee's estate}}{\text{Diminution in transferor's estate}}$$

## [¶6-475]   Intestate rules

(*Administration of Estates Act* 1925, s. 46(1) and Sch. 1A)

**Note:** See ¶26-500 for succession and intestacy rules applicable in Scotland.

| Surviving family | Beneficiaries | |
| | Deaths before 1 October 2014[1] | Deaths on or after 1 October 2014[2] |
|---|---|---|
| **Spouse or civil partner but no issue** Spouse or civil partner only (no issue, parents, brothers or sisters of the whole blood (or their issue)). | Spouse or civil partner takes everything, absolutely. | Spouse or civil partner takes everything, absolutely. |
| Spouse or civil partner (no issue) and parent or whole blood brother or sister, or issue of whole blood brother or sister. | Spouse or civil partner takes: <ul><li>personal chattels;</li><li>£450,000 absolutely (or the entire estate where this is less);</li><li>one-half share of residue (if any) absolutely.</li></ul> | Spouse or civil partner takes everything, absolutely. |
| | Remainder distributable to: <ul><li>parent(s);</li><li>failing a parent then on trust for the deceased's whole blood brothers and sisters, (nephews and nieces step into their parent's shoes if the latter is dead).</li></ul> | Parents/siblings receive nothing. |

| Surviving family | Beneficiaries | |
| --- | --- | --- |
| | **Deaths before 1 October 2014**[1] | **Deaths on or after 1 October 2014**[2] |
| **Spouse or civil partner and issue** | Spouse or civil partner takes:<br>• personal chattels (e.g. furniture, pictures, clothing, jewellery, etc.), absolutely;<br>• £250,000 absolutely (or the entire estate where this is less);<br>• **life interest** in one-half of the residue (if any).<br><br>Issue receive:<br>• one half of residue (if any) on statutory trusts;<br>• the other half of residue on statutory trusts upon the death of the spouse or civil partner. | Spouse or civil partner takes:<br>• personal chattels (e.g. furniture, pictures, clothing, jewellery, etc.), absolutely;<br>• £250,000[3] absolutely (or the entire estate where this is less);<br>• one half of the residue (if any) **absolutely**.<br><br>Issue receive:<br>• one half of residue (if any) on statutory trusts. |
| **No spouse or civil partner** | Everything is taken by:<br>• Issue, but if none;<br>• Parent(s), but if none;<br>• Brothers and sisters of the whole blood (nephews and nieces step into their parent's shoes), but if none;<br>• Brothers and sisters of the half blood (nephews and nieces step into their parent's shoes), but if none;<br>• Grandparents, but if none;<br>• Uncles and aunts of the whole blood and the issue of any deceased uncle or aunt, but if none;<br>• Uncles and aunts of the half blood and the issue of any deceased uncle or aunt, but if none;<br>• the Crown. | |

**Notes**

[1] For deaths on or after 1 February 2009 under the *Administration of Estates Act* 1925, s. 46(1); not applicable in Scotland.

[2] For deaths after 1 October 2014 (2014/2039) under the *Administration of Estates Act* 1925, s. 46(1) (as amended by the *Inheritance and Trustees' Powers Act* 2014); not applicable in Scotland.

[3] The fixed sum statutory legacy is to be index-linked using the consumer prices index and amended by statutory instrument (*Administration of Estates Act* 1925, Sch. 1A (as inserted by the *Inheritance and Trustees' Powers Act* 2014)).

## [¶6-500]   Instalment option

(IHTA 1984, s. 227)

(Tax Reporter: ¶183-215)

Interest-free:

• controlling shareholdings;

• holdings of 10% or more of unquoted shares with value over £20,000;

• certain other death transfers of unquoted shares;

- business or interest in business;
- agricultural value of agricultural property; and
- woodlands.

Not interest-free:

- land, wherever situated, other than within categories above; and
- shareholdings in certain land investment and security dealing companies, or market makers or discount houses.

## [¶6-550]   Fall in value relief

(IHTA 1984, s. 179, 191 and 197A)

(Tax Reporter: ¶627-900)

| Type of property | Period after death |
|---|---|
| Quoted securities sold | One year |
| Qualifying investments[1] | One year |
| Interests in land – deaths after 15 March 1990 | Four years |

**Note**

[1] Qualifying investments mean shares or securities which are quoted at the date of death in question, holdings in a unit trust which at that date is an authorised unit trust, shares in an open-ended investment company and shares in any common investment fund established under the *Administration of Justice Act* 1982, s. 42.

## [¶6-600]   Taper relief

(IHTA 1984, s. 7(4))

(Tax Reporter: ¶611-400)

| Years between gift and death | | Percentage of full tax charge at death – rates actually due |
|---|---|---|
| More than | Not more than | % |
| 3 | 4 | 80 |
| 4 | 5 | 60 |
| 5 | 6 | 40 |
| 6 | 7 | 20 |

## [¶6-650]   Pre-owned assets

(FA 2004, s. 84 and Sch. 15)

(Tax Reporter: ¶614-800)

A freestanding income tax charge where individuals continue to enjoy property previously owned by them with effect from 6 April 2005. The charge to tax arises under three main heads, relating to:

- land;
- chattels; and
- intangible property in settlor interested trusts.

In determining whether charges arise in respect of land or chattels, certain transactions are excluded and there are a number of exemptions.

Limited reliefs prevent double charges to tax. Special rules apply to individuals not resident or not domiciled in the UK. Provisions allow for opting out of the pre-owned assets charge arising in respect of any property, with inheritance tax consequences.

### Land

The chargeable amount in the case of land or any interest in land is the 'appropriate rental value' less an amount paid under any legal obligation in respect of the occupation of the land. The appropriate rental value is:

$$R \times \frac{DV}{V}$$

Where:

R is the 'rental value' of the relevant land for the 'taxable period';

DV is the value at the 'valuation date' of the interest in the relevant land that was disposed of by the chargeable person or, where the disposal was a non-exempt sale, the appropriate proportion of that value; and

V is the value of the relevant land at the valuation date.

The 'taxable period' is the year of assessment, or part of the year of assessment, during which the relevant conditions are met.

The 'rental value' is based on the assumption of a letting from year-to-year where the tenant pays the taxes, rates and charges and the landlord is responsible for repair and insurance. Land may be valued on a five-yearly rather than an annual valuation (SI 2005/724).

### Chattels

In respect of chattels, the chargeable amount is the 'appropriate amount' less an amount paid under a legal obligation to the owner of the chattel. The 'appropriate amount' is:

$$N \times \frac{DV}{V}$$

Where:

N is the notional interest for the taxable period, at the prescribed rate, on the value of the chattel at the valuation date;

DV is the value at the valuation date of the interest in the relevant chattel that was disposed of by the chargeable person or, where the disposal was a non-exempt sale, the appropriate proportion of that asset; and

V is the value of the chattel at the valuation date.

Inheritance Tax

**Intangible property in settlor interested trusts**

The chargeable amount in relation to the relevant property is:

N – T

Where:

N is the notional amount of interest for the taxable period, at the prescribed rate, on the value of the property at the valuation date; and

T is the amount of income tax or capital gains tax payable by the chargeable person in the taxable period on gains from contracts of life assurance, income where settlor retains an interest, transfer of assets abroad, charge on settlor with interest in settlement and attribution of gains to settlors with interest in non-resident or dual resident settlements.

Where the aggregate amount attributable to a chargeable person in respect of land, chattels and intangibles does not exceed £5,000, there is no income tax payable. If benefits exceed £5,000, the charge is on the full amount including the first £5,000.

## [¶6-700]  Delivery of accounts

(IHTA 1984, s. 216)

Reporter: ¶180-725)

| Nature of transfer | Due Date |
| --- | --- |
| Chargeable lifetime transfer | Later of:<br>– 12 months after end of month in which transfer occurred<br>– three months after person became liable |
| Potentially exempt transfers which have become chargeable | 12 months after end of month in which death of transferor occurred |
| Transfers on death | Later of:<br>– 12 months after end of month in which death occurred<br>– three months after personal representatives first act or have reason to believe an account is required |
| Gifts subject to reservation included in donor's estate at death | 12 months after end of month in which death occurred |
| National heritage property | Six months after end of month in which chargeable event occurred |
| Relevant property settlements: ten-year anniversary and exit charges | Six months from end of month in which the occasion occurs[(1)] |

**Note**
[(1)] Chargeable transfers on or after 6 April 2014 (previously 12 months from the end of the month in which the transfer is made or if later, three months from the date when the trustee first becomes liable for the tax).

**Values below which no account required**

(SI 2008/605)

(Tax Reporter: ¶180-775)

| Excepted lifetime chargeable transfers on or after 6 April 2007 | £ |
|---|---|
| Where the property given away, or in which the interest subsists, is wholly attributable to cash or quoted stocks and securities, the cumulative total of all chargeable transfers made by the transfer in the seven years before the transfer must not exceed the nil-rate band. | |
| Where the property given away, or in which the interest subsists, is wholly or partly attributable to property other than cash or quoted stocks and securities:<br>(1)  the value transferred by the chargeable transfer together with the cumulative total of all chargeable transfers made by the transferor in the seven years before the transfer must not exceed 80% of the relevant IHT nil-rate band;<br>(2)  the value transferred must not exceed the nil-rate band that is available to the transferor at the time the disposal takes place. | |
| **Excepted lifetime chargeable transfers from 1 April 1981 to 5 April 2007** | |
| Transfer in question, together with all other chargeable transfers in same 12-month period ending on 5 April | 10,000 |
| Transfer in question, together with all previous chargeable transfers during preceding ten years | 40,000 |

**Excepted settlements**

(SI 2008/606)

(Tax Reporter: ¶180-905)

| Excepted settlements: chargeable events on or after 6 April 2007 |
|---|
| **No qualifying interest in possession subsists and:**<br>**Either:**<br>• Cash is and has always been the only property comprised in the settlement;<br>• No further property has been added to the settlement (since it was made);<br>• The trustees are and have always been UK resident;<br>• Gross value of settled property less than **£1,000** throughout; and<br>• No related settlements.<br>**Or:**<br>• UK domiciled settlor (when settlement made until earlier of the chargeable event or death of settlor);<br>• Trustees are and have always been UK resident;<br>• No related settlements; and<br>• One of following conditions satisfied. |

Inheritance Tax

> ### Chargeable event:
> 1) **Ten-year anniversary** (IHTA 1984, s. 64)
>    Value transferred does not exceed 80% of IHT threshold.
> 2) **Exit charge before first ten-year anniversary** (IHTA 1984, s. 65)
>    Value transferred does not exceed 80% of IHT threshold.
> 3) **Exit charge after one or more ten-year anniversaries** (IHTA 1984, s. 65)
>    Value transferred (under IHTA 1984, s. 66(3), taking into account s. 69) does not exceed 80% of IHT threshold.
> 4) **Exit charge age 18–25 trusts** (IHTA 1984, s. 71E)
>    Value transferred (under IHTA 1984, s. 71F) does not exceed 80% of IHT threshold.

## Excepted estates

(SI 2004/2543)

(Tax Reporter: ¶180-855)

*Domiciled in the United Kingdom*

| Deaths on and after | But on or before | Total gross value[1][2][3][4][5] £ | Total gross value of property outside UK £ | Total value of settled property £ | Aggregate value of 'specified transfers' £ |
|---|---|---|---|---|---|
| 6 April 2017 | 5 April 2018 | 325,000 | 100,000 | 150,000 | 150,000 |
| 6 April 2009 | 5 April 2017 | 325,000 | 100,000 | 150,000 | 150,000 |

**Notes**

[1] The aggregate of the gross value of that person's estate, the value transferred by any specified transfers made by that person, and the value transferred by any specified exempt transfers made by that person, must not exceed the IHT threshold. (Where the deceased dies after 5 April and before 6 August and application for probate or confirmation is made before 6 August in the same year as death, the inheritance tax threshold used is that for the preceding tax year.)

[2] An estate will qualify as an excepted estate where the gross value of the estate, plus the chargeable value of any transfers in the seven years to death, does not exceed £1m and the net chargeable estate after deduction of spouse or civil partner and/or charity exemption only is less than the IHT threshold, and the total value transferred on that person's death by a spouse, civil partner or charity transfer must be greater than nil (SI 2004/2543).

[3] For deaths on or after 6 April 2002, the limit applies to the aggregate of the gross value of the estate *plus* the value of 'specified transfers' which is extended and includes chargeable transfers, within seven years prior to death, of cash, quoted shares or securities, or an interest in land and furnishings and chattels disposed of at the same time to the same person (excluding property transferred subject to a reservation or property which becomes settled property).

[4] For deaths after 5 April 2010, the IHT threshold for these purposes is increased by 100% where (SI 2004/2543):
(a) the deceased is a surviving spouse or civil partner;
(b) a claim has been made for the transfer of the unused nil-rate band of their deceased spouse or civil partner;
(c) all of the first deceased spouse's or civil partner's nil-rate band was unused; and
(d) the first deceased met similar criteria to those listed above for excepted estates.

[5] For deaths after 28 February 2011, where, in any tax year in the seven years prior to death, a person has transferred over £3,000 that is considered to be exempt as part of normal expenditure out of income, the amount will be included in the value of a person's estate for the purposes of determining whether the estate is an excepted estate, even though the transfer itself may qualify for the exemption (SI 2004/2543).

# [¶6-750] Due dates for payment

(IHTA 1984, s. 226)

(Tax Reporter: ¶183-205)

| Transfer | Due date |
|---|---|
| Chargeable lifetime transfers between 6 April and 30 September | 30 April in following year |
| Chargeable lifetime transfers between 1 October and 5 April | Six months after end of month in which transfer made |
| Potentially exempt transfers which become chargeable | Six months after end of month in which death occurred |
| Transfers on death; extra tax payable on chargeable lifetime transfers within seven years before death | Six months after end of month in which death occurred or on delivery of accounts by personal representatives, if earlier |
| Relevant property settlements: ten-year anniversary and exit charges | Six months after end of month in which the occasion occurs[1] |

**Note**
[1] Chargeable transfers on or after 6 April 2014 (previously 30 April in the following year for chargeable events before 1 October (in any tax year), otherwise six months after the end of the month in which the event occurs).

# [¶6-800] Penalties for failure in relation to obligations falling due after 22 July 2004

(IHTA 1984, s. 245–253; FA 2007, Sch. 24; FA 2008, Sch. 36)

(Tax Reporter: ¶181-550)

| Failure to deliver an IHT account (IHTA 1984, s. 245) | Account outstanding at end of statutory period | Fixed penalty of £100 (but not exceeding tax due) |
|---|---|---|
| | Daily penalty after failure declared by a court or the tribunal | Up to £60 a day |
| | Penalty after six months from end of statutory period, if proceedings for declaring the failure not started before then | Fixed penalty of further £100 (but not exceeding tax due) |
| | Penalty after 12 months from end of statutory period where tax is payable | Up to £3,000 |

Inheritance Tax

| | | |
|---|---|---|
| **Failure by professional person to deliver a return of a settlement by a UK-domiciled person but with non-resident trustees** (IHTA 1984, s. 245A) | Account outstanding at end of statutory period (three months from making of settlement) | Up to £300 |
| | Daily penalty after failure declared by a court or the tribunal | Up to £60 a day |
| **Failure to report a deed of variation which increases the IHT liability** (IHTA 1984, s. 245A) | Penalty for failure to report within 18 months of deed of variation being executed | Up to £3,000 |
| | Penalty | Up to £100 |
| | Daily penalty after failure declared by a court or the tribunal | Up to £60 a day |
| **Failure to comply with a notice requiring information** (FA 2008, Sch. 36) | Penalty | Up to £300 |
| | Daily penalty | Up to £60 a day |
| | Penalty where continued failure and significant tax at stake, determined by tribunal | Tax related |
| **Incorrect information or document** provided in compliance with information notice (FA 2008, Sch. 36) | Penalty | Up to £3,000 per inaccuracy |
| **Incorrect information provided by any person** (IHTA 1984, s. 247(3)) | Fraud or negligence | Up to £3,000 |
| **Before 1 April 2013:** Person assisting in providing incorrect information, etc. (IHTA 1984, s. 247(4)) | Penalty | Up to £3,000 |
| **Error in taxpayer's document** (careless or deliberate) (FA 2007, Sch. 24, para. 1)[1] For reductions for disclosure, see ¶1-350 (but note FA 2016, Sch. 22 increases in offshore penalties apply for inheritance tax purposes in relation to transfers of value occurring on or after 1 April 2017). | Standard amount (careless behaviour) Where the inaccuracy is deliberate but not concealed Where the inaccuracy is deliberate and concealed | 30% of potential revenue lost 70% of potential lost revenue 100% of the potential lost revenue |

| Error in taxpayer's document attributable to another person (FA 2007, Sch. 24, para. 1A)[2] | Penalty | Tax geared |
|---|---|---|
| **Offshore asset moves** (FA 2015, Sch. 21) | Additional penalty for offshore asset moves from specified territory[3] to non-specified territory on or after 26 March 2015 following an original deliberate failure penalty under: FA 2007, Sch. 24, para. 1; or FA 2009, Sch. 55, para. 6. | 50% of original penalty |
| **Enabling offshore tax evasion or non-compliance** (FA 2016, Sch. 20) from 1 January 2017 <br><br> Penalty for engaging in offshore tax evasion of non-compliance where the tax at stake is inheritance tax. | Standard penalty: | The higher of: 100% of the potential lost revenue; or £3,000 |
| | Where a penalty under FA 2015, Sch. 21, para. 1 arises: | The higher of: 50% of the potential lost revenue; or £3,000 |
| **Asset based penalty for offshore inaccuracies and failures:** (FA 2016, Sch. 22) in relation to transfers of value made on or after 1 April 2017 <br><br> Additional penalty where one or more standard offshore penalties and the offshore potential lost revenue in relation to a tax year exceeds £25,000. Standard offshore penalties means penalties under: FA 2007, Sch. 24, para. 1; or FA 2009, Sch. 55, para. 6 imposed involving offshore matters or offshore transfers and deliberate behaviour. | Lower of 10% of value of asset and offshore PLR x 10. | |

Inheritance Tax

| Reductions for: | Reduction factors | |
| --- | --- | --- |
|  | **Unprompted disclosure** | **Prompted disclosure** |
| • disclosing to HMRC<br>• providing a reasonable value<br>• providing information or access to records to assist HMRC value the asset<br>• special circumstances | 50% | 20% |

**Notes**

[1] FA 2008, Sch. 40 extended the new penalty regime in FA 2007, Sch. 24 to inheritance tax from 1 April 2009 where documents are due to be filed on or after 1 April 2010.

[2] FA 2007, Sch. 24, para. 1A as added by FA 2008, Sch. 40 allows a penalty to be charged where an inaccuracy in the liable person's document was attributable to another person. Where it can be shown that the other person deliberately withheld information or supplied false information to the liable person, with the intention that the account or return would contain an inaccuracy, a penalty may be charged on that other person. But that will not necessarily mean that the personal representative themselves may not also be chargeable to a penalty. If the withheld or false information gave rise to inconsistencies in the information they had received about the estate and they did not question those inconsistencies; the liable person may still be charged a penalty for failing to take reasonable care as well.

[3] See ¶1-370 for table of specified territories.

## [¶6-850] Prescribed rates of interest

(IHTA 1984, s. 233 and 235)

Interest is charged at the following rates on late payments or repayments of inheritance tax or capital transfer tax.

| Interest period | Interest rate % | Repayment interest rate % | Days |
| --- | --- | --- | --- |
| From 23 August 2016 | 2.75 | 0.5 | — |
| 29 September 2009 to 22 August 2016 | 3 | 0.5 | 2,520 |

**Note**

[1] Fixed by Treasury Order under SI 1989/1297. From September 2009, interest charged on late payments of tax will be the Bank of England base rate plus 2.5% and the interest rate on overpayments is the Bank of England rate minus 1, subject to a minimum rate of 0.5% on repayment.

# TAXATION OF COMPANIES

## [¶7-000]    Rates of corporation tax

(Tax Reporter: ¶704-000ff.)

| Financial year[1] | Main rate[2][4] | Main ring fence profits rate[3] | Small ring fence profits rate[3] | Special IP rate[5] | Diverted profits rate[6] |
|---|---|---|---|---|---|
| | % | % | % | % | % |
| 2017 | 19 | 30 | 19 | 10 | 25 |
| 2016 | 20 | 30 | 19 | 10 | 25 |
| 2015 | 20 | 30 | 19 | 10 | 25 |

**Notes**

[1] A financial year begins on 1 April and ends on 31 March. The financial year 2016 began on 1 April 2016 and will end on 31 March 2017.

[2] F(No. 2)A 2015, s. 7 sets the main rate of corporation tax for the financial years 2018 and 2019 at 19%. FA 2016, s. 46 reduces the rate set by F(No. 2)A 2015 for financial year 2020 from 18% to 17%.

[3] The small ring fence profits rate applies to profits falling below the lower limit of £300,000 and the main ring fence rate applies otherwise. However, where ring fence profits exceed the lower limit of £300,000 but do not exceed the upper limit of £1,500,000, the amount of corporation tax (calculated at the main rates) is reduced by an amount equal to:

$$R \times (U - A) \times \frac{N}{A}$$

Where:

R is the marginal relief fraction of 11/400ths;

U is the upper limit of £1,500,000;

A is the amount of the augmented profits (CTA 2010, s. 279G); and

N is the amount of the taxable total profits.

The lower and upper limits are reduced proportionally for accounting periods of less than 12 months; and where a company has one or more related 51% group companies by dividing the limits by one plus the number of those related 51% group companies (CTA 2010, Ch. 3A).

[4] Special rules apply to companies in liquidation and administration (CTA 2010, s. 628 and 630) and to open-ended investment companies and authorised unit trusts (CTA 2010, s. 614 and 618).

[5] For accounting periods beginning on or after 1 April 2013, qualifying companies may elect that relevant intellectual property profits of a trade are chargeable at a lower rate of corporation tax (CTA 2010, s. 357A) (see ¶7-050).

[6] From 1 April 2015, diverted profits tax is charged at a rate of 25% where multinational companies use artificial arrangements to divert profits overseas in order to avoid UK tax (FA 2015, Pt. 3).

[7] Recent and future changes:

- *Finance Act* 2016 reduces the restriction on the amount of banking companies' profits that can be offset by carried-forward losses to 25%, with effect for the purposes of determining the taxable profits of companies for accounting periods beginning on or after 1 April 2016 (with periods straddling 1 April 2016 treated as separate accounting periods before and after that date). The restriction was first introduced at 50% from 1 April 2015 (to ensure banks continued to contribute through corporation tax payments notwithstanding having large accumulated losses), subject to an exemption for losses incurred in the first five years of a bank's authorisation (CTA 2010, Pt. 7A).

- A restriction on corporation tax relief for the cost of 'goodwill' (the reputation and customer relationships associated with a business), with effect for all acquisitions and disposals on or after 8 July 2015 (CTA 2009, s. 816A). A restriction had already been introduced in respect of acquisitions of goodwill from a related individual or partnership, with effect for acquisitions on or after 3 December 2015 (CTA 2009, s. 849B–849D).

- Compensation expenses relating to banks' widespread misconduct and mis-selling have been made non-deductible for corporation tax purposes, with effect in relation to expenses incurred on or after 8 July 2015 (CTA 2009, s. 133A–133N).
- A special 45% rate of corporation tax on income is applied to restitution interest, with effect in relation to interest (whether arising before or on or after 21 October 2015) which falls within F(No. 2)A 2015, s. 38(11) (a determination by a court becoming final on or after 21 October 2015 or an agreement between HMRC and a company in final settlement of a claim for restitution made on or after 21 October 2015) (CTA 2009, Pt. 8C).
- New rules to limit the tax relief that companies can claim for their interest expenses with effect from 1 April 2017. These rules will limit deductions where a group has net interest expenses of more than £2m to 30% of the earnings before interest, tax, depreciation and amortisation (EBITDA) that is taxable in the UK. An optional group ratio rule, based on the net-interest to EBITDA ratio for the worldwide group, may permit a greater amount to be deducted in some cases. The legislation also provides for repeal of the existing debt cap legislation and its replacement by a modified debt cap which will ensure that the net UK interest deduction does not exceed the total net interest expense of the worldwide group. All groups will be able to deduct up to £2m of net interest expense per annum, so groups below this threshold will not need to apply the rules (Spring Budget 2017 (as previously announced); Finance Bill 2017).
- The ability for all companies to utilise carried forward losses arising on or after 1 April 2017 against profits from different types of income and other group companies, subject to a restriction on the use of carried forward losses so that they cannot reduce their profits arising on or after 1 April 2017 by more than 50%. This restriction will apply to a company or group's profits above £5m (banking companies remain subject to separate bank loss restriction). Profits and losses subject to the oil and gas ring-fence regime will be excluded from the loss reform (Spring Budget 2017 (as previously announced); Finance Bill 2017).

## [¶7-010]   Rates of corporation tax: financial years to 2014

(Tax Reporter: ¶704-000ff.)

| Financial year[1] | Main rate %[3] | Small profits rate %[2][3] | Limit for small profits rate (lower limit) £[2][4] | Limit for marginal relief (upper limit) £[2][4] | Standard fraction for marginal relief[2][3] | Special IP rate %[5] |
|---|---|---|---|---|---|---|
| 2014 | 21 | 20 | 300,000 | 1,500,000 | 1/400 | 10 |
| 2013 | 23 | 20 | 300,000 | 1,500,000 | 3/400 | 10 |
| 2012 | 24 | 20 | 300,000 | 1,500,000 | 1/100 | — |
| 2011 | 26 | 20 | 300,000 | 1,500,000 | 3/200 | — |

**Notes**

[1] A financial year begins on 1 April an ends on 31 March. The financial year 2014 began on 1 April 2014 and ended on 31 March 2015.

[2] The small profits rate for non-ring fence profits was abolished with effect for the financial year 2015 and subsequent financial years (FA 2014).

[3] 'Close investment holding companies' did not receive the benefit of the small profits rate or of marginal relief and so were taxable entirely at the main rate regardless of the level of their profits (former CTA 2010, s. 18).

For companies with ring fence profits, the rates were as above except that:

- the small profits rate of tax was 19% and the standard fraction was 11/400; and
- for financial years 2008 to 2014 the main rate is 30%.

Special rules applied to companies in liquidation and administration (CTA 2010, s. 628 and 630) and to open-ended investment companies and authorised unit trusts (CTA 2010, s. 614 and 618).

[4] The lower and upper limits for the small profits rate and marginal relief were reduced proportionally:

- for accounting periods of less than 12 months; and
- in the case of associated companies, by dividing the limits by the total number of associated companies (former CTA 2010, s. 24).

[5] For accounting periods beginning on or after 1 April 2013, qualifying companies could elect that relevant intellectual property profits of a trade be chargeable at a lower rate of corporation tax (CTA 2010, s. 357A) (see ¶7-050).

## [¶7-015] Marginal relief and effective marginal rates: up to financial year 2014

For marginal relief and marginal starting rate relief, there is an effective rate of tax in the margin, i.e. between the lower and upper limits given for each in the preceding table, which *exceeds* the main rate. These marginal rates are not prescribed by statute, but are derived from the appropriate corporation tax rates and fractions. The applicable rates are as follows.

| Financial year | Marginal rate % |
|---|---|
| 2014 | 21.25 |
| 2013 | 23.75 |
| 2012 | 25.00 |
| 2011 | 27.50 |

**Marginal relief**

(CTA 2010, s. 19)

(Tax Reporter: ¶704-200)

$$\text{Deduction} = (\text{Upper Limit} - \text{Augmented Profits}) \times \frac{\text{Taxable Total Profits}}{\text{Augmented Profits}} \times \text{Standard Fraction}$$

**'Augmented Profits'** (formerly 'Profits') means a company's taxable total profits *plus* franked investment income *excluding* franked investment income received from companies in the same group (CTA 2010, s. 32). Distributions are treated as coming from within the group if they are received from a company which is either a 51% subsidiary or a consortium company (the recipient being a member of the consortium).

**'Franked investment income'** means a distribution in respect of which the company is entitled to a tax credit (CTA 2010, s. 1126). This includes a distribution which is exempt for the purposes of CTA 2009, Pt. 9A (CTA 2010, s. 1109).

**'Taxable Total Profits'** (formerly 'Basic Profits') means profits as finally computed for corporation tax purposes (CTA 2010, s. 4(2)).

## [¶7-020] Charge on loan to participators

(CTA 2010, s. 455)

(Tax Reporter: ¶776-900ff.)

| Loans and benefits conferred | Rate |
|---|---|
| On or after 6 April 2016 | 32.5%[1] |
| Pre-5 April 2016 | 25.00% |

**Note**

[1] *Finance Act* 2016 set the rate as such percentage as corresponds to the dividend upper rate specified in ITA 2007, s. 8(2) for the tax year in which the loan or advance is made.

The charge itself is separate from other liabilities, being treated as if it were an amount of corporation tax chargeable on the company.

The charge is not applied to qualifying loans or advances made on or after 25 November 2015, by close companies to charity trustees for charitable purposes (CTA 2010, s. 456(2A)).

## [¶7-050]  Patent profits election
(CTA 2010, Pt. 8A)

(Tax Reporter: ¶705-000ff.)

The patent box enables companies to apply a lower rate of corporation tax to profits earned after 1 April 2013 from its patented inventions and certain other innovations. The lower rate of corporation tax to be applied is 10%. The relief is subject to a number of conditions.

A company must elect into the regime, the election must be in writing, and specify the first accounting period for which the election will apply. The election will apply for all subsequent accounting periods until the election is revoked by notice in writing.

Any revocation must be in writing, specifying the accounting period for which it is to take effect. Any new election will have no effect for any accounting period which begins less than five years after the last day of the accounting period following the period identified in the revocation notice.

In order to avoid complications where losses and other reliefs are claimed, the reduced 10% rate is applied by subtracting an additional trading deduction from corporation tax profits as calculated below.

**Additional deduction**

The amount of the deduction is:

$$RP \times FY\% \times (\frac{MR - IPR}{MR})$$

Where:

RP is the relevant IP (patent box) profits of the trade of the company;

FY% is the appropriate percentage for each financial year;

MR is the main rate of corporation tax; and

IPR is the special IP rate of corporation tax.

| Financial year | Appropriate percentage |
|---|---|
| 2013 | 60% |
| 2014 | 70% |
| 2015 | 80% |
| 2016 | 90% |
| 2017 and subsequent years | 100% |

## ¶7-100]  Additional relief for research and development
(CTA 2009, Pt. 13)

(Tax Reporter: ¶715-000ff.)

Additional relief is available for companies incurring expenditure on qualifying research and development (R&D). The relief is subject to a number of conditions. SMEs with losses can claim a payable tax credit.

| | Expenditure incurred on or after | | | | | |
|---|---|---|---|---|---|---|
| | 1 April 2016 | 1 April 2015 | 1 April 2014 | 1 April 2013 | 1 April 2012 | 1 April 2011 |
| Additional deduction where SME qualifies for main or pre-trading relief | 130% | 130% | 125% | 125% | 125% | 100% |
| Rate of payable tax credit (SME only) | 14.5% | 14.5% | 14.5% | 11% | 11% | 12.5% |
| Additional deduction where R&D subcontracted to SME | —[1] | 30% | 30% | 30% | 30% | 30% |
| Additional deduction where expenditure of SME is subsidised or capped | —[1] | 30% | 30% | 30% | 30% | 30% |
| Additional deduction for non-SME | —[1] | 30% | 30% | 30% | 30% | 30% |
| R&D expenditure credit[1] | 11% | 11% | 10% | 10% | — | — |

**Notes**

[1] The 'above the line credit' (ATL) scheme is mandatory from 1 April 2016. The credit is taxable but paid net of tax to companies with no corporation tax liability. Prior to 31 March 2016, the ATL scheme was optional, as an alternative to (but not in addition to) the former large company enhanced deduction scheme of R&D relief. The ATL scheme first became available with effect for expenditure incurred on or after 1 April 2013 and although not previously mandatory, once a company had opted to claim the ATL credit, it could not revert back to the enhanced deduction scheme. Companies that did not opt to claim the ATL credit prior to 1 April 2016 were able to continue claiming R&D relief under the former large company scheme.

[2] For the rates of relief applying before 1 August 2008, see Tax Reporter: ¶714-000ff.

**Limits applying for SMEs (expenditure incurred on or after 1 August 2008):**

A company must pass the headcount test and either the turnover test or the Balance Sheet total test.

| | |
|---|---|
| Staff headcount less than | 500 |
| Turnover not exceeding | €100m |
| Balance sheet total not exceeding | €86m |

## [¶7-125]   Creative industry tax reliefs

(CTA 2009, Pt. 15, 15A, 15B, 15C and 15D)

(Tax Reporter: ¶714-000ff.)

Creative industry tax reliefs are a group of four corporation tax reliefs that allow qualifying companies to claim a larger deduction, or in some circumstances, claim a payable tax credit when calculating their taxable profits. The reliefs work by increasing the amount of allowable expenditure, which may be surrendered in exchange for a payable tax credit if the company makes a loss.

Additional relief is available for companies incurring expenditure on (i) qualifying film production, (ii) animation and high-end television production (including children's television programmes), (iii) video games development, (iv) theatrical productions and (v) production of orchestral concerts.

The creative industry tax reliefs are all subject to a number of conditions (in particular, that the film, animation, high-end television programme or game must be certified as culturally British to qualify).

| | Financial year | | | |
|---|---|---|---|---|
| | From 2016–17 | 2015–16 | 2014–15 | 2013–14 (and earlier) |
| **Minimum expenditure** (% of core expenditure) | | | | |
| Film (UK expenditure) | 10% | 10% | 10% | 25% |
| Animation/television (UK expenditure) | 10% | 10% | 25% | 25% |
| Video games development/theatrical productions/orchestral concert production (EEA expenditure) | 25% | 25% | 25% | 25% |
| **Additional deduction** (% of qualifying core expenditure) | | | | |
| Film: limited budget[1] | 100% | 100% | 100% | 100% |
| Film: any other[1] | 100% | 100% | 80% | 80% |
| Animation/television/video games development/theatrical productions/ orchestral concert production[2] | 100% | 100% | 100% | 100% |
| Maximum qualifying core expenditure (% of total core expenditure) | 80% | 80% | 80% | 80% |
| **Tax credits** (% of surrendered loss) | | | | |
| Film: first £20m | 25% | 25% | 25% | — |
| Film: remainder[3] | 25% | 25% | 20% | — |
| Film: limited budget[1] | — | — | — | 25% |
| Film: any other | — | — | — | 20% |
| Animation/television/video games development/theatrical productions/ orchestral concert production[2] | 25% | 25% | 25% | 25% |

**Notes**

[1] Limited-budget films are those with a total core expenditure of £20m or less. Definition of limited budget film was omitted and the rate of enhancement increased to 100% for all films by FA 2015, s. 29, with effect from 1 April 2015 (SI 2015/1741).

[2] Film production relief has been available since 1 January 2007. Animation and television reliefs were introduced from 1 April 2013, video games development relief from 1 April 2014, theatrical productions relief from 1 September 2014 and orchestra tax relief from 1 April 2016.

[3] Rate of film tax relief increased to 25% for all qualifying expenditure by FA 2015, s. 29, with effect from 1 April 2015 (SI 2015/1741).

## [¶7-130]   Museum and galleries tax relief

(Finance Bill 2017)

Spring Budget 2017 confirmed, as announced at Budget 2016 and Autumn Statement 2016, that from 1 April 2017, a new corporation tax relief will be introduced for museums and galleries who develop new exhibitions including those that are toured.

| Expenditure incurred on or after 1 April 2017 and before 31 March 2022 | |
| --- | --- |
| **Additional deduction** | |
| Non-touring exhibitions | 20% |
| Touring exhibitions | 25% |
| **Payable tax credit** | |
| Non-touring exhibitions | up to £80,000 |
| Touring exhibitions | up to £100,000 |
| Maximum equivalent expenditure cap | £500,000 |

## [¶7-150]   Gifts to the nation

(FA 2012, Sch. 14)

(Tax Reporter: ¶716-685ff.)

For accounting periods beginning on or after 1 April 2012, a reduction in corporation tax is available where a company makes a gift of pre-eminent property to be held for the benefit of the public or the nation. The tax reduction is 20% of the value of the gift. A gift offer must be made and registered in accordance with the scheme and relief is available against the company's liability for the accounting period in which the gift offer is registered.

Pre-eminent property includes any picture, print, book, manuscript, work of art, scientific object or other thing that is pre-eminent for its national, scientific, historic or artistic interest, collections of such items and any object kept in a significant building where it is desirable that it remain associated with the building.

## [¶7-200]   Car hire

(CTA 2009, s. 56ff.)

(Tax Reporter: ¶707-860ff.)

Leased cars, where the lease begins from 1 April 2009, suffer a 15% disallowance of relevant payments if $CO_2$ emissions exceed the limits set out below, otherwise no disallowance. This applies to all cars (not just those costing more than £12,000).

| | $CO_2$ emissions |
| --- | --- |
| From 1 April 2013 | Over 130g/km |
| 1 April 2009 to 31 March 2013 | Over 160g/km |

For leased cars where the lease began before 1 April 2009, the restricted deduction for hire charges of motor cars with a retail price greater than £12,000 is calculated as follows:

$$\text{Allowable amount} = \frac{£12,000 + \tfrac{1}{2}\,(\text{retail price} - £12,000)}{\text{retail price}} \times \text{hire charge}$$

# [¶7-300]  Bank levy

(FA 2011, Sch. 19)

(Tax Reporter: ¶807-000)

The rates of charge are as follows:

| Period | Chargeable equity and long-term chargeable liabilities[1][2]<br>% | Short-term chargeable liabilities[1][2]<br>% |
|---|---|---|
| 1 Jan. 2017–31 Dec. 2017 | 0.085 | 0.17 |
| 1 Jan. 2016–31 Dec. 2016 | 0.09 | 0.18 |
| 1 Jan. 2015–31 Dec. 2015 | 0.105 | 0.21 |
| 1 Jan. 2014–31 Dec. 2014 | 0.078 | 0.156 |
| 1 Jan. 2013–31 Dec. 2013 | 0.065 | 0.130 |
| 1 Jan. 2012–31 Dec. 2012 | 0.044 | 0.088 |
| 1 May 2011–31 Dec. 2011 | 0.0375 | 0.075 |
| 1 Mar. 2011–30 Apr. 2011 | 0.05 | 0.10 |
| 1 Jan. 2011–28 Feb. 2011 | 0.025 | 0.05 |

**Notes**

[1] F(No. 2)A 2015, s. 16 and Sch. 2 set future long-term and short-term rates as follows:

| Period | Long-term rate | Short-term rate |
|---|---|---|
| 1 Jan. 2018–31 Dec. 2018 | 0.08% | 0.16% |
| 1 Jan. 2019–31 Dec. 2019 | 0.075% | 0.15% |
| 1 Jan. 2020–31 Dec. 2020 | 0.07% | 0.14% |
| Any time on or after 1 Jan. 2021 | 0.05% | 0.10% |

[2] Double tax relief is available against the UK bank levy for payments made to the Eurozone Single Resolution Fund. Affected banks may claim relief in relation to accounting periods ending on or after 1 January 2016 (SI 2016/1212).

[3] As announced at Summer Budget 2015, the bank levy charge will be restricted to UK balance sheet liabilities from 1 January 2021, subject to an exemption for certain UK liabilities relating to the funding of non-UK companies and an exemption for UK liabilities relating to the funding of non-UK branches (Autumn Statement 2016; Finance Bill 2017–18).

# [¶7-325]  Banking companies: surcharge

(CTA 2010, Pt. 7A, Ch. 4)

(Tax Reporter: ¶807-000)

| Accounting periods beginning on or after | Surcharge[1] |
|---|---|
| 1 January 2016 | 8% |

**Note**

[1] A surcharge of 8% is levied on the taxable profits of banking companies arising on or after 1 January 2016. Taxable profits will be calculated before the offset of losses that arise before the commencement date or from non-banking companies, and before the surrender of group relief from non-banking companies. An annual surcharge allowance of £25m will be available to groups and individual banking companies which will reduce the profits liable to the surcharge.

## [¶7-350]   Annual tax on enveloped dwellings (ATED)

(FA 2013, Pt. 3; SI 2014/854; SI 2016/1244)

(Tax Reporter: ¶807-800ff.)

From 1 April 2013, annual tax on enveloped dwellings (ATED) is a tax payable by companies and other corporate bodies (partnerships with corporate partners or other collective investment vehicle) that own UK residential property valued at over £2m.

The tax is charged for the chargeable period concerned. Chargeable periods are the period beginning 1 April 2013 and ending with 31 March 2014, and each subsequent 12-month period beginning with 1 April.

| Property value | | Annual charge[1] | | | | |
|---|---|---|---|---|---|---|
| More than £ | Less than £ | 2017–18 £ | 2016–17 £ | 2015–16 £ | 2014–15 £ | 2013–14 £ |
| 500,000 | 1,000,000 | 3,500 | 3,500 | 0 | 0 | 0 |
| 1,000,000 | 2,000,000 | 7,050 | 7,000 | 7,000 | 0 | 0 |
| 2,000,000 | 5,000,000 | 23,550 | 23,350 | 23,350 | 15,400 | 15,000 |
| 5,000,000 | 10,000,000 | 54,950 | 54,450 | 54,450 | 35,900 | 35,000 |
| 10,000,000 | 20,000,000 | 110,100 | 109,050 | 109,050 | 71,850 | 70,000 |
| 20,000,000 | | 220,350 | 218,200 | 218,200 | 143,750 | 140,000 |

**Note**
[1] The annual charge will be increased by consumer prices index inflation each year.

| Reliefs[1] | References |
|---|---|
| Property rental businesses | FA 2013, s. 133 (Tax Reporter: ¶807-922) |
| Rental property: preparation for sale, etc. | FA 2013, s. 134 |
| Dwellings opened to the public | FA 2013, s. 137 (Tax Reporter: ¶807-923) |
| Property developers | FA 2013, s. 138 |
| Property developers: exchange of dwellings | FA 2013, s. 139 |
| Property traders | FA 2013, s. 141 |
| Financial institutions acquiring dwellings in the course of lending | FA 2013, s. 143 |
| Occupation by certain employees or partners | FA 2013, s. 145 (Tax Reporter: ¶807-924) |
| Farmhouses | FA 2013, s. 148 (Tax Reporter: ¶807-925) |
| Providers of social housing | FA 2013, s. 150 |

Taxation of Companies

| Exemptions | References |
|---|---|
| Charitable companies | FA 2013, s. 151 (Tax Reporter: ¶807-927) |
| Public bodies | FA 2013, s. 153 (Tax Reporter: ¶807-928) |
| Bodies established for national purpose | FA 2013, s. 154 (Tax Reporter: ¶807-929) |
| Dwelling conditionally exempt from inheritance tax | FA 2013, s. 155 (Tax Reporter: ¶807-930) |

**Note**
[1] *Finance Act* 2016 extends the reliefs available from ATED (and the 15% higher rate of SDLT) to equity release schemes (home reversion plans) and properties occupied by employees from 1 April 2016 (FA 2013, s. 144A and 145).

# Administration

## 00]   Filing deadlines

(FA 1998, Sch. 18, para. 14)

(Tax Reporter: ¶181-075ff.)

The filing date for a return of profits (CT600) is generally the **later** of the dates outlined below:

● 12 months from the end of the return period;

● where the period of account is 18 months or less, 12 months from the end of the period of account;

● where the period of account is greater than 18 months, 30 months from the start of the period of account; and

● three months after the issue of a notice to deliver a corporation tax return.

**Notes**
Obligation to file a return is not automatic but is imposed by notice.
Every company which is chargeable to corporation tax in respect of any accounting period, and which has not made a return of its profits for that period, nor received a notice to make such a return, is under a duty to give notice to the inspector that it is so chargeable. The notice must be given not later than 12 months after the end of that accounting period.
A company must notify HMRC that its first accounting period has begun within three months of the accounting period beginning. This also applies to dormant companies which cease to be dormant.
An amended return under self-assessment may not be made later than 12 months after the filing date stipulated above.

Taxation of Companies

# [¶7-450]  Due and payable dates

(TMA 1970, s. 59D–59FA; ITA 2007, Pt. 15; SI 1998/3175)

(Tax Reporter: ¶183-410ff.; ¶117-000ff.)

| Liability | Due date |
|---|---|
| Corporation tax | Nine months and one day after end of an accounting period[1] |
| Corporation tax in instalments[2][4] | The 14th day of the 7th, 10th, 13th and 16th months after start of a 12-month accounting period |
| Income tax on interest, annual payments, etc. | 14 days after end of return period[3] |

**Notes**

[1] The *Taxes Management Act* 1970, s. 59G provides for companies to enter into voluntary payment plans with HMRC under which corporation tax liabilities can be paid in instalments spread equally before and after the due date. It should be noted that only corporation tax payable in accordance with TMA 1970, s. 59D (i.e. tax payable nine months and one day after the end of the accounting period) can be the subject of a managed payment plan. This excludes corporation tax payable by large companies in accordance with the quarterly instalment payment scheme. In addition, companies which have entered into a group payment arrangement can not enter into a managed payment plan.

[2] The *Taxes Management Act* 1970, s. 59E and SI 1998/3175 provide for the payment of corporation tax by 'large' companies (defined in accordance with the small profits marginal relief upper limit) in instalments.

Companies which are 'large' because of the number of associated companies or because of substantial dividend income will not have to pay by instalments if their corporation tax liabilities are less than £10,000. Companies which become 'large' in an accounting period, having previously had profits below the upper limit, may be exempt from instalment arrangements in certain circumstances. Groups containing 'large' companies are able to pay corporation tax on a group-wide basis.

For accounting periods ending after 30 June 2005, corporation tax and the supplementary charge payable by oil companies on ring fence profits are payable in three equal instalments. Corporation tax due on other profits (i.e. non-ring fence) continues to be payable in quarterly instalments as above.

The payment dates for the three instalments once the transitional period (see below) has passed are as follows:

(1) one-third payable six months and 13 days from the start of the accounting period (unless the date for instalment (3) is earlier);

(2) one-third payable three months from the first instalment due date (unless (3) is earlier); and

(3) the balance payable 14 days from the end of the accounting period (regardless of the length of the period).

Transitional arrangements apply for the first accounting period affected. These arrangements leave the first two quarterly instalments unchanged (at one-quarter each of the estimated liability for the period) but then require payment of the remainder of the estimated liability on ring fence profits for that accounting period to be paid on the new third instalment date.

[3] Return periods end on 31 March, 30 June, 30 September, 31 December and at the end of an accounting period.

The requirement for companies to deduct and account for income tax on certain payments is removed with effect for payments after 31 March 2001 of:

• interest, royalties, annuities and other annual payments made to companies within the charge to UK corporation tax on that income; and

• interest on quoted Eurobonds paid to non-residents.

[4] Summer Budget 2015 announced that the Government will introduce new payment dates for companies with annual taxable profits of £20m or more. Where a company is a member of a group, the £20m threshold will be divided by the number of companies in the group. Affected companies will be required to pay corporation tax in quarterly instalments in the third, sixth, ninth and twelfth months of their accounting period. The measure was due to apply to accounting periods starting on or after 1 April 2017, however, the commencement of rules has been deferred for two years, so will now have effect for accounting periods commencing on or after 1 April 2019 (Budget 2016).

## 00] Penalties

(Tax Reporter: ¶181-350ff.)

| Infringement penalised[9] | Maximum penalty | Provision |
|---|---|---|
| Failure to notify chargeability[1]<br>• deliberate and concealed act or failure<br>• deliberate but not concealed act or failure<br>• any other case | *Standard amount*<br><br>100% of potential lost revenue<br>70% of potential lost revenue<br><br>30% of potential lost revenue | FA 2008, Sch. 41, para. 1, 6 |
| Failure to make return[2]<br>• up to three months after filing date<br>• more than three months after filing date<br><br>• at least 18 months but less than 24 months after end of return period<br>• 24 months or more after end of return period | *Fixed rate penalty*[3]<br>£100 (persistent failure, £500)<br><br>£200 (persistent failure, £1,000)<br>*Tax-geared penalty*[4]<br>10% of tax unpaid at 18 months after end of return period<br>20% of tax unpaid at 18 months after end of return period | FA 1998, Sch. 18, para. 17(2), (3)<br><br><br>FA 1998, Sch. 18, para. 18 |
| Error in a return (careless or deliberate)<br>• standard amount<br>• where the inaccuracy is deliberate but not concealed<br>• where the inaccuracy is deliberate and concealed | <br>30% of potential lost revenue<br>70% of potential lost revenue<br><br>100% of potential lost revenue | FA 2007, Sch. 24, para. 4 |
| Failure to keep and preserve records (subject to specific exceptions) | Up to £3,000 | FA 1998, Sch. 18, para. 23 |
| Failure to produce document required in connection with an enquiry[5]<br>• standard amount<br>• continued failure | <br><br>£300<br>daily penalty of £60 | FA 2008, Sch. 36, para. 39 and 40 |

**Notes**

[1] *Finance Act* 2008, Sch. 41 applies with effect from 1 April 2010. Prior to that date, a penalty was provided for by FA 1998, Sch. 18, para. 2(3) and (4). The standard penalty imposed by FA 2008, Sch. 41 can be reduced where disclosure is made or where there are special circumstances.

[2] From a date yet to be announced, FA 2009 introduced a new flat-rate and tax-geared penalty regime for the late filing of corporation tax returns (FA 2009, Sch. 55).

[3] Fixed rate penalty does not apply if return filed by date allowed by registrar of companies.

[4] Tax geared penalty is charged in addition to fixed penalty. Where more than one tax-geared penalty is incurred the total penalty shall not exceed the largest individual penalty on that part.

[5] An additional tax-related penalty can be imposed under FA 2008, Sch. 36, para. 50.

Taxation of Companies

[6] Prior to 1 April 2010, a penalty was chargeable in accordance with TMA 1970, s. 98 where a company failed to notify HMRC of the start of an accounting period under the obligation at FA 2004, s. 55.

[7] From a date yet to be announced, FA 2009 introduced a new penalty regime for late payment of corporation tax (FA 2009, Sch. 56).

[8] For financial years beginning on or after 21 July 2009, the senior accounting officer of a qualifying company is obliged to ensure that the company establishes and maintains appropriate tax accounting arrangements, and to provide a certificate to HMRC indicating whether or not this was the case for each financial year (FA 2009, Sch. 46; see Tax Reporter: ¶191-660ff.). Qualifying companies are obliged to provide details of their senior accounting officer to HMRC. Failure to comply with these requirements will make the senior accounting officer and/or the company liable to a penalty.

[9] Autumn Statement 2015 announced that the Government will introduce a new criminal offence for corporates which fail to prevent their agents from criminally facilitating tax evasion by an individual or entity.

## [¶7-550] Interest on overdue tax

(Tax Reporter: ¶183-430ff.)

| Interest on | Interest runs from | Provision in TMA 1970 |
|---|---|---|
| Overdue corporation tax | Date tax due and payable (nine months and one day after end of accounting period)[1] | s. 87A |
| Corporation tax payable in instalments | Date instalment is due to be paid | s. 87A[2] |
| Overdue income tax deducted from certain payments | 14 days after end of return period | s. 87 |
| Overdue tax due on loans to participators | Date tax due and payable | s. 109 |

**Notes**

[1] Where one group company is liable to interest and another group company with the same accounting period is due a repayment of corporation tax an election may be made for the overpayment to be surrendered so as to reduce the interest liability of the first company which will be treated as having paid tax at the same time as the surrendering company (CTA 2010, s. 963).

[2] As modified by SI 1998/3175, reg. 7.

[3] *Finance (No. 3) Act* 2010 contains provisions to apply the harmonised interest regime introduced by FA 2009 to corporation tax and PRT. The provisions will be brought into force by Treasury Order.

## [¶7-650] Interest on tax repayments

(ICTA 1988, s. 826; SI 1998/3175, reg. 8)

(Tax Reporter: ¶183-430ff.)

Repayment interest on corporation tax runs from later of:

(1) due and payable date (nine months after end of accounting period); and

(2) date of actual payment except for:

  (a) overpayments of instalments of corporation tax, when interest runs from the first instalment date on which the excess amount would have been due and payable or, if later, the date on which that excess arises; and

(b)  for companies outside the instalments regime, if tax was paid earlier than the normal due date, then interest on repayments in advance of agreement of liability runs from the first instalment date on which the excess amount would have been due and payable had the instalments regime applied or, the date on which the amount repayable was originally paid, whichever is later.

Interest on repayments of income tax deducted at source from income will run from the day after the end of the accounting period in which the income was received for accounting periods under self-assessment.

*Finance (No. 3) Act* 2010 contains provisions to apply the harmonised interest regime introduced by *Finance Act* 2009 to corporation tax and PRT. The provisions will be brought into force by Treasury Order.

# [¶7-700]  Rates of interest

With effect for interest periods commencing on 6 February 1997, the rates of interest for the purposes of corporation tax are different from those for other taxes. The rate of interest on corporation tax will depend on the accounting period for which the tax is due and, under self-assessment, the nature of the tax due or repayable.

## Self-assessment

For accounting periods within the self-assessment regime (CTSA), i.e. APs on or after 1 July 1999, the rates of interest are distinct from those for pre-CTSA periods, because the interest is taxable and tax deductible (see below).

In addition, there are separate provisions for:

● overpaid instalments of corporation tax; and

● payments of corporation tax made after the normal due date.

## Pre-self-assessment

For accounting periods before the start of self-assessment, there are two rates of interest applicable depending on whether the accounting period is within the Pay and File regime (APs ending after 30 September 1993) or not (i.e. periods ending before 1 October 1993).

## CTSA

### 1.  CT (other than instalments and CT not due by instalments)

| From | Late payment % | Repayment % |
|------|----------------|-------------|
| 23 August 2016 | 2.75 | 0.5 |
| 29 September 2009 to 22 August 2016 | 3.00 | 0.50 |

### 2.  Instalments and CT not due by instalments

| From | Late payment % | Repayment % |
|------|----------------|-------------|
| 15 August 2016 | 1.25 | 0.5 |
| 21 September 2009 to 14 August 2016 | 1.50 | 0.50 |

**Pre-CTSA**

| From | Late payment | | Repayment | |
|---|---|---|---|---|
| | Pre Pay and File % | Pay and File % | Pre Pay and File % | Pay and File % |
| 23 August 2016 | 2.75 | 2.75 | 0.5 | 0.5 |
| 29 September 2009 to 22 August 2016 | 3.00 | 3.00 | 0.50 | 0.50 |

# [¶7-900]   Time limits for elections and claims

(Tax Reporter: ¶191-835)

In the absence of any provision to the contrary (some of which are considered below), the normal rule is that a claim must be made within four years of the end of the accounting period to which it relates (six years prior to 1 April 2010) (FA 1998, Sch. 18, para. 55).

In certain cases, HMRC *may* permit an extension of the strict time limit in relation to certain elections and claims.

| Provision | Time limit | References |
|---|---|---|
| Stock transferred to a connected party on cessation of trade to be valued at higher cost or sale price | Two years from end of accounting period in which trade ceased | CTA 2009, s. 167(4) |
| Carry-forward of trading losses | Relief is given automatically | CTA 2010, s. 45 |
| Set-off of trading losses against profits of the same, or an earlier, accounting period[1] | Two years from end of accounting period in which loss incurred | CTA 2010, s. 37(7) |
| Group relief | Claims to group relief must be made (or withdrawn) by the later of:<br>(1) 12 months after the claimant company's filing date for the return for the accounting period covered by the claim;<br>(2) 30 days after a closure notice is issued on the completion of an enquiry[2];<br>(3) 30 days after HMRC issue a notice of amendment to a return following the completion of an enquiry (issued where the company fails to amend the return itself); or<br>(4) 30 days after the determination of any appeal against an HMRC amendment (as in (3) above). | FA 1998, Sch. 18, para. 74 |
| Set-off of loss on disposal of shares in unquoted trading company against income of investment company | Two years from end of accounting period | CTA 2010, s. 70(4) |
| Surrender of company tax refund within group | Before refund made to surrendering company | CTA 2010, s. 963(3) |

| Provision | Time limit | References |
|---|---|---|
| Election to reallocate a chargeable gain or an allowable loss within a group[3] | Two years from end of transferring company's accounting period during which the gain or loss accrues | TCGA 1992, s. 171A |
| Relief for a non-trading deficit on loan relationships (including any non-trading exchange losses)<br>– set off against profits of deficit or earlier periods<br>– carry forward to later periods | <br><br><br>– two years from end of period in which deficit arises<br>– two years from end of the accounting period following the deficit period, or such further period as an officer of HMRC allows | CTA 2009, s. 458(2) and 460(1) |
| Appropriation of asset to trading stock: election to adjust trading profit by the amount of the gain or loss on the deemed disposal at market value | Two years from the end of the accounting period in which the asset is appropriated as trading stock | TCGA 1992, s. 161(3) |
| Terminal loss relief on cessation of trade | Two years from end of the loss making accounting period | CTA 2010, s. 39 |
| Intangible fixed assets: election to write down cost for tax purposes at fixed rate | Two years from end of accounting period in which company creates or acquires the asset | CTA 2009, s. 730 |
| Election by recipient that company distribution should not be exempt | Second anniversary of end of accounting period in which distribution received | CTA 2009, s. 931R |
| Claims included in a company tax return, including research and development tax relief claim, land remediation tax credits and life assurance company tax credits, and film tax credits | One year from filing date for return or a later date if an officer of HMRC allows it | FA 1998, Sch. 18, para. 83E, 83K, 83W |
| Election for special treatment of profits from patents, etc. (patent box) | Two years from end of first accounting period to which it relates | CTA 2010, s. 357G |

**Notes**
[1] The carry-back period is extended to three years for accounting periods ending in the period 23 November 2008 to 24 November 2010 (FA 2009, s. 23, Sch. 6).
[2] 'Enquiry' in the above does not include a restricted enquiry into an amendment to a return (restricted because the time limit for making an enquiry into the return itself has expired), where the amendment consists of a group relief claim or withdrawal of claim.
These time limits have priority over any other general time limits for amending returns and are subject to HMRC permitting an extension to the time limits.
[3] Following the enactment of FA 2009, it is now possible for chargeable gains and allowable losses to be transferred within a group. For gains and losses made before 21 July 2009, this result could only be achieved by electing for the notional transfer of an asset before its disposal to a third party (TCGA 1992, s. 171A prior to the changes made by FA 2009, s. 31, Sch. 12). The election had to be made jointly on or before the second anniversary of the end of the actual vendor group company's accounting period in which it made the disposal.

# CAPITAL ALLOWANCES

## [¶8-000]    Plant and machinery: overview of allowances
(CAA 2001)

(Tax Reporter: ¶235-000ff.)

Plant and machinery allowances are normally given by way of:

*   annual investment allowances: see ¶8-100;
*   first-year allowances: see ¶8-200; or
*   writing-down allowances: see ¶8-300.

In specified circumstances, balancing allowances may be due or balancing charges may be made.

## [¶8-100]    Plant and machinery: annual investment allowances
(CAA 2001, s. 51A)

(Tax Reporter: ¶236-400ff.)

|                                          | Maximum (£)   |
| ---------------------------------------- | ------------- |
| 1 January 2016                           | 200,000       |
| 1/6 April 2014 to 31 December 2015       | 500,000[1]    |
| 1 January 2013 to 31 March/5 April 2014  | 250,000[1]    |
| 1/6 April 2012 to 31 December 2012       | 25,000        |
| 1/6 April 2010 to 31 March/5 April 2012  | 100,000       |

**Note**
[1] Temporary increase in the annual invesment allowance initially for the period of two years beginning with 1 January 2013 (FA 2013, s. 7 and Sch. 1) was extended to 31 December 2015 (and increased to £500,000) by FA 2014, s. 10 and Sch. 2.

This figure is adjusted pro rata for chargeable periods shorter or longer than one year.

Where a chargeable period spans the above dates of change (i.e. 1/6 April 2014, or 1 January 2016), the maximum AIA is calculated by splitting the chargeable period into separate periods falling before and after each of the dates of change. Transitional rules are then applied to determine the maximum AIA available in respect of the total chargeable period and the maximum AIA that may be allocated against qualifying expenditure incurred in each of the separate periods (FA 2014, Sch. 2; FA 2013, Sch. 1; FA 2011, s. 11).

Groups of companies, companies and qualifying activities carried on by individuals or partnerships, under common control which share premises and carry on similar activities are entitled to a single annual investment allowance only.

# [?0] Plant and machinery: 100% first-year allowances

(A 2001, s. 52)

(Tax Reporter: ¶237-000ff.)

Subject to the general exclusions listed at ¶8-210, full 100% allowances are available for the following types of expenditure incurred by a business of any size. If full FYAs are not claimed, WDA is normally available on a reducing balance basis (see ¶8-300).

| Nature of expenditure | Authority (CAA 2001) | Notes |
|---|---|---|
| Energy-saving plant or machinery | s. 45A–45C | Loss-making companies may claim tax rebate[1][2] (CAA 2001, Sch. A1). |
| Cars with low $CO_2$ emissions | s. 45D | On expenditure incurred until 31 March 2018 (as extended from 31 March 2015 and to be further extended to April 2021 (Budget 2016)). See also ¶8-500. |
| Zero-emission goods vehicles | s. 45DA | On expenditure incurred before 1 April 2018 (corporation tax) or 6 April 2018 (income tax) (as extended from 31 March/5 April 2015). |
| Plant or machinery for certain refuelling stations | s. 45E | Expenditure incurred until 31 March 2018 (for both corporation tax and income tax) (as extended from 31 March 2015). |
| Plant or machinery (other than a long life asset) for use by a company wholly in a ring fence trade | s. 45F | |
| Environmentally beneficial plant or machinery | s. 45H–45J | Loss-making companies may claim tax rebate[2] |
| Expenditure on plant and machinery for use in designated assisted areas | s. 45K | Initially due to end on 31 March 2017 but extended to 31 March 2020. |

**Notes**

[1] FYAs are not available on expenditure incurred on or after 1 April 2012 (corporation tax) or 6 April 2012 (income tax) on plant or machinery to generate renewable electricity or heat where tariff payments are received under the Feed-in Tariff or Renewable Heat Incentive schemes. In the case of expenditure incurred on a combined heat and power system, this restriction applies from 1 April 2014 (corporation tax) or 6 April 2014 (income tax). FYAs granted in respect of expenditure incurred from April 2012 (or April 2014 for CHP installations) will be withdrawn if FIT or RHI tariffs are paid subsequently (CAA 2001, s. 45AA).

[2] First-year tax credits, for companies surrendering losses attributable to their expenditure on designated energy-saving or environmentally beneficial plant or machinery has been extended for a further five years until 31 March 2018 (SI 2013/464).

## [¶8-210]    Plant and machinery: first-year allowances – general exclusions

(CAA 2001, s. 46(2))

(Tax Reporter: ¶237-150)

No first-year allowances are available for:

*   expenditure incurred in the final chargeable period;
*   cars (other than those with very low $CO_2$ emissions);
*   [certain ships and railway assets (pre-1 April 2013)][1];
*   items excluded from the long-life asset treatment only by virtue of the transitional provisions in CAA 2001, Sch. 3, para. 20;
*   plant or machinery for leasing;
*   in certain anti-avoidance cases where the obtaining of a FYA is linked to a change in the nature or conduct of a trade;
*   where an asset was initially acquired for purposes other than those of the qualifying activity;
*   where an asset was acquired by way of a gift; and
*   where plant or machinery that was provided for long funding leasing starts to be used for other purposes.

**Note**
[1] Exclusion from first-year allowances for expenditure incurred on either ships or railway assets omitted with effect for qualifying expenditure incurred on or after 1 April 2013.

## [¶8-300]    Plant and machinery: writing-down allowances

(CAA 2001, s. 56)

(Tax Reporter: ¶238-050ff.)

|                        | Standard rate (%) | Special rate (%) |
| ---------------------- | ----------------- | ---------------- |
| From April 2012        | 18                | 8                |
| April 2008 to April 2012 | 20              | 10               |

**Note**
Different rules apply for certain cars (see ¶8-500).

### WDA for small pools

Main pool or special rate pool only where tax written down value brought forward plus expenditure added to the pool during the period minus disposal receipts deducted from the pool during the period totals less than or equal to £1,000 (apportioned for periods of more or less than one year), an allowance may be claimed for the former amount in place of the standard rates above (CAA 2001, s. 56A).

### Pooling

Expenditure is allocated to the main pool unless it is allocated to either a single asset pool or single class pool. Single asset and single class pools are as follows:

Capital Allowances

Single asset pools
- short life asset (CAA 2001, s. 86);
- ship (CAA 2001, s. 127);
- assets with partial non-qualifying use (CAA 2001, s. 206);
- expenditure in relation to which a partial depreciation subsidy is received (CAA 2001, s. 211); and
- contribution allowances: plant and machinery (CAA 2001, s. 538).

Single class pools
- special rate expenditure (see below) (CAA 2001, s. 104A); and
- overseas leasing (CAA 2001, s. 107).

**Special rate expenditure**

| Expenditure | Incurred on or after | Provision |
|---|---|---|
| Thermal insulation of buildings | 1 April 2008 (corporation tax) or 6 April 2008 (income tax) | CAA 2001, s. 28 |
| Integral features | 1 April 2008 (corporation tax) or 6 April 2008 (income tax) | CAA 2001, s. 33A |
| Long life asset expenditure | 26 November 1996, or 1 January 2001 in pursuance of a contract entered into before 26 November 1996 or incurred before 26 November 1996 but allocated to a pool in a chargeable period beginning on or after that date | CAA 2001, Ch. 10 |
| Cars (excluding main rate cars (first registered before 1 March 2001, cars with low $CO_2$ emissions, electrically-propelled cars)) | 1 April 2009 (corporation tax) or 6 April 2009 (income tax) | CAA 2001, s. 104AA |
| Provision of cushion gas | 1 April 2010 | CAA 2001, s. 70J(7) |
| Solar panels | 1 April 2012 (corporation tax) or 6 April 2012 (income tax) | CAA 2001, s. 104A(1)(g) |

# [¶8-400]  Plant and machinery: integral features

(CAA 2001, s. 33A)

(Tax Reporter: ¶243-400ff.)

The following assets are designated as integral features:
- electrical systems (including lighting systems);
- cold water systems;
- space or water heating systems, powered systems of ventilation, air cooling or air purification, and any floor or ceiling comprised in such systems;
- lifts, escalators and moving walkways; and
- external solar shading.

## [¶8-410]  Plant and machinery: expenditure unaffected by statutory restrictions re buildings

(CAA 2001, s. 23)

(Tax Reporter: ¶245-550)

The restrictions in CAA 2001, s. 21 and 22 (buildings, structures and other assets) do not apply to the following categories of expenditure:

*   thermal insulation of buildings (CAA 2001, s. 28);
*   personal security (CAA 2001, s. 33);
*   integral features (CAA 2001, s. 33A); and
*   software and rights to software (CAA 2001, s. 71).

**Note**

Before 1 April 2013, expenditure on safety at designated sports grounds, safety at regulated stands at sports grounds and safety at other sports grounds was also included in the list of exclusions.

The restrictions in CAA 2001, s. 21 and 22 (buildings, structures and other assets) also do not apply to expenditure in List C at CAA 2001, s. 23. List C, as amended, is as follows:

(1)   machinery (including devices for providing motive power) not within any other item in this list;

(2)   gas and sewerage systems provided mainly:

    (a)   to meet the particular requirements of the qualifying activity;

    (b)   to serve particular plant or machinery used for the purposes of the qualifying activity;

(3)   [omitted by *Finance Act* 2008];

(4)   manufacturing or processing equipment; storage equipment (including cold rooms); display equipment; and counters, checkouts and similar equipment;

(5)   cookers, washing machines, dishwashers, refrigerators and similar equipment; washbasins, sinks, baths, showers, sanitary ware and similar equipment; and furniture and furnishings;

(6)   hoists;

(7)   sound insulation provided mainly to meet the particular requirements of the qualifying activity;

(8)   computer, telecommunication and surveillance systems (including their wiring or other links);

(9)   refrigeration or cooling equipment;

(10)  fire alarm systems, sprinkler and other equipment for extinguishing or containing fires;

(11)  burglar alarm systems;

(12)  strong rooms in bank or building society premises, safes;

(13)  partition walls, where moveable and intended to be moved in the course of the qualifying activity;

(14)  decorative assets provided for the enjoyment of the public in hotel, restaurant or similar trades;

(15)  advertising hoardings, signs, displays and similar assets;

Capital Allowances

(16)    swimming-pools (including diving boards, slides and structures on which such boards or slides are mounted);

(17)    any glasshouse constructed so that the required environment (namely, air, heat, light, irrigation and temperature) for the growing of plants is provided automatically by means of devices forming an integral part of its structure;

(18)    cold stores;

(19)    caravans provided mainly for holiday lettings;

(20)    buildings provided for testing aircraft engines run within the buildings;

(21)    moveable buildings intended to be moved in the course of the qualifying activity;

(22)    the alteration of land for the purpose only of installing plant or machinery;

(23)    the provision of dry docks;

(24)    the provision of any jetty or similar structure provided mainly to carry plant or machinery;

(25)    the provision of pipelines or underground ducts or tunnels with a primary purpose of carrying utility conduits;

(26)    the provision of towers to support floodlights;

(27)    the provision of:

   (a)    any reservoir incorporated into a water treatment works; or

   (b)    any service reservoir of treated water for supply within any housing estate or other particular locality;

(28)    the provision of:

   (a)    silos provided for temporary storage; or

   (b)    storage tanks;

(29)    the provision of slurry pits or silage clamps;

(30)    the provision of fish tanks or fish ponds;

(31)    the provision of rails, sleepers and ballast for a railway or tramway;

(32)    the provision of structures and other assets for providing the setting for any ride at an amusement park or exhibition;

(33)    the provision of fixed zoo cages.

Items (1)–(16) of the above list do not, however, include any asset with the principal purpose of insulating or enclosing the interior of a building or of providing an interior wall, floor or ceiling that is intended to remain permanently in place (CAA 2001, s. 33A).

## [¶8-420]    Assets treated as buildings

(CAA 2001, s. 21)

(Tax Reporter: ¶245-550)

Plant and machinery allowances are not available on expenditure on the provision of a building, including its construction or acquisition. Building includes:

- an asset incorporated in the building;
- although not incorporated in the building (whether because the asset is moveable or for any other reason), is in the building and is of a kind normally incorporated in a building; or
- is in, or connected with the building and is in list A as follows:
    - walls, floors, ceilings, doors, gates, shutters, windows and stairs;
    - mains services, and systems, for water, electricity and gas;
    - waste disposal systems;
    - sewerage and drainage systems;
    - shafts or other structures in which lifts, hoists, escalators and moving walkways are installed;
    - fire safety systems.

## [¶8-430] Excluded structures and other assets

(CAA 2001, s. 22)

Plant and machinery does not include expenditure on the provision of a structure or other asset within list B, or any works involving the alteration of land. List B is as follows:

(1) a tunnel, bridge, viaduct, aqueduct, embankment or cutting;

(2) a way, hard standing (such as a pavement), road, railway, tramway, a park for vehicles or containers, or an airstrip or runway;

(3) an inland navigation, including a canal or basin or a navigable river;

(4) a dam, reservoir or barrage, including any sluices, gates, generators and other equipment associated with the dam, reservoir or barrage;

(5) a dock, harbour, wharf, pier, marina or jetty or any other structure in or at which vessels may be kept, or merchandise or passengers may be shipped or unshipped;

(6) a dike, sea wall, weir or drainage ditch;

(7) any structure not within items (1)–(6) other than:

(a) a structure (but not a building) within the meaning of 'industrial building';

(b) a structure in use for the purposes of an undertaking for the extraction, production, processing or distribution of gas; and

(c) a structure in use for the purposes of a trade which consists in the provision of telecommunication, television or radio services.

**Note**
Structure means a fixed structure of any kind, other than a building (as defined by s. 21(3) (see ¶8-420 above)).
Land does not include buildings or other structures.

## [¶8-450] Fixtures

(CAA 2001, s. 187A)

From April 2012, purchasers of buildings which include fixtures on which capital allowances have previously been claimed will only be able to claim capital allowances on the fixtures if either:

(1)    the fixed value requirement is met whereby the value of the fixtures transferred is agreed within two years of the transfer either:

   •    between the seller and purchaser by joint election under CAA 2001, s. 198–199; or

   •    by determination of the First-tier Tribunal; or

(2)    the purchaser obtains a written statement from the seller that the fixed value requirement has not been met and is no longer capable of being met and the purchaser obtains from a past owner a written statement of the disposal value brought into account by that owner (this will apply in cases where the seller is an intermediate owner or lessee not entitled to claim allowances but who acquired the fixtures from a past owner who was entitled to claim allowances).

From April 2014, it will also be necessary to show that historic expenditure has been pooled, or that the past owner claimed a first year allowance on the expenditure (or any part of it) before a subsequent transfer to another person.

# [¶8-500]   Plant and machinery: allowances for cars

2001, s. 104A and 104AA)

eporter: ¶238-500ff.)

| | CO$_2$ emissions | | | |
|---|---|---|---|---|
| | **2018–19 to 2020–21**[1] | **2015–16 to 2017–18** | **2013–14 & 2014–15** | **2012–13 (from 2009–10)** |
| 100% FYAs (CAA 2001, s. 45D) (see also ¶8-200) | 50g/km or less | 75g/km or less | 95g/km or less | 110g/km or less |
| Main rate pool (18%) | Over 50g/km up to 110g/km | Over 75g/km up to 130g/km | Over 95g/km up to 130g/km | Over 110g/km up to 160g/km |
| Special rate pool (8%) | Over 110g/km | Over 130g/km | Over 130g/km | Over 160g/km |

**Note**
[1] Rates announced at Budget 2016.

Cars with private use go to a single asset pool but still with WDA as above, but then adjusted for private use percentage.

### Cars acquired before April 2009

(Former CAA 2001, s. 74ff.)

(Tax Reporter: ¶238-880)

Under rules which applied until April 2009, cars costing more than £12,000 were allocated to a single asset pool and had the annual WDA capped at £3,000. The £3,000 restriction continued for cars owned at April 2009 until the car was disposed of or if it was still owned on the first day of the first chargeable period beginning on or after 1 April 2014 (corporation tax) or 6 April 2014 (income tax) ('the third relevant date'), then any unrelieved old expenditure was carried forward to the main plant and machinery pool at that time (whatever the level of vehicle emissions).

## [¶8-550]   Enterprise zones: 100% capital allowances
(CAA 2001, s. 45K–45N)

(Tax Reporter: ¶237-610)

First year allowances (at 100%) are available in respect of expenditure incurred by companies (not unincorporated businesses) on new and unsued plant and machinery for use primarily in designated assisted areas in enterprise zones. The allowances are available for expenditure incurred during the period of eight years beginning with the date on which the area is (or is treated as) designated by Treasury Order[1]. Expenditure must be incurred for the purposes of a new or expanding business carried on by the company, must not be replacement expenditure and is limited to €125m per single investment project (as defined) (CAA 2001, s. 45K–45N). A full list of current zones and designated assisted areas is available at:

*   http://enterprisezones.communities.gov.uk (see also maps at www.gov.uk/government/publications/enterprise-zones);
*   http://business.wales.gov.uk/enterprisezones/enhanced-capital-allowances;
*   www.scotland.gov.uk/Topics/Economy/EconomicStrategy/Enterprise-Areas/Incentives/Capital-Allowances.

**Note**
[1] The period of availability was originally introduced as five years beginnning with 1 April 2012 (FA 2012, s. 44 and Sch. 11, para. 3), extended to eight years from the same date by FA 2014, s. 64(5)(a) and has been further extended to eight years from the date of designation by FA 2016, s. 69.

## [¶8-650]   Enterprise zones: industrial buildings, hotels, commercial buildings or structures
(Former CAA 2001, s. 271ff.; FA 2008, Sch. 27, para. 31)

(Tax Reporter: ¶250-950ff.)

No IBAs are given for any chargeable period beginning after 1 or 6 April 2011. For enterprise zone expenditure only, a balancing charge can still be incurred up to 5 April 2018.

Initial allowances (at 100%) or writing-down allowances (at 25%) were formerly available for certain buildings in enterprise zones (industrial buildings; hotels and commercial buildings or structures).

Enterprise zones can be valid for up to a maximum of 20 years in total. Those that still fall within that 20-year period are as follows:

| Statutory Instrument | Area | Start date |
|---|---|---|
| 1996/106 | Tyne Riverside (North Tyneside) | 19 February 1996 |
| 1996/1981 | Tyne Riverside (Silverlink North Scheme) | 26 August 1996 |
| 1996/1981 | Tyne Riverside (Silverlink Business Park Scheme) | 26 August 1996 |
| 1996/1981 | Tyne Riverside (Middle Engine Lane Scheme) | 26 August 1996 |
| 1996/1981 | Tyne Riverside (New York Industrial Park Scheme) | 26 August 1996 |
| 1996/1981 | Tyne Riverside (Balliol Business Park West Scheme) | 26 August 1996 |
| 1996/2435 | Tyne Riverside (Baltic Enterprise Park Scheme) | 21 October 1996 |
| 1996/2435 | Tyne Riverside (Viking Industrial Park – Wagonway West Scheme) | 21 October 1996 |
| 1996/2435 | Tyne Riverside (Viking Industrial Park – Blackett Street Scheme) | 21 October 1996 |
| 1996/2435 | Tyne Riverside (Viking Industrial Park – Western Road Scheme) | 21 October 1996 |

# [¶8-800]   Other allowances

| Allowance | Date expenditure incurred (from) | Initial allowance (%) | WDA (%) | CAA 2001 | Tax Reporter |
|---|---|---|---|---|---|
| Business premises renovation[3] | 11 April 2007 (to 31 March or 5 April 2017) | 100 | 25 | s. 360A | ¶252-500 |
| [Flat conversion[1]] | [11 May 2001 (to 31 March or 5 April 2013)] | [100] | [25] | [former s. 393A] | ¶254-000 |
| Mineral extraction[4] | 1 April 1986 | — | 25 | s. 394 | ¶255-500 |
| Research and development | 6 November 1962 | 100 | — | s. 437 | ¶256-000 |
| Know-how[2] | 1 April 1986 | — | 25 | s. 452 | ¶257-000 |
| Patents[2] | 1 April 1986 | — | 25 | s. 464 | ¶257-500 |
| Dredging | 6 November 1962 | — | 4 | s. 484 | ¶258-000 |
| Assured tenancy | 10 March 1982 (to 31 March 1992) | — | 4 | s. 490 | ¶258-500 |

**Notes**
[1] Flat conversion allowances are abolished in respect of expenditure incurred on or after 1 April 2013 for corporation tax purposes and 6 April 2013 for income tax purposes (FA 2012, s. 227 and Sch. 39, para. 36 and 37). The entitlement to claim writing-down allowances on any residual expenditure is also withdrawn from that date.
[2] Capital allowances for know-how and patents still apply for income tax but were replaced for most corporation tax purposes by the intangible assets regime with effect from 1 April 2002.
[3] With effect from 1/6 April 2014, FA 2014 amended CAA 2001, Pt. 3A to: specify qualifying expenditure for BPRA; prevent claims where another form of state aid has or will be received on the same investment project; introduce a time limit for works to be completed after expenditure has been incurred (and relief claimed) of 36 months (otherwise relief is withdrawn and the expenditure is treated as incurred when the works are provided); and reduce the period in which balancing adjustments must be made if certain events occur from seven years to five years.
[4] With effect in relation to claims made on or after 1 April 2014 (corporation tax) or 6 April 2014 (income tax), the treatment of MEAs is aligned with the existing principles for plant and machinery allowances and a mineral extraction trade for the purposes of MEAs must consist of activity within the charge to UK tax. *Finance Act* 2014 also amends the legislation to confirm that activity of an exempt foreign permanent establishment (FPE) is treated as a separate mineral extraction trade for the purposes of MEAs and to confirm that notional allowances will be given automatically in calculating the profits or losses of the exempt FPE as if the exempt FPE were within the charge to UK tax (with effect in relation to elections under CTA 2009, s. 18A which start to have effect on or after 1 April 2014). With effect from 17 July 2014, expenditure incurred on seeking planning permission qualifies as expenditure on mineral exploration and access, whether the planning permission is successful or not. Previously, where planning permission was granted, the expenditure was treated as acquiring a mineral asset and eligible for relief at the lower rate of 10%.

# [¶8-950]   Time limits for elections and claims
(CAA 2001, s. 3; TMA 1970, s. 43; FA 1998, Sch. 18, para. 54–60)

(Tax Reporter: ¶235-050)

Capital allowances must be claimed in a tax return. However, the rules for claims outside a return for income tax (TMA 1970, s. 42) and corporation tax (FA 1998, Sch. 18, para. 54–60) apply in certain instances:

- special leasing plant and machinery allowance claims; and
- claims for patent allowances on non-trading expenditure (in income tax cases).

| Provision | Time limit | Statutory reference |
|---|---|---|
| General claim to capital allowances under corporation tax self-assessment | Claims to capital allowances must be made (or amended or withdrawn) by the later of:<br><br>(1) 12 months after the claimant company's filing date for the return for the accounting period covered by the claim;<br><br>(2) 30 days after a closure notice is issued on the completion of an enquiry;<br><br>(3) 30 days after HMRC issue a notice of amendment to a return following the completion of an enquiry (issued where the company fails to amend the return itself); or<br><br>(4) 30 days after the determination of any appeal against an HMRC amendment (as in (3) above).<br><br>'Enquiry' in the above does not include a restricted enquiry into an amendment to a return (restricted because the time limit for making an enquiry into the return itself has expired), where the amendment consists of making, amending or withdrawing a claim for capital allowances. These time limits have priority over any other general time limits for amending returns to the extent that an amendment makes, amends or withdraws a claim for capital allowances. A claim for capital allowances may be made, amended or withdrawn at a later time if an officer of HMRC allows it. | FA 1998, Sch. 18, para. 82 |
| Certain plant and machinery treated as 'short life' assets (income tax elections) | 12 months from 31 January next following the tax year in which ends the chargeable period in which the qualifying expenditure was incurred | CAA 2001, s. 85 |

Capital Allowances

| Provision | Time limit | Statutory reference |
|---|---|---|
| Certain plant and machinery treated as 'short life' assets (corporation tax elections) | Two years from end of the chargeable period in which the qualifying expenditure was incurred | CAA 2001, s. 85 |
| Set-off of capital allowances on special leasing (corporation tax) | Two years from end of accounting period | CAA 2001, s. 260(3), (6) |
| Business successions: election between connected parties to transfer plant and machinery at tax written down value | Two years from date on which succession takes effect | CAA 2001, s. 266(4) |
| Transfer between connected parties of certain assets treated as being at market value; election for sale to be treated as being for an alternative amount value | Two years from date of sale | CAA 2001, s. 570(5) |
| Purchase of interest in land that includes a fixture – election to fix apportionment of disposal proceeds | Two years from the date of purchase | CAA 2001, s. 198, 201 |
| Lease of interest in land that includes a fixture – election to fix apportionment of disposal proceeds | Two years from the date the lease is granted | CAA 2001, s. 199, 201 |

# NATIONAL INSURANCE CONTRIBUTIONS

## [¶9-000]   NIC rates: general

(NIC Reporter: ¶305-000ff.)

There are six classes of National Insurance contributions (NICs) payable according to the individual circumstances of the payer.

### Class 1 contributions

Class 1 contributions are earnings-related and payable by employer and employee on earnings above the earnings thresholds. The primary threshold (PT) applies for employees and the secondary threshold (ST) for employers. Employees pay at the main rate up to the upper earnings limit (UEL) and the additional rate above the limit.

Where the employee is a member of the employer's contracted-out pension scheme, a contracted-out rebate reduces the contributions due from both on any earnings between the lower earnings limit (LEL) and the upper accruals point (UAP). Earnings between the LEL and the PT/ST attract the rebate despite there being no contributions due at that level.

The *Pensions Act* 2014 abolishes the contracting-out for salary-related occupational pensions schemes (from 6 April 2016) and introduces a new single-component state pension to replace the existing state pension comprising basic state pension and additional state pension (from 6 April 2016).

Contracting out for money purchase schemes (COMPS), mixed benefit schemes (COMB) contracted-out on a defined contribution basis, appropriate personal pension schemes (APP) and APP stakeholder schemes was abolished on 5 April 2012.

The reduced rate applies to married women or widows with a valid certificate of election and affects only primary contributions.

Individuals over state pension age pay no primary contributions, though employers still pay the secondary contribution regardless of the previous category of contribution liability. Children under 16 and their employers pay no contributions.

### Employer NIC for the under 21s and apprentices under 25

(SSCBA 1992, s. 9A and 9B)

From 6 April 2015, employers with employees under the age of 21 are no longer required to pay Class 1 secondary NICs on earnings up to the upper earning limit (UEL), for those employees.

From 6 April 2016, employers of apprentices under the age of 25 are no longer required to pay secondary Class 1 (employer) NICs on earnings up to the UEL, for those employees.

National Insurance Contributions

## [¶9-005] National Insurance rate ceilings

(NIC(RC)A 2015)

(NIC Reporter: ¶305-600)

The *National Insurance Contributions (Rate Ceilings) Act* 2015 sets a ceiling on the main and additional primary percentages, the secondary percentage and the upper earnings limit in relation to Class 1 NICs. The Act came into force on 17 December 2015, with effect for a tax years beginning after that date but before the date of the first Parliamentary general election after that day (i.e. from 2016–17 until the tax year starting before the next general election thereafter). The Act prescribes the following limits:

| Contribution/limit | Ceiling |
|---|---|
| Class 1 main primary percentage | 12% |
| Class 1 additional primary percentage | 2% |
| Class 1 secondary percentage | 13.8% |
| Upper earnings limit | $\dfrac{\text{HRT}^{(1)}}{52}$ |

**Note**

(1) HRT is the proposed higher rate threshold for the tax year calculated as the sum of the basic rate limit for income tax for the tax year as proposed in the pre-budget proposals for that year, and the personal allowance for income tax for the tax year as so proposed.

## [¶9-010] Class 1 NIC: 2017–18

(SSCBA 1992; NICA 2014, s. 1, 8–9; SI 2001/1004, reg. 10–11 and 131)

Reporter: ¶305-575ff.)

### Class 1 contributions

| Class 1 primary (employee) contributions 2017–18 | |
|---|---|
| Lower earnings limit (LEL)[4] | £113 weekly<br>£490[2] monthly<br>£5,876[2] yearly |
| Primary threshold (PT)[4][5] | £157 weekly<br>£680[3] monthly<br>£8,164[3] yearly |
| Upper earnings limit (UEL) | £866 weekly<br>£3,750[3] monthly<br>£45,000[3] yearly |
| Rate on earnings up to PT[1] | 0% |
| Rate | 12% on £157.01 to £866 weekly<br>2% on excess over £866 weekly |
| Reduced rate | 5.85% on £157.01 to £866 weekly<br>2% on excess over £866 |

**Notes**

(1) No National Insurance contributions (NICs) are actually payable but a notional Class 1 NIC is deemed to have been paid in respect of earnings between the LEL and PT to protect contributory benefit entitlement.

(2) Monthly and annual LEL and UAP figures are calculated as per SI 2001/1004, reg. 11.

(3) Monthly and annual PT and UEL figures are prescribed by SI 2001/1004, reg. 11 and amended by Statutory Instrument. Rates for 2017–18 figures have yet to be specified and the amounts shown are calculated amounts (by reference to prior year equivalents) and may be subject to change.
(4) These thresholds are uprated by CPI.
(5) Primary threshold aligned with secondary (employer) threshold from April 2017 (Autumn Statement 2016; Spring Budget 2017).

| Class 1 secondary (employer) contributions 2017–18 | |
| --- | --- |
| Secondary earnings threshold (ST)[4][6] | £157 weekly<br>£680[1] monthly<br>£8,164[1] yearly |
| Upper secondary threshold (UST) for under 21s[2] | £866 weekly<br>£3,750[1] monthly<br>£45,000[1] yearly |
| Apprentice upper secondary threshold (AUST) for under 25s[3] | £866 weekly<br>£3,750[1] monthly<br>£45,000[1] yearly |
| Rate | 13.8% on earnings above ST/UST[2]/AUST[3] |
| Employment allowance[5] | £3,000 per year, per employer |

**Notes**
(1) Monthly and annual ST, UST and AUST figures are prescribed by SI 2001/1004, reg. 11 and amended by Statutory Instrument. Rates for 2017–18 figures have yet to be specified and the amounts shown are calculated amounts (by reference to prior year equivalents) and may be subject to change.
(2) Upper secondary threshold (UST) introduced from April 2015 for employees under the age of 21. The rate of secondary NICs for employees under the age of 21 on earnings between the ST and UST is 0%.
(3) Apprentice upper secondary threshold (AUST) introduced from April 2016. The rate of secondary NICs for employees under the age of 25 on earnings between the ST and AUST is 0%.
(4) The weekly secondary threshold is uprated by CPI.
(5) From 6 April 2016, companies where the director is the sole employee are longer be able to claim the allowance (NICA 2014, s. 2(4A)).
(6) Secondary threshold aligned with primary (employee) threshold from April 2017 (Autumn Statement 2016).

## [¶9-015]   Class 1 NIC: 2016–17
(SSCBA 1992, NICA 2014, s. 1, 8–9; SI 2001/1004, reg. 10–11 and 131)
(NIC Reporter: ¶305-575ff.)

### Class 1 contributions

| Class 1 primary (employee) contributions 2016–17 | |
| --- | --- |
| Lower earnings limit (LEL)[4] | £112 weekly<br>£486[2] monthly<br>£5,824[2] yearly |
| Primary threshold (PT)[4] | £155 weekly<br>£672[3] monthly<br>£8,060[3] yearly |
| Upper earnings limit (UEL) | £827 weekly<br>£3,583[3] monthly<br>£43,000[3] yearly |

National Insurance Contributions

| Class 1 primary (employee) contributions 2016–17 | |
|---|---|
| Rate on earnings up to PT[1] | 0% |
| Rate | 12% on £155.01 to £827 weekly<br>2% on excess over £827 weekly |
| Reduced rate | 5.85% on £155.01 to £827 weekly<br>2% on excess over £827 weekly |

**Notes**
[1] No National Insurance contributions (NICs) are actually payable but a notional Class 1 NIC is deemed to have been paid in respect of earnings between the LEL and PT to protect contributory benefit entitlement.
[2] Monthly and annual LEL and UAP figures are calculated as per SI 2001/1004, reg. 11.
[3] Monthly and annual PT and UEL figures are prescribed by SI 2001/1004, reg. 11 and amended by Statutory Instrument.
[4] These thresholds are uprated by CPI.

| Class 1 secondary (employer) contributions 2016–17 | |
|---|---|
| Secondary earnings threshold (ST)[4] | £156 weekly<br>£676[1] monthly<br>£8,112[1] yearly |
| Upper secondary threshold (UST) for under 21s[2] | £827 weekly<br>£3,583[1] monthly<br>£43,000[1] yearly |
| Apprentice upper secondary threshold (AUST) for under 25s[3] | £827 weekly<br>£3,583[1] monthly<br>£43,000[1] yearly |
| Rate | 13.8% on earnings above ST/UST[2]/AUST[3] |
| Employment allowance[5] | £3,000 per year, per employer |

**Notes**
[1] Monthly and annual ST, UST and AUST figures are prescribed by SI 2001/1004, reg. 11 and amended by Statutory Instrument.
[2] Upper secondary threshold (UST) introduced from April 2015 for employees under the age of 21. The rate of secondary NICs for employees under the age of 21 on earnings between the ST and UST is 0%.
[3] Apprentice upper secondary threshold (AUST) introduced from April 2016. The rate of secondary NICs for apprentices under the age of 25 on earnings between the ST and AUST is 0%.
[4] The weekly secondary threshold is uprated by CPI.
[5] From 6 April 2016, companies where the director is the sole employee are no longer be able to claim the allowance (NICA 2014, s. 2(4A)).

# [¶9-020]   Class 1 NIC: 2015–16

(NIC Reporter: ¶305-575ff.)

## Class 1 contributions

| Class 1 primary (employee) contributions 2015–16 | |
|---|---|
| Lower earnings limit (LEL)[4] | £112 weekly<br>£486[2] monthly<br>£5,824[2] yearly |
| Primary threshold (PT)[4] | £155 weekly<br>£672[3] monthly<br>£8,060[3] yearly |

| Class 1 primary (employee) contributions 2015–16 | |
|---|---|
| Upper earnings limit (UEL) | £815 weekly<br>£3,532[3] monthly<br>£42,385[3] yearly |
| Upper accruals point (UAP) | £770 weekly<br>£3,337[2] monthly<br>£40,040[2] yearly |
| Rate on earnings up to PT[1] | 0% |
| Not contracted-out rate | 12% on £155.01 to £815 weekly<br>2% on excess over £815 weekly |
| Contracted-out rate | 10.6% on £155.01 to £770 weekly<br>12% on £770.01 to £815 weekly<br>2% on excess over £815 weekly |
| Reduced rate | 5.85% on £155.01 to £815 weekly<br>2% on excess over £815 (no rebate even if contracted out) |

**Notes**

[1] Earnings from the LEL, up to and including the PT, count towards the employee's basic state pension, even though no contributions are paid on those earnings. Similarly, earnings between the LEL and the PT count towards the employee's entitlement to certain benefits including the second state pension (S2P). Employees in contracted-out employment earn no S2P rights and receive a rebate of contributions of 1.4%. This applies from the LEL to the UAP, so earnings from LEL to PT attract a 'negative' contribution of 1.4% and the rate for earnings from PT to UAP becomes 10.6%. Earnings from UAP to UEL are subject to the main not contracted-out rate.
[2] Monthly and annual LEL and UAP figures are calculated as per SI 2001/1004, reg. 11.
[3] Monthly and annual PT and UEL figures are prescribed by SI 2001/1004, reg. 11 and amended by Statutory Instrument.
[4] These thresholds are uprated by CPI.

| Class 1 secondary (employer) contributions 2015–16 | |
|---|---|
| Secondary earnings threshold (ST)[4] | £156 weekly<br>£676[2] monthly<br>£8,112[2] yearly |
| Upper secondary threshold (UST) for under 21s[3] | £815 weekly<br>£3,532 monthly<br>£42,385 yearly |
| Not contracted-out rate | 13.8% on earnings above ST |
| Contracted-out rate[1] | 10.4% for salary related (COSR) on earnings from ST to UAP (plus 3.4% rebate for earnings from LEL to ST), then 13.8% above UAP |
| Employment allowance[5] | £2,000 per year, per employer |

**Notes**

[1] Although employer contributions do not per se give any benefit entitlements, earnings between the LEL and ST are those classed as relevant for S2P. Employers with contracted-out occupational pension schemes receive a rebate of contributions for scheme members of 3.4% (COSR). This applies from the LEL to the UAP, so earnings from LEL to ST attract a 'negative' contribution and the rate for earnings from ST to UAP is reduced as shown.
[2] Monthly and annual ST figures are prescribed by SI 2001/1004, reg. 11 and amended by Statutory Instrument.
[3] Upper secondary threshold (UST) introduced from April 2015 for employees under the age of 21. The rate of secondary NICs for employees under the age of 21 on earnings between the ST and UST will be 0%.
[4] The weekly secondary threshold is uprated by RPI.
[5] From 6 April 2015, the allowance is extended to care and support workers (NICA 2014, s. 2(3A)).

National Insurance Contributions

# [¶9-025]   Class 1 NIC: 2014–15

(NIC Reporter: ¶305-575ff.)

## Class 1 contributions

| Class 1 primary (employee) contributions 2014–15 | |
|---|---|
| Lower earnings limit (LEL) | £111 weekly<br>£481[2] monthly<br>£5,772[2] yearly |
| Primary threshold (PT) | £153 weekly<br>£663[3] monthly<br>£7,956[3] yearly |
| Upper earnings limit (UEL) | £805 weekly<br>£3,489[3] monthly<br>£41,865[3] yearly |
| Upper accruals point (UAP) | £770 weekly<br>£3,337[2] monthly<br>£40,040[2] yearly |
| Rate on earnings up to PT[1] | 0% |
| Not contracted-out rate | 12% on £153.01 to £805 weekly<br>2% on excess over £805 weekly |
| Contracted-out rate | 10.6% on £153.01 to £770 weekly<br>12% on £770.01 to £805 weekly<br>2% on excess over £805 weekly |
| Reduced rate | 5.85% on £153.01 to £805 weekly<br>2% on excess over £805 (no rebate even if contracted-out) |

**Notes**

[1] Earnings from the LEL, up to and including the PT, count towards the employee's basic state pension, even though no contributions are paid on those earnings. Similarly, earnings between the LEL and the PT count towards the employee's entitlement to certain benefits including the second state pension (S2P). Employees in contracted-out employment earn no S2P rights and receive a rebate of contributions of 1.4%. This applies from the LEL to the UAP, so earnings from LEL to PT attract a 'negative' contribution of 1.4% and the rate for earnings from PT to UAP becomes 10.6%. Earnings from UAP to UEL are subject to the main not contracted-out rate.

[2] Monthly and annual LEL and UAP figures are calculated as per SI 2001/1004, reg. 11.

[3] Monthly and annual PT and UEL figures are prescribed by SI 2001/1004, reg. 11 and amended by Statutory Instrument.

| Class 1 secondary (employer) contributions 2014–15 | |
|---|---|
| Secondary earnings threshold (ST) | £153 weekly<br>£663[2] monthly<br>£7,956[2] yearly |
| Not contracted-out rate | 13.8% on earnings above ST |

| Class 1 secondary (employer) contributions 2014–15 | |
|---|---|
| Contracted-out rate[1] | 10.4% for salary related (COSR) on earnings from ST to UAP (plus 3.4% rebate for earnings from LEL to ST), then 13.8% above UAP |
| Employment allowance | £2,000 (per year, per employer) |

**Notes**

[1] Although employer contributions do not per se give any benefit entitlements, earnings between the LEL and ST are those classed as relevant for S2P. Employers with contracted-out occupational pension schemes receive a rebate of contributions for scheme members of 3.4% (COSR). This applies from the LEL to the UAP, so earnings from LEL to ST attract a 'negative' contribution and the rate for earnings from ST to UAP is reduced as shown.

[2] Monthly and annual ST figures are prescribed by SI 2001/1004, reg. 11 and amended by Statutory Instrument.

# [¶9-030]   Class 1 NIC: 2013–14

(NIC Reporter: ¶305-575ff.)

## Class 1 contributions

| Class 1 primary (employee) contributions 2013–14 | |
|---|---|
| Lower earnings limit (LEL) | £109 weekly<br>£473[2] monthly<br>£5,668[2] yearly |
| Primary threshold (PT) | £149 weekly<br>£646 monthly<br>£7,755 yearly |
| Upper earnings limit (UEL) | £797 weekly<br>£3,454 monthly<br>£41,450 yearly |
| Upper accruals point (UAP) | £770 weekly<br>£3,337[2] monthly<br>£40,040[2] yearly |
| Rate on earnings up to PT[1] | 0% |
| Not contracted-out rate | 12% on £149.01 to £797 weekly<br>2% on excess over £797 weekly |
| Contracted-out rate | 10.6% on £149.01 to £770 weekly<br>12% on £770.01 to £797 weekly<br>2% on excess over £797 weekly |
| Reduced rate | 5.85% on £149.01 to £797 weekly<br>2% on excess over £797 (no rebate even if contracted-out) |

**Notes**

[1] Earnings from the LEL, up to and including the PT, count towards the employee's basic state pension, even though no contributions are paid on those earnings. Similarly, earnings between the LEL and the PT count towards the employee's entitlement to certain benefits including the second state pension (S2P). Employees in contracted-out employment earn no S2P rights and receive a rebate of contributions of 1.4%. This applies from the LEL to the UAP, so earnings from LEL to PT attract a 'negative' contribution of 1.4% and the rate for earnings from PT to UAP becomes 10.6%. Earnings from UAP to UEL are subject to the main not contracted-out rate.

[2] Monthly and annual LEL and UAP figures are calculated as per SI 2001/1004, reg. 11.

National Insurance Contributions

| Class 1 secondary (employer) contributions 2013–14[2] | |
|---|---|
| Secondary earnings threshold (ST) | £148 weekly<br>£641 monthly<br>£7,696 yearly |
| Not contracted-out rate | 13.8% on earnings above ST |
| Contracted-out rate[1] | 10.4% for salary related (COSR) on earnings from ST to UAP (plus 3.4% rebate for earnings from LEL to ST), then 13.8% above UAP |

**Notes**
[1] Although employer contributions do not per se give any benefit entitlements, earnings between the LEL and ST are those classed as relevant for S2P. Employers with contracted-out occupational pension schemes receive a rebate of contributions for scheme members of 3.4% (COSR). This applies from the LEL to the UAP, so earnings from LEL to ST attract a 'negative' contribution and the rate for earnings from ST to UAP is reduced as shown.
[2] From 22 June 2010 until 5 September 2013, qualifying businesses will be exempt (when a claim is made and accepted) from the first £5,000 of Class 1 NICs due in respect of the first ten qualifying employees hired in the first year of business (*National Insurance Contributions Act* 2011, s. 4).

## [¶9-035]    Class 1 NIC: 2012–13

(NIC Reporter: ¶305-575ff.)

### Class 1 contributions

| Class 1 primary (employee) contributions 2012–13 | |
|---|---|
| Lower earnings limit (LEL)[1] | £107 weekly<br>£464[2] monthly<br>£5,564[2] yearly |
| Primary threshold (PT) | £146 weekly<br>£634 monthly<br>£7,605 yearly |
| Upper earnings limit (UEL) | £817 weekly<br>£3,540 monthly<br>£42,475 yearly |
| Upper accrual point (UAP) | £770 weekly<br>£3,337[2] monthly<br>£40,040[2] yearly |
| Rate on earnings up to PT[1] | 0% |
| Not contracted-out rate | 12% on £146.01 to £817 weekly<br>2% on excess over £817 weekly |
| Contracted-out rate | 10.6% on £146.01 to £770 weekly<br>12% on £770.01 to £817 weekly<br>2% on excess over £817 weekly |
| Reduced rate | 5.85% on £146.01 to £817 weekly<br>2% on excess over £817 (no rebate even if contracted-out) |

**Notes**

(1) Earnings from the LEL, up to and including the PT, count towards the employee's basic state pension, even though no contributions are paid on those earnings. Similarly, earnings between the LEL and the PT count towards the employee's entitlement to certain benefits including the second state pension (S2P). Employees in contracted-out employment earn no S2P rights and receive a rebate of contributions of 1.4%. This applies from the LEL to the UAP, so earnings from LEL to PT attract a 'negative' contribution of 1.4% and the rate for earnings from PT to UAP becomes 10.6%. Earnings from UAP to UEL are subject to the main not contracted-out rate.

(2) Monthly and annual LEL and UAP figures are calculated as per SI 2001/1004, reg. 11.

| Class 1 secondary (employer) contributions 2012–13[2] | |
| --- | --- |
| Secondary earnings threshold (ST) | £144 weekly<br>£624 monthly<br>£7,488 yearly |
| Not contracted-out rate | 13.8% on earnings above the ST |
| Contracted-out rate[1] | 10.4% for salary-related (COSR) on earnings from ST to UAP (plus 3.4% rebate for earnings from LEL to ST), then 13.8% above UAP |

**Notes**

(1) Although employer contributions do not per se give any benefit entitlements, earnings between the LEL and ST are those classed as relevant for S2P. Employers with contracted-out occupational pension schemes receive a rebate of contributions for scheme members of 3.4% (COSR). This applies from the LEL to the UAP, so earnings from LEL to ST attract a 'negative' contribution and the rate for earnings from ST to UAP is reduced as shown.

(2) From 22 June 2010 until 5 September 2013, qualifying businesses will be exempt (when a claim is made and accepted) from the first £5,000 of Class 1 NICs due in respect of the first ten qualifying employees hired in the first year of business (*National Insurance Contributions Act* 2011, s. 4).

## [¶9-350]   Class 1A contributions

(SSCBA 1992, s. 10)

(NIC Reporter: ¶310-000ff.)

From 2016–17, employers (but not employees) pay NIC on an annual basis on benefits in kind provided to all employees (other than lower paid ministers of religion). Prior to 5 April 2016 (since 6 April 2000), NICs were payable only on benefits provided to employees earning at a rate of £8,500 p.a. or more or to directors (SSCBA 1992, s. 10). Contributions for the year are due by 19 July following the end of the tax year to which they relate (22 July for electronic payment). Rates applying are always the full Class 1 secondary (employer) rate for each year, as follows:

| Period | % |
| --- | --- |
| 2011–12 to 2017–18 | 13.8 |

For rates of interest on late paid Class 1A contributions, see ¶9-650.

National Insurance Contributions

## [¶9-400]  Return deadlines for Class 1 and 1A contributions

(NIC Reporter: ¶310-425; ¶340-000ff.)

| Forms | Date | Penalty provision |
|---|---|---|
| **Real time employers (RTI)** (see ¶4-930) | Each time a payment is made to an employee | FA 2009, Sch. 55 (see also ¶4-942) (previously TMA 1970, s. 98A) |
| **Non-real time employers** End of year returns P14, P35, P38 and P38A | 19 May following year of assessment | TMA 1970, s. 98A |
| **All employers** P11D(b) | 6 July following year of assessment | SI 2001/1004, reg. 81(2) |

**Note**
In cases of PAYE and NIC default, there are provisions to prevent double charging. Class 1A contributions are recorded annually in arrears.

## [¶9-450]  Class 1B contributions

(SSCBA 1992, s. 10A)

(NIC Reporter: ¶311-400ff.)

Class 1B contributions are payable by employers on the amount of earnings in a PAYE settlement agreement (PSA) that are chargeable to Class 1 or Class 1A NICs, together with the total amount of income tax payable under the agreement (SSCBA 1992, s. 10A). Class 1B contributions are charged at the same rate as Class 1A contributions (see above) and are payable by 19 October after the end of the tax year to which the PSA applies (22 October for electronic payment).

## [¶9-500]  Class 2 contributions

(SSCBA 1992, s. 11)

(NIC Reporter: ¶315-000ff.)

Class 2 contributions are paid at a flat rate by a self-employed person. From 2015–16, the contributions are collected through self-assessment alongside income tax and Class 4 contributions and only those with profits at or above the small profits threshold (SPT) are liable to Class 2 NICs. Prior to 2015–16, a person had to pay Class 2 NICs unless he had applied for and been granted exception because his earnings were below the small earnings exception (SEE) limit. Persons with profits below the small profits threshold (or who were previously granted exception for earnings below the SEE limit) can (could) still pay voluntary contributions in order to protect entitlement to contributory benefits.

Spring Budget 2017 reconfirmed that, as previously announced, Class 2 NICs will be abolished from April 2018 and following abolition, self-employed contributory benefit entitlement will be accessed through Class 3 and Class 4 NICs.

## Rates and small profits threshold

| Tax year | Weekly contribution rate[1] | | | Small profits threshold[2] £ |
| | Rate £ | Share fishermen £ | Volunteer development workers £ | |
|---|---|---|---|---|
| 2017–18 | 2.85 | 3.50 | 5.65 | 6,025 |
| 2016–17 | 2.80 | 3.45 | 5.60 | 5,965 |
| 2015–16 | 2.80 | 3.45 | 5.60 | 5,965 |
| 2014–15 | 2.75 | 3.40 | 5.55 | 5,885 |
| 2013–14 | 2.70 | 3.35 | 5.45 | 5,725 |
| 2012–13 | 2.65 | 3.30 | 5.35 | 5,595 |
| 2011–12 | 2.50 | 3.15 | 5.10 | 5,315 |

**Notes**

[1] These rates are uprated by CPI.

[2] The 'small profits threshold' replaced the 'small earnings exception' from 6 April 2015. This threshold is uprated by CPI.

## [¶9-550]   Class 3 contributions

(SSCBA 1992, s. 13)

(NIC Reporter: ¶320-000ff.)

Class 3 contributions are paid voluntarily by persons not liable for contributions, or who have been excepted from Class 2 contributions, or whose contribution record is insufficient to qualify for benefits (i.e. Class 3 contributions allow people to fill gaps in their contributions record for basic state pension purposes). They are paid at a flat-rate. Class 3 contributions may not be paid where an individuals earnings factor (earnings on which primary Class 1 or Class 2 contributions have been paid) equals or exceeds the qualifying limit for the year.

Autumn Statement 2016 announced that following the abolition of Class 2 NICs (from April 2018), self-employed contributory benefit entitlement will be accessed through Class 3 and Class 4 NICs.

### Rate and earnings factor

| Tax year | Weekly contribution rate[1] £ | Earnings factor for each contribution in col. 2 £ |
|---|---|---|
| 2017–18 | 14.25 | 113.00 |
| 2016–17 | 14.10 | 112.00 |
| 2015–16 | 14.10 | 112.00 |
| 2014–15 | 13.90 | 111.00 |
| 2013–14 | 13.55 | 109.00 |
| 2012–13 | 13.25 | 107.00 |
| 2011–12 | 12.60 | 102.00 |

**Note**

[1] Rate is uprated by CPI.

National Insurance Contributions

## [¶9-570] Class 3A contributions

(SSCBA 1992, s. 14A–14C; PA 2014, Sch. 15, para. 4; SI 2014/3240)

(NIC Reporter: ¶321-500)

From 12 October 2015 until 5 April 2017, existing pensioners and those reaching state pension age before 6 April 2016 have the opportunity to gain additional state pension by paying Class 3A voluntary NICs. There are two conditions:

• contributors must have entitlement to a UK state pension; and

• contributors must reach state pension age before 6 April 2016.

The measure is in addition to Class 3 voluntary contributions (see above).

The amount of a Class 3A contribution needed to obtain a unit of additional pension is determined by reference to the age of the person who is paying the contribution per the table below. Where a person had not reached state pension age on the date of payment but would do so before 6 April 2016, the amount of contribution needed to obtain a unit of additional pension is the amount that would be needed if the person had reached pensionable age.

The maximum number of units of additional pension that a person can obtain is 25 and each unit is equivalent to £1 per week of additional pension (i.e. a maximum of £25 per week of additional pension can be acquired).

A cooling-off period of 90 days applies for the contributor to apply for a repayment, beginning with the date of payment.

| Age at payment date (12 October 2015 to 5 April 2017) | Rate for each additional pension unit of £1 per week £ | Age at payment date (12 October 2015 to 5 April 2017) | Rate for each additional pension unit of £1 per week £ |
|---|---|---|---|
| 62 (women only) | 956 | 82 | 484 |
| 63 (women only) | 934 | 83 | 454 |
| 64 (women only) | 913 | 84 | 424 |
| 65 | 890 | 85 | 394 |
| 66 | 871 | 86 | 366 |
| 67 | 847 | 87 | 339 |
| 68 | 827 | 88 | 314 |
| 69 | 801 | 89 | 291 |
| 70 | 779 | 90 | 270 |
| 71 | 761 | 91 | 251 |
| 72 | 738 | 92 | 232 |
| 73 | 719 | 93 | 216 |
| 74 | 694 | 94 | 200 |
| 75 | 674 | 95 | 185 |
| 76 | 646 | 96 | 172 |
| 77 | 625 | 97 | 159 |
| 78 | 596 | 98 | 148 |
| 79 | 574 | 99 | 137 |
| 80 | 544 | 100 | 127 |
| 81 | 514 | | |

## [¶9-600]   Class 4 contributions

(SSCBA 1992, s. 15)

(NIC Reporter: ¶317-650ff.)

Self-employed people whose profits or gains are over a certain amount have to pay Class 4 contributions as well as Class 2 contributions. These contributions are earnings-related and paid at a main rate on trading profits (earnings) between the lower and upper annual limits (which are the same as the Class 1 earnings threshold and upper earnings limit), with an additional 2% on profits above the upper limit since 6 April 2011.

Autumn Statement 2016 announced that following the abolition of Class 2 NICs (from April 2018), self-employed contributory benefit entitlement will be accessed through Class 3 and Class 4 NICs.

| Tax year | Rate on profits between upper and lower limits[2] % | Annual lower profits limit[1] £ | Annual upper profits limit £ | Rate on profits in excess of upper limit % | Maximum contribution £ |
|---|---|---|---|---|---|
| 2017–18 | 9 | 8,164 | 45,000 | 2 | unlimited |
| 2016–17 | 9 | 8,060 | 43,000 | 2 | unlimited |
| 2015–16 | 9 | 8,060 | 42,385 | 2 | unlimited |
| 2014–15 | 9 | 7,956 | 41,865 | 2 | unlimited |
| 2013–14 | 9 | 7,755 | 41,450 | 2 | unlimited |
| 2012–13 | 9 | 7,605 | 42,475 | 2 | unlimited |
| 2011–12 | 9 | 7,225 | 42,475 | 2 | unlimited |

**Notes**
[1] This threshold is uprated by CPI.
[2] Spring Budget 2017 announced that the main rate of Class 4 NICs would be increased from 9% to 10% in April 2018, and to 11% in April 2019. However, on 15 March 2017, in a Statement to the House, the Chancellor announced that the proposed increases will not go ahead and there will be no increases in NICs rates in this Parliament.

## [¶9-650]   Rates of interest on National Insurance contributions

(NIC Reporter: ¶341-875ff.)

(SSCBA 1992, Sch. 1, para. 6(2))

The same rates of interest apply in relation to overdue and overpaid National Insurance as apply in relation to overdue and overpaid income tax (see ¶1-500).

From 15 September 2016, late payment interest rates and the special repayment rate for debts owed to or by HMRC under a court judgment or order are extended to National Insurance related debts (F(No.2)A 2015, s. 52) (see ¶1-500).

Interest on **overdue** National Insurance contributions is payable from the due date of payment:

- **Class 1:** from 2014–15, see ¶4-948: interest on certain PAYE paid late (previously 19 April, or 22 April (electronic payments) following end of the tax year in respect of which the NIC was due (SI 2001/1004, Sch. 4, para. 17(3))).
- **Class 1A:** 19 July, or 22 July (where payment is made electronically) following the end of the tax year in respect of which the NIC was due to the date of payment (SI 2004/1004, reg. 76(3)).

- **Class 1B:** 19 October, or 22 October (where payment is made electronically) following the end of the tax year in respect of which the NIC was due to the date of payment (SI 2004/1004, Sch. 4, para. 17(3)).

The qualifying period for repayment interest on **overpaid** National Insurance contributions is as set out below:

- **Class 1:** from 2014–15, see ¶4-948: interest on certain PAYE paid late (previously from 19 April following the end of the tax year in respect of which the NIC was paid to the date on which the order for the repayment is issued. Contributions paid late, i.e. after 19 April, and later repaid carry interest from the actual date of payment (SI 2001/1004, Sch. 4, para. 18(3))).

- **Class 1A:** from 19 April following the end of the tax year in respect of which the NIC was paid, or if the contribution was paid later, from the date of actual payment – usually 19 July in practice – to the date on which the order for the repayment is issued (SI 2001/1004, reg. 77(2)).

- **Class 1B:** from 19 October following the end of the tax year in respect of which the NIC was paid to the date on which the order for the repayment is issued. Contributions paid late, i.e. after 19 October, and later repaid carry interest from the actual date of payment (SI 2001/1004, Sch. 4, para. 18(3)).

# TAX CREDITS

## [¶10-000]  Working tax credits
(SI 2002/2005)

Maximum rates 2012–13 to 2017–18

| Element | 2017–18[1] £ | 2016–17[1] £ | 2015–16 £ | 2014–15 £ | 2013–14 £ | 2012–13 £ |
|---|---|---|---|---|---|---|
| Basic element | 1,960 | 1,960 | 1,960 | 1,940 | 1,920 | 1,920 |
| Disabled worker element | 3,000 | 2,970 | 2,970 | 2,935 | 2,855 | 2,790 |
| Severe disability element | 1,290 | 1,275 | 1,275 | 1,255 | 1,220 | 1,190 |
| 30-hour element | 810 | 810 | 810 | 800 | 790 | 790 |
| Couple and lone parent element | 2,010 | 2,010 | 2,010 | 1,990 | 1,970 | 1,950 |
| Childcare element: percentage of eligible costs covered | 70% | 70% | 70% | 70% | 70% | 70% |
| • maximum eligible cost for one child (per week) | 175 | 175 | 175 | 175 | 175 | 175 |
| • maximum eligible cost of two or more children (per week) | 300 | 300 | 300 | 300 | 300 | 300 |

**Note**
[1] Working age benefits, including tax credits and the local housing allowances (but excluding disability benefits which will continue to be indexed by CPI) frozen for four years from 2016–17 to 2019–20 (Summer Budget 2015).

## [¶10-100]  Child tax credits
(SI 2002/2007)

Maximum rates 2012–13 to 2017–18

| Element | Circumstance | 2017–18[1] £ | 2016–17[1] £ | 2015–16 £ | 2014–15 £ | 2013–14 £ | 2012–13 £ |
|---|---|---|---|---|---|---|---|
| Family[3] | Normal case | 545 | 545 | 545 | 545 | 545 | 545 |
| Individual | Each child or young person[2] | 2,780 | 2,780 | 2,780 | 2,750 | 2,720 | 2,690 |
| | Each disabled child or young person | 5,955 | 5,920 | 5,920 | 5,850 | 5,735 | 5,640 |
| | Each severely disabled child or young person | 7,245 | 7,195 | 7,195 | 7,105 | 6,955 | 6,830 |

Income thresholds and withdrawal rates 2012–13 to 2017–18

| | 2017–18[1] | 2016–17[1] | 2015–16 | 2014–15 | 2013–14 | 2012–13 |
|---|---|---|---|---|---|---|
| First income threshold | £6,420 | £6,420 | £6,420 | £6,420 | £6,420 | £6,420 |
| First withdrawal rate | 41% | 41% | 41% | 41% | 41% | 41% |
| First threshold for those entitled to child tax credit only | £16,105 | £16,105 | £16,105 | £16,010 | £15,910 | £15,860 |
| Income rise disregard | £2,500 | £2,500 | £5,000 | £5,000 | £5,000 | £10,000 |
| Income fall disregard | £2,500 | £2,500 | £2,500 | £2,500 | £2,500 | £2,500 |

**Notes**
[1] Working age benefits, including tax credits and the local housing allowances (but excluding disability benefits which will continue to be indexed by CPI) frozen for four years from 2016–17 to 2019–20 (Summer Budget 2015).
[2] Tax credits support to be limited to two children from April 2017 (Summer Budget 2015).
[3] Not available to those starting a family after April 2017 (Summer Budget 2015).

# STATE BENEFITS AND STATUTORY PAYMENTS

## [¶10-500]   Taxable state benefits
(ITEPA 2003, s. 577, 660)

(Tax Reporter: ¶490-000ff.)

The following benefits are liable to income tax.

Rates were most recently updated by SI 2016/230.

| | Weekly rate from | | | | | |
|---|---|---|---|---|---|---|
| **Benefit** | **April 2017 £** | **April 2016[5] £** | **April 2015 £** | **April 2014 £** | **April 2013 £** | **April 2012 £** |
| **Bereavement** | | | | | | |
| Bereavement allowance[3] | 113.70 | 112.55 | 112.55 | 111.20 | 108.30 | 105.95 |
| Widowed parent's allowance[4] | 113.70 | 112.55 | 112.55 | 111.20 | 108.30 | 105.95 |
| **Carer's allowance** | 62.70 | 62.10 | 62.10 | 61.35 | 59.75 | 58.45 |
| **Dependent adults** | | | | | | |
| with retirement pension[1] | 66.35 | 65.70 | 65.70 | 64.90 | 63.20 | 61.85 |
| with carer's allowance[1] | 36.90 | 36.55 | 36.55 | 36.10 | 35.15 | 34.40 |
| with long-term incapacity | 61.80 | 61.20 | 61.20 | 60.45 | 58.85 | 57.60 |
| with short-term incapacity (under pensionable age) | 48.15 | 47.65 | 47.65 | 47.10 | 45.85 | 44.85 |
| with short-term incapacity (over pensionable age) | 59.50 | 58.90 | 58.90 | 58.20 | 56.65 | 55.45 |
| **Employment & support allowance** | | | | | | |
| Age 25+ contributions-based ESA | 73.10 | 73.10 | 73.10 | 72.40 | 71.70 | 71.00 |
| **Industrial death benefit: Widow's pension** | | | | | | |
| Permanent rate: | | | | | | |
| higher | 122.30 | 119.30 | 115.95 | 113.10 | 110.15 | 107.45 |
| lower | 36.69 | 35.79 | 34.79 | 33.93 | 33.05 | 32.24 |
| **Widower's pension** | 122.30 | 119.30 | 115.95 | 113.10 | 110.15 | 107.45 |
| **Incapacity benefit (long-term)** | | | | | | |
| Rate | 106.40 | 105.35 | 105.35 | 104.10 | 101.35 | 99.15 |
| Increase for age: | | | | | | |
| higher rate | 11.25 | 11.15 | 11.15 | 11.00 | 10.70 | 11.70 |
| lower rate | 6.25 | 6.20 | 6.20 | 6.15 | 6.00 | 5.90 |
| **Jobseeker's allowance** See ¶10-600. | | | | | | |

| Benefit | Weekly rate from | | | | | |
|---|---|---|---|---|---|---|
| | April 2017 £ | April 2016[5] £ | April 2015 £ | April 2014 £ | April 2013 £ | April 2012 £ |
| **Incapacity benefit (short-term)** | | | | | | |
| Higher rate: | | | | | | |
| under pensionable age[2] | 95.00 | 94.05 | 94.05 | 92.95 | 90.50 | 88.55 |
| over pensionable age[2] | 106.40 | 105.35 | 105.35 | 104.10 | 101.35 | 99.15 |
| **Non-contributory retirement pension** | | | | | | |
| Standard rate[6] | 73.30 | 71.50 | 69.50 | 67.80 | 66.00 | 64.40 |
| Age addition (at age 80) | 0.25 | 0.25 | 0.25 | 0.25 | 0.25 | 0.25 |
| **Retirement pension** | | | | | | |
| Standard rate | 122.30 | 119.30 | 115.95 | 113.10 | 110.15 | 107.45 |
| Age addition (at age 80) | 0.25 | 0.25 | 0.25 | 0.25 | 0.25 | 0.25 |
| **SSP, SMP, SPP and SAP** See ¶10-650ff. | | | | | | |
| **New state pension** | 159.55 | 155.65 | — | — | — | — |
| **Widow's pension**[3] | 113.70 | 112.55 | 112.55 | 111.20 | 108.30 | 105.95 |
| **Widowed mother's allowance**[4] | 113.70 | 112.55 | 112.55 | 111.20 | 108.30 | 105.95 |

**Notes**

[1] No new claims for adult dependency increases payable with the state retirement pension or the carer's allowance may be made on or after 6 April 2010. Adult dependency increases already in payment immediately before 6 April 2010 will be phased out between 2010 and 2020.

[2] A man born before 6 December 1953 still attains pensionable age at age 65, whilst a woman born before 6 April 1950 attained pensionable age at age 60. The date the pensionable age is attained by individuals born after those dates is set out in the tables at ¶3-175.

[3] Bereavement allowance replaced widow's pension from 9 April 2001 for all new claims by widows and widowers.

[4] Widowed parent's allowance replaced widowed mother's allowance from 9 April 2001 for all new claims.

[5] Working age benefits, including tax credits and the local housing allowances (but excluding SMA, SMP, SPP, SSP and disability benefits which will continue to be indexed by CPI) frozen for four years from 2016–17 to 2019–20 (Summer Budget 2015).

From April 2011, the consumer price index is used for the indexation of benefits.

## [¶10-550] Non-taxable state benefits

(ITEPA 2003, s. 677(1): see also EIM76100)

(Tax Reporter: ¶490-000ff.)

The following UK social security benefits are wholly exempt from tax, except where indicated otherwise.

- Attendance allowance
- Back to work bonus (see EIM76223)
- Bereavement payment (see EIM76171)
- Child benefit
- Child's special allowance
- Child tax credit
- Constant attendance allowance: see industrial disablement benefit
- Council tax benefit

- Disability living allowance
- Income related employment and support allowance (see EIM76186)
- Exceptionally severe disablement allowance: see industrial disablement benefit
- Guardian's allowance
- Housing benefit
- Incapacity benefit for first 28 weeks of entitlement, taxable thereafter (see EIM76180)
- Income support, certain payments (see EIM76190)
- Industrial injuries benefit, a general term covering industrial injuries pension, reduced earnings allowance, retirement allowance, constant attendance allowance and exceptionally severe disablement allowance
- Invalidity benefit, replaced by incapacity benefit from April 1995 but still payable where invalidity commenced before April 1995
- In-work credit, In-work emergency discretion fund payment, In-work emergency fund payment
- Maternity allowance (see EIM76361)
- Pensioner's Christmas bonus
- Personal independence payment
- State pension credit
- Reduced earnings allowance: see industrial disablement benefit
- Retirement allowance: see industrial injuries benefit
- Return to work credit and self-employment credit
- Severe disablement allowance
- Social fund payments – help with maternity expenses, funeral costs, financial crisis, community care grants and interest free loans.
- Universal credit
- War widow's pension (see EIM76103)
- Winter fuel payment (or 'cold weather payment')
- Working tax credit

With regard to wounds and disability pensions for service with the forces see EIM74302 and for allowances payable to civilians in respect of war injuries see EIM74700.

Certain foreign social security payments are exempt from UK tax (see EIM76009).

The new bereavement support payment, which is due to replace three current benefits paid in respect of bereavement from April 2017 (*Pensions Act* 2014) will be exempt from income tax (Autumn Statement 2014).

**Benefit rates**

| | Weekly rate from | | | | | |
|---|---|---|---|---|---|---|
| Benefit | April 2017 £ | April 2016[6] £ | April 2015 £ | April 2014 £ | April 2013 £ | April 2012 £ |
| **Attendance allowance** | | | | | | |
| Higher rate | 83.10 | 82.30 | 82.30 | 81.30 | 79.15 | 77.45 |
| Lower rate | 55.65 | 55.10 | 55.10 | 54.45 | 53.00 | 51.85 |
| **Child benefit**[1] | | | | | | |
| For the eldest qualifying child | 20.70 | 20.70 | 20.70 | 20.50 | 20.30 | 20.30 |
| For each other child | 13.70 | 13.70 | 13.70 | 13.55 | 13.40 | 13.40 |

State Benefits and Statutory Payments

| Benefit | Weekly rate from | | | | | |
|---|---|---|---|---|---|---|
| | April 2017 £ | April 2016[6] £ | April 2015 £ | April 2014 £ | April 2013 £ | April 2012 £ |
| **Guardian's allowance** | 16.70 | 16.55 | 16.55 | 16.35 | 15.90 | 15.55 |
| **Child dependency addition** | | | | | | |
| Payable with: state pension; widowed mothers/parents allowance; short-term incapacity benefit – higher rate or over state pension age; long-term incapacity benefit; carer's allowance; severe disablement unemployability supplement. | 11.35 | 11.35 | 11.35 | 11.35 | 11.35 | 11.35 |
| Reduced rate[2] | 8.00 | 8.00 | 8.00 | 8.05 | 8.10 | 8.10 |
| **Constant attendance allowance** | | | | | | |
| Exceptional rate | 135.80 | 134.40 | 134.40 | 132.80 | 129.40 | 126.60 |
| Intermediate rate | 101.85 | 100.80 | 100.80 | 99.60 | 97.05 | 94.95 |
| Normal maximum rate | 67.90 | 67.20 | 67.20 | 66.40 | 64.70 | 63.30 |
| Part-time rate | 33.95 | 33.60 | 33.60 | 33.20 | 32.35 | 31.65 |
| Exceptionally severe disablement allowance | 67.90 | 67.20 | 67.20 | 66.40 | 64.70 | 63.30 |
| **Employment & support allowance – income-related based (ESA(IR))** | | | | | | |
| Involves over 30 potential components | | | | | | |
| **Maternity allowances** (where SMP not available) | | | | | | |
| Standard rate | 140.98 | 139.58 | 139.58 | 138.18 | 136.78 | 135.45 |
| MA threshold | 30.00 | 30.00 | 30.00 | 30.00 | 30.00 | 30.00 |
| **Disability living allowance (care component)[5]** | | | | | | |
| Higher rate | 83.10 | 82.30 | 82.30 | 81.30 | 79.15 | 77.45 |
| Middle rate | 55.65 | 55.10 | 55.10 | 54.45 | 53.00 | 51.85 |
| Lower rate | 22.00 | 21.80 | 21.80 | 21.55 | 21.00 | 20.55 |

| Benefit | Weekly rate from | | | | | |
|---|---|---|---|---|---|---|
| | April 2017 £ | April 2016[6] £ | April 2015 £ | April 2014 £ | April 2013 £ | April 2012 £ |
| **Disability living allowance (mobility component)[5]** | | | | | | |
| Higher rate | 58.00 | 57.45 | 57.45 | 56.75 | 55.25 | 54.05 |
| Lower rate | 22.00 | 21.80 | 21.80 | 21.55 | 21.00 | 20.55 |
| **Incapacity benefit (short-term)[3]** | | | | | | |
| Lower rate: | | | | | | |
| under pensionable age[4] | 80.25 | 79.45 | 79.45 | 78.50 | 76.45 | 74.80 |
| over pensionable age[4] | 102.10 | 101.10 | 101.10 | 99.90 | 97.25 | 95.15 |
| **Severe disablement allowance** | | | | | | |
| Basic rate Age addition (from Dec 90) | 75.40 | 74.65 | 74.65 | 73.75 | 71.80 | 69.00 |
| • Higher rate | 11.25 | 11.15 | 11.15 | 11.00 | 10.70 | 11.70 |
| • Middle rate | 6.25 | 6.20 | 6.20 | 6.15 | 6.00 | 5.90 |
| • Lower rate | 6.25 | 6.20 | 6.20 | 6.15 | 6.00 | 5.90 |
| Adult dependency increase | 37.10 | 36.75 | 36.75 | 36.30 | 35.35 | 34.60 |
| **Pensions credit** | | | | | | |
| **Standard** | | | | | | |
| Single | 159.35 | 155.60 | 151.20 | 148.35 | 145.40 | 142.70 |
| Couple | 243.25 | 237.55 | 230.85 | 226.50 | 222.05 | 217.90 |
| **Additional amount for severe disability** | | | | | | |
| Single | 62.45 | 61.85 | 61.85 | 61.10 | 59.50 | 58.20 |
| Couple (one qualifies) | 62.45 | 61.85 | 61.85 | 61.10 | 59.50 | 58.20 |
| Couple (both qualify) | 124.90 | 123.70 | 123.70 | 122.20 | 119.00 | 116.40 |
| **Additional amount for carers** | 34.95 | 34.60 | 34.60 | 34.20 | 33.30 | 32.60 |
| **Savings credit** | | | | | | |
| Threshold – single | 137.35 | 133.82 | 126.50 | 120.35 | 115.30 | 111.80 |
| Threshold – couple | 218.42 | 212.97 | 201.80 | 192.00 | 183.90 | 178.35 |
| Maximum award – single | 13.20 | 13.07 | 14.82 | 16.80 | 18.06 | 18.54 |
| Maximum award – couple | 14.90 | 14.75 | 17.43 | 20.70 | 22.89 | 23.73 |

| | Weekly rate from | | | | | |
|---|---|---|---|---|---|---|
| Benefit | April 2017 £ | April 2016[6] £ | April 2015 £ | April 2014 £ | April 2013 £ | April 2012 £ |
| **Polygamous marriage amounts** | | | | | | |
| Claimant and first spouse | 243.25 | 237.55 | 230.85 | 226.50 | 222.05 | 217.90 |
| Additional amount for additional spouse | 83.90 | 81.95 | 79.65 | 78.15 | 76.65 | 75.20 |
| **Personal independence payment[5]** | | | | | | |
| **Daily living component** | | | | | | |
| Standard rate | 83.10 | 82.30 | 55.10 | 54.45 | 53.00 | — |
| Enhanced rate | 55.65 | 55.10 | 82.30 | 81.30 | 79.15 | — |
| **Mobility component** | | | | | | |
| Standard rate | 58.00 | 57.45 | 21.80 | 21.55 | 21.00 | — |
| Enhanced rate | 22.00 | 21.80 | 57.45 | 56.75 | 55.25 | — |

**Notes**

(1) High income child benefit charge applies from 7 January 2013 (see ¶1-110).

(2) The rate of child dependency increase is adjusted where it is payable for the eldest child for whom child benefit is also paid. The weekly rate in such cases is reduced by the difference between ChB rates for the eldest and subsequent children.

(3) Incapacity benefit and contributory employment & support allowance (ESA(C)) are taxable, under the *Income Tax (Earnings and Pensions) Act* 2003, Pt. 10, Ch. 3, except for short-term benefit payable at the lower rate. It is not taxable, however, if the recipient started receiving invalidity benefit or sickness benefit before 6 April 1995 and has continued receiving long-term incapacity benefit since then.

(4) A man born before 6 December 1953 still attains pensionable age at age 65, whilst a woman born before 6 April 1950 attained pensionable age at age 60. The date the pensionable age is attained by individuals born after those dates is set out in the tables at ¶3-175.

(5) Personal independence payment (PIP) is replacing disability living allowance for claimants aged 16–64 (but not children under 16 or people aged 65 and over already in receipt of disability living allowance). PIPs were phased in between April 2013 and 2015.

(6) Working age benefits, including tax credits and the local housing allowances (but excluding SMA, SMP, SPP, SSP and disability benefits which will continue to be indexed by CPI) frozen for four years from 2016–17 to 2019–20 (Summer Budget 2015).

From April 2011, the consumer price index is used for the indexation of benefits.

# [¶10-560]　Childcare accounts

(CPA 2014; SI 2015/448; SI 2015/522)

(Tax Reporter: ¶434-500)

The *Childcare Payments Act* 2014 introduces a new scheme which provides financial support to help working families with the cost of childcare. Once the scheme is implemented, the Government will make a top-up payment of £2 for every £8 which a person pays towards childcare. Government support will be capped at a maximum of £4,000 in the case of a disabled child and £2,000 in the case of any other child, per year, although there will be no restriction on the number of children for whom support is available. The scheme will be managed by HMRC and rolled out in 2017 following a trial which will run for six months from 14 November 2016 to 15 May 2017 (SI 2016/1083).

A person will be eligible to receive government support (referred to as a 'top-up payment') if they meet the eligibility conditions; provide information to demonstrate their eligibility in a declaration to HMRC, and HMRC agree, based on that information, that they are eligible; have a child who qualifies for support (broadly, a child under the age of 12 years old, or if disabled, 17 years old); have opened a childcare account in accordance with the scheme; and they, or another person, pay money into the childcare account.

Existing tax and NIC reliefs (see ¶4-815) will be withdrawn from employees and employers where the employee enters a childcare voucher or directly contracted childcare scheme after the new scheme has come into force, however, as part of the transition to tax-free childcare, employer-supported childcare will remain open to new entrants until April 2018 (Budget 2016).

A top-up payment made into a childcare account is not to be regarded as income of the account holder for the purposes of the Income Tax Acts (CPA 2014, s. 66).

## [¶10-600]   Income support and jobseeker's allowance

(Tax Reporter: ¶490-250)

| | Weekly rate from | | | | | |
|---|---|---|---|---|---|---|
| Benefit: Income support | April 2017 £ | April 2016(1) £ | April 2015 £ | April 2014 £ | April 2013 £ | April 2012 £ |
| **Single** | | | | | | |
| Under 25 | 57.90 | 57.90 | 57.90 | 57.35 | 56.80 | 56.25 |
| 25 or over | 73.10 | 73.10 | 73.10 | 72.40 | 71.70 | 71.00 |
| **Lone parent** | | | | | | |
| Under 18 | 57.90 | 57.90 | 57.90 | 57.35 | 56.80 | 56.25 |
| 18 or over | 73.10 | 73.10 | 73.10 | 72.40 | 71.70 | 71.00 |
| **Couple** | | | | | | |
| Both under 18 | 57.90 | 57.90 | 57.90 | 57.35 | 56.80 | 56.25 |
| Both under 18 – higher rate | 87.50 | 87.50 | 87.50 | 86.65 | 85.80 | 84.95 |
| One under 18, one under 25 | 57.90 | 57.90 | 57.90 | 57.35 | 56.80 | 56.25 |
| One under 18, one 25 and over | 73.10 | 73.10 | 73.10 | 72.40 | 71.70 | 71.00 |
| Both 18 or over | 114.85 | 114.85 | 114.85 | 113.70 | 112.55 | 111.45 |
| **Dependent children** | 66.90 | 66.90 | 66.90 | 66.33 | 65.62 | 64.99 |

State Benefits and Statutory Payments

| Benefit: Jobseeker's allowance | Weekly rate from | | | | | |
|---|---|---|---|---|---|---|
| | April 2017 £ | April 2016[1] £ | April 2015 £ | April 2014 £ | April 2013 £ | April 2012 £ |
| **Contributions based JSA – personal rates** | | | | | | |
| under 25 | 57.90 | 57.90 | 57.90 | 57.35 | 56.80 | 56.25 |
| 25 or over | 73.10 | 73.10 | 73.10 | 72.40 | 71.70 | 71.00 |
| **Income based JSA – personal allowances** | | | | | | |
| under 25 | 57.90 | 57.90 | 57.90 | 57.35 | 56.80 | 56.25 |
| 25 or over | 73.10 | 73.10 | 73.10 | 72.40 | 71.70 | 71.00 |
| **Lone parent** | | | | | | |
| Under 18 | 57.90 | 57.90 | 57.90 | 57.35 | 56.80 | 56.25 |
| 18 or over | 73.10 | 73.10 | 73.10 | 72.40 | 71.70 | 71.00 |
| **Couple** | | | | | | |
| Both under 18 | 57.90 | 57.90 | 57.90 | 57.35 | 56.80 | 56.25 |
| Both under 18 – higher rate | 87.50 | 87.50 | 87.50 | 86.65 | 85.80 | 84.95 |
| One under 18, one under 25 | 57.90 | 57.90 | 57.90 | 57.35 | 56.80 | 56.25 |
| One under 18, one 25 and over | 73.10 | 73.10 | 73.10 | 72.40 | 71.70 | 71.00 |
| Both 18 or over | 114.85 | 114.85 | 114.85 | 113.70 | 112.55 | 111.45 |
| **Dependent children** | 66.90 | 66.90 | 66.90 | 66.33 | 65.62 | 64.99 |

| Premium: Income support and Jobseeker's allowance | Weekly rate from | | | | | |
|---|---|---|---|---|---|---|
| | April 2017 £ | April 2016[1] £ | April 2015 £ | April 2014 £ | April 2013 £ | April 2012 £ |
| Family/lone parent | 17.45 | 17.45 | 17.45 | 17.45 | 17.40 | 17.40 |
| Pensioner | | | | | | |
| Single (JSA only) | 86.25 | 82.50 | 78.10 | 75.95 | 73.70 | 71.70 |
| Couple | 128.40 | 122.70 | 116.00 | 112.80 | 109.50 | 106.45 |
| Disability | | | | | | |
| Single | 32.55 | 32.25 | 32.25 | 31.85 | 31.00 | 30.35 |
| Couple | 46.40 | 45.95 | 45.95 | 45.40 | 44.20 | 43.25 |
| Enhanced disability | | | | | | |
| Single | 15.90 | 15.75 | 15.75 | 15.55 | 15.15 | 14.80 |
| Disabled child | 24.78 | 24.43 | 24.43 | 24.08 | 23.45 | 22.89 |
| Couple | 22.85 | 22.60 | 22.60 | 22.35 | 21.75 | 21.30 |
| Severe disability | | | | | | |
| Single | 62.45 | 61.85 | 61.85 | 61.10 | 59.50 | 58.20 |
| couple (lower rate) | 62.45 | 61.85 | 61.85 | 61.10 | 59.50 | 58.20 |
| couple (higher rate) | 124.90 | 123.70 | 123.70 | 122.20 | 119.00 | 116.40 |
| Disabled child | 60.90 | 60.06 | 60.06 | 59.50 | 57.89 | 56.63 |
| Carer | 34.95 | 34.60 | 34.60 | 34.20 | 33.30 | 32.60 |

**Note**
(1) Working age benefits, including tax credits and the local housing allowances (but excluding SMA, SMP, SPP, SSP and disability benefits which will continue to be indexed by CPI) frozen for four years from 2016–17 to 2019–20 (Summer Budget 2015).

From April 2011, the consumer price index is used for the indexation of benefits.

## [¶10-625]   Benefits cap
(SI 2006/213, reg. 75CA; SI 2013/376, reg. 80A)

The benefits cap limits the total amount of benefit that working age people can receive.

| Benefit capped | Limits from | | |
|---|---|---|---|
| | 7 Nov. 2016 | | 15 Apr. 2013 |
| **Housing benefit** | Annual £ | Weekly(1) £ | Weekly £ |
| *Single claimants* | | | |
| Greater London | 15,410 | 296.35 | 350.00 |
| Outside Greater London | 13,400 | 257.69 | 350.00 |
| *Couples and lone parents* | | | |
| Greater London | 23,000 | 442.31 | 500.00 |
| Outside Greater London | 20,000 | 384.62 | 500.00 |
| **Universal credit** | Annual £ | Monthly(2) £ | Monthly £ |
| *Single claimants with no dependent children* | | | |
| Greater London | 15,410 | 1,284.17 | 1,517 |
| Outside Greater London | 13,400 | 1,116.67 | 1,517 |
| *Joint claimants and single claimants with children* | | | |
| Greater London | 23,000 | 1,916.67 | 2,167 |
| Outside Greater London | 20,000 | 1,666.67 | 2,167 |

**Notes**
(1) Rates expressed as annual limits with weekly amount calculated as annual limit divide by 52, rounding up or down to the nearest whole penny (SI 2006/213, reg. 75CA).
(2) Rates expressed as annual rates with monthly equivalent calculated as annual rates divide by 12 (SI 2013/376, reg. 80A(1)).

### Benefits to which cap is applicable
The cap will apply to household income from the following:
- Bereavement Allowance
- Child Benefit
- Child Tax Credit
- Employment and Support Allowance (except where paid with support component)
- Housing Benefit
- Incapacity Benefit
- Income Support
- Jobseeker's Allowance
- Maternity Allowance
- Severe Disablement Allowance

State Benefits and Statutory Payments

- Widowed Parent's Allowance (or widowed mother's allowance or widow's pension)
- Universal credit

**Note**
Carer's allowance and Guardian's allowance added to list of excluded benefits from 7 November 2016 (SI 2013/376, reg. 83).

### Households not affected by the cap

A partner or any dependant child qualifies for Working Tax Credit, or in receipt of any of the following:

- Armed Forces Compensation Scheme
- Armed Forces Independence Payment
- Attendence Allowance
- Carer's Allowance
- Disability Living Allowance
- Employment and Support Allowance
- Guardian's Allowance
- Industrial Injuries Benefit
- Personal Independence Payment
- Universal Credit (payments towards carer's costs or for 'limited capability for work and work-related activity')
- War pensions
- War Widow's or Widower's pension

## [¶10-650]   Statutory sick pay (SSP)

Employers are liable to pay SSP in any period of incapacity for work to a maximum of 28 weeks at the SSP rate in force. Statutory sick pay is treated as wages and is subject to PAYE income tax and to National Insurance contributions. Statutory sick pay is not payable for certain periods in which statutory maternity pay is being paid.

The amount of SSP payable to an employee depends on the earnings band into which he or she falls. The earnings bands and the associated SSP payments are as follows:

| Period (from) | Average gross weekly earnings £ | Weekly SSP rate[1] £ |
|---|---|---|
| 6 April 2017 | 113.00 or more | 89.35 |
| 6 April 2016 | 112.00 or more | 88.45 |
| 6 April 2015 | 112.00 or more | 88.45 |
| 6 April 2014 | 111.00 or more | 87.55 |
| 6 April 2013 | 109.00 or more | 86.70 |
| 6 April 2012 | 107.00 or more | 85.85 |
| 6 April 2011 | 102.00 or more | 81.60 |

**Notes**
[1] The daily rate of SSP is ascertained by dividing the weekly rate by the number of qualifying days in the week (beginning on Sunday), then multiplying by the number of qualifying days of incapacity in the week, rounded up to the nearest penny.

From April 2011, the consumer price index is used for the indexation of benefits.

Statutory payments will continue to be indexed by CPI (Summer Budget 2015).

### Maximum entitlement

An employee reaches his maximum entitlement to SSP in one spell of incapacity when he has been paid 28 times the appropriate rate, i.e. £89.35 × 28 = £2,501.80.

## [¶10-700] Statutory maternity pay (SMP)

Women expecting a baby who satisfy the qualifying conditions are entitled to a maximum of 39 weeks' SMP. These include having 'average weekly earnings' of:

* £113 if their baby is due between 16 July 2017 and 14 July 2018;
* £112 if their baby is due between 19 July 2015 and 15 July 2017;
* £111 if their baby is due between 20 July 2014 and 18 July 2015;
* £109 if their baby is due between 14 July 2013 and 19 July 2014;
* £107 if their baby is due between 15 July 2012 and 13 July 2013; and
* £102 if their baby is due between 17 July 2011 and 14 July 2012.

In other words, 'average weekly earnings' must reach or exceed the then-current NIC LEL in the eight weeks leading up to the fifteenth week before the expected week of childbirth (or placement of an adopted child).

| Period (from) | First six weeks | Remaining weeks |
|---|---|---|
| 6 April 2017 | 90% average weekly earnings | Lower of 90% average weekly earnings and £140.98 |
| 6 April 2016 | 90% average weekly earnings | Lower of 90% average weekly earnings and £139.58 |
| 6 April 2015 | 90% average weekly earnings | Lower of 90% average weekly earnings and £139.58 |
| 6 April 2014 | 90% average weekly earnings | Lower of 90% average weekly earnings and £138.18 |
| 6 April 2013 | 90% average weekly earnings | Lower of 90% of weekly earnings and £136.78 |
| 6 April 2012 | 90% average weekly earnings | Lower of 90% of weekly earnings and £135.45 |

**Note**
From April 2011, the consumer price index is used for the indexation of benefits.

Statutory payments will continue to be indexed by CPI (Summer Budget 2015).

## [¶10-725] Statutory shared parental pay (ShPP)

Shared parental leave (SPL) and statutory shared parental pay (ShPP) is available in respect of:

* children with an expected week of birth ending on or after 5 April 2015;
* children placed for adoption on or after 5 April 2015.

SPL is available where both parents are eligible and one partner ends maternity or adoption leave or pay (or maternity allowance) early. The remaining leave will be available as SPL. The remaining weeks of pay will be available as ShPP.

State Benefits and Statutory Payments

The mother must take a minimum of two weeks' maternity leave following the birth (four if she works in a factory). Thereafter:

- the rest of the 52 weeks of leave (up to a maximum of 50 weeks) can be taken as SPL;
- the rest of the 39 weeks of pay or maternity allowance (up to a maximum of 37 weeks) can be taken as ShPP.

ShPP is paid at the rate of £140.98 (2017–18) a week or 90% of average weekly earnings, whichever is lower. This is the same as statutory maternity pay (see ¶10-700) except that during the first six weeks, SMP is paid at 90% of earnings (with no maximum).

## [¶10-750]   Statutory paternity pay (SPP)

From April 2015, statutory paternity leave and pay is replaced with shared parental pay and leave (see ¶10-725), with effect for children with an expected week of birth ending on or after 5 April 2015.

SPP was introduced from 6 April 2003 and is payable for a maximum of two weeks (ordinary SPP). For babies due to be born on or after 3 April 2011 and before 6 April 2015, a mother could return to work early and pass her entitlement to leave and lower rate benefit to the father, for up to 26 weeks (additional SPP). Weekly rates of SPP (standard rate and additional rate) are the same as the standard rate of statutory maternity pay (see ¶10-700).

## [¶10-800]   Statutory adoption pay (SAP)

SAP was introduced in April 2003.

Employees who are adopting a child and are notified that they have been matched with a child or received official notification that they are eligible to adopt a child from abroad who satisfy the qualifying conditions are entitled to a maximum of 39 weeks' SAP. These include having average weekly earnings of:

| Eligible to adopt on or after | Average weekly earnings |
|---|---|
| 2 April 2017 | £113.00 |
| 5 April 2015 | £112.00 |
| 6 April 2014 | £111.00 |
| 31 March 2013 | £109.00 |
| 1 April 2012 | £107.00 |
| 3 April 2011 | £102.00 |

The weekly rate of statutory adoption pay is the same as the standard rate of statutory maternity pay (see ¶10-700). The adoptive parents are treated in effect as if they have had a baby and qualified for SMP.

# [¶10-900]   Universal credit
(SI 2013/376)
(Tax Reporter: ¶490-670)

Universal credit is a new benefit that has started to replace six existing benefits with a single monthly payment. Universal credit will eventually replace all of the following tax credits and benefits:

* tax credits – both child tax credit and working tax credit;
* income-based Jobseeker's Allowance;
* income-related employment and support allowance;
* income support; and
* housing benefit.

Universal credit will not replace child benefit.

Universal credit started to be introduced in stages from April 2013. Existing claimants of the above benefits will be moved to universal credit during 2016 and 2017. Universal credit is exempt from income tax.

| Universal credit | Per month | | | | |
|---|---|---|---|---|---|
| | 2017 £ | 2016(1) £ | 2015 £ | 2014 £ | 2013 £ |
| **Universal credit amounts** | | | | | |
| Standard allowance | | | | | |
|   – single under 25 | 251.77 | 251.77 | 251.77 | 249.28 | 246.81 |
|   – single over 25 | 317.82 | 317.82 | 317.82 | 314.67 | 311.55 |
|   – joint claimants, both under 25 | 395.20 | 395.20 | 395.20 | 391.29 | 387.42 |
|   – joint claimants, one or both 25 or over | 498.89 | 498.89 | 498.89 | 493.95 | 489.06 |
| Child element | | | | | |
|   – first child(2) | 277.08 | 277.08 | 277.08 | 274.58 | 272.08 |
|   – second/subsequent child(2) | 231.67 | 231.67 | 231.67 | 229.17 | 226.67 |
| Disabled child additions | | | | | |
|   – lower rate | 126.11 | 126.11 | 126.11 | 124.86 | 123.62 |
|   – higher rate | 372.30 | 367.92 | 367.92 | 362.92 | 352.92 |
| LCW and WRA elements | | | | | |
|   – limited capability for work | 126.11 | 126.11 | 126.11 | 124.86 | 123.62 |
|   – limited capability for work and work related activity | 318.76 | 315.60 | 315.60 | 311.86 | 303.66 |
| Carer element | 151.89 | 150.39 | 150.39 | 148.61 | 144.70 |
| Childcare costs element | | | | | |
|   – max for one child | 646.35 | 646.35 | 532.29 | 532.29 | 532.29 |
|   – max for two or more children | 1,108.04 | 1,108.04 | 912.50 | 912.50 | 912.50 |

| Universal credit | Per month | | | | |
|---|---|---|---|---|---|
| | 2017 £ | 2016(1) £ | 2015 £ | 2014 £ | 2013 £ |
| **Non-dependants' housing cost contributions** | 70.06 | 69.37 | 69.37 | 68.68 | 68.00 |
| **Work allowances** | | | | | |
| Higher work allowance (no housing element) | | | | | |
|   – single claimant, no dependent children | Nil | Nil | 111.00 | 111.00 | 111.00 |
|   – single claimant, one or more children | 397.00 | 397.00 | 734.00 | 734.00 | 734.00 |
|   – single claimant, limited capability for work | 397.00 | 397.00 | 647.00 | 647.00 | 647.00 |
|   – joint claimant, no dependent children | Nil | Nil | 111.00 | 111.00 | 111.00 |
|   – joint claimant, one or more children | 397.00 | 397.00 | 536.00 | 536.00 | 536.00 |
|   – joint claimant, limited capability for work | 397.00 | 397.00 | 647.00 | 647.00 | 647.00 |
| Lower work allowance | | | | | |
|   – single claimant, no dependent children | Nil | Nil | 111.00 | 111.00 | 111.00 |
|   – single claimant, one or more children | 192.00 | 192.00 | 263.00 | 263.00 | 263.00 |
|   – single claimant, limited capability for work | 192.00 | 192.00 | 192.00 | 192.00 | 192.00 |
|   – joint claimant, no dependent children | Nil | Nil | 111.00 | 111.00 | 111.00 |
|   – joint claimant, one or more children | 192.00 | 192.00 | 222.00 | 222.00 | 222.00 |
|   – joint claimant, limited capability for work | 192.00 | 192.00 | 192.00 | 192.00 | 192.00 |
| **Assumed income from capital** (for every £250 or part thereof) | 4.35 | 4.35 | 4.35 | 4.35 | 4.35 |

**Notes**
(1) Working age benefits (but excluding disability benefits which will continue to be indexed by CPI) frozen for four years from 2016–17 to 2019–20 (Summer Budget 2015).
(2) New claims from April 2017 limited to two children and first child premium also withdrawn for new claims from April 2017 (Summer Budget 2015).

# GENERAL

## Retail prices index

### [¶11-000]   Retail prices index: general

The retail prices index (RPI), issued by the Office for National Statistics, is used to calculate the indexation allowance for the purposes of calculating capital gains on corporation tax. (Since April 1998, the indexation allowance has ceased to be available when calculating gains liable to capital gains tax.) Certain personal and other reliefs are also linked to RPI subject to Parliament determining otherwise, although since April 2011, the consumer price index (CPI) has been used for the indexation of benefits, tax credits and public service pensions. Historically, the RPI was used for indexation of pensions and state benefits.

With effect from February 1987, the reference date to which the price level in each subsequent month is related was changed from 'January 1974 = 100' to 'January 1987 = 100'.

Movements in the RPI in the months after January 1987 are calculated with reference to January 1987 = 100. (With a base of January 1974 = 100, January 1987's RPI was 394.5). A new formula was provided by the then Department of Employment for calculating movements in the index over periods which span January 1987:

> 'The index for the later month (January 1987 = 100) is multiplied by the index for January 1987 (January 1974 = 100) and divided by the index for the earlier month (January 1974 = 100). 100 is subtracted to give the percentage change between the two months.'

CCH has prepared the following table in accordance with this formula:

|        | 1982  | 1983  | 1984  | 1985  | 1986  | 1987  | 1988  | 1989  | 1990  | 1991  |
|--------|-------|-------|-------|-------|-------|-------|-------|-------|-------|-------|
| Jan.   |       | 82.61 | 86.84 | 91.20 | 96.25 | 100.0 | 103.3 | 111.0 | 119.5 | 130.2 |
| Feb.   |       | 82.97 | 87.20 | 91.94 | 96.60 | 100.4 | 103.7 | 111.8 | 120.2 | 130.9 |
| March  | 79.44 | 83.12 | 87.48 | 92.80 | 96.73 | 100.6 | 104.1 | 112.3 | 121.4 | 131.4 |
| April  | 81.04 | 84.28 | 88.64 | 94.78 | 97.67 | 101.8 | 105.8 | 114.3 | 125.1 | 133.1 |
| May    | 81.62 | 84.64 | 88.97 | 95.21 | 97.85 | 101.9 | 106.2 | 115.0 | 126.2 | 133.5 |
| June   | 81.85 | 84.84 | 89.20 | 95.41 | 97.79 | 101.9 | 106.6 | 115.4 | 126.7 | 134.1 |
| July   | 81.88 | 85.30 | 89.10 | 95.23 | 97.52 | 101.8 | 106.7 | 115.5 | 126.8 | 133.8 |
| Aug.   | 81.90 | 85.68 | 89.94 | 95.49 | 97.82 | 102.1 | 107.9 | 115.8 | 128.1 | 134.1 |
| Sept.  | 81.85 | 86.06 | 90.11 | 95.44 | 98.30 | 102.4 | 108.4 | 116.6 | 129.3 | 134.6 |
| Oct.   | 82.26 | 86.36 | 90.67 | 95.59 | 98.45 | 102.9 | 109.5 | 117.5 | 130.3 | 135.1 |
| Nov.   | 82.66 | 86.67 | 90.95 | 95.92 | 99.29 | 103.4 | 110.0 | 118.5 | 130.0 | 135.6 |
| Dec.   | 82.51 | 86.89 | 90.87 | 96.05 | 99.62 | 103.3 | 110.3 | 118.8 | 129.9 | 135.7 |

|        | 1992  | 1993  | 1994  | 1995  | 1996  | 1997  | 1998  | 1999  | 2000  | 2001  |
|--------|-------|-------|-------|-------|-------|-------|-------|-------|-------|-------|
| Jan.   | 135.6 | 137.9 | 141.3 | 146.0 | 150.2 | 154.4 | 159.5 | 163.4 | 166.6 | 171.1 |
| Feb.   | 136.3 | 138.8 | 142.1 | 146.9 | 150.9 | 155.0 | 160.3 | 163.7 | 167.5 | 172.0 |
| March  | 136.7 | 139.3 | 142.5 | 147.5 | 151.5 | 155.4 | 160.8 | 164.1 | 168.4 | 172.2 |
| April  | 138.8 | 140.6 | 144.2 | 149.0 | 152.6 | 156.3 | 162.6 | 165.2 | 170.1 | 173.1 |
| May    | 139.3 | 141.1 | 144.7 | 149.6 | 152.9 | 156.9 | 163.5 | 165.6 | 170.7 | 174.2 |
| June   | 139.3 | 141.0 | 144.7 | 149.8 | 153.0 | 157.5 | 163.4 | 165.6 | 171.1 | 174.4 |
| July   | 138.8 | 140.7 | 144.0 | 149.1 | 152.4 | 157.5 | 163.0 | 165.1 | 170.5 | 173.3 |

General

|  | 1992 | 1993 | 1994 | 1995 | 1996 | 1997 | 1998 | 1999 | 2000 | 2001 |
|---|---|---|---|---|---|---|---|---|---|---|
| Aug. | 138.9 | 141.3 | 144.7 | 149.9 | 153.1 | 158.5 | 163.7 | 165.5 | 170.5 | 174.0 |
| Sept. | 139.4 | 141.9 | 145.0 | 150.6 | 153.8 | 159.3 | 164.4 | 166.2 | 171.7 | 174.6 |
| Oct. | 139.9 | 141.8 | 145.2 | 149.8 | 153.8 | 159.5 | 164.5 | 166.5 | 171.6 | 174.3 |
| Nov. | 139.7 | 141.6 | 145.3 | 149.8 | 153.9 | 159.6 | 164.4 | 166.7 | 172.1 | 173.6 |
| Dec. | 139.2 | 141.9 | 146.0 | 150.7 | 154.4 | 160.0 | 164.4 | 167.3 | 172.2 | 173.4 |

|  | 2002 | 2003 | 2004 | 2005 | 2006 | 2007 | 2008 | 2009 | 2010 | 2011 |
|---|---|---|---|---|---|---|---|---|---|---|
| Jan. | 173.3 | 178.4 | 183.1 | 188.9 | 193.4 | 201.6 | 209.8 | 210.1 | 217.9 | 229.0 |
| Feb. | 173.8 | 179.3 | 183.8 | 189.6 | 194.2 | 203.1 | 211.4 | 211.4 | 219.2 | 231.3 |
| March | 174.5 | 179.9 | 184.6 | 190.5 | 195.0 | 204.4 | 212.1 | 211.3 | 220.7 | 232.5 |
| April | 175.7 | 181.2 | 185.7 | 191.6 | 196.5 | 205.4 | 214.0 | 211.5 | 222.8 | 234.4 |
| May | 176.2 | 181.5 | 186.5 | 192.0 | 197.7 | 206.2 | 215.1 | 212.8 | 223.6 | 235.2 |
| June | 176.2 | 181.3 | 186.8 | 192.2 | 198.5 | 207.3 | 216.8 | 213.4 | 224.1 | 235.2 |
| July | 175.9 | 181.3 | 186.8 | 192.2 | 198.5 | 206.1 | 216.5 | 213.4 | 223.6 | 234.7 |
| Aug. | 176.4 | 181.6 | 187.4 | 192.6 | 199.2 | 207.3 | 217.2 | 214.4 | 224.5 | 236.1 |
| Sept. | 177.6 | 182.5 | 188.1 | 193.1 | 200.1 | 208.0 | 218.4 | 215.3 | 225.3 | 237.9 |
| Oct. | 177.9 | 182.6 | 188.6 | 193.3 | 200.4 | 208.9 | 217.7 | 216.0 | 225.8 | 238.0 |
| Nov. | 178.2 | 182.7 | 189.0 | 193.6 | 201.1 | 209.7 | 216.0 | 216.6 | 226.8 | 238.5 |
| Dec. | 178.5 | 183.5 | 189.9 | 194.1 | 202.7 | 210.9 | 212.9 | 218.0 | 228.4 | 239.4 |

|  | 2012 | 2013 | 2014 | 2015 | 2016 | 2017 | 2018 | 2019 | 2020 | 2021 |
|---|---|---|---|---|---|---|---|---|---|---|
| Jan. | 238.0 | 245.8 | 252.6 | 255.4 | 258.8 |  |  |  |  |  |
| Feb. | 239.9 | 247.6 | 254.2 | 256.7 | 260.0 |  |  |  |  |  |
| March | 240.8 | 248.7 | 254.8 | 257.1 | 261.1 |  |  |  |  |  |
| April | 242.5 | 249.5 | 255.7 | 258.0 | 261.4 |  |  |  |  |  |
| May | 242.4 | 250.0 | 255.9 | 258.5 | 262.1 |  |  |  |  |  |
| June | 241.8 | 249.7 | 255.9 | 258.9 | 263.1 |  |  |  |  |  |
| July | 242.1 | 249.7 | 256.0 | 258.6 | 263.4 |  |  |  |  |  |
| Aug. | 243.0 | 251.0 | 257.0 | 259.8 | 264.4 |  |  |  |  |  |
| Sept. | 244.2 | 251.9 | 257.6 | 259.6 | 264.9 |  |  |  |  |  |
| Oct. | 245.6 | 251.9 | 257.7 | 259.5 | 264.8 |  |  |  |  |  |
| Nov. | 245.6 | 252.1 | 257.1 | 259.8 | 265.5 |  |  |  |  |  |
| Dec. | 246.8 | 253.4 | 257.5 | 260.6 | 267.1 |  |  |  |  |  |

## [¶11-020]   Indexation allowance up to 5 April 1998

(TCGA 1992, s. 53 and 54)

Indexation allowance in respect of changes shown by the retail prices indices for months after April 1998 shall be allowed only for the purposes of corporation tax. For disposals made by individuals, trustees and personal representatives after April 1998 and before 6 April 2008, indexation allowance up to 5 April 1998 and taper relief could be obtained.

The table below sets out the figure that is determined by the formula of (RD – RI)/RI where RD is the RPI for April 1998 and RI is the RPI for the later of March 1982 and the date that the item of relevant allowable expenditure was incurred. The indexation allowance is the aggregate of the indexed rise in each item of relevant allowable expenditure. In relation to each item of expenditure, the indexed rise is a sum produced by multiplying the amount of that item of expenditure by the appropriate figure in the table below.

| | Jan. | Feb. | Mar. | Apr. | May | Jun. | Jul. | Aug. | Sep. | Oct. | Nov. | Dec. |
|---|---|---|---|---|---|---|---|---|---|---|---|---|
| **1982** | — | — | 1.047 | 1.006 | 0.992 | 0.987 | 0.986 | 0.985 | 0.987 | 0.977 | 0.967 | 0.971 |
| **1983** | 0.968 | 0.960 | 0.956 | 0.929 | 0.921 | 0.917 | 0.906 | 0.898 | 0.889 | 0.883 | 0.876 | 0.871 |
| **1984** | 0.872 | 0.865 | 0.859 | 0.834 | 0.828 | 0.823 | 0.825 | 0.808 | 0.804 | 0.793 | 0.788 | 0.789 |
| **1985** | 0.783 | 0.769 | 0.752 | 0.716 | 0.708 | 0.704 | 0.707 | 0.703 | 0.704 | 0.701 | 0.695 | 0.693 |
| **1986** | 0.689 | 0.683 | 0.681 | 0.665 | 0.662 | 0.663 | 0.667 | 0.662 | 0.654 | 0.652 | 0.638 | 0.632 |
| **1987** | 0.626 | 0.620 | 0.616 | 0.597 | 0.596 | 0.596 | 0.597 | 0.593 | 0.588 | 0.580 | 0.573 | 0.574 |
| **1988** | 0.574 | 0.568 | 0.562 | 0.537 | 0.531 | 0.525 | 0.524 | 0.507 | 0.500 | 0.485 | 0.478 | 0.474 |
| **1989** | 0.465 | 0.454 | 0.448 | 0.423 | 0.414 | 0.409 | 0.408 | 0.404 | 0.395 | 0.384 | 0.372 | 0.369 |
| **1990** | 0.361 | 0.353 | 0.339 | 0.300 | 0.288 | 0.283 | 0.282 | 0.269 | 0.258 | 0.248 | 0.251 | 0.252 |
| **1991** | 0.249 | 0.242 | 0.237 | 0.222 | 0.218 | 0.213 | 0.215 | 0.213 | 0.208 | 0.204 | 0.199 | 0.198 |
| **1992** | 0.199 | 0.193 | 0.189 | 0.171 | 0.167 | 0.167 | 0.171 | 0.171 | 0.166 | 0.162 | 0.164 | 0.168 |
| **1993** | 0.179 | 0.171 | 0.167 | 0.156 | 0.152 | 0.153 | 0.156 | 0.151 | 0.146 | 0.147 | 0.148 | 0.146 |
| **1994** | 0.151 | 0.144 | 0.141 | 0.128 | 0.124 | 0.124 | 0.129 | 0.124 | 0.121 | 0.120 | 0.119 | 0.114 |
| **1995** | 0.114 | 0.107 | 0.102 | 0.091 | 0.087 | 0.085 | 0.091 | 0.085 | 0.080 | 0.085 | 0.085 | 0.079 |
| **1996** | 0.083 | 0.078 | 0.073 | 0.066 | 0.063 | 0.063 | 0.067 | 0.062 | 0.057 | 0.057 | 0.057 | 0.053 |
| **1997** | 0.053 | 0.049 | 0.046 | 0.040 | 0.036 | 0.032 | 0.032 | 0.026 | 0.021 | 0.019 | 0.019 | 0.016 |
| **1998** | 0.019 | 0.014 | 0.011 | — | — | — | — | — | — | — | — | — |

General

# [¶11-350]   RPI: October 2016 to December 2016

Tables follow showing the indexed rise to be used for disposals between October 2016 and December 2016. The amount of indexation allowances is restricted where the indexation allowance gives rise to a loss.

### RD Month (October 2016 to December 2016) January 1987 = 100

|            |        | 2016 | | |
|------------|--------|------|------|------|
| **RI Month** |      | **Oct.** | **Nov.** | **Dec.** |
| **1982**   | Mar.   | 2.333 | 2.342 | 2.362 |
|            | April  | 2.268 | 2.276 | 2.296 |
|            | May    | 2.244 | 2.253 | 2.272 |
|            | June   | 2.235 | 2.244 | 2.263 |
|            | July   | 2.234 | 2.243 | 2.262 |
|            | Aug.   | 2.233 | 2.242 | 2.261 |
|            | Sept.  | 2.235 | 2.244 | 2.263 |
|            | Oct.   | 2.219 | 2.228 | 2.247 |
|            | Nov.   | 2.203 | 2.212 | 2.231 |
|            | Dec.   | 2.209 | 2.218 | 2.237 |
| **1983**   | Jan.   | 2.205 | 2.214 | 2.233 |
|            | Feb.   | 2.192 | 2.200 | 2.219 |
|            | Mar.   | 2.186 | 2.194 | 2.214 |
|            | April  | 2.142 | 2.150 | 2.169 |
|            | May    | 2.129 | 2.137 | 2.156 |
|            | June   | 2.121 | 2.129 | 2.148 |
|            | July   | 2.104 | 2.113 | 2.131 |
|            | Aug.   | 2.091 | 2.099 | 2.117 |
|            | Sept.  | 2.077 | 2.085 | 2.104 |
|            | Oct.   | 2.066 | 2.074 | 2.093 |
|            | Nov.   | 2.055 | 2.063 | 2.082 |
|            | Dec.   | 2.047 | 2.055 | 2.074 |
| **1984**   | Jan.   | 2.049 | 2.057 | 2.076 |
|            | Feb.   | 2.037 | 2.045 | 2.063 |
|            | Mar.   | 2.027 | 2.035 | 2.053 |
|            | April  | 1.987 | 1.995 | 2.013 |
|            | May    | 1.976 | 1.984 | 2.002 |
|            | June   | 1.969 | 1.976 | 1.994 |

| RI Month | | 2016 | | |
|---|---|---|---|---|
| | | Oct. | Nov. | Dec. |
| | July | 1.972 | 1.980 | 1.998 |
| | Aug. | 1.944 | 1.952 | 1.970 |
| | Sept. | 1.938 | 1.946 | 1.964 |
| | Oct. | 1.920 | 1.928 | 1.946 |
| | Nov. | 1.911 | 1.919 | 1.937 |
| | Dec. | 1.914 | 1.922 | 1.939 |
| 1985 | Jan. | 1.903 | 1.911 | 1.929 |
| | Feb. | 1.880 | 1.888 | 1.905 |
| | Mar. | 1.853 | 1.861 | 1.878 |
| | April | 1.794 | 1.801 | 1.818 |
| | May | 1.781 | 1.789 | 1.805 |
| | June | 1.775 | 1.783 | 1.799 |
| | July | 1.781 | 1.788 | 1.805 |
| | Aug. | 1.773 | 1.780 | 1.797 |
| | Sept. | 1.775 | 1.782 | 1.799 |
| | Oct. | 1.770 | 1.778 | 1.794 |
| | Nov. | 1.761 | 1.768 | 1.785 |
| | Dec. | 1.757 | 1.764 | 1.781 |
| 1986 | Jan. | 1.751 | 1.758 | 1.775 |
| | Feb. | 1.741 | 1.748 | 1.765 |
| | Mar. | 1.738 | 1.745 | 1.761 |
| | April | 1.711 | 1.718 | 1.735 |
| | May | 1.706 | 1.713 | 1.730 |
| | June | 1.708 | 1.715 | 1.731 |
| | July | 1.715 | 1.723 | 1.739 |
| | Aug. | 1.707 | 1.714 | 1.731 |
| | Sept. | 1.694 | 1.701 | 1.717 |
| | Oct. | 1.690 | 1.697 | 1.713 |
| | Nov. | 1.667 | 1.674 | 1.690 |
| | Dec. | 1.658 | 1.665 | 1.681 |
| 1987 | Jan. | 1.648 | 1.655 | 1.671 |
| | Feb. | 1.637 | 1.644 | 1.660 |
| | Mar. | 1.632 | 1.639 | 1.655 |

General

| RI Month | | 2016 | | |
|---|---|---|---|---|
| | | Oct. | Nov. | Dec. |
| | April | 1.601 | 1.608 | 1.624 |
| | May | 1.599 | 1.605 | 1.621 |
| | June | 1.599 | 1.605 | 1.621 |
| | July | 1.601 | 1.608 | 1.624 |
| | Aug. | 1.594 | 1.600 | 1.616 |
| | Sept. | 1.586 | 1.593 | 1.608 |
| | Oct. | 1.573 | 1.580 | 1.596 |
| | Nov. | 1.561 | 1.568 | 1.583 |
| | Dec. | 1.563 | 1.570 | 1.586 |
| **1988** | Jan. | 1.563 | 1.570 | 1.586 |
| | Feb. | 1.554 | 1.560 | 1.576 |
| | Mar. | 1.544 | 1.550 | 1.566 |
| | April | 1.503 | 1.509 | 1.525 |
| | May | 1.493 | 1.500 | 1.515 |
| | June | 1.484 | 1.491 | 1.506 |
| | July | 1.482 | 1.488 | 1.503 |
| | Aug. | 1.454 | 1.461 | 1.475 |
| | Sept. | 1.443 | 1.449 | 1.464 |
| | Oct. | 1.418 | 1.425 | 1.439 |
| | Nov. | 1.407 | 1.414 | 1.428 |
| | Dec. | 1.401 | 1.407 | 1.422 |
| **1989** | Jan. | 1.386 | 1.392 | 1.406 |
| | Feb. | 1.369 | 1.375 | 1.389 |
| | Mar. | 1.358 | 1.364 | 1.378 |
| | April | 1.317 | 1.323 | 1.337 |
| | May | 1.303 | 1.309 | 1.323 |
| | June | 1.295 | 1.301 | 1.315 |
| | July | 1.293 | 1.299 | 1.313 |
| | Aug. | 1.287 | 1.293 | 1.307 |
| | Sept. | 1.271 | 1.277 | 1.291 |
| | Oct. | 1.254 | 1.260 | 1.273 |
| | Nov. | 1.235 | 1.241 | 1.254 |
| | Dec. | 1.229 | 1.235 | 1.248 |

| RI Month | | 2016 | | |
|---|---|---|---|---|
| | | Oct. | Nov. | Dec. |
| **1990** | Jan. | 1.216 | 1.222 | 1.235 |
| | Feb. | 1.203 | 1.209 | 1.222 |
| | Mar. | 1.181 | 1.187 | 1.200 |
| | April | 1.117 | 1.122 | 1.135 |
| | May | 1.098 | 1.104 | 1.116 |
| | June | 1.090 | 1.096 | 1.108 |
| | July | 1.088 | 1.094 | 1.106 |
| | Aug. | 1.067 | 1.073 | 1.085 |
| | Sept. | 1.048 | 1.053 | 1.066 |
| | Oct. | 1.032 | 1.038 | 1.050 |
| | Nov. | 1.037 | 1.042 | 1.055 |
| | Dec. | 1.038 | 1.044 | 1.056 |
| **1991** | Jan. | 1.034 | 1.039 | 1.051 |
| | Feb. | 1.023 | 1.028 | 1.040 |
| | Mar. | 1.015 | 1.021 | 1.033 |
| | April | 0.989 | 0.995 | 1.007 |
| | May | 0.984 | 0.989 | 1.001 |
| | June | 0.975 | 0.980 | 0.992 |
| | July | 0.979 | 0.984 | 0.996 |
| | Aug. | 0.975 | 0.980 | 0.992 |
| | Sept. | 0.967 | 0.973 | 0.984 |
| | Oct. | 0.960 | 0.965 | 0.977 |
| | Nov. | 0.953 | 0.958 | 0.970 |
| | Dec. | 0.951 | 0.957 | 0.968 |
| **1992** | Jan. | 0.953 | 0.958 | 0.970 |
| | Feb. | 0.943 | 0.948 | 0.960 |
| | Mar. | 0.937 | 0.942 | 0.954 |
| | April | 0.908 | 0.913 | 0.924 |
| | May | 0.901 | 0.906 | 0.917 |
| | June | 0.901 | 0.906 | 0.917 |
| | July | 0.908 | 0.913 | 0.924 |
| | Aug. | 0.906 | 0.911 | 0.923 |
| | Sept. | 0.900 | 0.905 | 0.916 |

General

| RI Month | | 2016 | | |
|---|---|---|---|---|
| | | Oct. | Nov. | Dec. |
| | Oct. | 0.893 | 0.898 | 0.909 |
| | Nov. | 0.895 | 0.901 | 0.912 |
| | Dec. | 0.902 | 0.907 | 0.919 |
| **1993** | Jan. | 0.920 | 0.925 | 0.937 |
| | Feb. | 0.908 | 0.913 | 0.924 |
| | Mar. | 0.901 | 0.906 | 0.917 |
| | April | 0.883 | 0.888 | 0.900 |
| | May | 0.877 | 0.882 | 0.893 |
| | June | 0.878 | 0.883 | 0.894 |
| | July | 0.882 | 0.887 | 0.898 |
| | Aug. | 0.874 | 0.879 | 0.890 |
| | Sept. | 0.866 | 0.871 | 0.882 |
| | Oct. | 0.867 | 0.872 | 0.884 |
| | Nov. | 0.870 | 0.875 | 0.886 |
| | Dec. | 0.866 | 0.871 | 0.882 |
| **1994** | Jan. | 0.874 | 0.879 | 0.890 |
| | Feb. | 0.863 | 0.868 | 0.880 |
| | Mar. | 0.858 | 0.863 | 0.874 |
| | April | 0.836 | 0.841 | 0.852 |
| | May | 0.830 | 0.835 | 0.846 |
| | June | 0.830 | 0.835 | 0.846 |
| | July | 0.839 | 0.844 | 0.855 |
| | Aug. | 0.830 | 0.835 | 0.846 |
| | Sept. | 0.826 | 0.831 | 0.842 |
| | Oct. | 0.824 | 0.829 | 0.840 |
| | Nov. | 0.822 | 0.827 | 0.838 |
| | Dec. | 0.814 | 0.818 | 0.829 |
| **1995** | Jan. | 0.814 | 0.818 | 0.829 |
| | Feb. | 0.803 | 0.807 | 0.818 |
| | Mar. | 0.795 | 0.800 | 0.811 |
| | April | 0.777 | 0.782 | 0.793 |
| | May | 0.770 | 0.775 | 0.785 |
| | June | 0.768 | 0.772 | 0.783 |

| RI Month | | 2016 | | |
| --- | --- | --- | --- | --- |
| | | Oct. | Nov. | Dec. |
| | July | 0.776 | 0.781 | 0.791 |
| | Aug. | 0.767 | 0.771 | 0.782 |
| | Sept. | 0.758 | 0.763 | 0.774 |
| | Oct. | 0.768 | 0.772 | 0.783 |
| | Nov. | 0.768 | 0.772 | 0.783 |
| | Dec. | 0.757 | 0.762 | 0.772 |
| 1996 | Jan. | 0.763 | 0.768 | 0.778 |
| | Feb. | 0.755 | 0.759 | 0.770 |
| | Mar. | 0.748 | 0.752 | 0.763 |
| | April | 0.735 | 0.740 | 0.750 |
| | May | 0.732 | 0.736 | 0.747 |
| | June | 0.731 | 0.735 | 0.746 |
| | July | 0.738 | 0.742 | 0.753 |
| | Aug. | 0.730 | 0.734 | 0.745 |
| | Sept. | 0.722 | 0.726 | 0.737 |
| | Oct. | 0.722 | 0.726 | 0.737 |
| | Nov. | 0.721 | 0.725 | 0.736 |
| | Dec. | 0.715 | 0.720 | 0.730 |
| 1997 | Jan. | 0.715 | 0.720 | 0.730 |
| | Feb. | 0.708 | 0.713 | 0.723 |
| | Mar. | 0.704 | 0.708 | 0.719 |
| | April | 0.694 | 0.699 | 0.709 |
| | May | 0.688 | 0.692 | 0.702 |
| | June | 0.681 | 0.686 | 0.696 |
| | July | 0.681 | 0.686 | 0.696 |
| | Aug. | 0.671 | 0.675 | 0.685 |
| | Sept. | 0.662 | 0.667 | 0.677 |
| | Oct. | 0.660 | 0.665 | 0.675 |
| | Nov. | 0.659 | 0.664 | 0.674 |
| | Dec. | 0.655 | 0.659 | 0.669 |
| 1998 | Jan. | 0.660 | 0.665 | 0.675 |
| | Feb. | 0.652 | 0.656 | 0.666 |
| | Mar. | 0.647 | 0.651 | 0.661 |

General

| RI Month | | 2016 | | |
|---|---|---|---|---|
| | | Oct. | Nov. | Dec. |
| | April | 0.629 | 0.633 | 0.643 |
| | May | 0.620 | 0.624 | 0.634 |
| | June | 0.621 | 0.625 | 0.635 |
| | July | 0.625 | 0.629 | 0.639 |
| | Aug. | 0.618 | 0.622 | 0.632 |
| | Sept. | 0.611 | 0.615 | 0.625 |
| | Oct. | 0.610 | 0.614 | 0.624 |
| | Nov. | 0.611 | 0.615 | 0.625 |
| | Dec. | 0.611 | 0.615 | 0.625 |
| **1999** | Jan. | 0.621 | 0.625 | 0.635 |
| | Feb. | 0.618 | 0.622 | 0.632 |
| | Mar. | 0.614 | 0.618 | 0.628 |
| | April | 0.603 | 0.607 | 0.617 |
| | May | 0.599 | 0.603 | 0.613 |
| | June | 0.599 | 0.603 | 0.613 |
| | July | 0.604 | 0.608 | 0.618 |
| | Aug. | 0.600 | 0.604 | 0.614 |
| | Sept. | 0.593 | 0.597 | 0.607 |
| | Oct. | 0.590 | 0.595 | 0.604 |
| | Nov. | 0.588 | 0.593 | 0.602 |
| | Dec. | 0.583 | 0.587 | 0.597 |
| **2000** | Jan. | 0.589 | 0.594 | 0.603 |
| | Feb. | 0.581 | 0.585 | 0.595 |
| | Mar. | 0.572 | 0.577 | 0.586 |
| | April | 0.557 | 0.561 | 0.570 |
| | May | 0.551 | 0.555 | 0.565 |
| | June | 0.548 | 0.552 | 0.561 |
| | July | 0.553 | 0.557 | 0.567 |
| | Aug. | 0.553 | 0.557 | 0.567 |
| | Sept. | 0.542 | 0.546 | 0.556 |
| | Oct. | 0.543 | 0.547 | 0.557 |
| | Nov. | 0.539 | 0.543 | 0.552 |
| | Dec. | 0.538 | 0.542 | 0.551 |

| RI Month | | 2016 | | |
|---|---|---|---|---|
| | | Oct. | Nov. | Dec. |
| **2001** | Jan. | 0.548 | 0.552 | 0.561 |
| | Feb. | 0.540 | 0.544 | 0.553 |
| | Mar. | 0.538 | 0.542 | 0.551 |
| | April | 0.530 | 0.534 | 0.543 |
| | May | 0.520 | 0.524 | 0.533 |
| | June | 0.518 | 0.522 | 0.532 |
| | July | 0.528 | 0.532 | 0.541 |
| | Aug. | 0.522 | 0.526 | 0.535 |
| | Sept. | 0.517 | 0.521 | 0.530 |
| | Oct. | 0.519 | 0.523 | 0.532 |
| | Nov. | 0.525 | 0.529 | 0.539 |
| | Dec. | 0.527 | 0.531 | 0.540 |
| **2002** | Jan. | 0.528 | 0.532 | 0.541 |
| | Feb. | 0.524 | 0.528 | 0.537 |
| | Mar. | 0.517 | 0.521 | 0.531 |
| | April | 0.507 | 0.511 | 0.520 |
| | May | 0.503 | 0.507 | 0.516 |
| | June | 0.503 | 0.507 | 0.516 |
| | July | 0.505 | 0.509 | 0.518 |
| | Aug. | 0.501 | 0.505 | 0.514 |
| | Sept. | 0.491 | 0.495 | 0.504 |
| | Oct. | 0.488 | 0.492 | 0.501 |
| | Nov. | 0.486 | 0.490 | 0.499 |
| | Dec. | 0.483 | 0.487 | 0.496 |
| **2003** | Jan. | 0.484 | 0.488 | 0.497 |
| | Feb. | 0.477 | 0.481 | 0.490 |
| | Mar. | 0.472 | 0.476 | 0.485 |
| | April | 0.461 | 0.465 | 0.474 |
| | May | 0.459 | 0.463 | 0.472 |
| | June | 0.461 | 0.464 | 0.473 |
| | July | 0.461 | 0.464 | 0.473 |
| | Aug. | 0.458 | 0.462 | 0.471 |
| | Sept. | 0.451 | 0.455 | 0.464 |
| | Oct. | 0.450 | 0.454 | 0.463 |

General

| RI Month | | 2016 | | |
|---|---|---|---|---|
| | | Oct. | Nov. | Dec. |
| | Nov. | 0.449 | 0.453 | 0.462 |
| | Dec. | 0.443 | 0.447 | 0.456 |
| 2004 | Jan. | 0.446 | 0.450 | 0.459 |
| | Feb. | 0.441 | 0.445 | 0.453 |
| | Mar. | 0.434 | 0.438 | 0.447 |
| | April | 0.426 | 0.430 | 0.438 |
| | May | 0.420 | 0.424 | 0.432 |
| | June | 0.418 | 0.421 | 0.430 |
| | July | 0.418 | 0.421 | 0.430 |
| | Aug. | 0.413 | 0.417 | 0.425 |
| | Sept. | 0.408 | 0.411 | 0.420 |
| | Oct. | 0.404 | 0.408 | 0.416 |
| | Nov. | 0.401 | 0.405 | 0.413 |
| | Dec. | 0.394 | 0.398 | 0.407 |
| 2005 | Jan. | 0.402 | 0.406 | 0.414 |
| | Feb. | 0.397 | 0.400 | 0.409 |
| | Mar. | 0.390 | 0.394 | 0.402 |
| | April | 0.382 | 0.386 | 0.394 |
| | May | 0.379 | 0.383 | 0.391 |
| | June | 0.378 | 0.381 | 0.390 |
| | July | 0.378 | 0.381 | 0.390 |
| | Aug. | 0.375 | 0.379 | 0.387 |
| | Sept. | 0.371 | 0.375 | 0.383 |
| | Oct. | 0.370 | 0.374 | 0.382 |
| | Nov. | 0.368 | 0.371 | 0.380 |
| | Dec. | 0.364 | 0.368 | 0.376 |
| 2006 | Jan. | 0.369 | 0.373 | 0.381 |
| | Feb. | 0.364 | 0.367 | 0.375 |
| | Mar. | 0.358 | 0.362 | 0.370 |
| | April | 0.348 | 0.351 | 0.359 |
| | May | 0.339 | 0.343 | 0.351 |
| | June | 0.334 | 0.338 | 0.346 |
| | July | 0.334 | 0.338 | 0.346 |
| | Aug. | 0.329 | 0.333 | 0.341 |

| RI Month | | 2016 | | |
|---|---|---|---|---|
| | | Oct. | Nov. | Dec. |
| | Sept. | 0.323 | 0.327 | 0.335 |
| | Oct. | 0.321 | 0.325 | 0.333 |
| | Nov. | 0.317 | 0.320 | 0.328 |
| | Dec. | 0.306 | 0.310 | 0.318 |
| 2007 | Jan. | 0.313 | 0.317 | 0.325 |
| | Feb. | 0.304 | 0.307 | 0.315 |
| | Mar. | 0.295 | 0.299 | 0.307 |
| | April | 0.289 | 0.293 | 0.300 |
| | May | 0.284 | 0.288 | 0.295 |
| | June | 0.277 | 0.281 | 0.288 |
| | July | 0.285 | 0.288 | 0.296 |
| | Aug. | 0.277 | 0.281 | 0.288 |
| | Sept. | 0.273 | 0.276 | 0.284 |
| | Oct. | 0.268 | 0.271 | 0.279 |
| | Nov. | 0.263 | 0.266 | 0.274 |
| | Dec. | 0.256 | 0.259 | 0.266 |
| 2008 | Jan. | 0.262 | 0.265 | 0.273 |
| | Feb. | 0.253 | 0.256 | 0.263 |
| | Mar. | 0.248 | 0.252 | 0.259 |
| | April | 0.237 | 0.241 | 0.248 |
| | May | 0.231 | 0.234 | 0.242 |
| | June | 0.221 | 0.225 | 0.232 |
| | July | 0.223 | 0.226 | 0.234 |
| | Aug. | 0.219 | 0.222 | 0.230 |
| | Sept. | 0.212 | 0.216 | 0.223 |
| | Oct. | 0.216 | 0.220 | 0.227 |
| | Nov. | 0.226 | 0.229 | 0.237 |
| | Dec. | 0.244 | 0.247 | 0.255 |
| 2009 | Jan. | 0.260 | 0.264 | 0.271 |
| | Feb. | 0.253 | 0.256 | 0.263 |
| | Mar. | 0.253 | 0.257 | 0.264 |
| | April | 0.252 | 0.255 | 0.263 |
| | May | 0.244 | 0.248 | 0.255 |
| | June | 0.241 | 0.244 | 0.252 |

General

| RI Month | | 2016 | | |
|---|---|---|---|---|
| | | Oct. | Nov. | Dec. |
| | July | 0.241 | 0.244 | 0.252 |
| | Aug. | 0.235 | 0.238 | 0.246 |
| | Sept. | 0.230 | 0.233 | 0.241 |
| | Oct. | 0.226 | 0.229 | 0.237 |
| | Nov. | 0.223 | 0.226 | 0.233 |
| | Dec. | 0.215 | 0.218 | 0.225 |
| 2010 | Jan. | 0.215 | 0.218 | 0.226 |
| | Feb. | 0.208 | 0.211 | 0.219 |
| | Mar. | 0.200 | 0.203 | 0.210 |
| | April | 0.189 | 0.192 | 0.199 |
| | May | 0.184 | 0.187 | 0.195 |
| | June | 0.182 | 0.185 | 0.192 |
| | July | 0.184 | 0.187 | 0.195 |
| | Aug. | 0.180 | 0.183 | 0.190 |
| | Sept. | 0.175 | 0.178 | 0.186 |
| | Oct. | 0.173 | 0.176 | 0.183 |
| | Nov. | 0.168 | 0.171 | 0.178 |
| | Dec. | 0.159 | 0.162 | 0.169 |
| 2011 | Jan. | 0.156 | 0.159 | 0.166 |
| | Feb. | 0.145 | 0.148 | 0.155 |
| | Mar. | 0.139 | 0.142 | 0.149 |
| | April | 0.130 | 0.133 | 0.140 |
| | May | 0.126 | 0.129 | 0.136 |
| | June | 0.126 | 0.129 | 0.136 |
| | July | 0.128 | 0.131 | 0.138 |
| | Aug. | 0.122 | 0.125 | 0.131 |
| | Sept. | 0.113 | 0.116 | 0.123 |
| | Oct. | 0.113 | 0.116 | 0.122 |
| | Nov. | 0.110 | 0.113 | 0.120 |
| | Dec. | 0.106 | 0.109 | 0.116 |
| 2012 | Jan. | 0.113 | 0.116 | 0.122 |
| | Feb. | 0.104 | 0.107 | 0.113 |
| | Mar. | 0.100 | 0.103 | 0.109 |

| RI Month | | 2016 | | |
|---|---|---|---|---|
| | | Oct. | Nov. | Dec. |
| | April | 0.092 | 0.095 | 0.101 |
| | May | 0.092 | 0.095 | 0.102 |
| | June | 0.095 | 0.098 | 0.105 |
| | July | 0.094 | 0.097 | 0.103 |
| | Aug. | 0.090 | 0.093 | 0.099 |
| | Sept. | 0.084 | 0.087 | 0.094 |
| | Oct. | 0.078 | 0.081 | 0.088 |
| | Nov. | 0.078 | 0.081 | 0.088 |
| | Dec. | 0.073 | 0.076 | 0.082 |
| 2013 | Jan. | 0.077 | 0.080 | 0.087 |
| | Feb. | 0.069 | 0.072 | 0.079 |
| | Mar. | 0.065 | 0.068 | 0.074 |
| | Apr. | 0.061 | 0.064 | 0.071 |
| | May | 0.059 | 0.062 | 0.068 |
| | June | 0.060 | 0.063 | 0.070 |
| | July | 0.060 | 0.063 | 0.070 |
| | Aug. | 0.055 | 0.058 | 0.064 |
| | Sept. | 0.051 | 0.054 | 0.060 |
| | Oct. | 0.051 | 0.054 | 0.060 |
| | Nov. | 0.050 | 0.053 | 0.060 |
| | Dec. | 0.048 | 0.051 | 0.057 |
| 2014 | Jan. | 0.048 | 0.051 | 0.057 |
| | Feb. | 0.042 | 0.044 | 0.051 |
| | Mar. | 0.039 | 0.042 | 0.048 |
| | Apr. | 0.036 | 0.038 | 0.045 |
| | May | 0.035 | 0.038 | 0.044 |
| | June | 0.033 | 0.036 | 0.042 |
| | July | 0.034 | 0.037 | 0.043 |
| | Aug. | 0.030 | 0.033 | 0.039 |
| | Sept. | 0.028 | 0.031 | 0.037 |
| | Oct. | 0.028 | 0.030 | 0.036 |
| | Nov. | 0.030 | 0.033 | 0.039 |
| | Dec. | 0.028 | 0.031 | 0.037 |

General

| RI Month | | 2016 | | |
|---|---|---|---|---|
| | | Oct. | Nov. | Dec. |
| **2015** | Jan. | 0.037 | 0.040 | 0.046 |
| | Feb. | 0.032 | 0.034 | 0.041 |
| | Mar. | 0.030 | 0.033 | 0.039 |
| | Apr. | 0.026 | 0.029 | 0.035 |
| | May | 0.024 | 0.027 | 0.033 |
| | June | 0.023 | 0.025 | 0.032 |
| | July | 0.024 | 0.027 | 0.033 |
| | Aug. | 0.019 | 0.022 | 0.028 |
| | Sept. | 0.020 | 0.023 | 0.029 |
| | Oct. | 0.020 | 0.023 | 0.029 |
| | Nov. | 0.019 | 0.022 | 0.028 |
| | Dec. | 0.016 | 0.019 | 0.025 |
| **2016** | Jan. | 0.023 | 0.026 | 0.032 |
| | Feb. | 0.018 | 0.021 | 0.027 |
| | Mar. | 0.014 | 0.017 | 0.023 |
| | Apr. | 0.013 | 0.016 | 0.022 |
| | May | 0.010 | 0.013 | 0.019 |
| | June | 0.006 | 0.009 | 0.015 |
| | July | 0.005 | 0.008 | 0.014 |
| | Aug. | 0.002 | 0.004 | 0.010 |
| | Sept. | Nil | 0.002 | 0.008 |
| | Oct. | Nil | 0.003 | 0.009 |
| | Nov. | | Nil | 0.006 |
| | Dec. | | Nil | Nil |

# Foreign exchange rates

## [¶12-000]   Foreign exchange rates: general

HMRC publish annually currency exchange rates for the purposes of converting foreign currencies into sterling.

The currency exchange rates for the US dollar, German deutschmark, Japanese yen and euro are reproduced below.

**Average exchange rates for year to 31 December**

| Average for year to 31 December | US $ | DM | Yen | Euro |
|---|---|---|---|---|
| 1989 | 1.6387 | 3.0786 | 225.64 | |
| 1990 | 1.7854 | 2.8749 | 257.45 | |
| 1991 | 1.7696 | 2.9247 | 237.69 | |
| 1992 | 1.7655 | 2.7528 | 230.90 | |
| 1993 | 1.5023 | 2.4828 | 166.9335 | |
| 1994 | 1.5318 | 2.4826 | 156.4429 | |
| 1995 | 1.5783 | 2.2603 | 148.283 | |
| 1996 | 1.5619 | 2.3506 | 169.593 | |
| 1997 | 1.638 | 2.8391 | 198.189 | |
| 1998 | 1.6573 | 2.9147 | 216.6834 | 1.4783[1] |
| 1999 | 1.6181 | 2.9702 | 183.969 | 1.5207 |
| 2000 | 1.5163 | 3.2114 | 163.378 | 1.6427 |
| 2001 | 1.4401 | 3.1461 | 174.8889 | 1.6085 |
| 2002 | 1.5023 | N/A | 187.8315 | 1.5906 |
| 2003 | 1.6348 | N/A | 189.3354 | 1.4457 |
| 2004 | 1.8318 | N/A | 198.065 | 1.474 |
| 2005 | 1.8195 | N/A | 200.1041 | 1.4626 |
| 2006 | 1.8424 | N/A | 214.3005 | 1.4666 |
| 2007 | 2.0020 | N/A | 235.6273 | 1.4604 |
| 2008 | 1.8511 | N/A | 192.26 | 1.2586 |
| 2009 | 1.5633 | N/A | 146.366 | 1.1235 |
| 2010 | 1.5457 | N/A | 136.104 | 1.1664 |
| 2011 | 1.603844 | N/A | 128.003692 | 1.151701 |
| 2012 | 1.582875 | N/A | 126.15025 | 1.233473 |
| 2013 | 1.562598 | N/A | 151.646301 | 1.178398 |
| 2014 | 1.65073 | N/A | 173.790568 | 1.224907 |
| 2015 | 1.530538 | N/A | 185.286343 | 1.37576 |
| 2016 | 1.376045 | N/A | 150.168417 | 1.240784 |

**Note**
[1] Former European Currency Unit.

**Average exchange rates for year to 31 March**

| Average for year to 31 March | US $ | DM | Yen | Euro |
|---|---|---|---|---|
| 1985 | 1.2500 | 3.7300 | 305.00 | |
| 1986 | 1.3700 | 3.7100 | 285.00 | |
| 1987 | 1.4900 | 3.0300 | 238.00 | |
| 1988 | 1.7000 | 2.9800 | 234.76 | |
| 1989 | 1.7970 | 3.2460 | 229.33 | |
| 1990 | 1.6305 | 2.9144 | 235.64 | |
| 1991 | 1.8682 | 2.9090 | 258.31 | |
| 1992 | 1.7350 | 2.9113 | 230.80 | |
| 1993 | 1.6924 | 2.6526 | 218.72 | |
| 1994 | 1.5066 | 2.5203 | 162.2872 | |
| 1995 | 1.5553 | 2.4256 | 154.3941 | |
| 1996 | 1.5656 | 2.2375 | 150.75 | |
| 1997 | 1.5866 | 2.4642 | 178.8762 | |
| 1998 | 1.642 | 2.912 | 201.5651 | |
| 1999 | 1.6542 | 2.878 | 211.499 | 1.4647 |
| 2000 | 1.6114 | 3.0548 | 179.386 | 1.563 |
| 2001 | 1.4793 | 3.1886 | 163.482 | 1.6304 |
| 2002 | 1.432 | 3.1677 | 179.0169 | 1.6202 |
| 2003 | 1.5466 | N/A | 188.3036 | 1.5573 |
| 2004 | 1.6939 | N/A | 190.9326 | 1.4400 |
| 2005 | 1.8445 | N/A | 198.171 | 1.467 |
| 2006 | 1.79738 | N/A | 201.2374 | 1.4664 |
| 2007 | 1.8932 | N/A | 221.4527 | 1.475 |
| 2008 | 2.0080 | N/A | 229.3116 | 1.4178 |
| 2009 | 1.7138 | N/A | 173.793 | 1.2042 |
| 2010 | 1.5962 | N/A | 148.193 | 1.1298 |
| 2011 | 1.55345 | N/A | 133.404 | 1.1779 |
| 2012 | 1.5958134 | N/A | 126.098730 | 1.158234 |
| 2013 | 1.580925 | N/A | 130.738615 | 1.228351 |
| 2014 | 1.584390 | N/A | 158.325192 | 1.185417 |
| 2015 | 1.598652 | N/A | 176.516505 | 1.270009 |
| 2016 | 1.508298 | N/A | 181.381545 | 1.368138 |

# [¶12-640]   Foreign exchange rates 2016–17

**Average for the year to 31 December 2016**

| Country | Unit of currency | Average for the year to 31 December 2016 | |
| --- | --- | --- | --- |
| | | Sterling value of currency unit £ | Currency units per £1 |
| Abu Dhabi | Dirham | 0.1978 | 5.056488 |
| Albania | Lek | 0.0059 | 170.723375 |
| Algeria | Dinar | 0.0067 | 150.356917 |
| Angola | Readj Kwanza | 0.0045 | 223.259667 |
| Antigua | E Caribbean Dollar | 0.269 | 3.716987 |
| Argentina | Peso | 0.0499 | 20.039292 |
| Armenia | Dram | 0.0015 | 661.087208 |
| Aruba | Florin | 0.4058 | 2.464473 |
| Australia | Dollar | 0.5398 | 1.852649 |
| Azerbaijan | New Manat | 0.4582 | 2.182317 |
| Bahamas | Dollar | 0.7267 | 1.376045 |
| Bahrain | Dinar | 1.9263 | 0.519127 |
| Bangladesh | Taka | 0.0093 | 108.051708 |
| Barbados | Dollar | 0.3632 | 2.753181 |
| Belarus | Rouble | 0.3887 | 2.57286 |
| Belize | Dollar | 0.3632 | 2.753017 |
| Benin | CFA Franc | 0.0012 | 814.319917 |
| Bermuda | Dollar (US) | 0.7267 | 1.376045 |
| Bhutan | Ngultrum | 0.0108 | 92.449 |
| Bolivia | Boliviano | 0.1052 | 9.505183 |
| Bosnia-Herzegovina | Marka | 0.4119 | 2.428067 |
| Botswana | Pula | 0.0665 | 15.039908 |
| Brazil | Real | 0.206 | 4.854893 |
| Brunei | Dollar | 0.2934 | 3.408618 |
| Bulgaria | Lev | 0.4118 | 2.428196 |
| Burkina Faso | CFA Franc | 0.0012 | 814.319917 |
| Burundi | Franc | 0.0004 | 2222.357583 |
| Cambodia | Riel | 0.0002 | 5330.036625 |

General

| Country | Unit of currency | Average for the year to 31 December 2016 | |
| | | Sterling value of currency unit £ | Currency units per £1 |
|---|---|---|---|
| Cameroon Republic | CFA Franc | 0.0012 | 814.319917 |
| Canada | Dollar | 0.5501 | 1.817877 |
| Cape Verde Islands | Escudo | 0.0073 | 136.919417 |
| Cayman Islands | Dollar | 0.8858 | 1.128863 |
| Central African Republic | CFA Franc | 0.0012 | 814.319917 |
| Chad | CFA Franc | 0.0012 | 814.319917 |
| Chile | Peso | 0.0011 | 937.166708 |
| China | Yuan | 0.1099 | 9.098112 |
| Colombia | Peso | 0.0002 | 4207.046542 |
| Comoros | Franc | 0.0016 | 610.738583 |
| Congo (Brazzaville) | CFA Franc | 0.0012 | 814.319917 |
| Congo (DemRep) | Congo Franc | 0.0008 | 1217.051375 |
| Costa Rica | Colon | 0.0013 | 745.827167 |
| Cote d'Ivoire | CFA Franc | 0.0012 | 814.319917 |
| Croatia | Kuna | 0.1069 | 9.354187 |
| Cuba | Peso | 0.7264 | 1.376575 |
| Czech Republic | Koruna | 0.0298 | 33.553167 |
| Denmark | Krone | 0.1082 | 9.239276 |
| Djibouti | Franc | 0.0041 | 244.655458 |
| Dominica | E Caribbean Dollar | 0.269 | 3.716987 |
| Dominican Republic | Peso | 0.0158 | 63.174 |
| Dubai | Dirham | 0.1978 | 5.056488 |
| Ecuador | Dollar | 0.7267 | 1.376045 |
| Egypt | Pound | 0.0784 | 12.756667 |
| El Salvador | Colon | 0.083 | 12.041875 |
| Equatorial Guinea | CFA Franc | 0.0012 | 814.319917 |

| Country | Unit of currency | Average for the year to 31 December 2016 | |
| | | Sterling value of currency unit £ | Currency units per £1 |
|---|---|---|---|
| Eritrea | Nakfa | 0.0484 | 20.6435 |
| Ethiopia | Birr | 0.0334 | 29.935083 |
| Eurozone | Euro | 0.8059 | 1.240784 |
| Fiji Islands | Dollar | 0.3469 | 2.88288 |
| Fr. Polynesia | CFP Franc | 0.0068 | 148.136792 |
| Gabon | CFA Franc | 0.0012 | 814.319917 |
| Gambia | Dalasi | 0.0173 | 57.703958 |
| Georgia | Lari | 0.3119 | 3.206053 |
| Ghana | Cedi | 0.1853 | 5.395412 |
| Grenada | E Caribbean Dollar | 0.269 | 3.716987 |
| Guatemala | Quetzal | 0.0954 | 10.486725 |
| Guinea Bissau | CFA Franc | 0.0012 | 814.319917 |
| Guinea Republic | Franc | 0.0001 | 9424.586583 |
| Guyana | Dollar | 0.0035 | 285.108708 |
| Haiti | Gourde | 0.0116 | 86.077125 |
| Honduras | Lempira | 0.0319 | 31.304417 |
| Hong Kong | Dollar | 0.0937 | 10.676933 |
| Hungary | Forint | 0.0026 | 386.828917 |
| Iceland | Krona | 0.0059 | 168.441917 |
| India | Rupee | 0.0108 | 92.449 |
| Indonesia | Rupiah | 0.0001 | 18335.22346 |
| Iraq | Dinar | 0.0006 | 1616.382625 |
| Israel | Shekel | 0.1892 | 5.285135 |
| Jamaica | Dollar | 0.0058 | 171.248417 |
| Japan | Yen | 0.0067 | 150.168417 |
| Jordan | Dinar | 1.0244 | 0.976191 |
| Kazakhstan | Tenge | 0.0021 | 469.985917 |
| Kenya | Schilling | 0.0072 | 139.787417 |
| Kuwait | Dinar | 2.4045 | 0.415885 |
| Kyrgyz Republic | Som | 0.0104 | 96.609792 |
| Lao People's Dem Rep | Kip | 0.0001 | 11193.88567 |

| Country | Unit of currency | Average for the year to 31 December 2016 | |
| | | Sterling value of currency unit £ | Currency units per £1 |
| --- | --- | --- | --- |
| Lebanon | Pound | 0.0005 | 2076.391292 |
| Lesotho | Loti | 0.049 | 20.421333 |
| Liberia | Dollar (US) | 0.7216 | 1.385863 |
| Libya | Dinar | 0.5337 | 1.873744 |
| Macao | Pataca | 0.0909 | 11.001733 |
| Macedonia | Denar | 0.0131 | 76.4425 |
| Madagascar | Malagasy Ariary | 0.0002 | 4370.964 |
| Malawi | Kwacha | 0.001 | 975.086042 |
| Malaysia | Ringgit | 0.1767 | 5.660823 |
| Maldive Islands | Rufiyaa | 0.0475 | 21.074542 |
| Mali Republic | CFA Franc | 0.0012 | 814.319917 |
| Mauritania | Ouguiya | 0.0021 | 481.10375 |
| Mauritius | Rupee | 0.0205 | 48.857917 |
| Mexico | Mexican Peso | 0.0393 | 25.431792 |
| Moldova | Leu | 0.0366 | 27.330792 |
| Mongolia | Tugrik | 0.0003 | 2891.671958 |
| Montserrat | E Caribbean Dollar | 0.269 | 3.716987 |
| Morocco | Dirham | 0.0742 | 13.476167 |
| Mozambique | Metical | 0.012 | 83.258833 |
| Myanmar | Kyat | 0.0006 | 1693.940542 |
| Nepal | Rupee | 0.0068 | 147.969542 |
| New Caledonia | CFP Franc | 0.0068 | 148.136792 |
| New Zealand | Dollar | 0.5039 | 1.984533 |
| Nicaragua | Gold Cordoba | 0.0255 | 39.258144 |
| Niger Republic | CFA Franc | 0.0012 | 814.319917 |
| Nigeria | Naira | 0.0029 | 347.059917 |
| Norway | Norwegian Krone | 0.0865 | 11.563583 |
| Oman | Rial | 1.8866 | 0.53006 |
| Pakistan | Rupee | 0.0069 | 144.189208 |
| Panama | Balboa | 0.7264 | 1.376654 |
| Papua New Guinea | Kina | 0.2325 | 4.301563 |

| Country | Unit of currency | Average for the year to 31 December 2016 | |
| --- | --- | --- | --- |
| | | Sterling value of currency unit £ | Currency units per £1 |
| Paraguay | Guarani | 0.0001 | 7789.234917 |
| Peru | New Sol | 0.2157 | 4.635137 |
| Philippines | Peso | 0.0154 | 65.009792 |
| Poland | Zloty | 0.1851 | 5.402822 |
| Qatar | Riyal | 0.1995 | 5.01264 |
| Romania | New Leu | 0.1794 | 5.575248 |
| Russia | Rouble | 0.0108 | 92.835625 |
| Rwanda | Franc | 0.0009 | 1075.026417 |
| Saotome and Principe | Dobra | 0 | 27787.62243 |
| Saudi Arabia | Riyal | 0.1938 | 5.160259 |
| Senegal | CFA Franc | 0.0012 | 814.319917 |
| Serbia | Dinar | 0.0065 | 152.777667 |
| Seychelles | Rupee | 0.0546 | 18.33075 |
| Sierra Leone | Leone | 0.0002 | 6389.390333 |
| Singapore | Dollar | 0.5272 | 1.896978 |
| Soloman Islands | Dollar | 0.092 | 10.874433 |
| Somali Republic | Schilling | 0.0012 | 819.771 |
| South Africa | Rand | 0.049 | 20.428208 |
| South Korea | Won | 0.0006 | 1598.662625 |
| Sri Lanka | Rupee | 0.005 | 200.72675 |
| St Christopher and Anguilla | E Caribbean Dollar | 0.269 | 3.716987 |
| St Lucia | E Caribbean Dollar | 0.269 | 3.716987 |
| St Vincent | E Caribbean Dollar | 0.269 | 3.716987 |
| Sudan Republic | Pound | 0.1187 | 8.427427 |
| Surinam | Dollar | 0.121 | 8.26306 |
| Swaziland | Lilangeni | 0.049 | 20.421575 |
| Sweden | Krona | 0.0857 | 11.667417 |
| Switzerland | Franc | 0.7393 | 1.35263 |
| Taiwan | Dollar | 0.0225 | 44.499375 |

| Country | Unit of currency | Average for the year to 31 December 2016 | |
| --- | --- | --- | --- |
| | | Sterling value of currency unit £ | Currency units per £1 |
| Tanzania | Schilling | 0.0003 | 3009.647958 |
| Thailand | Baht | 0.0206 | 48.517458 |
| Togo Republic | CFA Franc | 0.0012 | 814.319917 |
| Tonga Islands | Pa'anga (AUS) | 0.5398 | 1.852649 |
| Trinidad/Tobago | Dollar | 0.1097 | 9.113027 |
| Tunisia | Dinar | 0.3423 | 2.921115 |
| Turkey | Turkish Lira | 0.2453 | 4.076891 |
| Turkmenistan | New Manat | 0.2074 | 4.821745 |
| UAE | Dirham | 0.1978 | 5.056488 |
| Uganda | Schilling | 0.0002 | 4676.453958 |
| Ukraine | Hryvnia | 0.0286 | 34.921333 |
| Uruguay | Peso | 0.0239 | 41.794083 |
| USA | Dollar | 0.7267 | 1.376045 |
| Uzbekistan | Sum | 0.0002 | 4039.4335 |
| Vanuatu | Vatu | 0.0066 | 152.664458 |
| Venezuela | Bolivar Fuerte | 0.0812 | 12.311973 |
| Vietnam | Dong | 0 | 30756.86363 |
| Wallis and Futuna Islands | CFP Franc | 0.0068 | 148.136792 |
| Western Samoa | Tala | 0.285 | 3.509119 |
| Yemen (Rep of) | Rial | 0.003 | 329.298792 |
| Zambia | Kwacha | 0.0703 | 14.221917 |
| Zimbabwe | Dollar | 0.002 | 498.20875 |

**Table of spot rates on 31 December 2016**

| Country | Unit of currency | Spot rate on 31 December 2016 | |
| --- | --- | --- | --- |
| | | Sterling value of currency unit £ | Currency units per £1 |
| Australia | Dollar | 0.586 | 1.7065 |
| Canada | Dollar | 0.6035 | 1.6571 |
| Denmark | Krone | 0.1148 | 8.7108 |
| Eurozone | Euro | 0.8536 | 1.1715 |
| Hong Kong | Dollar | 0.1044 | 9.5802 |
| Japan | Yen | 0.0069 | 144.12 |
| Norway | Norwegian Krone | 0.0941 | 10.63 |
| South Africa | Rand | 0.0592 | 16.89 |
| Sweden | Krona | 0.0891 | 11.22 |
| Switzerland | Franc | 0.7962 | 1.2559 |
| USA | Dollar | 0.8093 | 1.2357 |

General

# Residence of individuals

## [¶13-000]   Statutory residence: from 2013–14

(FA 2013, Sch. 45)

(Tax Reporter: ¶199-000ff.)

From 6 April 2013, with effect for the tax year 2013–14 and subsequent tax years, a new statutory residence test (SRT) applies to determine the residence of an individual for tax purposes. The test applies for the purposes of income tax, capital gains tax and so far as relevant inheritance tax and corporation tax.

| Tests | Status |
|---|---|
| Automatic overseas test is satisfied | Not resident |
| Automatic UK residence test is satisfied (at least one of the automatic tests is satisfied **and** none of the automatic overseas tests are satisfied) | Resident |
| None of automatic overseas or automatic UK tests are satisfied:<br>• sufficient ties test is satisfied;<br>• sufficient ties test is not satisfied. | • UK resident<br>• Not resident |

### Automatic tests

An individual is automatically resident or not resident if they meet any of the four tests:

| Automatic overseas test (any one) | Automatic UK test (any one plus none of the overseas tests) |
|---|---|
| Resident in the UK for one or more of the three previous tax years and spend fewer than 16 days in the UK in the current tax year | Spend at least 183 days in the UK during the tax year |
| Not resident in the UK for any of the previous three tax years and spend fewer than 46 days in the UK in the current tax year | A period of more than 90 days, part of which falls into the tax year, when the individual has a home in the UK, and no overseas home (disregarding any home at which they are present for fewer than 30 days in the tax year) |

General

| Automatic overseas test (any one) | Automatic UK test (any one plus none of the overseas tests) |
|---|---|
| Work full-time overseas in the tax year and spends fewer than 91 days in the UK in the tax year, incl. fewer than 31 working days | Work full time in the UK in the current tax year |
| Die in the current tax year subject to conditions which include spending fewer than 46 days in the current tax year | Die in current tax year subject to conditions which include having been UK resident in the previous three tax years |

## Sufficient ties tests

Where none of the automatic overseas and none of the automatic UK tests are satisfied, an individual will need to look at the number of ties in conjunction with the number of days spent in the UK during the tax year and whether they have been resident in the previous three tax years to determine whether the sufficient ties test is satisfied. Ties to be considered are as follows:

* UK resident family;
* Substantive UK employment (including self-employment);
* Available accommodation in the UK;
* More than 90 days spent in the UK in either or both of the previous two tax years; and
* A country tie (but only if individual resident in one or more three previous tax years).

| Days spent in the UK during the tax year | Number of ties that are sufficient | |
|---|---|---|
| | Not resident in previous three tax years | Resident in any of the previous three tax years |
| More than 15 but not more than 45 | [Automatic overseas test is satisfied] | At least four |
| More than 45 but not more than 90 | All four | At least three |
| More than 90 but not more than 120 | At least three | At least two |
| More than 120 | At least two | At least one |

| Definition of ties |
| --- |
| **Family tie (either):** |
| • Individual has a UK resident spouse (unless separated), or partner (if living together as husband and wife or civil partners); |
| • Individual has a UK resident child under 18-years old (unless spends fewer than 61 days with the child in the tax year), |
| (an individual will not be considered to have a family tie with a child who is UK resident and under 18 years who is in full-time education and would not be a UK resident if the time spent in full-time education were disregarded and the child spends fewer than 21 days in the UK outside term time (half-term counts as term time)). |
| **Work tie** |
| Individual does more than three hours of work a day in the UK on at least 40 days in that year (whether continuously or intermittently). [NB. special rules apply as to what constitutes three hours work for workers on board a vehicle, aircraft or ship.] |
| **Accommodation tie** |
| Individual has a place to live in the UK (including a home, holiday home, temporary retreat of other accommodation) that is: |
| • available for a continuous period of 91 days or more during the year; |
| • the individual spends one or more nights there during the year; or |
| • if it is at the home of a close relative (parent, grandparent, sibling, child or grandchild over 18 years old), the individual spends 16 or more nights there during the year. |
| **90-day tie** |
| Individual spends more than 90 days (counting midnights) in the UK in either or both of the previous two tax years |
| **Country tie** |
| **(applicable only where resident in any of previous three tax years)** |
| UK is the country in which the individual was present at midnight for the greatest number of days in the tax year. |
| If the number of days an individual is present in a country at midnight is the same for two or more countries in a tax year, and one of those countries is the UK, then the individual will have a country tie for that tax year if that is the greatest number of days spent in any country in that tax year. |

## [¶13-400]   Split year treatment

(FA 2013, Sch. 45, Pt. 3)

(Tax Reporter: ¶199-375)

Under the SRT, an individual is either UK resident or non-UK resident for a full tax year and at all times in that tax year. However, if during a year that individual either starts to live or work abroad or comes from abroad to live or work in the UK, the tax year will be split into two parts if their circumstances meet specific criteria:

• a UK part for which they are charged to UK tax as a UK resident;

• an overseas part for which, for most purposes, they are charged to UK tax as a non-UK resident.

General

The taxpayer must be UK resident for a tax year under the SRT to meet the criteria for split year treatment for that year. They will not meet the split year criteria for a tax year for which they are non-UK resident under the SRT. Split year treatment only applies to an individual in their individual capacity and not to individuals acting as personal representatives. It applies in a limited way to individuals acting as trustee of a settlement.

## [¶13-500]   Abolition of ordinary residence

(FA 2013, Sch. 46)

(Tax Reporter: ¶199-975)

The concept of ordinary resident for tax purposes has been abolished for tax years 2013–14 onwards. Transitional provisions apply to ensure those who currently benefit from being ordinarily resident will continue to be able to benefit for a maximum of two complete tax years.

## [¶13-600]   Overseas workday relief

(ITEPA 2013, Pt. 2, Ch. 5)

(Tax Reporter: ¶199-960ff.)

Overseas workday relief (OWR) is available to certain resident, but non-UK domiciled individuals with an employment the duties of which are carried out partly in the UK and partly overseas. If relevant conditions are met, the earnings which relation to the duties performed overseas are only taxable on the remittance basis and if not remitted, are not taxable – this is OWR. OWR is available to all non-UK domiciled individuals who arrive in the UK after 5 April 2013 having been non-UK resident for the previous three tax years. It will be available for the whole of the tax year that the individual becomes resident in the UK (or for the UK part of the year if that year is a split year) and for the following two tax years.

## [¶13-800]   Remittance basis

(ITA 2007, Pt. 14, Ch. A1)

(Tax Reporter: ¶199-675)

Non-domiciled individuals can elect to pay tax on the remittance basis so that UK tax is paid on foreign income or gains only to the extent that (and when) they are brought into the UK. A charge for claiming the remittance basis applies where the individual satisfies one of the three residence tests (is a 'long-term UK resident'), as shown in the table below.

| No. of years UK resident | Remittance basis charge[1][2][3] | | | |
|---|---|---|---|---|
| | 2017–18 £ | 2015–16 to 2016–17 £ | 2012–13 to 2014–15 £ | 2008–09 to 2011–12 £ |
| 7-year test (7 out of past 9 tax years) | 30,000 | 30,000 | 30,000 | 30,000 |
| 12-year test (12 out of past 14 tax years) | 60,000 | 60,000 | 50,000 | — |
| 17-year test (17 out of past 20 tax years) | — | 90,000 | — | — |

**Notes**
[1] Since 2008, where the remittance basis is claimed, the individual is not entitled to any personal allowance, blind person's allowance, tax reductions for married couples or civil partners, life assurance payments relief or capital gains tax annual exempt amount (ITA 2007, s. 809G).
[2] The remittance basis applies automatically (without a claim) to:
- individuals whose unremitted foreign income or gains for the year are less than £2,000 (unless they satisfy the conditions for the exemption from income tax for non-domiciliaries on foreign income described under ITA 2007, s. 828B, or give notice that the remittance basis is not to apply) (ITA 2007, s. 809D);
- individuals who:
  - do not have UK source income or gains (other than taxed investment income) exceeding £100 for the tax year concerned;
  - do not remit in that year any foreign income or gains which arose in a year in which the remittance basis has applied; and
  - have been UK resident for not more than six of the immediately preceding nine tax years, or are under the age of 18 throughout the tax year concerned (ITA 2007, s. 809E).
[3] Where a claim for the remittance basis is made, the claimant is required to 'nominate' all or part of his unremitted foreign income or gains for the year of claim, to be taxed on the arising basis. That amount must be such as would produce a 'relevant tax increase' of not more than the amount of the charge that applies (depending on which of the residence tests is satisfied) (ITA 2007, s. 809C(2)–(4)). These amounts are termed the 'applicable amounts' (ITA 2007, s. 809H(5A)).

## Reform of domicile rules

(Draft Finance Bill 2017)

Draft Finance Bill 2017 legislates for a series of reforms announced at the Summer 2015 Budget to the tax rules for individuals who are not domiciled in the UK under the general law.

The reforms will broadly align the existing inheritance tax deemed domicile provisions for individuals with the proposed changes for income tax and capital gains tax.

Individuals who are not domiciled in the UK will be deemed to be UK domiciled for tax purposes if they are either resident in the UK for 15 of the past 20 tax years, or if they are born in the UK with a UK domicile of origin and return to the UK having obtained a domicile of choice elsewhere. They will be taxed on any arising worldwide income and gains in the same way as UK domiciles. At the same time, the existing inheritance tax deeming provisions will be aligned with the new 15 out of 20 rule.

Transitional protections will be given where an individual becomes deemed-UK domicile under the 15 out of 20 rule in April 2017, including the facility to rebase offshore assets for capital gains tax purposes. Those who become deemed domicile in April 2017, excepting those who were born in the UK with a UK domicile of origin, will be able to treat the cost base of their non-UK based assets as the market value of that asset on 5 April 2017.

General

The new rules will also ensure that any non-dom who sets up a qualifying trust before becoming deemed domiciled would not pay income tax/capital gains tax on income/ gains in the trust, as long as they did not receive a benefit from the trust. However, once a benefit is taken, capital gains tax would be payable on trust gains and income tax on family benefits received.

There will also be a facility for remittance basis taxpayers to rearrange their overseas mixed funds to allow them to remit clean capital from overseas ahead of income and gains. Non-doms will be able to segregate amounts of income, gains and capital within their overseas mixed funds to provide certainty on how amounts remitted to the UK will be taxed. This treatment will be extended by government amendment to income, gains and capital held in mixed funds from years before 2007–08, as well as those from subsequent years.

## [¶14-000]   Double tax treaties

The following table lists all the territories with which the UK has concluded agreements to avoid international double taxation and also facilitate the exchange of information to prevent tax evasion.

Albania (C)
Algeria (C)
Andorra (EC)
Anguilla (SIE/TIE)
Antigua and Barbuda (C/TIE)
Argentina (C)
Aruba (SIE/TIE)
Armenia (C)
Australia (C)
Austria (C)
Azerbaijan (C)
Bahamas (TIE)
Bahrain (C)
Bangladesh (C)
Barbados (C)
Belarus (C)[(1)]
Belgium (C)
Belize (C/TIE)
Bermuda (TIE/IGA)
Bolivia (C)
Bosnia-Herzegovina (C)[(2)]
Botswana (C)
Brazil (SA/AC/TIE)
British Virgin Islands (SIE/TIE/IGA)
Brunei Darussalam (C)
Bulgaria (C)
Burma (C)
Cameroon (A)
Canada (C)
Cayman Islands (C/SIE/IGA)
Chile (C)[(3)]
China (C/A)
Croatia (C)
Cyprus (C)
Czech Republic (C)
Denmark (C)
Dominica (TIE)
Egypt (C)
Estonia (C)[(1)]
Ethiopia (C/A)
Falkland Islands (C)
Faroe Islands (C)
Fiji (C)
Finland (C)
France (includes Guadeloupe, Guyane, Martinique and Réunion (C/EIG)
Gambia (C)
Georgia (C)
Germany (C)
Ghana (C)
Gibraltar (SIE/IGA)
Greece (C)

Grenada (C/TIE)
Guernsey (includes Alderney, Herm and Lithou) (C/TIE/IGA)
Guyana (C)
Hong Kong SAR (C/SA)
Hungary (C)
Iceland (C)
India (C/EIG)[(3)]
Indonesia (C)
Iran (A)
Ireland (C/EIG)
Isle of Man (SIE) (C/TIE/IGA)
Israel (C)
Italy (C/EIG)
Ivory Coast (Cote d'Ivoire) (C)
Jamaica (C)
Japan (C)
Jersey (SIE/C/TIE/IGA)
Jordan (C)
Kazakstan (C)
Kenya (C)
Kiribati and Tuvalu (C)
Korea (C)
Kosovo (C)
Kuwait (C)
Latvia (C)
Lebanon (SA)
Lesotho (C)
Liberia (TIE)
Libya (C)
Liechtenstein (EC/TIE/C)
Lithuania (C)
Luxembourg (C)
Macao (TIE)
Macedonia (C)
Malawi (C)
Malaysia (C)
Malta (C)
Marshall Islands (TIE)
Mauritius (C)
Mexico (C)
Moldova (C)
Monaco (EC/TIE)
Mongolia (C)
Montenegro (C)[(2)]
Montserrat (SIE/C/TIE/IGA)
Morocco (C)
Namibia (C)
Netherlands (C/EIG/BT)
Netherlands Antilles (SIE/TIE)
New Zealand (C)
Nigeria (C)
Norway (C)

Oman (C)
Pakistan (EIG unchecked[(3)]/C)
Panama (C)
Papua New Guinea (C)
Philippines (C)
Poland (C)
Portugal (C)
Qatar (C)
Romania (C)
Russia (C)
St Christopher (St. Kitts) & Nevis (C/TIE)
St Lucia (TIE)
St Vincent and the Grenadines (TIE)
San Marino (EC/TIE)
Saudi Arabia (C/A)
Senegal (C)
Serbia (C)[(2)]
Sierra Leone (C)
Singapore (C)
Slovak Republic (C)
Slovenia (C)
Solomon Islands (C)
South Africa (C/EIG)
Spain (C)
Sri Lanka (C)
Sudan (C)
Swaziland (C)
Sweden (C/EIG)
Switzerland (TC/C/EC/EIG/EC/TIE)
Taiwan (C)
Tajikistan (C)
Thailand (C)
Trinidad and Tobago (C)
Tunisia (C)
Turkey (C)
Turkmenistan (C)[(1)]
Turks & Caicos Islands (SIE/TIE/IGA)
Tuvula (UK/Gilbert and Ellice Islands) (C)
Uganda (C)
Ukraine (C)
United Arab Emirates (C)
Uruguay (C/TIE)
USA (C/EIG)
Uzbekistan (C)
Venezuela (C)
Vietnam (C)
Zaire (SA)
Zambia (C)
Zimbabwe (C)

General

These agreements may be of various types which are indicated below by the following letters:

- (C) – comprehensive agreements covering a wide range of areas of possible double taxation of income and capital gains;
- (SA) – agreements limited to shipping and air transport profits;
- (A) – agreements limited to air transport profits only;
- (AC) – agreements limited to salaries of aircrew only;
- (EIG) – agreements relating to tax on estates, inheritances and gifts;
- (SIE) – tax information exchange agreements: agreements relating to the EU Directive on taxation of savings income in the form of interest payments;
- (TIE) – tax information exchange agreements: bilateral agreements for co-operation in tax matters through exchange of information;
- (EC) – tax information exchange agreements concluded by the EC on behalf of its member states with third countries;
- (TC) – tax co-operation agreements;
- (BT) – convention in respect of bank taxes; and
- (IGA) – inter-governmental agreement to improve international tax compliance.

**Notes**
[1] The Convention of 31 July 1985 with the former USSR is regarded as continuing in force (see SP 04/01). The Convention between UK and Turkmenistan was signed on 10 June 2016 but has not yet entered into force.
[2] The Convention of 5 November 1981 with the former Yugoslavia is regarded as continuing in force (see SP 03/07).
[3] The estate, inheritance and gifts agreements with India and Pakistan have not been formally terminated despite the fact that estate duties in those countries were abolished on 15 March 1985 and 29 July 1979 respectively.

# Recognised exchanges

## [¶15-000]   Recognised stock exchanges

(ITA 2007, s. 1005)

With effect from 19 July 2007, a 'recognised stock exchange' is defined for the purposes of the Income Tax Acts as being one which is designated as such by an Order of the Commissioners for HMRC and which falls within one of two categories:

- 'recognised investment exchanges' designated by the Financial Conduct Authority (formerly the Financial Services Authority); and
- markets outside the UK (see below).

**Designated 'recognised stock exchanges' by Order**

Below is a list of stock exchanges designated as 'recognised stock exchanges' by Order of the Commissioners for HMRC, together with the date of recognition.

| | |
|---|---|
| The Athens[1] Stock Exchange | 14 Jun 1993 |
| The Australian[1] Stock Exchange and any of its subsidiaries | 22 Sep 1988 |
| The Bahamas International Securities Exchange | 19 Apr 2010 |
| The Bermuda Stock Exchange | 4 Dec 2007 |
| The Bond Exchange of South Africa[1] | 16 Apr 2008 |
| The Cayman Islands Stock Exchange | 4 Mar 2004 |
| The Colombo[1] Stock Exchange | 21 Feb 1972 |
| The Copenhagen[1] Stock Exchange | 22 Oct 1970 |
| The Cyprus[1] Stock Exchange | 22 Jun 2009 |
| The Dutch Caribbean Securities Exchange | 8 Dec 2014 |
| Euronext London Ltd | 4 Feb 2015 |
| European Wholesale Securities Market | 18 Jan 2013 |
| Gibraltar Stock Exchange Limited | 16 Aug 2016 |
| Global Board of Trade | 30 Jul 2013 |
| GXG Official List | 16 May 2013 |
| GXG Main Quote[1] | 23 Sep 2013 |
| The Helsinki[1] Stock Exchange | 22 Oct 1970 |
| The Iceland[1] Stock Exchange | 31 Mar 2006 |
| ICAP Securities[1] & Derivatives Exchange Ltd | 25 Apr 2013 |
| The Johannesburg[1] Stock Exchange | 22 Oct 1970 |
| The Korea[1] Stock Exchange | 10 Oct 1994 |
| The Kuala Lumpa[1] Stock Exchange | 10 Oct 1994 |
| LIFFE[1] Administration and Management | 26 Sep 2011 |
| The London[1] Stock Exchange | 19 Jul 2007 |
| The Malta Stock Exchange | 29 Dec 2005 |
| The Mexico[1] Stock Exchange | 10 Oct 1994 |

General

| The MICEX[1] Stock Exchange | 5 Jan 2011 |
|---|---|
| The NASDAQ OMX Tallinn[1] | 5 May 2010 |
| The NASDAQ OMX Vilnius[1] | 12 Mar 2012 |
| The National Stock Exchange of Australia | 19 Jun 2014 |
| The New Zealand[1] Stock Exchange | 22 Sep 1988 |
| The Rio De Janeiro Stock Exchange | 17 Aug 1995 |
| The Sao Paulo[1] Stock Exchange | 11 Dec 1995 |
| The Singapore Exchange Limited (SGX) | 7 Oct 2014 (30 Jun 1977) |
| The Stockholm[1] Stock Exchange | 16 Jul 1985 |
| The Stock Exchange of Mauritius[1] | 31 Jan 2011 |
| The Stock Exchange of Thailand[1] | 10 Oct 1994 |
| The Swiss Stock Exchange | 12 May 1997 |
| The Warsaw[1] Stock Exchange | 25 Feb 2010 |

**Note**

[1] Markets of the above recognised exchanges on which securities would not meet HMRC definition of 'listed' are as follows:

- Athens Stock Exchange: The Alternative Market (EN.A)
- Australian Stock Exchange: The Sydney Futures Exchange (SFX)
- Bond Exchange of South Africa: Over-the Counter (OTC) market
- Colombo Stock Exchange: Diri Savi Board
- Copenhagen Stock Exchange (part of the OMX Nordic Exchange which is part of the NASDAQ OMX Group): First North
- Cyprus Stock Exchange: Emerging Companies Market (a Multi-lateral trading facility)
- GXG Main Quote: GXG Main Quote
- Helsinki Stock Exchange (part of the OMX Nordic Exchange which is part of the NASDAQ OMX Group): First North
- Iceland Stock Exchange (part of the OMX Nordic Exchange which is part of the NASDAQ OMX Group): First North
- ICAP Securities & Derivatives Exchange Ltd: ISDX Growth Market and ISDX Secondary Market
- Johannesburg Stock Exchange: Alt-X, Venture Capital Market (VCM) and Development Capital Market (DCM)
- Korean Stock Exchange: KOSDAQ and Korean Derivatives Market
- Kuala Lumpa Stock Exchange: ACE Market
- LIFFE Administration and Management (LIFFE A&M): London International Financial Futures and Options Market (LIFFE) the Derivatives Market
- London Stock Exchange: the Alternative Investment Market (AIM), Specialist Fund Market (SFM) and High Growth Segment (HGS)
- Mexico Stock Exchange: OTC Market
- MICEX Stock Exchange: Quotation list B, Quotation list V, Quotation list I, Over the Counter and unlisted security segments
- NASDAQ OMX Tallinn: First North
- NASDAQ OMX Vilnius: First North
- New Zealand Stock Exchange: NZAX Market (Alternative Market)
- Sao Paulo Stock Exchange: Over-the-Counter (OTC) market
- Stockholm Stock Exchange (part of the OMX Nordic Exchange which is part of the NASDAQ OMX Group): First North
- Stock Exchange of Mauritius: Development and Enterprise Market (DEM)
- Stock Exchange of Thailand: Market for Alternative Investment (MAI) and the Thailand Futures Exchange (TFEX), and securities traded over the counter (OTC)
- Warsaw Stock Exchange: New Connect Market and Catalyst Market for Bonds (Retail Market) Multi-lateral Trading Facility (MTF)

In addition, a recognised stock exchange is any stock exchange in the following countries which is a stock exchange within the meaning of the law of the particular country relating to stock exchanges (or as specified below).

| | |
|---|---|
| Austria[1] | 22 Oct 1970 |
| Belgium[1] | 22 Oct 1970 |
| Canada[1] (any stock exchange prescribed for the purpose of the Canadian Income Tax Act) | 22 Oct 1970 |
| France[1] | 22 Oct 1970 |
| Germany[1] | 5 Aug 1971 |
| Guernsey[2] | 10 Dec 2002 |
| Hong Kong[1] | 26 Feb 1971 |
| Ireland[1], Republic of | 22 Oct 1970 |
| Italy | 3 May 1972 |
| Japan | 22 Oct 1970 |
| Luxembourg | 21 Feb 1972 |
| Netherlands[1] | 22 Oct 1970 |
| Norway | 22 Oct 1970 |
| Portugal | 21 Feb 1972 |
| Spain | 5 Aug 1971 |
| USA[1] (any exchange registered with the Securities and Exchange Commission of the United States as a national securities exchange) | 22 Oct 1970 |

**Notes**
[1] Markets of the above recognised exchanges on which securities would not meet HMRC definition of 'listed' are as follows:
- Austria: Third Market or Dritter Market
- Belgium: NYSE Alternext
- Canada: NEX
- France: NYSE Alternext
- Germany: Freiverkehr markets, Entry Markets (also known as open or unofficial markets)
- Hong Kong: The Growth and Enterprise Market (GEM)
- Ireland (Republic of): Enterprise Securities Market (ESM)
- Netherlands: NYSE Alternext
- USA: Over the counter transactions, Over the Counter Bulletin Board (OTCBB) and Pink Sheets

[2] The Channel Islands Stock Exchange restructured on 20 December 2013 with the business of the exchange being transferred to The Channel Islands Securities Exchange Authority Limited.

## Alternative finance investment bonds

(TCGA 1992, s. 151N; ITA 2007, s. 564G; CTA 2009, s. 507)

'Alternative finance investment bonds' (Sharia compliant financial instruments commonly known as 'sukuk') must be listed on a recognised stock exchange. An alternative finance investment bond listed on an exchange recognised under ITA 2007, s. 1005 will meet this requirement. In addition, certain other exchanges are designated as recognised stock exchanges **solely** for the purposes of ITA 2007, s. 564G. These are listed below, together with the dates of recognition.

| | |
|---|---|
| Abu Dhabi Securities Market | 1 April 2007 |
| Bahrain Stock Exchange | 1 April 2007 |
| Dubai Financial Market | 1 April 2007 |
| NASDAQ Dubai (formerly the 'Dubai International Financial Exchange') | 1 April 2007 |
| Labuan International Financial Exchange | 1 April 2007 |
| Saudi Stock Exchange (Tadawul) | 1 April 2007 |
| Surabaya Stock Exchange | 1 April 2007 |

## [¶15-050] Recognised futures exchanges
(TCGA 1992, s. 288(6))

The following futures exchanges have been designated by the Board of Her Majesty's Revenue and Customs as 'recognised futures exchanges' (when the Board recognises a futures exchange this is announced in the *London Gazette*):

| Exchange | Date |
|---|---|
| International Petroleum Exchange of London London Metal Exchange | From 6 August 1985 |
| London Gold Market London Silver Market | From 12 December 1985 |
| CME Group (formerly Chicago Mercantile Exchange and Chicago Board of Trade[3]) Philadelphia Board of Trade New York Mercantile Exchange | From 19 December 1986 |
| Montreal Exchange Mid-America Commodity Exchange | From 29 July 1987 |
| Hong Kong Futures Exchange | From 15 December 1987 |
| Commodity Exchange, Inc (COMEX) | From 25 August 1988 |
| Sydney Futures Exchange Ltd | From 31 October 1988 |
| OM Stockholm OMLX (formerly OM London) | From 18 March 1992 |
| Euronext (London International Financial Futures and Options Exchange)[1] | From 22 March 1992 |
| New York Board of Trade[2] | From 10 June 2004 |
| Eurex Deutschland | From 13 March 2015 |

**Notes**

[1] Euronext (merged with NYSE group in 2007 to form NYSE Euronext) acquired London International Financial Futures and Options Exchange in January 2002. On 22 March 1992, London International Financial Futures Exchange and the London Traded Options Market merged forming London International Financial Futures and Options Exchange. In 1996, the LIFFE merged with the London Commodity Exchange (formerly FOX). Markets incorporated within former London Commodity Exchange, recognised from 6 August 1985 include: Baltic International Freight Futures Exchange; London Cocoa Terminal Market; London Coffee Terminal Market; London Futures and Options Exchange;

London Grain Futures Market; London Meat Futures Market; London Potato Futures Market; London Rubber Market; London Soya Bean Meal Futures Market and London Sugar Terminal Market.
[(2)] In June 2004, the New York Coffee Sugar and Cocoa Exchange (CS&CE) merged with the New York Cotton Exchange (NYCE) to form the New York Board of Trade. As a result of this merger, all previous exchanges and subsidiaries ceased to exist, including the Coffee, Sugar, & Cocoa Exchange, the New York Cotton Exchange, the Citrus Associates of the New York Cotton Exchange, the New York Futures Exchange (NYFE), and the FINEX Exchange. All markets are now referred to as the New York Board of Trade or NYBOT. [NY CS&CE was designated from 15 December 1987, and NYCE and Citrus Associates of the NYCE from 25 August 1988.]
[(3)] Chicago Board of Trade recognised from 24 April 1987.

## [¶15-150]   Recognised investment exchanges

(ITEPA 2003, s. 702)

(Tax Reporter: ¶494-300)

A 'recognised investment exchange' (RIE) is an investment exchange in relation to which a recognition order made by the Financial Conduct Authority (FCA) (formerly Financial Services Authority) is in force (*Financial Services and Markets Act* 2000, s. 285ff.).

Where the FCA does issue a recognition order for a 'recognised investment exchange' this has consequences for the rules relating to the operation of PAYE on the provision of 'readily convertible asset' for employees. If an employer provides an employee with an asset that can be sold, or otherwise realised, on a recognised investment exchange (RIE); the London Bullion Market; the New York Stock Exchange; or any market specified in PAYE Regulations, that asset is a 'readily convertible asset' and the employer is obliged to operate PAYE (ITEPA 2003, s. 696, 702). Similarly, any asset, such as a gold bar, capable of sale or realisation on the London Bullion Market is a 'readily convertible asset'. As at November 2013, the FCA has currently issued recognition orders for the following RIEs:

| Investment exchange | Effective date |
|---|---|
| **UK** | |
| ICE Futures Europe | 22 November 2001 |
| BATS Trading Limited | 11 July 2013 |
| ICAP Securities & Derivatives Exchange Limited | 19 July 2007 |
| LIFFE Administration and Management | 22 November 2001 |
| London Stock Exchange plc | 22 November 2001 |
| The London Metal Exchange Limited | 22 November 2001 |
| **Overseas** | |
| Australian Securities Exchange Limited | 30 January 2002 |
| Chicago Board of Trade [CBOT] | 23 November 2001 |
| EUREX [Zurich] | 23 November 2001 |
| ICE Futures U.S., Inc | 17 May 2007 |
| National Association of Securities Dealers Automated Quotations [NASDAQ] | 23 November 2001 |
| New York Mercantile Exchange Inc. [NYMEX Inc.] | 23 November 2001 |
| NYSE Liffe US | 29 September 2009 |
| SIX Swiss Exchange AG | 23 November 2001 |
| The Chicago Mercantile Exchange [CME] | 23 November 2001 |

General

## [¶15-200]  Recognised growth markets

(FA 1986, s. 99A)

*Finance Act* 2014 introduces an exemption from stamp duty and stamp duty reserve tax for transfers of securities admitted to trading on recognised growth markets, with effect from 28 April 2014.

To qualify as a recognised growth market, a market must be a recognised stock exchange (see ¶15-000) and meet one of two conditions:

- a majority of companies trading on that market are companies with market capitalisations of less than £170m in the qualifying period; or

- the market's rules require that companies seeking admission demonstrate at least 20% compounded annual growth in revenue or employment over the three years preceding admission.

### List of recognised growth markets

| Name | Effective date |
| --- | --- |
| Alternative Investment Market | 28 April 2014 |
| Enterprise Securities Market (ESM) | 28 April 2014 |
| GXG Markets A/S | 28 April 2014 |
| High Growth Segment | 28 April 2014 |
| ICAP Securities and Derivatives Exchange Limited (ISDX) | 28 April 2014 |

# HMRC information

**Note:** See ¶26-000 for opinions from Revenue Scotland in respect of Scottish taxes.

## [¶15-500]   Clearances and approvals

(Source: www.gov.uk/seeking-clearance-or-approval-for-a-transaction)

HMRC may be able to provide advance clearance or approval to some transactions. HMRC will not provide clearances on the following matters:

- application of the 'settlements legislation' in ITTOIA 2005, Pt. 5, Ch. 5; or
- the tax consequences of executing non-charitable trust deeds or settlements.

### Clearances and the General Anti-Abuse Rule (GAAR)

HMRC will not give either formal or informal clearances that the GAAR does not apply. However, as part of its model of direct engagement with large businesses and wealthy individuals HMRC will discuss commercial arrangements and confirm where appropriate that it does not regard particular arrangements as tax avoidance.

### Code of Practice on Taxation for Banks

A bank which adopts the Code of Practice on Taxation for Banks commits not to undertake any tax planning that achieves a tax result contrary to the intentions of Parliament. When approached by a bank under the code, Customer Relationship Managers will continue to give HMRC's view of whether a transaction is 'code compliant'.

## [¶15-550]   Non-statutory clearances

(Source: www.gov.uk/seeking-clearance-or-approval-for-a-transaction)

| Transaction | Applications to: |
|---|---|
| **Company migrations**<br>Notification of company migration and approval of arrangements for payment of tax liabilities in accordance with TMA 1970, s. 109B–109F (previously FA 1988, s. 130) (see SP 2/90). | Nicola Harris<br>HM Revenue & Customs<br>CTIS Business International,<br>Foreign Profits Team<br>100 Parliament Street<br>London<br>SW1A 2BQ<br>Telephone: 03000 543 476 |

General

| Transaction | Applications to: |
|---|---|
| **Controlled Foreign Companies** Clearances in relation to Controlled Foreign Companies (CFC) in accordance with TIOPA 2010, Pt. 9A (new CFC rules) or ICTA 1988, s. 747–756 and Sch. 24–26 (old CFC Rules). | Electronically to Mary Sharp and copied to the UK group's Customer Relationship Manager or Customer Co-ordinator. (No paper copies of an application are needed.) If it is not possible to send applications for clearance electronically, applications should be sent to the following address: CTIS, Foreign Profits Team Registry (CFC clearances) 3rd floor 100 Parliament Street London SW1A 2BQ Telephone: 03000 585 623 |
| **Inward Investment Support service** For information on inward investment and to discuss the tax implications of an investment. | Inward Investment Support HM Revenue & Customs CTIAA Business International 100 Parliament Street London SW1A 2BQ E-mail: inwardinvestmentsupport@hmrc. gsi.gov.uk. |
| **Business Investment Relief Provisions** For HMRC's view on whether a proposed investment can be treated as a qualifying investment as defined in ITA 2007, s. 809VC use the checklist at www.gov.uk/government/uploads/system/ uploads/attachment_data/file/377647/ annex-b.pdf. | Business Investment Relief HM Revenue & Customs BX9 1BN Telephone: 03000 527 416 |
| **Creative Industries** Advice on the workings of the scheme as it applies to film tax, animation tax, high-end television tax and video games development reliefs. | Creative Industries Unit (film, television/ animation and video games tax reliefs) Local Compliance S0717 PO Box 3900 Glasgow G70 6AA Telephone: 03000 510 191 |
| **Enterprise investment scheme (EIS), seed enterprise investment scheme (SEIS) and venture capital trust (VCT) scheme** Advice on the workings of these schemes, as well as providing non-statutory advance assurance to companies seeking investment under these schemes. | Local Compliance Small Company Enterprise Centre Admin Team SO777 PO Box 3900 Glasgow G70 6AA Telephone: 0300 123 1083 |

| Transaction | Applications to: |
|---|---|
| **Research and development tax relief: advance assurance** <br> Confirmation that a company will get R&D tax relief. | Apply online at www.gov.uk/government/ publications/research-and-development-tax-relief-application-for-advance-assurance-for-research-and-development-tax-relief-ct-rd-aa <br> By post to: <br> Local Compliance <br> I & R Unit Manchester (AA) <br> SO717 <br> Newcastle upon Tyne <br> NE98 1ZZ |

**Other non-statutory clearances**

(Source: www.gov.uk/non-statutory-clearance-service-guidance)

HMRC offer a further clearance service for customers and their advisers who need clarification on guidance or legislation in relation to a specific transaction that is not covered by a more appropriate clearance or approval route. HMRC will usually reply within 28 days.

HMRC will not provide advice under this service where:

- all the necessary information (per the checklists below) has not been provided;
- HMRC do not think that there are genuine points of uncertainty – they will explain why they think this and where the relevant online guidance can be found;
- the request is for HMRC to give tax planning advice, or to 'approve' tax planning products or arrangements;
- the application is about treatment of transactions which, in HMRC's view, are for the purposes of avoiding tax;
- HMRC are already checking the tax position for the period in question, in which case contact should be directed to the officer dealing with the check;
- any related return for the period in question is final; or
- there is a statutory clearance applicable for the transaction.

| Other non-statutory clearances | Applications to: |
|---|---|
| **All transactions other than Business Investment Relief and Business Property Relief** <br> See Annex A checklist at www.gov.uk/government/uploads/system/ uploads/attachment_data/file/377646/ annex-a.pdf – head the application letter 'Clearance service'. | HMRC Non-Statutory Clearance Team, <br> 5th Floor Alexander House, <br> 21 Victoria Avenue, <br> Southend on Sea, Essex <br> SS99 1AA <br> E-mail: hmrc.southendteam@hmrc.gsi.gov.uk <br> (HMRC Non-Statutory Clearance Team) |

General

| Other non-statutory clearances | Applications to: |
| --- | --- |
| **Advance assurance on Business Investment Relief for non-domiciled persons taxed on the remittance basis** See Annex B checklist at www.gov.uk/government/uploads/system/ uploads/attachment_data/file/377647/ annex-b.pdf – head the application letter 'Advance Assurance for Business Investment Relief'. | HM Revenue & Customs Business Investment Relief Team S1278 PO Box 202 Bootle L69 9AL |
| **Inheritance Tax Business Property Relief clearances** See Annex C checklist at www.gov.uk/government/uploads/system/ uploads/attachment_data/file/377648/ annex-c.pdf. | By e-mail to: mailpoint.e@hmrc.gsi.gov.uk (Trusts & Estates Technical Team (Clearances)). Please quote reference BP102/P1/08E By post to: HMRC Trusts & Estates Technical Team (Clearances) Ferrers House Castle Meadow Road Nottingham NG2 1BB |
| **VAT clearances** See Annex D checklist at www.gov.uk/government/uploads/system/ uploads/attachment_data/file/423806/ Annex_D_final_150416-5.pdf. | HM Revenue and Customs Non-Statutory Clearance Team 5th Floor Alexander House 21 Victoria Avenue Southend on Sea Essex SS99 1AA E-mail: hmrc.southendteam@hmrc.gsi. gov.uk |

## [¶15-600] Statutory clearance or approval

| Transaction | Applications to: |
| --- | --- |
| **Qualifying life assurance policies ICTA 1988, Sch. 15** Applications to approve certification of qualifying life assurance policies. | HM Revenue & Customs CTISA Corporation Tax and Business Income Tax Financial Services Team 3rd Floor 100 Parliament Street London SW1A 2BQ Telephone: 03000 585 911 |

| Transaction | Applications to: |
|---|---|
| **Transfers of long-term business between life assurance companies under FA 2012, s. 133**<br>Applications for clearance, including cases where the parties include non-UK resident companies or friendly societies | The transferor company's Customer Relationship Manager and to:<br>HM Revenue & Customs<br>CTISA Corporation Tax and Business Income Tax<br>Financial Services Team<br>3rd Floor<br>100 Parliament Street<br>London<br>SW1A 2BQ<br>Telephone: 03000 585911<br>Alternatively, by e-mail to Anthony Fawcett via link at www.hmrc.gov.uk/cap/ |
| **Transactions in shares or debentures under ICTA 1988, s. 765 and 765A**<br>The Treasury Consents regime was repealed by *Finance Act* 2009. Events or transactions taking place on or after 1 July 2009 are subject to a new reporting regime, detail of which can be found in HMRC's *International Manual*. | |
| **Transfer pricing (advance pricing agreements)**<br>HMRC have run an Advanced Pricing Agreements programme since 1999 to assist businesses in identifying solutions for complex transfer pricing issues. HMRC issued Statement of Practice (SP) 2/10 in December 2010 to update an earlier Statement of Practice (SP 3/99) on Advance Pricing Agreements (APAs). The SP is intended as general guidance as to how HMRC interpret the APA legislation and how HMRC operate the UK APA Programme. | Nicholas Stevart (APA Team Leader)<br>HM Revenue & Customs<br>CTIS Business International<br>East Spur, Euston Tower,<br>286 Euston Road,<br>London NW1 3UH<br>Telephone: 03000 585 659<br>Fax: 03000 543 795 |
| **Stamp taxes**<br>Queries on stamp taxes should be directed first to the Stamp Taxes Helpline and if the helpline is unable to answer the question, in writing to the Stamp Office. The Clearance and Counteraction Team (see below) does not handle applications for stamp duty land tax (SDLT) adjudications. | **Stamp Taxes Helpline**<br>Tel: 0300 200 3510<br><br>Birmingham Stamp Office<br>9th Floor<br>City Centre House<br>30 Union Street<br>Birmingham<br>B2 4AR |

General

| Transaction | Applications to: |
|---|---|
| **Statutory applications for advance clearance** HMRC's Clearance and Counteraction Team, Counter-Avoidance handles requests where advance clearance is required under statutory provisions relating to any one or more of the following: | Please ensure a 'Market sensitive' application is marked for the attention of 'The Team leader', and send it to: HM Revenue & Customs CA Clearance SO528 PO Box 194 Merseyside L69 9AA |
| *Capital gains:* • share exchanges (TCGA 1992, s. 138(1)) • reconstruction involving the transfer of a business (TCGA 1992, s. 139(5)) • collective investment schemes: exchanges, mergers and schemes of reconstruction (TCGA 1992, s. 103K) • transfer of a UK trade between EU member states (TCGA 1992, s. 140B and 140D) | Telephone: 03000 589 004 Fax: 03000 589 802 E-mail: reconstructions@hmrc.gsi.gov.uk (Clearance and Counteraction Team) Where clearance is required under any one or more of the statutory provisions, a single letter should be sent to the Clearance and Counteraction Team, Counter-Avoidance at the address above. No extra copy is required as the same person will deal with each of the clearances asked for. A single response will be given covering all of these. Please make clear at the top of the letter what clearances are being requested. |
| *Other shares, securities, demergers and reorganisations* • purchase of own shares by unquoted trading companies (CTA 2010, s. 1044) • demergers (CTA 2010, s. 1091) • EIS shares (acquisition by new company) (ITA 2007, s. 247(1)(f)) • Company reorganisation involving intangible fixed assets (CTA 2009, s. 831) • Transactions in securities (CTA 2010, s. 748 and ITA 2007, s. 701) | Please note the following points: • HMRC acknowledge only those applications that request an acknowledgement; • if a reply by e-mail is required, please write 'I confirm that I understand and accept the risks involved in using e-mail'. HMRC do not e-mail market sensitive applications; |
| *Transactions in land* • under CTA 2009, s. 237 (for corporation tax purposes) and ITTOIA 2005, s. 300 (for income tax purposes) – confirmation of the customer's view of the tax consequences of assigning a lease granted at under value • under CTA 2010, s. 831 (for corporation tax purposes) and ITA 2007, s. 770 (for income tax purposes). | • enquiries about the progress of an application or making general enquiries should be made by telephone: 03000 589 004. Please allow ten days after receiving an acknowledgement before you contact to check progress; |

| Transaction | Applications to: |
|---|---|
| **Company finance**<br>• CTA 2009, s. 426/7 (loan relationships transfers) and 437 (loan relationships: mergers)<br>• CTA 2009, s. 677 (derivative contracts: transfers) and 686 (derivative contracts: mergers)<br><br>**Targeted Anti-Avoidance Rule 3 (Capital Gains)**<br>Informal clearances: companies and their representatives may make requests for advice about the legislation in TCGA 1992, s. 184G–184H, including whether the provisions will apply to a planned series of transactions that may constitute an arrangement.<br><br>**Cross border transfers** of a loan relationship, derivative contract or intangible fixed assets under TIOPA 2010, s. 117(4).<br>**Seed enterprise investment scheme (SEIS)** continuity of relief under ITA 2007, s. 257HB. | • HMRC regard information that could affect the price of a stock market quoted company and information concerning the financial affairs of well known individuals as sensitive;<br>• in March, September and December HMRC receive high volumes of applications which increases turn around time. Please bear this in mind when applying during these times. |

## [¶15-650]   HMRC websites

HMRC's homepage and website content has moved to the GOV.UK website and all content is now accessible through the GOV.UK site only.

### HMRC home page

www.gov.uk/government/organisations/hm-revenue-customs

The HMRC section of the GOV.UK website contains full details of contact addresses and numbers, including in particular the following:

• Helplines and postal addresses for all taxes, National Insurance and VAT queries: www.gov.uk/government/organisations/hm-revenue-customs/contact;

• Dedicated helplines and contacts for authorised agents: www.gov.uk/topic/dealing-with-hmrc/tax-agent-guidance.

General

Other useful parts of the HMRC content are:

**HMRC forms**

http://search.hmrc.gov.uk/kb5/hmrc/forms/home.page

**HMRC leaflets, factsheets and booklets**

www.gov.uk/government/collections/hm-revenue-and-customs-leaflets-factsheets-and-booklets

**HMRC manuals**

www.gov.uk/government/collections/hmrc-manuals

**HMRC self-assessment pages**

www.gov.uk/personal-tax/self-assessment

**HMRC employers information**

www.gov.uk/business-tax/paye

**HMRC tax credits**

www.gov.uk/topic/benefits-credits/tax-credits

**VAT**

www.gov.uk/topic/business-tax/vat

**Construction industry scheme**

www.gov.uk/topic/business-tax/construction-industry-scheme

# [¶15-800]   Other useful websites

**Adjudicator**

www.adjudicatorsoffice.gov.uk/

**CIOT**

www.tax.org.uk

**Government Information Service**

UK: www.direct.gov.uk
Scotland: www.scotland.gov.uk
Wales: http://wales.gov.uk/splash?orig=/

**ICAEW Tax Faculty**

www.icaew.com/en/technical/tax/tax-faculty

**Legislation**

www.legislation.gov.uk/

**Parliament**

UK: www.parliament.uk/

Scotland: www.scottish.parliament.uk/

Wales: www.assembly.wales/en/Pages/Home.aspx

**Parliamentary Ombudsman**

www.ombudsman.org.uk/

**Revenue Scotland**

www.revenue.scot/

**Treasury Home Page**

www.gov.uk/government/organisations/hm-treasury

**Tribunals service**

www.justice.gov.uk/tribunals/tax

**Valuation Office Agency**

www.voa.gov.uk/

# Finance Acts

## [¶15-950] Finance Acts

| Year | Budget | | Royal Assent | |
|---|---|---|---|---|
| 1980 | 26 March | 1980 | 1 August | 1980 |
| 1981 | 10 March | 1981 | 27 July | 1981 |
| 1982 | 9 March | 1982 | 30 July | 1982 |
| 1983 | 15 March | 1983 | 13 May | 1983 |
| 1983 (No. 2) | 15 March | 1983 | 26 July | 1983 |
| 1984 | 13 March | 1984 | 26 July | 1984 |
| 1985 | 19 March | 1985 | 25 July | 1985 |
| 1986 | 18 March | 1986 | 25 July | 1986 |
| 1987 | 17 March | 1987 | 15 May | 1987 |
| 1987 (No. 2) | 17 March | 1987 | 23 July | 1987 |
| 1988 | 15 March | 1988 | 29 July | 1988 |
| 1989 | 14 March | 1989 | 27 July | 1989 |
| 1990 | 20 March | 1990 | 26 July | 1990 |
| 1991 | 19 March | 1991 | 26 July | 1991 |
| 1992 | 10 March | 1992 | 16 March | 1992 |
| 1992 (No. 2) | 10 March | 1992 | 16 July | 1992 |
| 1993 | 16 March | 1993 | 27 July | 1993 |
| 1994 | 30 November | 1993 | 3 May | 1994 |
| 1995 | 29 November | 1994 | 1 May | 1995 |
| 1996 | 28 November | 1995 | 29 April | 1996 |
| 1997 | 26 November | 1996 | 19 March | 1997 |
| 1997 (No. 2) | 2 July | 1997 | 31 July | 1997 |
| 1998 | 17 March | 1998 | 31 July | 1998 |
| 1999 | 9 March | 1999 | 27 July | 1999 |
| 2000 | 21 March | 2000 | 28 July | 2000 |
| 2001 | 7 March | 2001 | 11 May | 2001 |
| 2002 | 17 April | 2002 | 24 July | 2002 |
| 2003 | 9 April | 2003 | 10 July | 2003 |
| 2004 | 17 March | 2004 | 22 July | 2004 |
| 2005 | 16 March | 2005 | 7 April | 2005 |
| 2005 (No. 2) | 16 March | 2005 | 20 July | 2005 |
| 2006 | 22 March | 2006 | 19 July | 2006 |
| 2007 | 21 March | 2007 | 19 July | 2007 |
| 2008 | 12 March | 2008 | 21 July | 2008 |
| 2009 | 22 April | 2009 | 21 July | 2009 |
| 2010 | 24 March | 2010 | 8 April | 2010 |
| 2010 (No. 2) | 22 June | 2010 | 27 July | 2010 |
| 2010 (No. 3) | 22 June | 2010 | 16 December | 2010 |
| 2011 | 23 March | 2011 | 19 July | 2011 |
| 2012 | 21 March | 2012 | 17 July | 2012 |
| 2013 | 20 March | 2013 | 17 July | 2013 |
| 2014 | 19 March | 2014 | 17 July | 2014 |
| 2015 | 18 March | 2015 | 26 March | 2015 |
| 2015 (No. 2) | 8 July | 2015 | 18 November | 2015 |
| 2016 | 16 March | 2016 | 15 September | 2016 |
| 2017 | 8 March | 2017 | | |

General

# STAMP TAXES

## Stamp duty land tax

**Note:** See ¶26-200 for rates applicable in Scotland from 1 April 2015.

### [¶16-000]   Stamp duty land tax: general

(FA 2003, Pt. 4; SDLTA 2015)

(SLDT Reporter: ¶50-100ff.)

Applies to contracts entered into (or varied) after 10 July 2003 and completed after 30 November 2003 and to leases granted after that date.

SDLT also applies to transfers of an interest in land into or out of a partnership, and to an acquisition of an interest in a partnership where the partnership property includes an interest in land (from 22 July 2004). From 19 July 2006, SDLT additionally applies to transfers of partnership interests but only where the sole or main activity of the partnership is investing or dealing in interests in land.

### [¶16-010]   SDLT: residential property rates

(FA 2003, s. 55; SDLTA 2015)

(SDLT Reporter: ¶50-105; ¶50-106)

**Rate on portion of value above threshold**

| Period | Portion of value £ | Rate % | Additional property rate[5] % |
|---|---|---|---|
| On or after 1 April 2016 | 0–125,000 | 0 | 3 |
| | 125,001–250,000 | 2 | 5 |
| | 250,001–925,000 | 5 | 8 |
| | 925,001–1,500,000 | 10 | 13 |
| | 1,500,001 and over | 12 | 15 |
| | Over 500,000 | 15[1][2][3][4] | |
| On or after 4 December 2014 | 0–125,000 | 0 | — |
| | 125,001–250,000 | 2 | — |
| | 250,001–925,000 | 5 | — |
| | 925,001–1,500,000 | 10 | — |
| | 1,500,001 and over | 12 | — |
| | Over 500,000 | 15[1][2][3] | — |

## Rate on entire property value

| Period | Band £ | Rate % |
|---|---|---|
| 20 March 2014 to 3 December 2014 | 0–125,000 | 0 |
| | 125,001–250,000 | 1 |
| | 250,001–500,000 | 3 |
| | 500,001–1,000,000 | 4 |
| | 1,000,001–2,000,000 | 5 |
| | Over 2,000,000 | 7 |
| | Over 500,000 | 15[(1)(2)(3)] |
| 22 March 2012 to 19 March 2014 | 0–125,000 | 0 |
| | 125,001–250,000 | 1 |
| | 250,001–500,000 | 3 |
| | 500,001–1,000,000 | 4 |
| | 1,000,001–2,000,000 | 5 |
| | Over 2,000,000 | 7 |
| | Over 2,000,000 | 15[(1)(2)(3)] |
| 6 April 2011 to 21 March 2012 | 0–125,000 | 0 |
| | 125,001–250,000 | 1 |
| | 250,001–500,000 | 3 |
| | 500,001–1,000,000 | 4 |
| | Over 1,000,000 | 5 |

**Notes**

[(1)] The 15% rate applies if the property is acquired by certain non-natural persons (e.g. companies, partnerships with corporate members and collective investment schemes) with effect from 21 March 2012. *Finance Act* 2014 reduces the threshold from £2m to £500,000 where the effective date is on or after 20 March 2014 with the £2m threshold continuing to apply, subject to exceptions, where contracts were entered into before that date.

[(2)] *Finance Act* 2013 introduced a number of reliefs to reduce the 15% rate to 7% with effect in relation to transactions with an effective date on or after 17 July 2013 (Royal Assent). The reliefs broadly match those where there is relief against the annual tax on enveloped dwellings. However, the SDLT reliefs will apply only if the property continues to satisfy the qualifying conditions throughout the following three years, otherwise, additional SDLT will become payable.

[(3)] *Finance Act* 2013 also introduced legislation to reform the stamp duty land tax rules for 'transfer of rights' with effect from 17 July 2013 (Royal Assent).

[(4)] Reliefs available from the 15% higher rate of SDLT extended to equity release schemes (home reversion plans), property development activities and properties occupied by employees from 1 April 2016 (FA 2003, Sch. 4A, as amended by FA 2016, s. 129-131).

[(5)] From 1 April 2016, higher rates of stamp duty land tax apply to purchases of additional residential properties, such as second homes and buy-to-let properties in England, Wales and Northern Ireland. Purchasers have 36 months to claim a refund of the higher rates if they buy a new main residence before disposing of their previous main residence. Purchasers also have 36 months between selling a main residence and replacing it with another without having to pay the higher rates. A share (of up to 50%) in a property which has been inherited within the 36 months prior to a transaction will not be considered as an additional property when applying the higher rates (FA 2003, s. 55 and Sch. 4ZA, as amended and inserted by FA 2016, s. 128).

## [¶16-020]  SDLT: non-residential or mixed property rates

(FA 2003, s. 55)

(SDLT Reporter: ¶50-110)

**Rate on portion of value above threshold**

| Period | Portion of value £ | Rate % |
|---|---|---|
| On or after 17 March 2016[(1)] | 0–150,000 | 0 |
| | 150,001–250,000 | 2 |
| | Over 250,000 | 5 |

**Note**

[(1)] Where contracts have been exchanged but transactions have not completed before 17 March 2016 purchasers will have a choice of whether the old or new structure and rates apply (FA 2016, s. 127(13)–(14)).

**Rate on entire property value**

| Period | Band £ | Rate % |
|---|---|---|
| 6 April 2011 to 16 March 2016 | 0–150,000 | 0 |
| | 150,001–250,000 | 1 |
| | 250,001–500,000 | 3 |
| | Over 500,000 | 4 |

## [¶16-030]  SDLT: lease rental rates

(FA 2003, Sch. 5)

(SDLT Reporter: ¶60-405)

**Residential**

| Period | Rate % | Net present value of rent £ |
|---|---|---|
| From 1 January 2010 | 0 | 0–125,000 |
| | 1 | Over 125,000 |

**Non-residential (on portion of value above threshold)**

| Period | Rate % | Net present value of rent £ |
|---|---|---|
| On or after 17 March 2016 | 0 | 0–150,000 |
| | 1 | 150,001–5,000,000 |
| | 2 | Over 5,000,000 |
| From 1 January 2010 | 0 | 0–150,000 |
| | 1 | 150,001–5,000,000 |

Stamp Taxes

Duty on premium is the same as for transfers of land (except special rules apply for premium where rent exceeds £1,000 annually.
*Finance Act* 2013 simplifies reporting requirements that apply when a lease continues after the expiry of its fixed-term and where an agreement for the lease is substantially performed before the actual lease is granted and abolishes the rules on abnormal rent increases with effect from 17 July 2013 (Royal Assent).

## [¶16-100]   Stamp duty land tax returns and payment dates

(FA 2003, s. 76 and 86)

(SDLT Reporter: ¶50-500)

| Event | Deadline[2] |
|---|---|
| Delivery of land transaction return | 30 days of the effective date[1] |
| Payment of tax | Not later than the filing date for the land transaction return |

**Notes**

[1] Where the transaction is completed by a conveyance, the effective dates of the transaction is the date of completion or, if earlier, the date the contract is substantially performed (FA 2003, s. 44).

[2] As announced at Autumn Statement 2015, the Government consulted in 2016 on changes to the SDLT filing and payment process, including a reduction in the filing and payment window from 30 days to 14 days. Spring Budget 2017 announced that the reduction in the filing and payment window will be delayed until after April 2018.

## [¶16-200]   Stamp duty land tax penalties

(SLDT Reporter: ¶100-400)

| | |
|---|---|
| Failure to deliver a land transaction return by the filing date (FA 2003, Sch. 10, para. 3 and 4) | £100 if return delivered within three months of filing date, otherwise £200. If not delivered within 12 months, maximum penalty of amount of tax chargeable |
| Failure to comply with a notice to deliver return within specified period (FA 2003, Sch. 10, para. 5) | Maximum of £60 for each day on which the failure continues after notification |
| Failure to keep or preserve records under FA 2003, Sch. 10, para. 9 or Sch. 11, para. 4 | Maximum of £3,000 unless other documentary evidence provided |

| Errors in returns[1] (FA 2007, Sch. 24) Errors in returns for periods starting 1 April 2009 where return is filed on or after 1 April 2010, or where liability arises on or after 1 April 2010: | **Percentage of potential lost revenue Category 1** | | |
|---|---|---|---|
| • careless action | 30% | | |
| • deliberate but not concealed action | 70% | | |
| • deliberate and concealed action | 100% | | |
| Reductions for disclosure: maximum reduction weighted according to quality of disclosure determined as: | **Standard penalty** | **Prompted disclosure minimum** | **Unprompted disclosure minimum** |
| • 30% for telling | 30% | 15% | 0% |
| • 40% for helping | 70% | 35% | 20% |
| • 30% for giving access | 100% | 50% | 30% |
| Error in taxpayer's document attributable to another person[1] (FA 2007, Sch. 24) | 100% potential lost revenue Subject to reductions for disclosure as above | | |
| Failure to notify HMRC of an under-assessment within 30 days[1] (FA 2007, Sch. 24) | 30% of potential lost revenue Subject to reductions for disclosure as above | | |
| Failure to comply with an information notice (FA 2008, Sch. 36) | Initial penalty £300 Up to £60 per day for each day for continued failure Tax-related penalty determined by tribunal where significant tax at stake | | |
| Inaccurate information/documents in complying with an information notice (FA 2008, Sch. 36) Inaccuracy careless or deliberate | Up to £3,000 for each inaccuracy | | |

**Note**
[1] No penalties for errors that occur despite taking reasonable care.

Stamp Taxes

# [¶16-250]  Stamp duty land tax interest

(SLDT Reporter: ¶100-000ff.)

The rates are as follows:

| Period of application | Rate % | |
|---|---|---|
| | Underpayments | Repayments |
| From 23 August 2016 | 2.75 | 0.50 |
| 29 September 2009 to 22 August 2016 | 3.00 | 0.50 |

*Finance Act* 2009, s. 101–104 and Sch. 53 and 54 contain provisions to harmonise interest regimes across all HMRC taxes and duties.

# Stamp duty

## [¶17-000]  Stamp duty rates

### Conveyance or transfer on sale of shares and securities

(FA 1986, s. 67(3); FA 1999, Sch. 13, para. 3)

| Instrument[1][2][3][4][5] | Rate of tax % |
|---|---|
| Stock transfer | 0.5 |
| Conversion of shares into depositary receipts | 1.5 |
| Take overs and mergers | 0.5 |
| Purchase by company of own shares | 0.5 |
| Letters of allotment | 0.5 |

**Notes**

[1]  Stamp duty is rounded up to the nearest multiple of £5 (FA 1999, s. 112).

[2]  Loan capital is generally exempt from transfer on sale duty subject to specific exclusions (designed to prevent exemption applying to quasi-equity securities) (FA 1986, s. 79).

[3]  Stamp duty is not chargeable on a transfer of stock or marketable securities where the amount or value of the consideration for the sale is £1,000 or under, and the instrument is certified at £1,000 (with effect in relation to instruments executed on or after 13 March 2008 and not stamped before 19 March 2008) (FA 1999, Sch. 13, para. 1(3A)).

[4]  From 28 April 2014, transfers of securities admitted to trading on recognised growth markets are exempt from stamp duty (FA 2014, Sch. 24). See ¶15-200 for a list of recognised growth markets.

[5]  Shares transferred to a clearance service or depositary receipt issuer as a result of the exercise of an option will now be charged the 1.5% higher rate of stamp duty based on either their market value or the option strike price, whichever is higher. This will prevent avoidance using 'Deep in the Money Options' (DITMOs), which are options with a strike price significantly below (for call options) or above (for put options) market value. Share transfers made other than to a clearance service or depositary receipt system as a result of exercising an option will be unaffected. The change will apply to options exercised on or after 23 March 2016 which were entered into on or after 25 November 2015. (FA 1986, s. 67 and 70, as amended by FA 2016, s. 138).

## [¶17-200]  Stamp duty penalties

| Type of document | Penalties applicable if document presented for stamping more than |
|---|---|
| Document executed in UK | 30 days after execution |
| Document executed abroad relating to UK land and buildings | 30 days after execution |
| Document executed abroad | 30 days after document first received in UK[1] |

**Note**

[1]  Free standing penalty (see table further below) may apply if written information confirming date of receipt in UK is incorrect.

The maximum penalties are:

- £300 or the amount of duty, whichever is less; on documents submitted up to one year late; and
- £300 or the amount of duty, whichever is greater; on documents submitted more than one year late.

## Mitigated penalties due on late stamping

The Stamp Office publishes tables of mitigated penalty levels that will be applied in straightforward cases at www.hmrc.gov.uk/sd/pay-penalties/penalties.htm#1.

### From 1 October 2014

| Length of delay | Penalty |
|---|---|
| Documents late by up to 12 months | 10% of the duty, capped at £300 |
| Documents late by 12 to 24 months | 20% of the duty |
| Documents late by more than 24 months | 30% of the duty |

### Before 1 October 2014

| Months late | Up to £300 | £305–£700 | £705–£1,350 | £1,355–£2,500 | £2,505–£5,000 | Over £5,000 |
|---|---|---|---|---|---|---|
| Under 3 | Nil | £20 | £40 | £60 | £80 | £100 |
| Under 6 | £20[(1)] | £40 | £60 | £80 | £100 | £150 |
| Under 9 | £40[(1)] | £60 | £80 | £100 | £150 | £200 |
| Under 12 | £60[(1)] | £80 | £100 | £150 | £200 | £300 |
| Under 15 | 15% of the duty or £100 if greater | | | | 20% of the duty | |
| Under 18 | 25% of the duty or £150 if greater | | | | 40% of the duty | |
| Under 21 | 35% of the duty or £200 if greater | | | | 60% of the duty | |
| Under 24 | 45% of the duty or £250 if greater | | | | 80% of the duty | |

**Note**

[(1)] Or the amount of the duty if that is less.

If a document is over 24 months late, the penalty is the higher of:

– the amount of stamp duty that's due;

– £300.

## Reasonable excuse

In all cases above, the penalties will not apply if the person responsible for stamping can show a 'reasonable excuse' for the failure to submit the document(s) within the time limit. Interest is due on any unpaid penalty.

## [¶17-250]   Stamp duty interest

In respect of instruments executed on or after 1 October 1999, interest is chargeable on stamp duty that is not paid within 30 days of execution of a stampable document, wherever execution takes place (SA 1891, s. 15A). Interest is payable on repayments of overpaid duty, calculated from the later of 30 days from the date of execution of the instrument, or lodgement with the Stamp Office of the duty repayable (FA 1999, s. 110). Interest is rounded down (if necessary) to the nearest multiple of £5. No interest is payable if that amount is under £25. The applicable interest rate is as prescribed under FA 1989, s. 178.

For interest periods from 1 October 1999 onwards, the rate of interest charged on underpaid or late paid stamp duty and SDRT exceeds that on repayments:

| | Rate % | |
|---|---|---|
| Period of application | Underpayments | Repayments |
| From 23 August 2016 | 2.75 | 0.50 |
| 29 September 2009 to 22 August 2016 | 3.00 | 0.50 |

*Finance Act* 2009, s. 101–104 and Sch. 53 and 54 contain provisions to harmonise interest regimes across all HMRC taxes and duties.

# Stamp duty reserve tax

## [¶18-000]   Stamp duty reserve tax rates
(FA 1986, s. 87, 93 and 96)

**Principal charge**

| Subject matter of charge | Rate of tax % |
|---|---|
| Agreements to transfer chargeable securities[(1)] for money or money's worth | 0.5 |
| Renounceable letters of allotment | 0.5 |
| Shares converted into depositary receipts[(2)(4)] | 1.5 |
| Chargeable securities[(1)] put into clearance system[(2)(4)] | 1.5 |

**Notes**

[(1)] Chargeable securities = stocks, shares, loan capital, units under unit trust scheme (FA 1986, s. 99(3)). From 28 April 2014, the definition of chargeable securities for SDRT purposes excludes securities admitted to trading on a recognised growth market (FA 1986, s. 99(4A) and 99A). See ¶15-200 for a list of recognised growth markets.

[(2)] Following the European Court of Justice judgment in *HSBC Holdings plc & Vidacos Nominees Ltd v R & C Commrs* (Case C-569/07) [2010] BTC 13, HMRC accept that art. 11(a) of Council Directive 69/335/EEC of 17 July 1969 concerning indirect taxes on the raising of capital, as amended by Council Directive 85/303/EEC of 10 June 1985 (now Council Directive 2008/7/EC) ('the EC Capital Directive') must be interpreted as meaning that it prohibits the levying of a duty such as the charge to SDRT imposed by FA 1986, s. 96 on the issue of shares to a depositary receipt issuer or a clearance service located within the European Union.

[(3)] From 30 March 2014, the stamp duty reserve tax charge for which fund managers are liable when investors surrender their units in UK unit trust schemes or shares in UK OEICs is abolished. Previously, the charge was at the 0.5% rate. Non-pro rata in specie redemptions remain subject to the principle SDRT charge (FA 2014, s. 114).

[(4)] Shares transferred to a clearance service or depositary receipt issuer as a result of the exercise of an option will now be charged the 1.5% higher rate of stamp duty based on either their market value or the option strike price, whichever is higher. This will prevent avoidance using 'Deep in the Money Options' (DITMOs), which are options with a strike price significantly below (for call options) or above (for put options) market value. Share transfers made other than to a clearance service or depositary receipt system as a result of exercising an option will be unaffected. The change will apply to options exercised on or after 23 March 2016 which were entered into on or after 25 November 2015 (FA 1986, s. 93 and 96, as amended by FA 2016, s. 139).

## [¶18-100]   Stamp duty reserve tax notification and payment deadlines
(SI 1986/1711, reg. 2 and 3)

| Transfer type | Deadline |
|---|---|
| Share transfers involving CREST (where notification and payment to HMRC is automatic) and any transfer that could have been made through CREST but was not | 14 calendar days after the date when the trade took place |
| Off-market share transfers (when shares are transferred off-market using a system other than CREST and the transfer could not have been made through CREST) | Seventh day of the month following the month when the trade took place |

## [¶18-200]   Stamp duty reserve tax penalties

| Errors in returns[1] (FA 2007, Sch. 24) | Percentage of potential lost revenue | | |
|---|---|---|---|
| Errors in returns for periods starting 1 April 2009 where return is filed on or after 1 April 2010, or where liability arises on or after 1 April 2010:<br>• careless action<br>• deliberate but not concealed action<br>• deliberate and concealed action | Category 1<br><br><br><br><br>30%<br>70%<br>100% | | |
| Reductions for disclosure: maximum reduction weighted according to quality of disclosure determined as: | Standard penalty | Prompted disclosure minimum | Unprompted disclosure minimum |
| • 30% for telling | 30% | 15% | 0% |
| • 40% for helping | 70% | 35% | 20% |
| • 30% for giving access | 100% | 50% | 30% |
| Failure to comply with an information notice (FA 2008, Sch. 36) | Initial penalty £300<br>Up to £60 per day for each day continued failure<br>Tax-related penalty determined by tribunal where significant tax at stake | | |
| Inaccurate information/documents in complying with an information notice (FA 2008, Sch. 36)<br>Inaccuracy careless or deliberate | Up to £3,000 for each inaccuracy | | |
| Failure to make return[2] (FA 2009, Sch. 55)<br>**From 1 January 2015** in relation to a charge to stamp duty reserve tax under regulations under FA 1986, s. 98 | | | |
| Failure to submit return | £100 | | |
| Continued failure – three months from penalty date | £10 per day for a period up to 90 days beginning with date specified in notice (maximum £900) | | |
| Continued failure – six months from penalty date | The greater of £300 or 5% of the liability to tax shown by the return | | |

| Failure still continues after 12 months after the penalty date | Greater of relevant percentage of liability shown by the return and £300 | | |
|---|---|---|---|
| | **Relevant percentage** | | |
| • withholding information deliberate and concealed | 100% | | |
| • withholding information deliberate but not concealed | 70% | | |
| • any other case | 5% | | |
| Reductions for disclosure: maximum reduction weighted according to quality of disclosure determined as: | **Standard penalty** | **Prompted disclosure minimum** | **Unprompted disclosure minimum** |
| • 30% for telling | 70% | 35% | 20% |
| • 40% for helping | 100% | 50% | 30% |
| • 30% for giving access | | | |
| Failure to notify HMRC and pay tax (TMA 1970, s. 93; SI 1986/1711) **Before 1 January 2015** | | | |
| Failure to give notice | £100 | | |
| Failure continues after 12 months | Penalty of amount of tax due | | |

**Notes**
[1] No penalties for errors that occur despite taking reasonable care.
[2] Defences of 'reasonable excuse' or 'special circumstances' may be available.

**Penalties for late payment of stamp duty reserve tax**

(FA 2009, Sch. 56)

**From 1 January 2015**

| Tax overdue | Penalty |
|---|---|
| 30 days | 5% of unpaid tax |
| 6 months | Further 5% of unpaid tax |
| 12 months | Further 5% of unpaid tax |

## [¶18-250]   Stamp duty reserve tax interest

(TMA 1970, s. 86; FA 1986, s. 92 and FA 1989, s. 178; FA 2009, s. 101 and 102; SI 1986/1711)

Late payment interest is charged on unpaid stamp duty reserve tax from the due date for payment (see ¶18-100) to the actual date of payment. Repayment interest is paid on amounts of overpaid stamp duty reserve tax of £25 or more and runs from the date of payment to the date of repayment.

| Period | Rate % | |
| --- | --- | --- |
| | Late payment | Repayment |
| From 23 August 2016 | 2.75 | 0.5 |
| 29 September 2009 to 22 August 2016[(1)] | 3.00 | 0.5 |

**Note**

[(1)] From 1 January 2015, FA 2009, s. 101 and 102 apply for the purposes of stamp duty reserve tax (including any penalties in relation to that tax) but only to a charge with a due and payable date falling after 31 December 2014. Late payment and repayment rates prior to 1 January 2015 were prescribed under FA 1989, as 3% and 0.5% respectively from 29 September 2009.

# VALUE ADDED TAX

## [¶19-000]   Rates
(VATA 1994, s. 2)

(Indirect Tax Reporter: ¶18-014)

| Period of application | Standard rate[1] % | VAT fraction % | Reduced rate[1][2][3] % | VAT fraction % |
|---|---|---|---|---|
| From 4 January 2011 | 20 | 1/6 | 5.0 | 1/21 |
| 1 January 2010 to 3 January 2011 | 17.5 | 7/47 | 5.0 | 1/21 |

**Notes**
[1] VAT lock: F(No. 2)A 2015, s. 2 sets a ceiling on the standard and reduced rates of VAT at 20% and 5% respectively, for the period beginning with 18 November 2015 and ending immediately before the date of the first Parliamentary general election after that day (the 'VAT lock period').
[2] Supplies of fuel and power for domestic, residential and charity non-business use and certain other supplies are charged at 5% (VATA 1994, Sch. 7A).
[3] Imports of certain works of art, antiques and collectors' items are charged at an effective rate of 5% from 27 July 1999 (VATA 1994, s. 21(4)–(6)).
The zero rate has applied from 1 April 1973 to date.

## [¶19-040]   Flat-rate scheme
(VATA 1994, s. 26B; SI 1995/2518, reg. 55A–55V; Notice 733; HMRC 'Flat-rate scheme' manual)

(Indirect Tax Reporter: ¶55-350)

### Limited cost businesses
From 1 April 2017, a flat rate of 16.5% applies to all limited cost businesses. A limited cost business is a business where the amount spent on 'relevant goods' including VAT is either:

- less than 2% of the business's VAT flat rate turnover; or
- greater than 2% of the business's VAT flat rate turnover but less than £1,000 per year (£250 per quarterly return period).

**Relevant goods** are goods that are used exclusively for the purposes of the business, but **do not include:**
- vehicle costs including fuel, unless the business is operating in the transport sector using its own, or a leased vehicle
- food or drink for the business or its staff
- capital expenditure goods of any value

Value Added Tax

- goods for resale, leasing, letting or hiring out if the main business activity does not ordinarily consist of selling, leasing, letting or hiring out such goods
- goods that are intended for re-sell or hire out, unless selling or hiring is the main business activity
- any services

| Examples of relevant goods | Examples of supplies that are not relevant goods |
|---|---|
| This is not an exhaustive list: | This is not an exhaustive list: |
| • stationery and other office supplies to be used exclusively for the business<br>• gas and electricity used exclusively for the business<br>• fuel for a taxi owned by a taxi firm<br>• stock for a shop<br>• cleaning products to be used exclusively for the business<br>• hair products to use to provide hairdressing services<br>• standard software, provided on a disk | • accountancy fees, these are services<br>• advertising costs, these are services<br>• an item leased/hired to the business, this counts as services, as ownership will never transfer to the business<br>• food and drink for the business or its staff, these are excluded goods<br>• fuel for a car this is excluded unless operating in the transport sector using owned, or a leased vehicle<br>• laptop or mobile phone for use by the business, this is excluded as it is capital expenditure<br>• anything provided electronically, for example a downloaded magazine, these are services<br>• rent, this is a service<br>• software you download, this is a service<br>• software designed specifically (bespoke software), this is a service even if it is not supplied electronically |

**Flat-rate percentages applying from 4 January 2011**

Generally, the percentage that applies to the flat-rate scheme (FRS) for small firms is cut by 1% for the first year of VAT registration.

| Category of business | Appropriate percentage | |
|---|---|---|
| | From 4 Jan. 2011 | 1 Jan. 2010 to 3 Jan. 2011 |
| Accountancy or book-keeping | 14.5 | 13 |
| Advertising | 11 | 10 |
| Agricultural services | 11 | 10 |
| Any other activity not listed elsewhere | 12 | 10.5 |
| Architect, civil and structural engineer or surveyor | 14.5 | 13 |
| Boarding or care of animals | 12 | 10.5 |

| | Appropriate percentage | |
|---|---|---|
| Category of business | From 4 Jan. 2011 | 1 Jan. 2010 to 3 Jan. 2011 |
| Business services that are not listed elsewhere | 12 | 10.5 |
| Catering services including restaurants and takeaways | 12.5 | 11 |
| Computer and IT consultancy or data processing | 14.5 | 13 |
| Computer repair services | 10.5 | 9.5 |
| Entertainment or journalism | 12.5 | 11 |
| Estate agency or property management services | 12 | 10.5 |
| Farming or agriculture that is not listed elsewhere | 6.5 | 6 |
| Film, radio, television or video production | 13 | 11.5 |
| Financial services | 13.5 | 12 |
| Forestry or fishing | 10.5 | 9.5 |
| General building or construction services[(1)] | 9.5 | 8.5 |
| Hairdressing or other beauty treatment services | 13 | 11.5 |
| Hiring or renting goods | 9.5 | 8.5 |
| Hotel or accommodation | 10.5 | 9.5 |
| Investigation or security | 12 | 10.5 |
| Labour-only building or construction services[(1)] | 14.5 | 13 |
| Laundry or dry-cleaning services | 12 | 10.5 |
| Lawyer or legal services | 14.5 | 13 |
| Library, archive, museum or other cultural activity | 9.5 | 8.5 |
| Management consultancy | 14 | 12.5 |
| Manufacturing fabricated metal products | 10.5 | 9.5 |
| Manufacturing food | 9 | 8 |
| Manufacturing that is not listed elsewhere | 9.5 | 8.5 |
| Manufacturing yarn, textiles or clothing | 9 | 8 |
| Membership organisation | 8 | 7 |
| Mining or quarrying | 10 | 9 |
| Packaging | 9 | 8 |
| Photography | 11 | 10 |
| Post offices | 5 | 4.5 |
| Printing | 8.5 | 7.5 |
| Publishing | 11 | 10 |
| Pubs | 6.5 | 6 |
| Real estate activity not listed elsewhere | 14 | 12.5 |
| Repairing personal or household goods | 10 | 9 |
| Repairing vehicles | 8.5 | 7.5 |

Value Added Tax

| | Appropriate percentage | |
|---|---|---|
| Category of business | From 4 Jan. 2011 | 1 Jan. 2010 to 3 Jan. 2011 |
| Retailing food, confectionary, tobacco, newspapers or children's clothing | 4 | 3.5 |
| Retailing pharmaceuticals, medical goods, cosmetics or toiletries | 8 | 7 |
| Retailing that is not listed elsewhere | 7.5 | 6.5 |
| Retailing vehicles or fuel | 6.5 | 6 |
| Secretarial services | 13 | 11.5 |
| Social work | 11 | 10 |
| Sport or recreation | 8.5 | 7.5 |
| Transport or storage, including couriers, freight, removals and taxis | 10 | 9 |
| Travel agency | 10.5 | 9.5 |
| Veterinary medicine | 11 | 10 |
| Wholesaling agricultural products | 8 | 7 |
| Wholesaling food | 7.5 | 6.5 |
| Wholesaling that is not listed elsewhere | 8.5 | 7.5 |

**Note**

[1] 'Labour-only building or construction services' means building or construction services where the value of materials suppls than 10% of relevant turnover from such services; any other building or construction services are 'general building or construction services'.

## [¶19-060]   Farmer's flat-rate scheme

(VATA 1994, s. 54; SI 1992/3220; SI 1992/3221; SI 1995/2518, reg. 202 ff.; Notice 700/46; HMRC 'VAT – Agricultural flat-rate scheme' manual)

(Indirect Tax Reporter: ¶53-500)

The rate which applies to the farmers' flat-rate scheme is 4%.

## [¶19-080]   Registration limits

### (1) Taxable supplies in the UK

(VATA 1994, Sch. 1; Notice 700/1)

(Indirect Tax Reporter: ¶43-025)

| Period of application | Past turnover 1 year £ | Future turnover 30 days £ | Unless turnover for next year will not exceed £ |
|---|---|---|---|
| From 1/4/17 | 85,000 | 85,000 | 83,000 |
| 1/4/16–31/3/17 | 83,000 | 83,000 | 81,000 |
| 1/4/15–31/3/16 | 82,000 | 82,000 | 80,000 |
| 1/4/14–31/3/15 | 81,000 | 81,000 | 79,000 |
| 1/4/13–31/3/14 | 79,000 | 79,000 | 77,000 |
| 1/4/12–31/3/13 | 77,000 | 77,000 | 75,000 |
| 1/4/11–31/3/12 | 73,000 | 73,000 | 71,000 |

**Notes**

Taxable supplies at both the zero rate and positive rates are included in the above limits.

All of a person's taxable supplies are considered, because it is 'persons' not 'businesses' who can or must register. If a person took over a business as a 'going concern', he is deemed to have made the vendor's supplies for the purposes of registration.

These limits are exclusive of VAT, as VAT is not chargeable unless a person is registered or liable to be registered.

The limit which applies for a particular past period is that which is in force at the end of the period.

There are two alternative tests of the liability to notify HMRC of a person's liability to register as a result of making taxable supplies:

(1)   past 12 months turnover limit; and

(2)   future 30 days turnover limit. Registration is required if there are reasonable grounds for believing that the value of taxable supplies in a period of 30 days will exceed the limit. This limit is the same as that for the past 12 months, but applies to 30 days from any time.

The following are excluded from the supplies for the purpose of applying the registration limits:

(1)   the value of capital supplies (other than of land); and

(2)   any taxable supplies which would not be taxable supplies apart from VATA 1994, s. 7(4), which concerns removal of goods to the UK.

Any supplies made at a previous time when the person was registered are disregarded if all necessary information was given to HMRC when the earlier registration was cancelled.

## (2)  Supplies from other member states (distance selling into the UK)

(VATA 1994, Sch. 2; Notice 700/1)

(Indirect Tax Reporter: ¶43-030)

| Period of application | Cumulative relevant supplies from 1 January in year to any day in same year £ |
|---|---|
| From 1/1/93 (VATA 1994, Sch. 2; Notice 700/1) | 70,000 |

Generally, the value of relevant supplies is of those made by persons in other member states to non-taxable persons in the UK.

If certain goods, which are subject to excise duty, are removed to the UK, the person who removes the goods is liable to register in the UK because all such goods must be taxed in the country of destination. There is no de minimis limit.

### (3) Acquisitions from other member states
(VATA 1994, Sch. 3; Notice 700/1)

(Indirect Tax Reporter: ¶43-035)

| Period of application | Cumulative relevant supplies from 1 January in year to any day in same year £ |
|---|---|
| From 1/4/17 | 85,000 |
| 1/4/16–31/3/17 | 83,000 |
| 1/4/15–31/3/16 | 82,000 |
| 1/4/14–31/3/15 | 81,000 |
| 1/4/13–31/3/14 | 79,000 |
| 1/4/12–31/3/13 | 77,000 |
| 1/4/11–31/3/12 | 73,000 |

Future prospects rule: a person is also liable to register at any time if there are reasonable grounds for believing that the value of his relevant acquisitions in the period of 30 days then beginning will exceed the given limit. This limit is the same as that for the period starting on 1 January above.

### (4) Assets supplied in the UK by overseas persons
(VATA 1994, Sch. 3A; Notice 700/1)

(Indirect Tax Reporter: ¶43-045)

From 21 March 2000, any person without an establishment in the UK making or intending to make 'relevant supplies' must VAT register, regardless of the value of those supplies.

'Relevant supplies' are taxable supplies of goods, including capital assets, in the UK where the supplier has recovered UK VAT under:

● Directive 2008/9 for a person in a member state as regards VAT incurred in another member state; or

● Directive 86/560 (the thirteenth VAT directive) for claimants established outside the member states.

This applies where:

● the supplier (or his predecessor in business) was charged VAT on the purchase of the goods, or on anything incorporated in them, and has either claimed it back or intends to do so; or

● the VAT being claimed back was VAT paid on the import of goods into the UK.

### (5) Electronic, telecommunication and broadcasting services
(VATA 1994, Sch. 3B and 3BA; Notice 700/1)

(Indirect Tax Reporter: ¶43-047)

A person can register if he makes or intends to make qualifying supplies, i.e. electronically supplied services to a person who belongs in the UK or another member state and who receives such services otherwise than for business purposes. The person who registers must have neither a business establishment nor a fixed establishment in the UK or in another member state in relation to any supply. Generally, the person must also be neither registered nor required to be registered for VAT in the UK or the Isle of Man or, under equivalent legislation, in another member state.

### Digital services in the EU from 1 January 2015 (VAT MOSS)

From 1 January 2015, there are new place of supply rules for VAT on the supply of digital services by businesses to consumers in the EU. VAT on digital services will be paid in the consumer's country, not the supplier's country. It will be charged at the rate that applies in the consumer's country. Suppliers of digital services to EU consumers can either:

- register for VAT in each EU country; or
- register to use the VAT Mini One Stop Shop (VAT MOSS) online service.

VAT MOSS enables businesses to account for the VAT due on business-to-consumer (B2C) sales in other EU countries by submitting a single quarterly return and payment to HMRC. HMRC will send an electronic copy of the appropriate part of the return, and any payment, to each relevant country's tax authority.

### (6) Non-established taxable persons

(VATA 1994, Sch. 1A; Notice 700/1)

(Indirect Tax Reporter: ¶43-049)

From 1 December 2012, if a person makes taxable supplies in the UK but has no establishment there, he must register for VAT regardless of the value of such supplies. Thus, non-UK established taxable persons (NETPs) no longer benefit from the UK VAT registration threshold.

A NETP is any person not normally resident in the UK, does not have a UK establishment and, in the case of a company, is not incorporated here.

# [¶19-100]   Deregistration limits

### (1) Taxable supplies in the UK

(VATA 1994, Sch. 1; Notice 700/11)

(Indirect Tax Reporter: ¶43-925)

| Period of application | Future turnover £ |
|---|---|
| From 1/4/17 | 83,000 |
| 1/4/16–31/3/17 | 81,000 |
| 1/4/15–31/3/16 | 80,000 |
| 1/4/14–31/3/15 | 79,000 |
| 1/4/13–31/3/14 | 77,000 |
| 1/4/12–31/3/13 | 75,000 |
| 1/4/11–31/3/12 | 71,000 |

**Notes**

A registered person ceases to be liable to be registered if, at any time, HMRC are satisfied that the value of his taxable supplies in the period of one year, then beginning will not exceed the limit.

The value of supplies of capital assets is excluded from the supplies for the purpose of applying the deregistration limits.

The deregistration limits exclude VAT.

Taxable supplies at both the zero rate and positive rates are included in the above limits.

Value Added Tax

### (2) Supplies from other member states (distance selling into the UK)

(VATA 1994, Sch. 2; Notice 700/11)

(Indirect Tax Reporter: ¶43-930)

| Period of application | Past relevant supplies in last year to 31 December £ | Future relevant supplies in immediately following year £ |
|---|---|---|
| From 1/1/93 | 70,000 | 70,000 |

Generally, the value of supplies is of those made by persons in other member states to non-taxable persons in the UK.

### (3) Acquisitions from other member states

(VATA 1994, Sch. 3; Notice 700/11)

(Indirect Tax Reporter: ¶43-940)

| Period of application | Past relevant acquisitions in last year to 31 December £ | Future relevant acquisitions in immediately following year £ |
|---|---|---|
| From 1/4/17 | 85,000 | 85,000 |
| 1/4/16–31/3/17 | 83,000 | 83,000 |
| 1/4/15–31/3/16 | 82,000 | 82,000 |
| 1/4/14–31/3/15 | 81,000 | 81,000 |
| 1/4/13–31/3/14 | 79,000 | 79,000 |
| 1/4/12–31/3/13 | 77,000 | 77,000 |
| 1/4/11–31/3/12 | 73,000 | 73,000 |

### (4) Assets supplied in the UK by overseas persons

(VATA 1994, Sch. 3A; Notice 700/11)

(Indirect Tax Reporter: ¶43-945)

If HMRC are satisfied that a person registered under VATA 1994, Sch. 3A has ceased to make relevant supplies, HMRC can deregister the person from the date on which he so ceased or from an agreed later date. However, HMRC must not deregister a person unless they are satisfied that he is not liable to be registered under another provision in VATA 1994.

### (5) Electronic services

(VATA 1994, Sch. 3B and 3BA; Notice 700/11)

(Indirect Tax Reporter: ¶43-946)

HMRC cancel a person's registration under VATA 1994, Sch. 3B if he notifies them, or they determine, that he ceased to make, or have the intention to make, qualifying supplies.

### (6) Non-established taxable persons

(VATA 1994, Sch. 1A; Notice 700/11)

(Indirect Tax Reporter: ¶43-920)

HMRC may cancel the registration of a non-UK established taxable person (NETP) under VATA 1994, Sch. 1A if they are satisfied that:

(1)    the person has ceased to make taxable supplies in the course or furtherance of a business; or

(2)    the person is no longer a person in relation to whom condition C in Sch. 1A, para. 1 is met, i.e. the person has a business establishment, or another fixed establishment, in the UK in relation to any business carried on by him.

## [¶19-120]   Special accounting limits

### Cash accounting scheme

(SI 1995/2518, reg. 56–65; Notice 731; HMRC 'VAT – Cash accounting scheme' manual)

(Indirect Tax Reporter: ¶55-450)

| Period of application | Joining threshold (next 12 months supplies)[(1)] £ | Leaving threshold (last 12 months supplies) £ |
|---|---|---|
| From 1/4/07 | 1,350,000 | 1,600,000 |

**Note**

[(1)] Includes zero-rated supplies, but excludes any capital assets previously used in the business. Exempt supplies are also excluded.

Outstanding VAT on supplies made and received while using the cash accounting scheme may be brought into account on a cash basis for a further six months after withdrawal from the scheme, but only where withdrawal was voluntary or because the turnover threshold was exceeded.

### Annual accounting scheme

(SI 1995/2518, reg. 49–55; Notice 732; HMRC 'VAT – Annual accounting scheme' manual)

(Indirect Tax Reporter: ¶55-300)

| Period of application | Joining threshold (next 12 months supplies)[(1)] £ | Leaving threshold (last 12 months supplies) £ |
|---|---|---|
| From 1/4/06 | 1,350,000 | 1,600,000 |

**Note**

[(1)] Positive and zero-rated supplies excluding any supplies of capital assets and any exempt supplies.

Persons with a taxable turnover of up to (from 10 April 2003) £150,000 may join the annual accounting scheme immediately, i.e. without having to be registered for at least 12 months.

### Flat-rate scheme for small businesses scheme

(SI 1995/2518, reg. 55A–55V; Notice 733; HMRC 'Flat-rate scheme' manual)

(Indirect Tax Reporter: ¶55-350)

| Period of application | Joining threshold (next 12 months taxable supplies)[(1)] £ | Leaving threshold (flat-rate turnover at anniversary or next 30 days) £ |
|---|---|---|
| From 1/4/09 | 150,000 | 230,000 |

Value Added Tax

## [¶19-140]   Zero-rated supplies

(VATA 1994, Sch. 8)

(Indirect Tax Reporter: ¶20-000)

A zero-rated supply is a taxable supply, but the tax rate is nil.

**VAT lock:** F(No. 2)A 2015, s. 2 provides that no goods, services or supply specified in VATA 1994, Sch. 8, at the beginning of the VAT lock period (period beginning with 18 November 2015 and ending immediately before the date of the first parliamentary general election after that day) may be removed from it under VATA 1994, s. 30(4) during that period.

| Group | |
|---|---|
| 1. | Food (this includes most food for human and animal consumption – the exceptions are mainly food supplied in the course of catering, confectionary, pet foods and hot take-away food) |
| 2. | Sewerage services and water (except distilled and bottled water) but not if supplied to industry |
| 3. | Books, pamphlets, newspapers, journals, maps, music, etc. (but not stationery and posters) |
| 4. | Talking books for the blind and handicapped and wireless sets for the blind |
| 5. | Construction of buildings, etc. |
| 6. | Protected buildings[1] |
| 7. | International services |
| 8. | Transport |
| 9. | Caravans and houseboats[2] |
| 10. | Gold |
| 11. | Bank notes |
| 12. | Drugs, medicines, aids for the handicapped, etc. |
| 13. | Imports, exports, etc. |

| Group | |
|---|---|
| 14. | (repealed for supplies made after 30 June 1999) Tax-free shops |
| 15. | Charities, etc. |
| 16. | Clothing and footwear |
| 17. | (for supplies made after 30 July 2009, but repealed for supplies made after 31 October 2010 when the reverse charge applies) Emissions allowances |
| 18. | European Research Infrastructure Consortia (ERIC; from 1 January 2013) |

**Notes**

Except for exported goods and certain transactions in commodities, generally a supply is not zero-rated *unless* it is specified in the zero-rated schedule (VATA 1994, Sch. 8). A supply which can be classified as zero-rated overrides exemption. A supply which is not outside the scope of VAT is standard-rated *unless* it falls within one of the categories of exempt or zero-rated or reduced-rate supplies.

(1) From 1 October 2015, alterations of listed buildings are omitted from the list bringing their VAT treatment in line with other non-listed buildings and repairs and maintenance for all buildings which are standard-rated.

(2) From 6 April 2013, criteria for zero-rating is amended to ensure 'holiday' caravans are consistently either standard-rated (tourers) or subject to the reduced rate of VAT (static, non-residential).

# [¶19-160]   Exempt supplies

(VATA 1994, Sch. 9)

(Indirect Tax Reporter: ¶27-000)

No VAT is chargeable on an exempt supply, but input tax cannot be reclaimed except as computed under the provisions on partial exemption.

| Group | |
|---|---|
| 1. | Land |
| 2. | Insurance |
| 3. | Postal services (restricted after 30 January 2011 to supplies of public postal services and incidental goods made by the universal service provider) |
| 4. | Betting, gaming, dutiable machine games and lotteries |
| 5. | Finance |
| 6. | Education |
| 7. | Health and welfare |
| 8. | Burial and cremation |
| 9. | Subscriptions to trade unions, professional bodies and other public interest bodies |
| 10. | Sport, sports competitions and physical education |
| 11. | Works of art, etc. |
| 12. | Fund-raising events by charities and other qualifying bodies |
| 13. | Cultural services, etc. |
| 14. | Supplies of goods where input tax cannot be recovered (from 1 March 2000) |

Value Added Tax

| Group | |
|---|---|
| 15. | Investment gold (from 1 January 2000) |
| 16. | Supplies of services by groups involving cost sharing (from 17 July 2012) |

**Note**

The descriptions of the zero-rated and exempt groups are for ease of reference only and do not affect the interpretation of the groups (VATA 1994, s. 96(10)). Some suppliers can unilaterally opt to tax certain land and buildings (VATA 1994, Sch. 10, para. 2–4).

# [¶19-180]  Reduced-rate supplies

(VATA 1994, Sch. 7A)

(Indirect Tax Reporter: ¶32-000)

VAT is chargeable at 5% on a reduced-rated supply

**VAT lock:** F(No. 2)A 2015, s. 2 provides that no goods, services or supply specified in VATA 1994, Sch. 7A, at the beginning of the VAT lock period (period beginning with 18 November 2015 and ending immediately before the date of the first parliamentary general election after that day) may be removed from it under VATA 1994, s. 30(4) during that period.

| Group | |
|---|---|
| 1. | Domestic fuel and power |
| 2. | Installation of energy-saving materials |
| 3. | Grant-funded installation of heating equipment or security goods or connection of gas supply |
| 4. | Women's sanitary products |
| 5. | Children's car seats |
| 6. | Residential conversions |
| 7. | Residential renovations and alterations |
| 8. | Contraceptive products (from 1 July 2006) |
| 9. | Welfare advice or information (from 1 July 2006) |
| 10. | Installation of mobility aids for the elderly (from 1 July 2007) |
| 11. | Smoking cessation products (from 1 July 2007) |
| 12. | Caravans (from 6 April 2013) |
| 13. | Cable-suspended passenger transport systems (from 1 April 2013) |

**Notes**

(1) The 'Listed Places of Worship Grants Scheme', which is administered by the Department for Culture, Media and Sport (DCMS), effectively leaves a listed place of worship bearing VAT at 5% on repairs by funding the difference between VAT at 5% and at the standard rate. This runs along with the scheme for UK charities which refunds the VAT charged on qualifying supplies made after 15 March 2005 in the construction, renovation and maintenance of certain memorials.

(2) From 6 April 2013, Group 12 'Caravans' is added to the list in VATA 1994, Sch. 7A by way of recategorisation of 'holiday' (static, non-residential) caravans previously treated as zero-rated.

## [¶19-200]   Partial exemption

(SI 1995/2518, reg. 99–111; Notice 706; HMRC 'Partial exemption' manual)

(Indirect Tax Reporter: ¶19-400)

The law on partial exemption may restrict the amount of deductible input tax.

Where input tax cannot be attributed directly to taxable or exempt supplies (residual input tax), the standard method apportions the residual input tax according to the values of taxable and exempt supplies made in a period. In relation to input tax incurred after 17 April 2002, persons must adjust the input tax deductible under the standard method at the end of their tax year if that amount is substantially different from an attribution based on the use of purchases. 'Substantially' means in excess of:

● £50,000; or

● 50% or more of the value of the residual input tax and £25,000.

Where the residual input tax is less than £50,000 per year, the standard method can be used, unless the person is defined as a group undertaking under the Companies Acts and the residual input tax is greater than £25,000 per year.

Generally, the established de minimis limit for applying the partial exemption rules is as follows:

| Period | Exempt input tax not exceeding |
|---|---|
| Tax years beginning after 30/11/94 | ● £625 per month on average; and<br>● 50% of total input tax for prescribed accounting period |

In order to establish whether the de minimis limit has been breached, for partial exemption years starting after 31 March 2010, some taxable persons need only carry out simplified tests, rather than carry out detailed partial exemption calculations. The simplest test is whether total input tax incurred by a taxable person is less than £625 per month on average. If so, as long as 50% or less of the turnover is exempt, the de minimis test is passed. If that test is failed, the next simplified test is to strip out all input tax that is directly and solely attributable to taxable supplies. If the remainder is less than £625 per month on average then, as long as the value of exempt supplies does not exceed one-half of the value of all supplies, the de minimis test is passed.

For accounting periods commencing after 31 March 2005, rounding up the recovery rate under the standard method to the next whole number is only allowed for persons incurring no more than £400,000 residual input tax per month on average. Other persons round to two decimal places.

HMRC's approval of a partial exemption special method from 1 April 2007 is subject to a declaration by the taxable person that to the best of his knowledge and belief the intended method is fair and reasonable.

Value Added Tax

## [¶19-220]   Capital goods scheme
(SI 1995/2518, reg. 112–116; Notice 706/2)

(Indirect Tax Reporter: ¶19-800)

The capital goods scheme affects the acquisition, etc. by a partially exempt person for use in a business of certain items as follows:

| Item | Value | Adjustment period |
|------|-------|-------------------|
| Computers and computer equipment | £50,000 or more | Five years |
| Land and buildings | £250,000 or more | Ten years (five years where interest had less than ten years to run on acquisition) |
| Aircraft, ships, boats and other vessels (from 1 January 2011) | £50,000 or more | Five years |

Where the capital goods scheme applies, any initial deduction of input tax is made in the ordinary way, but must then be reviewed over the adjustment period by reference to the use of the asset concerned.

## [¶19-240]   Particulars to be shown on a valid VAT invoice
(SI 1995/2518, reg. 14; Notice 700, para. 16.3ff. (August 2013))

(Indirect Tax Reporter: ¶55-800)

**VAT invoices generally where supplied to a person who is also in the UK**

VAT invoices must show:

- a sequential number based on one or more series which uniquely identifies the document;
- the time of supply (tax point);
- date of issue of the document (where different to the time of supply);
- trader's name, address and VAT registration number;
- customer's name and address;
- a description which identifies the goods or services supplied;
- for each **description**, the quantity of the goods or the extent of the services, and the rate of VAT and the amount payable, excluding VAT, expressed in any currency;
- the gross total amount payable, excluding VAT, expressed in any currency;
- the rate of any cash discount offered;
- the total amount of VAT chargeable, expressed in sterling;
- the unit price; and
- the reason for any zero rate or exemption.

The final bullet point refers to the following types of supply:

- supplies subject to a second-hand margin scheme;
- supplies subject to the Tour Operators Margin Scheme (TOMS);
- intra-EC exempt supplies;
- intra-EC reverse charge supplies; and
- intra-EC zero-rated supplies.

Generally, VAT officers adopt a 'light touch' for about one year after any change to the requirements for a valid VAT invoice in order to give reasonable time to change procedures and help minimise the cost of change.

Persons providing VAT invoices for leasing certain motor cars must state on the invoice whether the car is a qualifying vehicle. This enables the lessee to claim the correct proportion of the VAT charged by the lessor.

The requirements for invoices concerning supplies intra-EU member states are in the *Value Added Tax Regulations* 1995 (SI 1995/2518, reg. 14(2)).

Also, a VAT invoice must be provided for an exempt supply made to a person in another member state for the purposes of that person's business.

### Less detailed VAT and modified VAT invoices

For retail sales, a VAT invoice must be provided if the customer asks for one. However, it may be possible to issue a less detailed or modified VAT invoice as follows, otherwise a full VAT invoice must be issued:

| Value of charge made for individual sale | Less detailed invoice requirements |
|---|---|
| is **£250 or less** (including VAT) | <ul><li>name of supplier, address and VAT registration number;</li><li>the time of supply (tax point);</li><li>a description which identifies the goods or services supplied;</li><li>and for each VAT rate applicable, the total amount payable, including VAT and the VAT rate charged.</li></ul> Exempt supplies must not be included in this type of VAT invoice.<br><br>To work out the amount of VAT in a VAT-inclusive price, multiply the sale price by the VAT fraction. |
| **exceeds** £250 and you are asked for a VAT invoice | must issue either a:<ul><li>full VAT invoice; or</li><li>modified VAT invoice (see below).</li></ul> |

### Credit card sales

Where credit cards, such as Visa/Mastercard or Barclaycard, are accepted, the sales voucher given to the cardholder at the time of the sale may be adapted to serve as a less detailed VAT invoice.

---

**Requirements**

The credit card voucher should show:
- retailer's name and address;
- the charge made, including VAT; and
- the date of sale.

Additional requirements:
- VAT registration number;
- rate of VAT; and
- a description of the goods or services supplied.

---

## Modified VAT invoice

Can be issued provided the customer agrees.

---

**Requirements**

- the VAT-inclusive value of each standard-rated or reduced-rated supply (instead of the VAT-exclusive values).

At the foot of the invoice, separate totals must be shown of:
- VAT-inclusive value of the standard-rated or reduced rate supplies;
- VAT payable on those supplies shown in sterling;
- value, excluding VAT, of those supplies;
- value of any zero-rated supplies included on the invoice; and
- value of any exempt supplies included on the invoice.

In all other respects the invoice should show the details required for a full VAT invoice.

---

See Notice 700, for the rules on invoices concerning:
- petrol, derv, paraffin, and heating oil;
- credit cards;
- another form of modified VAT invoice for retailers;
- cash and carry wholesalers;
- computer invoicing; and
- calculation of VAT on invoices.

## Continuous supplies of services

Certain additional particulars are required to be shown on a VAT invoice for a supply of continuous services, if the supplier chooses to use the advance invoicing facility (SI 1995/2518, reg. 90). Similar provisions apply for advance invoicing in respect of long leases (reg. 85) and in respect of supplies of water, gas, power, heat, refrigeration and ventilation (reg. 86).

## [¶19-260]   'Blocked' input tax

(VATA 1994, s. 24)

(Indirect Tax Reporter: ¶19-004)

Any input tax charged on the following items is generally 'blocked', i.e. non-recoverable:

- motor cars, but:
  - any person can recover input tax on motor cars used exclusively for business; and
  - only 50% of VAT on car leasing charges is recoverable if lessee makes any private use of the car and if lessor recovered the VAT on buying the car.

  A list of particular makes and models of car derived vans and combi vans for the purposes of determining whether VAT can be reclaimed as input tax is available at www.gov.uk/government/publications/hm-revenue-and-customs-car-derived-vans-and-combi-vans;

- entertainment, except of employees. However, if there is a strict business purpose and if it is necessary for the business to make supplies, input tax is recoverable as regards entertaining overseas customers (HMRC Brief 44/2010 (2 November 2010));
- in the case of claims by builders, articles of a kind not ordinarily installed by builders as fixtures in new houses;
- goods supplied under the second-hand scheme;
- goods imported for private purposes;
- non-business element of supplies to be used only partly for business purposes. VAT incurred on supplies not intended for business use generally does not rank as input tax, so cannot be recovered. *Lennartz* accounting starting before 1 January 2011 should run its course. Generally, *Lennartz* accounting does not apply to VAT incurred after 31 December 2010; and
- goods and services acquired by a tour operator for re-supply as a designated travel service.

'Exempt input tax' is generally not recoverable by a partially exempt person.

## [¶19-280]   Input tax and mileage allowances (advisory fuel rates)

(SI 2005/3290)

(Indirect Tax Reporter: ¶19-071)

An employer can reclaim the VAT incurred by employees on fuel costs that are reimbursed by the employer on the basis of cost or via a mileage allowance. VAT can only be reclaimed by an employer on fuel which is used in the course of the business to make taxable supplies. However, the key practical change is that employers must obtain and retain a valid VAT invoice to support the reclaim. Generally, a retailer's invoice (also known as a 'less-detailed invoice') should suffice, because the amount of fuel that is purchased by an employee in a single supply is likely to be within the VAT-inclusive limit of £250 for a retailer's invoice.

Generally, the invoiced amount does not match the input tax claim for the fuel in any one claim period and invoices may concern more than one period. For example, if fuel is purchased towards the end of a period, it may not be fully used until a subsequent period. An invoice may cover more than one claim and this needs to be taken into account when checking the evidence to support claims. Another possible reason why the invoiced amount does not match the claim is that often some of the fuel is used by the employee for private journeys. Generally, the VAT can be reclaimed if the invoice(s) are for sufficient fuel to cover the claimed mileage, and cover the relevant period. Strictly, a claim cannot be supported by an invoice that is dated after the dates covered by the claim.

HMRC publish 'advisory fuel rates' to determine the business fuel cost, but rates set by recognised motoring agencies, such as the RAC and the AA, are usually acceptable. HMRC first published the rates in 2002 (www.gov.uk/advisory-fuel-rates-when-you-can-use-them).

**Transition to revised 'advisory fuel rate': one-month rule**

For one month from the date of change, employers may use either the previous or new current rates, as they choose.

| Engine size | Rate per mile | | |
|---|---|---|---|
|  | **Petrol** | **Diesel** | **LPG** |
| **For journeys from 1 March 2017** | | | |
| 1400cc or less | 11p | 9p | 7p |
| 1401cc to 1600cc | 14p | 9p | 9p |
| 1601cc to 2000cc | 14p | 11p | 9p |
| Over 2000cc | 22p | 13p | 14p |
| **For journeys from 1 December 2016** | | | |
| 1400cc or less | 11p | 9p | 7p |
| 1401cc to 1600cc | 14p | 9p | 9p |
| 1601cc to 2000cc | 14p | 11p | 9p |
| Over 2000cc | 21p | 13p | 13p |
| **For journeys from 1 September 2016** | | | |
| 1400cc or less | 11p | 9p | 7p |
| 1401cc to 1600cc | 13p | 9p | 9p |
| 1601cc to 2000cc | 13p | 11p | 9p |
| Over 2000cc | 20p | 13p | 13p |
| **For journeys from 1 June 2016** | | | |
| 1400cc or less | 10p | 9p | 7p |
| 1401cc to 1600cc | 13p | 9p | 9p |
| 1601cc to 2000cc | 13p | 10p | 9p |
| Over 2000cc | 20p | 12p | 13p |

| Engine size | Rate per mile | | |
|---|---|---|---|
| | **Petrol** | **Diesel** | **LPG** |
| **For journeys from 1 March 2016** | | | |
| 1400cc or less | 10p | 8p | 7p |
| 1401cc to 1600cc | 12p | 8p | 8p |
| 1601cc to 2000cc | 12p | 10p | 8p |
| Over 2000cc | 19p | 11p | 13p |
| **For journeys from 1 December 2015** | | | |
| 1400cc or less | 11p | 9p | 7p |
| 1401cc to 1600cc | 13p | 9p | 9p |
| 1601cc to 2000cc | 13p | 11p | 9p |
| Over 2000cc | 20p | 13p | 13p |
| **For journeys from 1 September 2015** | | | |
| 1400cc or less | 11p | 9p | 7p |
| 1401cc to 1600cc | 14p | 9p | 9p |
| 1601cc to 2000cc | 14p | 11p | 9p |
| Over 2000cc | 21p | 13p | 14p |
| **For journeys from 1 June 2015** | | | |
| 1400cc or less | 12p | 10p | 8p |
| 1401cc to 1600cc | 14p | 10p | 9p |
| 1601cc to 2000cc | 14p | 12p | 9p |
| Over 2000cc | 21p | 14p | 14p |
| **For journeys from 1 March 2015** | | | |
| 1400cc or less | 11p | 9p | 8p |
| 1401cc to 1600cc | 13p | 9p | 10p |
| 1601cc to 2000cc | 13p | 11p | 10p |
| Over 2000cc | 20p | 14p | 14p |
| **For journeys from 1 December 2014** | | | |
| 1400cc or less | 13p | 11p | 9p |
| 1401cc to 1600cc | 16p | 11p | 11p |
| 1601cc to 2000cc | 16p | 13p | 11p |
| Over 2000cc | 23p | 16p | 16p |

Value Added Tax

| Engine size | Rate per mile | | |
|---|---|---|---|
| | Petrol | Diesel | LPG |
| **For journeys from 1 September 2014** | | | |
| 1400cc or less | 14p | 11p | 9p |
| 1401cc to 1600cc | 16p | 11p | 11p |
| 1601cc to 2000cc | 16p | 13p | 11p |
| Over 2000cc | 24p | 17p | 16p |
| **For journeys from 1 June 2014** | | | |
| 1400cc or less | 14p | 12p | 9p |
| 1401cc to 1600cc | 16p | 12p | 11p |
| 1601cc to 2000cc | 16p | 14p | 11p |
| Over 2000cc | 24p | 17p | 16p |
| **For journeys from 1 March 2014** | | | |
| 1400cc or less | 14p | 12p | 9p |
| 1401cc to 1600cc | 16p | 12p | 11p |
| 1601cc to 2000cc | 16p | 14p | 11p |
| Over 2000cc | 24p | 17p | 17p |
| **For journeys from 1 December 2013** | | | |
| 1400cc or less | 14p | 12p | 9p |
| 1401cc to 1600cc | 16p | 12p | 11p |
| 1601cc to 2000cc | 16p | 14p | 11p |
| Over 2000cc | 24p | 17p | 16p |
| **For journeys from 1 September 2013** | | | |
| 1400cc or less | 15p | 12p | 10p |
| 1401cc to 1600cc | 18p | 12p | 11p |
| 1601cc to 2000cc | 18p | 15p | 11p |
| Over 2000cc | 26p | 18p | 16p |
| **For journeys from 1 June 2013** | | | |
| 1400cc or less | 15p | 12p | 10p |
| 1401cc to 1600cc | 17p | 12p | 12p |
| 1601cc to 2000cc | 17p | 14p | 12p |
| Over 2000cc | 25p | 18p | 18p |

| Engine size | Rate per mile | | |
|---|---|---|---|
| | Petrol | Diesel | LPG |
| **For journeys from 1 March 2013** | | | |
| 1400cc or less | 15p | 13p | 10p |
| 1401cc to 1600cc | 18p | 13p | 12p |
| 1601cc to 2000cc | 18p | 15p | 12p |
| Over 2000cc | 26p | 18p | 18p |
| **For journeys from 1 December 2012** | | | |
| 1400cc or less | 15p | 12p | 11p |
| 1401cc to 1600cc | 18p | 12p | 13p |
| 1601cc to 2000cc | 18p | 15p | 13p |
| Over 2000cc | 26p | 18p | 18p |
| **For journeys from 1 September 2012** | | | |
| 1400cc or less | 15p | 12p | 10p |
| 1400cc to 1600cc | 18p | 12p | 13p |
| 1600cc to 2000cc | 18p | 15p | 13p |
| Over 2000cc | 26p | 18p | 17p |
| **For journeys from 1 June 2012** | | | |
| 1400cc or less | 15p | 12p | 11p |
| 1400cc to 1600cc | 18p | 12p | 13p |
| 1600cc to 2000cc | 18p | 15p | 13p |
| Over 2000cc | 26p | 18p | 19p |
| **For journeys from 1 March 2012** | | | |
| 1400cc or less | 15p | 13p | 10p |
| 1401cc to 1600cc | 18p | 13p | 12p |
| 1601cc to 2000cc | 18p | 15p | 12p |
| Over 2000cc | 26p | 19p | 18p |
| **For journeys from 1 December 2011** | | | |
| 1400cc or less | 15p | 12p | 10p |
| 1401cc to 1600cc | 18p | 12p | 12p |
| 1601cc to 2000cc | 18p | 15p | 12p |
| Over 2000cc | 26p | 18p | 18p |

Value Added Tax

| Engine size | Rate per mile | | |
|---|---|---|---|
| | Petrol | Diesel | LPG |
| **For journeys from 1 September 2011** | | | |
| 1400cc or less | 15p | 12p | 11p |
| 1401cc to 1600cc | 18p | 12p | 12p |
| 1601cc to 2000cc | 18p | 15p | 12p |
| Over 2000cc | 26p | 18p | 18p |
| **For journeys from 1 June 2011** | | | |
| 1400cc or less | 15p | 12p | 11p |
| 1401cc to 1600cc | 18p | 12p | 13p |
| 1601cc to 2000cc | 18p | 15p | 13p |
| Over 2000cc | 26p | 18p | 18p |
| **For journeys from 1 March 2011** | | | |
| 1400cc or less | 14p | 13p | 10p |
| 1401cc to 2000cc | 16p | 13p | 12p |
| Over 2000cc | 23p | 16p | 17p |

## [¶19-300] VAT on private fuel (scale charges)

(VATA 1994, Sch. 6, para. B1; SI 2013/2911; Notice 700/64)

(Indirect Tax Reporter: ¶18-320ff.)

### From 1 May 2016

*Fuel scale charges for 12-month period*

| CO$_2$ band | VAT fuel scale charge, 12-month period £ | VAT on 12-month charge £ | VAT exclusive 12-month charge £ |
|---|---|---|---|
| 120 or less | 467.00 | 77.83 | 389.17 |
| 125 | 699.00 | 116.50 | 582.50 |
| 130 | 747.00 | 124.50 | 622.50 |
| 135 | 792.00 | 132.00 | 660.00 |
| 140 | 841.00 | 140.17 | 700.83 |
| 145 | 886.00 | 147.67 | 738.33 |
| 150 | 934.00 | 155.67 | 778.33 |
| 155 | 979.00 | 163.17 | 815.83 |
| 160 | 1,028.00 | 171.33 | 856.67 |
| 165 | 1,073.00 | 178.83 | 894.17 |

| CO$_2$ band | VAT fuel scale charge, 12-month period £ | VAT on 12-month charge £ | VAT exclusive 12-month charge £ |
|---|---|---|---|
| 170 | 1,121.00 | 186.83 | 934.17 |
| 175 | 1,166.00 | 194.33 | 971.67 |
| 180 | 1,214.00 | 202.33 | 1,011.67 |
| 185 | 1,259.00 | 209.83 | 1,049.17 |
| 190 | 1,308.00 | 218.00 | 1,090.00 |
| 195 | 1,353.00 | 225.50 | 1,127.50 |
| 200 | 1,401.00 | 233.50 | 1,167.50 |
| 205 | 1,446.00 | 241.00 | 1,205.00 |
| 210 | 1,495.00 | 249.17 | 1,245.83 |
| 215 | 1,540.00 | 256.67 | 1,283.33 |
| 220 | 1,588.00 | 264.67 | 1,323.33 |
| 225 or more | 1,633.00 | 272.17 | 1,360.83 |

## Fuel scale charges for 3-month period

| CO$_2$ band | VAT fuel scale charge, 3-month period £ | VAT on 3-month charge £ | VAT exclusive 3-month charge £ |
|---|---|---|---|
| 120 or less | 116.00 | 19.33 | 96.67 |
| 125 | 175.00 | 29.17 | 145.83 |
| 130 | 186.00 | 31.00 | 155.00 |
| 135 | 197.00 | 32.83 | 164.17 |
| 140 | 209.00 | 34.83 | 174.17 |
| 145 | 221.00 | 36.83 | 184.17 |
| 150 | 233.00 | 38.83 | 194.17 |
| 155 | 245.00 | 40.83 | 204.17 |
| 160 | 256.00 | 42.67 | 213.33 |
| 165 | 268.00 | 44.67 | 223.33 |
| 170 | 279.00 | 46.50 | 232.50 |
| 175 | 291.00 | 48.50 | 242.50 |
| 180 | 303.00 | 50.50 | 252.50 |
| 185 | 314.00 | 52.33 | 261.67 |
| 190 | 326.00 | 54.33 | 271.67 |
| 195 | 338.00 | 56.33 | 281.67 |
| 200 | 350.00 | 58.33 | 291.67 |

Value Added Tax

| CO$_2$ band | VAT fuel scale charge, 3-month period £ | VAT on 3-month charge £ | VAT exclusive 3-month charge £ |
|---|---|---|---|
| 205 | 362.00 | 60.33 | 301.67 |
| 210 | 373.00 | 62.17 | 310.83 |
| 215 | 384.00 | 64.00 | 320.00 |
| 220 | 396.00 | 66.00 | 330.00 |
| 225 or more | 408.00 | 68.00 | 340.00 |

*Fuel scale charges for 1-month period*

| CO$_2$ band | VAT fuel scale charge, 1-month period £ | VAT on 1-month charge £ | VAT exclusive 1-month charge £ |
|---|---|---|---|
| 120 or less | 38.00 | 6.33 | 31.67 |
| 125 | 58.00 | 9.67 | 48.33 |
| 130 | 61.00 | 10.17 | 50.83 |
| 135 | 65.00 | 10.83 | 54.17 |
| 140 | 69.00 | 11.50 | 57.50 |
| 145 | 73.00 | 12.17 | 60.83 |
| 150 | 77.00 | 12.83 | 64.17 |
| 155 | 81.00 | 13.50 | 67.50 |
| 160 | 85.00 | 14.17 | 70.83 |
| 165 | 89.00 | 14.83 | 74.17 |
| 170 | 92.00 | 15.33 | 76.67 |
| 175 | 96.00 | 16.00 | 80.00 |
| 180 | 101.00 | 16.83 | 84.17 |
| 185 | 104.00 | 17.33 | 86.67 |
| 190 | 108.00 | 18.00 | 90.00 |
| 195 | 112.00 | 18.67 | 93.33 |
| 200 | 116.00 | 19.33 | 96.67 |
| 205 | 120.00 | 20.00 | 100.00 |
| 210 | 123.00 | 20.50 | 102.50 |
| 215 | 128.00 | 21.33 | 106.67 |
| 220 | 132.00 | 22.00 | 110.00 |
| 225 or more | 135.00 | 22.50 | 112.50 |

**1 May 2015 to 30 April 2016**

*Fuel scale charges for 12-month period*

| CO$_2$ band | VAT fuel scale charge, 12-month period £ | VAT on 12-month charge £ | VAT exclusive 12-month charge £ |
|---|---|---|---|
| 120 or less | 536.00 | 89.33 | 446.67 |
| 125 | 802.00 | 133.67 | 668.33 |
| 130 | 857.00 | 142.83 | 714.17 |
| 135 | 909.00 | 151.50 | 757.50 |
| 140 | 965.00 | 160.83 | 804.17 |
| 145 | 1,016.00 | 169.33 | 846.67 |
| 150 | 1,072.00 | 178.67 | 893.33 |
| 155 | 1,123.00 | 187.17 | 935.83 |
| 160 | 1,179.00 | 196.50 | 982.50 |
| 165 | 1,231.00 | 205.17 | 1,025.83 |
| 170 | 1,286.00 | 214.33 | 1,071.67 |
| 175 | 1,338.00 | 223.00 | 1,115.00 |
| 180 | 1,393.00 | 232.17 | 1,160.83 |
| 185 | 1,445.00 | 240.83 | 1,204.17 |
| 190 | 1,501.00 | 250.17 | 1,250.83 |
| 195 | 1,552.00 | 258.67 | 1,293.33 |
| 200 | 1,608.00 | 268.00 | 1,340.00 |
| 205 | 1,660.00 | 276.67 | 1,383.33 |
| 210 | 1,715.00 | 285.83 | 1,429.17 |
| 215 | 1,767.00 | 294.50 | 1,472.50 |
| 220 | 1,822.00 | 303.67 | 1,518.33 |
| 225 or more | 1,874.00 | 312.33 | 1,561.67 |

*Fuel scale charges for 3-month period*

| CO$_2$ band | VAT fuel scale charge 3-month period £ | VAT on 3-month charge £ | VAT exclusive 3-month charge £ |
|---|---|---|---|
| 120 or less | 133.00 | 22.17 | 110.83 |
| 125 | 200.00 | 33.33 | 166.67 |
| 130 | 213.00 | 35.50 | 177.50 |

Value Added Tax

| CO$_2$ band | VAT fuel scale charge 3-month period £ | VAT on 3-month charge £ | VAT exclusive 3-month charge £ |
|---|---|---|---|
| 135 | 227.00 | 37.83 | 189.17 |
| 140 | 240.00 | 40.00 | 200.00 |
| 145 | 254.00 | 42.33 | 211.67 |
| 150 | 267.00 | 44.50 | 222.50 |
| 155 | 281.00 | 46.83 | 234.17 |
| 160 | 294.00 | 49.00 | 245.00 |
| 165 | 308.00 | 51.33 | 256.67 |
| 170 | 320.00 | 53.33 | 266.67 |
| 175 | 334.00 | 55.67 | 278.33 |
| 180 | 347.00 | 57.83 | 289.17 |
| 185 | 361.00 | 60.17 | 300.83 |
| 190 | 374.00 | 62.33 | 311.67 |
| 195 | 388.00 | 64.67 | 323.33 |
| 200 | 401.00 | 66.83 | 334.17 |
| 205 | 415.00 | 69.17 | 345.83 |
| 210 | 428.00 | 71.33 | 356.67 |
| 215 | 441.00 | 73.50 | 367.50 |
| 220 | 455.00 | 75.83 | 379.17 |
| 225 or more | 468.00 | 78.00 | 390.00 |

*Fuel scale charges for 1-month period*

| CO$_2$ band | VAT fuel scale charge, 1-month period £ | VAT on 1-month charge £ | VAT exclusive 1-month charge £ |
|---|---|---|---|
| 120 or less | 44.00 | 7.33 | 36.67 |
| 125 | 66.00 | 11.00 | 55.00 |
| 130 | 70.00 | 11.67 | 58.33 |
| 135 | 75.00 | 12.50 | 62.50 |
| 140 | 80.00 | 13.33 | 66.67 |
| 145 | 84.00 | 14.00 | 70.00 |
| 150 | 88.00 | 14.67 | 73.33 |
| 155 | 93.00 | 15.50 | 77.50 |
| 160 | 97.00 | 16.17 | 80.83 |

| CO$_2$ band | VAT fuel scale charge, 1-month period £ | VAT on 1-month charge £ | VAT exclusive 1-month charge £ |
|---|---|---|---|
| 165 | 102.00 | 17.00 | 85.00 |
| 170 | 106.00 | 17.67 | 88.33 |
| 175 | 111.00 | 18.50 | 92.50 |
| 180 | 115.00 | 19.17 | 95.83 |
| 185 | 119.00 | 19.83 | 99.17 |
| 190 | 124.00 | 20.67 | 103.33 |
| 195 | 129.00 | 21.50 | 107.50 |
| 200 | 133.00 | 22.17 | 110.83 |
| 205 | 138.00 | 23.00 | 115.00 |
| 210 | 142.00 | 23.67 | 118.33 |
| 215 | 146.00 | 24.33 | 121.67 |
| 220 | 151.00 | 25.17 | 125.83 |
| 225 or more | 155.00 | 25.83 | 129.17 |

1 May 2014 to 30 April 2015

*Fuel scale charges for the 12-month period*

| CO$_2$ band | VAT fuel scale charge 12-month period £ | VAT on 12-month charge £ | VAT exclusive 12-month charge £ |
|---|---|---|---|
| 120 or less | 627.00 | 104.50 | 522.50 |
| 125 | 939.00 | 156.50 | 782.50 |
| 130 | 1,004.00 | 167.33 | 836.67 |
| 135 | 1,064.00 | 177.33 | 886.67 |
| 140 | 1,129.00 | 188.17 | 940.83 |
| 145 | 1,190.00 | 198.33 | 991.67 |
| 150 | 1,255.00 | 209.17 | 1,045.83 |
| 155 | 1,315.00 | 219.17 | 1,095.83 |
| 160 | 1,381.00 | 230.17 | 1,150.83 |
| 165 | 1,441.00 | 240.17 | 1,200.83 |
| 170 | 1,506.00 | 251.00 | 1,255.00 |
| 175 | 1,567.00 | 261.17 | 1,305.83 |
| 180 | 1,632.00 | 272.00 | 1,360.00 |
| 185 | 1,692.00 | 282.00 | 1,410.00 |
| 190 | 1,757.00 | 292.83 | 1,464.17 |

Value Added Tax

| $CO_2$ band | VAT fuel scale charge 12-month period £ | VAT on 12-month charge £ | VAT exclusive 12-month charge £ |
|---|---|---|---|
| 195 | 1,818.00 | 303.00 | 1,515.00 |
| 200 | 1,883.00 | 313.83 | 1,569.17 |
| 205 | 1,943.00 | 323.83 | 1,619.17 |
| 210 | 2,008.00 | 334.67 | 1,673.33 |
| 215 | 2,069.00 | 344.83 | 1,724.17 |
| 220 | 2,134.00 | 355.67 | 1,778.33 |
| 225 or more | 2,194.00 | 365.67 | 1,828.33 |

*Fuel scale charges for the 3-month period*

| $CO_2$ band | VAT fuel scale charge 3-month period £ | VAT on 3-month charge £ | VAT exclusive 3-month charge £ |
|---|---|---|---|
| 120 or less | 156.00 | 26.00 | 130.00 |
| 125 | 234.00 | 39.00 | 195.00 |
| 130 | 251.00 | 41.83 | 209.17 |
| 135 | 266.00 | 44.33 | 221.67 |
| 140 | 282.00 | 47.00 | 235.00 |
| 145 | 297.00 | 49.50 | 247.50 |
| 150 | 313.00 | 52.17 | 260.83 |
| 155 | 328.00 | 54.67 | 273.33 |
| 160 | 345.00 | 57.50 | 287.50 |
| 165 | 360.00 | 60.00 | 300.00 |
| 170 | 376.00 | 62.67 | 313.33 |
| 175 | 391.00 | 65.17 | 325.83 |
| 180 | 408.00 | 68.00 | 340.00 |
| 185 | 423.00 | 70.50 | 352.50 |
| 190 | 439.00 | 73.17 | 365.83 |
| 195 | 454.00 | 75.67 | 378.33 |
| 200 | 470.00 | 78.33 | 391.67 |
| 205 | 485.00 | 80.83 | 404.17 |
| 210 | 502.00 | 83.67 | 418.33 |
| 215 | 517.00 | 86.17 | 430.83 |
| 220 | 533.00 | 88.83 | 444.17 |
| 225 or more | 548.00 | 91.33 | 456.67 |

*Fuel scale charges for the 1-month period*

| CO$_2$ band | VAT fuel scale charge 1-month period £ | VAT on 1-month charge £ | VAT exclusive 1-month charge £ |
|---|---|---|---|
| 120 or less | 52.00 | 8.67 | 43.33 |
| 125 | 78.00 | 13.00 | 65.00 |
| 130 | 83.00 | 13.83 | 69.17 |
| 135 | 88.00 | 14.67 | 73.33 |
| 140 | 94.00 | 15.67 | 78.33 |
| 145 | 99.00 | 16.50 | 82.50 |
| 150 | 104.00 | 17.33 | 86.67 |
| 155 | 109.00 | 18.17 | 90.83 |
| 160 | 115.00 | 19.17 | 95.83 |
| 165 | 120.00 | 20.00 | 100.00 |
| 170 | 125.00 | 20.83 | 104.17 |
| 175 | 130.00 | 21.67 | 108.33 |
| 180 | 136.00 | 22.67 | 113.33 |
| 185 | 141.00 | 23.50 | 117.50 |
| 190 | 146.00 | 24.33 | 121.67 |
| 195 | 151.00 | 25.17 | 125.83 |
| 200 | 156.00 | 26.00 | 130.00 |
| 205 | 161.00 | 26.83 | 134.17 |
| 210 | 167.00 | 27.83 | 139.17 |
| 215 | 172.00 | 28.67 | 143.33 |
| 220 | 177.00 | 29.50 | 147.50 |
| 225 or more | 182.00 | 30.33 | 151.67 |

Value Added Tax

## [¶19-320]   VAT publications having legal force
(Indirect Tax Reporter: ¶4-200)

Certain VAT publications that have legal force in whole or part are listed in Notice 747.

## [¶19-340]   VAT registration numbers: country code prefix
(SI 1995/2518, reg. 2(1); Notice 725, para. 16.19 (October 2012))

(Indirect Tax Reporter: ¶63-160)

Certain invoices should show the invoicer's registration number prefixed by the country code (also known as the alphabetical code).

| Member state | Country code |
|---|---|
| Austria | AT |
| Belgium | BE |
| Bulgaria[2] | BG |
| Croatia[3] | HR |
| Cyprus[1] | CY |
| Czech Republic[1] | CZ |
| Denmark | DK |
| Estonia[1] | EE |
| Finland | FI |
| France | FR |
| Germany | DE |
| Greece | EL |
| Hungary[1] | HU |
| Ireland | IE |
| Italy | IT |
| Latvia[1] | LV |
| Lithuania[1] | LT |
| Luxembourg | LU |
| Malta[1] | MT |
| Netherlands | NL |
| Poland[1] | PL |
| Portugal | PT |
| Romania[2] | RO |
| Slovakia[1] | SK |
| Slovenia[1] | SI |
| Spain | ES |
| Sweden | SE |
| United Kingdom | GB |

**Notes**

[1] This country joined the European Union on 1 May 2004.

[2] Bulgaria and Romania joined the EU on 1 January 2007.

[3] Croatia joined the EU on 1 July 2013.

# [¶19-344]   Territory of the EU

(Directive 2006/112, art. 5; Notice 60, para. 2.5; Notice 725, para. 2.4; Notice 741A, para. 21)

Comprehensive tables of VAT rates applied in the EU member states as at 1 September 2015 are available at http://ec.europa.eu/taxation_customs/resources/documents/taxation/vat/how_vat_works/rates/vat_rates_en.pdf.

| Member states |
|---|
| The territory of the EU for VAT purposes consists of the following member states: |
| (1)    Austria (including Jungholtz and Mittelberg); |
| (2)    Belgium; |
| (3)    Bulgaria (from 1 January 2007); |
| (4)    Croatia (from 1 July 2013); |
| (5)    Cyprus (from 1 May 2004, including the British Sovereign Base Areas of Akrotiri and Dhekelia); |
| (6)    Czech Republic (from 1 May 2004); |
| (7)    Denmark; |
| (8)    Estonia (from 1 May 2004); |
| (9)    Finland; |
| (10)   France (including Monaco); |
| (11)   Germany; |
| (12)   Greece; |
| (13)   Hungary (from 1 May 2004); |
| (14)   Ireland (the Republic of) (also known as Eire); |
| (15)   Italy; |
| (16)   Latvia (from 1 May 2004); |
| (17)   Lithuania (from 1 May 2004); |
| (18)   Luxembourg; |
| (19)   Malta (from 1 May 2004); |
| (20)   Netherlands (also known as Holland); |
| (21)   Poland (from 1 May 2004); |
| (22)   Portugal (including the Azores and Madeira); |
| (23)   Romania (from 1 January 2007); |
| (24)   Slovakia (from 1 May 2004); |
| (25)   Slovenia (from 1 May 2004); |
| (26)   Spain (including the Balearic Islands); |
| (27)   Sweden; and |
| (28)   UK (including the Isle of Man). |

Value Added Tax

| Excluded territories |
| --- |

**Excluded territories**

The following territories of member states are excluded from the 'territory of the country':

(1)  re Cyprus: the United Nations buffer zone and the part of Cyprus to the north of the buffer zone where the Republic of Cyprus does not exercise effective control;

(2)  re Denmark: the Faroe Islands and Greenland;

(3)  re Finland: the Åland Islands;

(4)  re France: Guadeloupe, French Guiana, Martinique, Mayotte, Réunion and Saint-Martin (French Republic);

(5)  re Germany:

    (a)  the Island of Heligoland; and

    (b)  Büsingen,

(6)  re Greece: Mount Athos (also known as Agion Oros);

(7)  re Italy:

    (a)  Campione d'Italia; and

    (b)  the Italian waters of Lake Lugano and Livigno;

(8)  re Netherlands: Antilles.

(9)  re Spain:

    (a)  the Canary Islands

    (b)  Ceuta; and

    (c)  Melilla; and

(10)  re UK:

    (a)  the Channel Islands; and

    (b)  Gibraltar.

### Included areas: Monaco and the Isle of Man

Monaco and the Isle of Man are not treated as 'third territories'. They are part of France and the UK respectively. Thus, transactions originating in or intended for:

(1)  Monaco are treated as transactions originating in or intended for France; and

(2)  the Isle of Man are treated as transactions originating in or intended for the UK.

### Areas not within the EU

Andorra, San Marino, the Vatican City and Liechtenstein are not within the EU for VAT purposes.

# [¶19-400]   EC Sales List (ESL)

(SI 1995/2518, reg. 21–23)

(Indirect Tax Reporter: ¶64-800ff.)

VAT-registered businesses in the UK supplying goods and services to VAT-registered customers in another EU country must tell HMRC about those supplies using an EC Sales list. An EC sales list reports:

- details of each EU customer;
- the sterling value of supplies made to them; and
- the customer's country code.

**Reporting of supplies to VAT-registered customers in other EU countries**

| Supplies of: | Value | Frequency |
|---|---|---|
| Goods | Over £35,000 threshold in current or four previous quarters | Monthly |
| Goods | Under £35,000 threshold in the current or previous four quarters | Quarterly |
| Services subject to reverse charge in customer's country | N/A | Quarterly (but monthly returns optional) |
| Goods and services where required to send monthly lists for goods | N/A | Monthly for all supplies or monthly for goods, and quarterly for services |
| Goods or services by traders submitting annual VAT returns | • taxable turnover does not exceed £145,000<br>• annual value of supplies to other EU countries is not more than £11,000<br>• sales do not include New Means of Transport | Annually (subject to application and approval by HMRC) |
| Goods only (not services) | • taxable turnover does not exceed £93,500<br>• supplies £11,000 or less<br>• supplies exclude New Means of transport | Annually (subject to application and approval by HMRC) |

**ESL deadlines**

| Submission | Due date (following end of period) |
|---|---|
| Paper | Within 14 days |
| Electronic | Within 21 days |

Value Added Tax

## [¶19-450]   Intrastat

(SI 1992/2790)

(Indirect Tax Reporter: ¶64-600)

All VAT-registered businesses show the total value of goods dispatched to other EU member states in box 8 and the total arrivals of goods acquired from other EU member states in box 9 of their VAT Return. In addition, those who trade in the EU above the Intrastat exemption threshold in force during the year must also complete a monthly Supplementary Declaration (SD). Larger businesses that trade above the Intrastat delivery terms threshold must also specify delivery terms information on their SD. The table below shows recent thresholds:

| Period | Acquisitions (Arrivals) £ | Supplies (Dispatches) £ | Delivery terms £ |
|---|---|---|---|
| From 1 January 2015 | 1,500,000 | 250,000 | 24,000,000 |
| From 1 January 2014 | 1,200,000 | 250,000 | 24,000,000 |
| From 1 January 2010 | 600,000 | 250,000 | 16,000,000 |

**Intrastat deadlines**

| Monthly submission | Due date (following end of period) |
|---|---|
| Online (only) | by 21st day following |

# Administration

## [¶19-500]   Civil penalties

(Notices 700/41 (Late registration penalty) and 700/50 (Default surcharge); HMRC 'Compliance handbook' manual; HMRC 'VAT – Civil penalties' manual)

(Indirect Tax Reporter: ¶59-600ff.)

| Offence | Civil penalty |
|---|---|
| • **Dishonest conduct by a tax agent** (FA 2012, Sch. 38 from 1 April 2013) | • no less than £5,000;<br>• no more than £50,000;<br>• but the penalty may be reduced below £5,000 if there are special circumstances;<br>• also HMRC may publish certain information about the tax agent if the penalty is more than £5,000. |

| Offence | Civil penalty |
|---|---|
| • Failure of a data-holder to comply with a notice requiring **data to be provided to HMRC** (FA 2011, Sch. 23, Pt. 4 from 1 April 2012) | • a fixed penalty of £300 for the failure; <br> • if the assessment of the £300 penalty has been notified, a further penalty of £60 for each subsequent day of default. If HMRC apply, the tribunal may increase the daily default penalty to £1,000 for each applicable day; |
| • Inaccurate data provided | • £3,000 if inaccurate data is provided. |
| • Failure of a company to notify HMRC of the name of its **senior accounting officer** for a financial year beginning after 20 July 2009 (FA 2009, s. 93 and Sch. 46, para. 7) | Penalty of £5,000 |
| • Failure of a senior accounting officer (1) to take reasonable steps to ensure that the company establishes and maintains **appropriate tax accounting arrangements** or (2) to provide an accurate **certificate** to HMRC (FA 2009, s. 93 and Sch. 46, para. 4 and 5 in relation to financial years beginning after 20 July 2009) | Penalty of £5,000 |
| • Failure of a third party to comply with a notice from HMRC requiring **contact details for a debtor** for the purpose of collecting VAT (FA 2009, Sch. 49, para. 5) | Penalty of £300 |
| • Failure to make **quarterly returns** on time (FA 2009, Sch. 55 from a date **to be appointed** to replace the default surcharge) | • a fixed £100 penalty that escalates by £100 for each subsequent failure up to a maximum of £400 per failure; <br> • a penalty of 5% of tax or £300 if greater at six and 12 months from the date of the failure; <br> • a penalty of up to 100% of tax or £300 if greater if, by failing to make the return, the taxpayer is deliberately withholding information to stop HMRC correctly assessing. |

Value Added Tax

| Offence | Civil penalty | | |
|---|---|---|---|
| • Failure to make **quarterly payments on time** (FA 2009, Sch. 56 from a date **to be appointed** to replace the default surcharge) | • a penalty of 2% of the unpaid tax for a second failure during a penalty period; <br> • a penalty of 3% of the unpaid tax for a third failure during a penalty period with further failures attracting a maximum penalty of 4%; <br> • if any of the failures are prolonged, additional penalties of 5% of the unpaid tax are charged at six and 12 months from the date of the failure. | | |
| • Deliberately **obstructing an officer** in the course of an inspection that has been pre-approved by the tribunal | • a fixed £300 penalty (FA 2008, Sch. 36, para. 39); and <br> • daily penalties of up to £60 for continuing default (Sch. 36, para. 40). | | |
| • Failure to notify liability for **registration** or change in nature of supplies by person exempted from registration or certain acquisitions of goods in the UK from another member state (FA 2008, Sch. 41, para. 1, in relation to an obligation arising after 31 March 2010)[4] | **Type of failure** | | **Percentage of the tax unpaid** |
| | Non-deliberate failure | | 30% |
| | Deliberate but not concealed | | 70% |
| | Deliberate and concealed | | 100% |
| • Unauthorised issue of VAT **invoice** (FA 2008, Sch. 41, para. 2, in relation to an unauthorised issue of an invoice taking place after 31 March 2010)[4] | Penalty is the same as for the late notification penalty under Sch. 41, para. 1 | | |
| • **Error** in taxpayer's document sent to HMRC (FA 2007, Sch. 24, para. 1)[1][2][4] | Maximum penalty, i.e. without disclosure, <br> • for careless action, 30% of the 'potential lost revenue' (PLR); <br> • for deliberate but not concealed action, 70% of the PLR; and <br> • for deliberate and concealed action, 100% of the PLR. | | |
| • **Failure to notify** HMRC within 30 days of an **underassessment** (FA 2007, Sch. 24, para. 2)[1] | 30% of the potential lost revenue[2] | | |
| • Inaccuracy **delays tax** (FA 2007, Sch. 24, para. 8) | 5% of the delayed tax for each year or a percentage of the delayed tax, for each separate period of delay of less than one year, equating to 5% p.a.[2] | | |
| • Evasion of VAT due on **imports** (FA 2003, s. 25) | Amount of import VAT evaded | | |

| Offence | Civil penalty | | |
|---|---|---|---|
| • Contravention of HMRC rules relating to **exports** (FA 2003, s. 26; *Customs (Contravention of a Relevant Rule) Regulations* 2003 (SI 2003/3113)) | Penalty of up to £2,500 | | |
| • Default **surcharge** (VATA 1994, s. 59 but from a date **to be appointed** to be replaced by the penalty in FA 2009, Sch. 55 and 56) | 1st default in surcharge period | | 2% |
| | 2nd | | 5% |
| | 3rd | | 10% |
| | 4th or later | | 15% |

If a return is late, but either no VAT is due or the VAT is paid on time, although a default is recorded, no surcharge is assessed.

HMRC generally only issue a surcharge assessment at the 2% or 5% rate if the assessment is at least £400. The surcharge may be suspended while there is an agreement for deferred payment (FA 2009, s. 108).

There is no automatic default surcharge for persons with an annual turnover of up to £150,000. Generally, by concession, such persons are first offered help and advice when they are late with a VAT payment. Small businesses are often allowed two defaults before a default surcharge is assessed: a first default should trigger a letter and a second default should trigger a surcharge liability notice.

The penalty regime in FA 2009, Sch. 55 and 56 is due to replace the default surcharge and apply to taxpayers who fail (1) to file their VAT returns on time or (2) to pay their VAT liabilities in full and on time. The revised penalties will treat late payment of VAT and late-filed returns separately and try to encourage filing and payment by the correct dates by imposing an escalating series of penalties, depending on the number of failures within a penalty period. Further penalties arise if there is a prolonged delay in filing returns or paying the VAT due. A late payment penalty may be avoided where the taxpayer has agreed a 'time to pay' arrangement with HMRC.

Value Added Tax

| Offence | Civil penalty | |
|---|---|---|
| • Incorrect **certificates** as to zero-rating and reduced-rate certificates re fuel and power, etc. (VATA 1994, s. 62) | VAT chargeable if certificate had been correct minus any VAT actually charged. | |
| • Inaccurate **EU sales statement** or **reverse charge sales statement** (VATA 1994, s. 65) | £100 for a material inaccuracy on a statement submitted within two years of a penalty notice (itself issued after a second materially inaccurate statement) | |
| • **Failure to submit** EU sales statement or reverse charge sales statement (VATA 1994, s. 66) | 1st default including that to which the default notice relates | £5 per day |
| | 2nd | £10 per day |
| | 3rd | £15 per day |
| | (Maximum: 100 days – minimum: £50) | |
| • Breach of **walking possession agreement** (VATA 1994, s. 68) | 50% of the VAT due or amount recoverable | |
| • Breach of **regulatory provision** (VATA 1994, s. 69) (The penalty cannot be imposed without a prior written warning (VATA 1994, s. 76(2))) | Failure to preserve records: £500 | |
| | • **Submission of return or payment is late** | |
| | **Number of relevant failures in two years before the failure** | **Greater of:** |
| | 0 | £5 or 1/6 of 1% of VAT due |
| | 1 | £10 or 1/3 of 1% of VAT due |
| | 2 or more | £15 or 1/2 of 1% of VAT due |
| | • **Other breaches** | |
| | **Number of relevant failures in two years before the failure** | **Prescribed daily rate** |
| | 0 | £5 |
| | 1 | £10 |
| | 2 or more | £15 |
| | Penalty: the number of days of failure (100 maximum) multiplied by above prescribed daily rate (minimum penalty £50) | |

| Offence | Civil penalty | | |
|---|---|---|---|
| • Failure to comply with requirements of scheme for **investment gold** (VATA 1994, s. 69A) | 20% of the value of the transaction concerned | | |
| • Breach of **record-keeping requirements** imposed by a direction (VATA 1994, s. 69B) | Penalty: the number of days of failure (30 maximum) multiplied by £200 daily rate | | |
| • Failure to notify acquisition of **excise duty goods** or **new means of transport** (VATA 1994, s. 75) | **Period of failure** | **Percentage of relevant VAT** | |
| | Three months or less | 5% | |
| | Over three months but not over six months | 10% | |
| | Over six months | 15% | |
| • **Failure to pay** on time correct amount of a relevant tax (such as VAT) (SI 2013/1894; formerly SI 1997/1431) | Taking control of goods (from 6 April 2014; formerly distress) | | |
| • Failure of certain persons to use an **electronic return system** to make a VAT return (SI 1995/2518, reg. 25A) | **Annual VAT-exclusive turnover** | **Penalty** | |
| | £22,800,001 or more | £400 | |
| | £5,600,001 to £22,800,000 | £300 | |
| | £100,001 to £5,600,000 | £200 | |
| | £100,000 and under | £100 | |

**Notes**
[1] The penalty under FA 2007, Sch. 24, para. 1 and 2 is calculated on the '**potential lost revenue**' (PLR) by reference to:
(a) the amount of VAT understated;
(b) the nature of the behaviour giving rise to the understatement; and
(c) the extent of the taxpayer's disclosure.

| Penalised behaviour | Maximum penalty, without disclosure, based on PLR | Minimum penalty, with prompted disclosure, based on PLR | Minimum penalty, with unprompted disclosure, based on PLR |
|---|---|---|---|
| Careless | 30% | 15% | Nil |
| Deliberate but not concealed | 70% | 35% | 20% |
| Deliberate and concealed | 100% | 50% | 30% |

If HMRC think it right, because of special circumstances, they may reduce a penalty. 'Special circumstances' excludes:
(a) ability to pay; or
(b) the fact that the PLR from one taxpayer is balanced by a potential over-payment by another.

The penalty regime includes the concept of suspended penalties for careless (not deliberate) action for up to two years where the taxpayer shows that his compliance has improved. In due course, any such suspended penalty is cancelled or becomes payable. Apparently, suspension will only be used for weaknesses in the system for accounting for VAT and not for a one-off error.

Value Added Tax

The 'potential lost revenue' (PLR) in respect of an inaccuracy in a VAT return is the additional amount due or payable in respect of VAT as a result of correcting the inaccuracy or assessment. If an inaccuracy resulted in VAT being declared later than it should have been ('the delayed tax'), the PLR is:

(a) 5% of the delayed tax for each year of the delay; or

(b) a percentage of the delayed tax, for each separate period of delay of less than a year, equating to 5% per year, i.e. the 5% is calculated pro rata for part-years.

(2) The penalty under FA 2007, Sch. 24 for incorrect returns, etc. applies from the **appointed date** which, subject to the transitional provisions in SI 2008/568 (C. 20), art. 3, is:

- 1 April 2008 in relation to relevant documents relating to tax periods commencing on or after 1 April 2008;

- 1 April 2008 in relation to assessments falling within FA 2007, Sch. 24, para. 2 for tax periods commencing on or after 1 April 2008;

- 1 July 2008 in relation to relevant documents relating to claims under the 13th VAT directive for years commencing on or after 1 July 2008;

- 1 January 2009 in relation to relevant documents relating to claims under the eighth VAT directive for years commencing on or after 1 January 2009;

- 1 April 2009 in relation to documents relating to all other claims for repayments of relevant tax made on or after 1 April 2009 which are not related to a tax period;

- 1 April 2009 in relation to documents given where a person's liability to pay relevant tax arises on or after 1 April 2009.

The penalty for under-assessment by HMRC applies from 1 April 2008 in relation to assessments under FA 2007, Sch. 24, para. 2 for tax periods commencing on or after that date, but no person is liable to the penalty in respect of a tax period for which a return is required to be made before 1 April 2009.

(3) HMRC may waive certain interest and surcharges on VAT that was paid late and was payable by those who were adversely affected by designated **national disasters**, e.g. certain severe flooding (FA 2008, s. 135).

(4) HMRC may publish certain details of **deliberate tax defaulters** as regards return periods starting after 31 March 2010 and for failing to meet obligations that arise after 31 March 2010 (FA 2009, s. 94). However, there is no publication of the details of an offender who made a full disclosure, either unprompted or prompted in a time considered appropriate by HMRC.

## Criminal offences relating to VAT

### (1)  Knowingly engaged in fraudulent evasion

If a person is knowingly concerned in, or in the taking of steps with a view to, the fraudulent evasion of VAT by him or another person, he is liable:

- on summary conviction, to a penalty of the statutory maximum (£5,000) or of three times the amount of the VAT, whichever is the greater, or to imprisonment for a term not exceeding six months or to both; or

- on conviction on indictment, to a penalty of any amount or to imprisonment for a term not exceeding seven years or to both

(VATA 1994, s. 72).

HMRC must prove fraud to criminal standards of proof, i.e. beyond reasonable doubt, rather than on a balance of probabilities.

The circumstances in which HMRC consider prosecution under the criminal law are described in Notice 700.

A tax evader may be charged with 'false accounting' or the common law offence of cheating the Public Revenue (*Theft Act* 1968, s. 32(1)).

Spring Budget 2017 confirmed that (as previously announced at Budget 2016 and confirmed at Autumn Statement 2016) the Government will legislate in Finance Bill 2017 to introduce a new and more effective penalty for participating in VAT fraud. It will be applied to businesses and company officers when they knew or should have known that their transactions were connected with VAT fraud. The penalty will improve the application of penalties to those facilitating orchestrated VAT fraud. The new penalty will be a fixed rate penalty of 30% for participants in VAT fraud. This will be implemented following Royal Assent of the Finance Bill 2017.

*(2)    Supplementary declarations (Intrastats)*

As regards supplementary declarations, a failure to submit a declaration under the Intrastat system can result on summary conviction in a fine up to £2,500 (level 4 on the standard scale) (SI 1992/2790, reg. 6).

*(3)    Impersonating an officer*

It is a criminal offence to impersonate an HMRC officer with a view to obtaining:

- admission to premises;
- information; or
- any other benefit.

On summary conviction the penalty is imprisonment for up to 51 weeks, a fine not exceeding level 5 on the standard scale (£5,000), or both (CRCA 2005, s. 30).

# [¶19-530]    Reckonable dates

(VATA 1994, s. 74; FA 2009, s. 101; Notice 700/43)

(Indirect Tax Reporter: ¶60-630)

The reckonable dates for VAT are:

- *interest on overdue VAT*: due date for submission of return (usually last day of month following end of return period);
- *interest on VAT incorrectly repaid*: seven days after issue of instruction directing payment of amount incorrectly repaid.

From 1 September 2008, HMRC may charge interest on a voluntary disclosure of underdeclared VAT even if the underdeclaration error is below the disclosure threshold. However, underdeclaration errors properly corrected on a return still avoid an interest charge.

### Proposed harmonisation of interest charged by HMRC

From a date to be appointed, interest charged on late paid VAT and certain other taxes is to be harmonised (FA 2009, s. 101 and Sch. 53).

Value Added Tax

## [¶19-560]   Interest on underpaid VAT (default interest)
(VATA 1994, s. 74; Notice 700/43; HMRC 'VAT default interest' manual)

(Indirect Tax Reporter: ¶60-630)

| Period of application | Days in period | Interest % |
|---|---|---|
| From 23/08/16 | — | 2.75 |
| 29/09/09 to 22/08/16 | 2520 | 3.00 |

### Proposed harmonisation of interest charged by HMRC
From a date to be appointed, interest charged on late paid VAT and certain other taxes is to be harmonised (FA 2009, s. 101 and Sch. 53).

## [¶19-590]   Interest on overpaid VAT (statutory interest)
(VATA 1994, s. 78)

(Indirect Tax Reporter: ¶60-680)

Interest on overpaid VAT (statutory interest) arises in certain cases of official error.

Such interest is not free of income or corporation tax.

| Period of application | Interest rate % |
|---|---|
| From 29/9/09 | 0.5 |

### Proposed harmonisation of interest on overpaid VAT
From a date to be appointed, interest on overpaid VAT and certain other taxes is to be harmonised (FA 2009, s. 102 and Sch. 54).

# INSURANCE PREMIUM TAX

## [¶20-000]   Rates

(FA 1994, Pt. III; Notice IPT 1; HMRC 'Insurance premium tax' manual)

Insurance premium tax (IPT) is imposed on certain insurance premiums where the risk is located in the UK.

| Period of application | Standard rate[1] % | Higher rate[2] % |
|---|---|---|
| From 1 June 2017 | 12.0[4] | 20.0 |
| From 1 October 2016[3] | 10.0 | 20.0 |
| From 1 November 2015 | 9.5 | 20.0 |
| From 4 January 2011 | 6.0 | 20.0 |

**Notes**

[1] Rate increase to 9.5% with effect in relation to premiums received on or after 1 November 2015. For insurers using the special accounting scheme, there will be a four-month concessionary period that will begin on 1 November 2015 and end on 29 February 2016, during which premiums received that relate to policies entered into before 1 November 2015 will continue to be liable to IPT at 6%. From 1 March 2016, all premiums received by insurers will be taxed at the new rate of 9.5%, regardless of when the policy was entered into.

[2] From 1 August 1998, the higher rate applies to all travel insurance.

[3] Standard rate of IPT increased from 9.5% to 10% with effect from 1 October 2016, with an exception for those insurers who use a special accounting scheme rather than the cash receipt method. The exception operates to require the new standard rate to be applied by them only to premiums received on or after 1 February 2017, where the premium relates to risks covered by the terms of a contract entered into before 1 October 2016 (FA 2016, s. 141).

[4] Increase in standard rate announced at Autumn Statement 2016 and confirmed at Spring Budget 2017. No announcement was made regarding any change to higher rate.

## [¶20-100]   Error correction

(SI 1994/1774, reg. 13)

If the underdeclarations or overdeclarations on previous returns do not exceed a limit, such errors may be corrected on the return for the period in which the errors are discovered.

For accounting periods starting after 30 June 2008, the limit is the greater of £10,000 and 1% of the net IPT turnover as per box 10 on the IPT return. However, this is subject to an upper limit of £50,000.

Insurance Premium Tax

# LANDFILL TAX

**Note:** See ¶26-300 for rates applicable in Scotland from 1 April 2015.

## [¶21-000]   Rates
(FA 1996, s. 42; Notices LFT 1; HMRC 'Landfill tax' manual)

Landfill tax was introduced on 1 October 1996 and is collected from landfill site operators. Landfill tax aims to encourage diversion of waste disposal from landfill sites.

| Type of waste | Rate (per tonne) £ |
|---|---|
| **Inactive waste liable to lower rate** | |
| From 1 April 2018 | 2.80[1] |
| From 1 April 2017 | 2.70 |
| From 1 April 2016 | 2.65 |
| 1 April 2015 to 31 March 2016 | 2.60 |
| 1 April 2008 to 31 March 2015 | 2.50 |
| 1 October 1996 to 31 March 2008 | 2.00 |
| **Active waste liable to standard rate** | |
| From 1 April 2018 | 88.95[1] |
| From 1 April 2017 | 86.10 |
| From 1 April 2016 | 84.40 |
| 1 April 2015 to 31 March 2016 | 82.60 |
| 1 April 2014 to 31 March 2015 | 80.00 |
| 1 April 2013 to 31 March 2014 | 72.00 |
| 1 April 2012 to 31 March 2013 | 64.00 |
| 1 April 2011 to 31 March 2012 | 56.00 |

**Note**
[1] Rates set by FA 2016, s. 143.

## [¶21-100]   Landfill communities fund: tax credit
(SI 1996/1527, reg. 31(3))

The Landfill Communities Fund Scheme encourages landfill site operators to fund local community environmental projects. Under the scheme, a landfill site operator can claim a tax credit worth 90% of any qualifying contributions made to approved environmental bodies (bodies enrolled by ENTRUST) for spending on an approved object, subject to a maximum percentage of the landfill tax liability during a contribution year as set out in the table below.

**Maximum percentage credit**

| Date | Maximum credit % |
|---|---|
| From 1 April 2017 | 5.3 |
| 1 April 2016 to 31 March 2017 | 4.2 |
| 1 April 2015 to 31 March 2016 | 5.7 |
| 1 April 2014 to 31 March 2015 | 5.1 |
| 1 April 2013 to 31 March 2014 | 6.8 |
| 1 April 2012 to 31 March 2013 | 5.6 |

## [¶21-150]   Error correction

(SI 1996/1527, reg. 13)

If the underdeclarations on previous returns do not exceed a limit, such errors may be corrected on the return for the period in which the errors are discovered.

For accounting periods starting after 30 June 2008, the limit is the greater of £10,000 and 1% of net VAT turnover as per Box 6 on the VAT return for the return period. However, this is subject to an upper limit of £50,000. If the person is not required to be VAT registered, there is a single limit of £10,000.

# AGGREGATES LEVY

## [¶22-000]   Rates

(FA 2001, s. 16; Notices AGL 1 and AGL 2; HMRC 'Aggregates levy' manual)

Aggregates levy seeks to incorporate the environmental costs imposed by aggregates extraction into the price of virgin aggregate, and to encourage the use of alternative materials such as wastes from construction and demolition.

Generally, 'aggregate' is rock, gravel or sand and whatever occurs or is mixed with it as well as, in certain circumstances, spoil, offcuts and by-products.

| Period of application | Rate (per tonne) £ |
|---|---|
| From 1 April 2017[1] | 2.00 |
| 1 April 2009 to 31 March 2017 | 2.00 |

**Note**
[1] The aggregates levy rate for 2017–18 will be frozen at £2 per tonne, continuing the freeze that has been in place since 2009 (Spring Budget 2017).

## [¶22-100]   Error correction

(SI 2002/761)

If the undercalculations or overcalculations on previous returns do not exceed a limit, such errors may be corrected on the return for the period in which the errors are discovered.

For accounting periods starting after 30 June 2008, the limit is the greater of £10,000 and 1% of net VAT turnover as per box 6 on the VAT return for the return period. However, this is subject to an upper limit of £50,000. If the person is not required to be VAT registered, there is a single limit of £10,000.

# CLIMATE CHANGE LEVY

## [¶23-000]   Rates: climate change levy

(FA 2000, Sch. 6)

CCL is a tax on the taxable supply of specified energy products ('taxable commodities') for use as fuels (that is for lighting, heating and power) by business consumers including consumers in industry, commerce, agriculture, public administration and other services. CCL does not apply to taxable commodities supplied for use by domestic consumers or to charities for non-business use. There are four groups of taxable commodities, as follows:

* electricity;
* natural gas when supplied by a gas utility;
* liquid petroleum gas (LPG) and other gaseous hydrocarbons in a liquid state; and
* coal and lignite; coke, and semi-coke of coal or lignite; and petroleum coke.

CCL is charged at a specific rate per unit of energy. There is a separate rate for each of the four categories of taxable commodity. The rates are based on the energy content of each commodity and are expressed in kilowatt-hours (kWh) for gas and electricity, and in kilograms for all other taxable commodities. The rates, including the reduced rate for participants of the climate change agreement scheme and for gas in Northern Ireland where a lower rate for gas applies, are set out in the following tables.

## [¶23-070]   Main rates from 1 April 2017, 2018 and 2019

(FA 2000, Sch. 6, para. 42, as prospectively amended by FA 2016, s. 144–148)

| Commodity | 1 April 2017 | | 1 April 2018 | | 1 April 2019 | |
|---|---|---|---|---|---|---|
| | Rate | Reduced rate | Rate | Reduced rate | Rate | Reduced rate |
| Electricity | 0.00568 | 10% | 0.00583 | 10% | 0.00847 | 7% |
| Natural gas | 0.00198 | 35% | 0.00203 | 35% | 0.00339 | 22% |
| Liquefied petroleum gas | 0.01272 | 35% | 0.01304 | 35% | 0.02175 | 22% |
| Any other taxable commodity | 0.01551 | 35% | 0.01591 | 35% | 0.02653 | 22% |

## [¶23-080]   Main rates from 1 April 2016

(FA 2000, Sch. 6, para. 42)

| Commodity | Rates from 1 April 2016 | Reduced rate for holders of a CCA |
|---|---|---|
| Electricity | £0.00559 per kilowatt hour | 10% |
| Natural gas | £0.00195 per kilowatt hour | 35% |
| Liquefied petroleum gas | £0.01251 per kilogram | 35% |
| Any other taxable commodity | £0.01526 per kilogram | 35% |

Climate Change Levy

**Note**
[1] Climate change levy (CCL) exemption for renewably sourced electricity abolished from 1 August 2015 (FA 2000, Sch. 6, para. 19(3)(za)), subject to a transitional period for suppliers to claim the CCL exemption on any renewable electricity that was generated before that date. *Finance Act* 2016 legislates for an end date to the transitional period of 31 March 2018 (FA 2000, Sch. 6, para. 19(1), as amended and prospectively repealed by FA 2016, s. 144).

## [¶23-090]  Main rates from 1 April 2015

(FA 2000, Sch. 6, para. 42)

| Commodity | Rates from 1 April 2015 | Reduced rate for holders of a CCA |
|---|---|---|
| Electricity[1] | £0.00554 per kilowatt hour | 10% |
| Natural gas | £0.00193 per kilowatt hour | 35% |
| Liquefied petroleum gas | £0.01240 per kilogram | 35% |
| Any other taxable commodity | £0.01512 per kilogram | 35% |

**Note**
[1] Climate change levy (CCL) exemption for renewably sourced electricity abolished from 1 August 2015 (FA 2000, Sch. 6, para. 19(3)(za)), subject to a transitional period for suppliers to claim the CCL exemption on any renewable electricity that was generated before that date.

## [¶23-100]  Rates from 1 April 2014

(FA 2000, Sch. 6, para. 42)

| Taxable commodity supplied | Unit | Rate from 1 April 2014 | | |
|---|---|---|---|---|
| | | Rate | Reduction on main commodity rate for holders of a CCA | Lower rate when used in approved metal recycling process |
| Electricity | per kWh | £0.00541 | 10% | 20% of full electricity rate |
| Natural gas | per kWh | £0.00188 | 35% | 20% of main gas rate |
| Liquefied petroleum gas and other gaseous hydrocarbons in a liquid state | per kilogram[1] | £0.01210 | 35% | 20% of main LPG, etc. rate |
| Any other taxable commodity | per kilogram | £0.01476 | 35% | 20% of rate for other taxable commodities |

**Note**
[1] For CCL purposes, the conversion rate of 2,000 litres per tonne is to be used when converting litres of butane and propane to kilograms.

# [¶23-200]   Rates from 1 April 2013
(FA 2000, Sch. 6, para. 42)

| Taxable commodity supplied | Unit | Rate from 1 April 2013 | | |
|---|---|---|---|---|
| | | Rate | Reduction on main commodity rate for holders of a CCA | Lower rate when used in approved metal recycling process |
| Electricity | per kWh | £0.00524 | 10% | 20% of main electricity rate |
| Natural gas (in GB) | per kWh | £0.00182 | 35% | 20% of main gas rate |
| Natural gas (in Northern Ireland) | per kWh | 0.00064 until 31 October 2013 (then GB rate applies) | n/a up to 31 October 2013 then 35% | n/a up to 31 October 2013 then 20% of main gas rate for GB |
| Liquefied petroleum gas and other gaseous hydrocarbons in a liquid state | per kilogram[(1)] | £0.01172 | 35% | 20% of main LPG, etc. rate |
| Any other taxable commodity | per kilogram | £0.01429 | 35% | 20% of rate for other taxable commodities |

**Note**
[(1)] For CCL purposes, the conversion rate of 2,000 litres per tonne is to be used when converting litres of butane and propane to kilograms.

## [¶23-300]   Rates from 1 April 2012

| Taxable commodity supplied | Unit | Rate from 1 April 2012 | | |
|---|---|---|---|---|
| | | Rate | Reduction on main commodity rate for holders of a CCA | Lower rate when used in approved metal recycling process |
| Electricity | per kWh | £0.00509 | 35% | 20% of main electricity rate |
| Natural gas (in GB) | per kWh | £0.00177 | 35% | 20% of main gas rate |
| Natural gas (in Northern Ireland) | per kWh | £0.00062 | Not available | Not available |
| Liquefied petroleum gas and other gaseous hydrocarbons in a liquid state | per kilogram[(1)] | £0.01137 | 35% | 20% of main LPG, etc. rate |
| Any other taxable commodity | per kilogram | £0.01387 | 35% | 20% of rate for other taxable commodities |

**Note**
[(1)] For CCL purposes, the conversion rate of 2,000 litres per tonne is to be used when converting litres of butane and propane to kilograms.

## [¶23-500]   Carbon price floor

(FA 2000, Sch. 6)

From 1 April 2013, supplies of solid fossil fuels, gas and liquefied petroleum gas (LPG) used in most forms of electricity generation are liable to newly created carbon price support (CPS) rates of climate change levy. The commodities liable to the CPS rates of CCL when they become the subject of a deemed supply for use in electricity generation on or after 1 April 2013 are:

- gas of a kind supplied by a gas utility;
- LPG; and
- coal and other solid fossil fuels (petroleum coke; lignite; coke and semi-coke of coal or lignite).

Electricity is not a CPS rate commodity and does not become the subject of a deemed supply if used in electricity generation. The CPS rates of CCL do not apply to offshore (outside the UK's 12-mile territorial limit) electricity generation.

# [¶23-600]   Carbon price support (CPS) rates of CCL from 1 April 2013

(FA 2000, Sch. 6; FA 2014, s. 98)

| CPS rates of CCL | 2016–17 [until 31 March 2020][1] | 2015–16 | 2014–15 | 2013–14 |
|---|---|---|---|---|
| Natural gas (£ per kilowatt hour) | 0.00331 | 0.00334 | 0.00175 | 0.00091 |
| LPG (£ per kilogram) | 0.05280 | 0.05307 | 0.02822 | 0.01460 |
| Coal and other taxable solid fossil fuels (£ per gross gigajoule) | 1.54790 | 1.56860 | 0.81906 | 0.44264 |

**Note**
[1] Rates per *Finance Act* 2014. At Spring Budget 2017, the Government confirmed the continued cap on CPS rates until 31 March 2020.

Climate Change Levy

# AIR PASSENGER DUTY

## [¶24-000]  Rates

(FA 1994, s. 30)

Air passenger duty (APD) is an excise duty which is due on chargeable passengers being carried from a UK airport on chargeable aircraft.

The rate of APD depends on the passengers' final destination which are allocated into bands based on the distance between London and the capital city of the destination country/territory. Each destination band has three rates of duty depending on the class of travel and the type of aircraft used.

| Air passenger duty rates from 1 April 2015[1][4] | | | | | | | | | | | |
|---|---|---|---|---|---|---|---|---|---|---|---|
| Band (approximate distance in miles from London) | Reduced rate (lowest class of travel) from 1 April | | | | Standard rate (other than lowest class of travel)[2] from 1 April | | | | Higher rate[3] from 1 April | | |
| | 2015 £ | 2016 £ | 2017[5] £ | 2018[6] £ | 2015 £ | 2016 £ | 2017[5] £ | 2018[6] £ | 2015 £ | 2016 £ | 2017[5] £ | 2018[6] £ |
| Band A (0–2,000 miles) | 13 | 13 | 13 | 13 | 26 | 26 | 26 | 26 | 78 | 78 | 78 | 78 |
| Band B (Over 2,000 miles) | 71 | 73 | 75 | 78 | 142 | 146 | 150 | 156 | 426 | 438 | 450 | 468 |

**Notes**

[1] From 1 April 2015, the number of destination bands was reduced from four to two by merging the former bands B, C and D and the higher rates that apply to aircraft with an authorised take off weight of 20 tonnes or more and with fewer than 19 seats was increased to six times the reduced rate (previously twice the standard rate).

[2] If any class of travel provides a seat pitch in excess of 1.016 metres (40 inches) the standard rate is the minimum rate that applies.

[3] The higher rate applies to flights aboard aircraft of 20 tonnes and above with fewer than 19 seats.

[4] From 1 May 2015, economy tickets for children under 12 are exempt from the reduced rate of APD. The exemption was extended to include children under 16 from 1 March 2016 (FA 1994, s. 31, as amended by FA 2015, s. 57).

[5] Rates confirmed at Spring Budget 2017 (Finance Bill 2017).

[6] Rates announced at Spring Budget 2017.

| Air Passenger Duty Rates[1][2] | | | | | | | | |
|---|---|---|---|---|---|---|---|---|
| **Bands (approximate distance in miles from the UK)** | **Reduced rate (lowest class of travel)** | | | **Standard rate (other than the lowest class of travel)[3]** | | | **Higher rate[4]** | |
| From | 1 April 2012 £ | 1 April 2013 £ | 1 April 2014 £ | 1 April 2012 £ | 1 April 2013 £ | 1 April 2014 £ | 1 April 2013 £ | 1 April 2014 £ |
| Band A (0–2,000 miles) | 13 | 13 | 13 | 26 | 26 | 26 | 52 | 52 |
| Band B (2,001–4,000 miles) | 65 | 67 | 69 | 130 | 134 | 138 | 268 | 276 |
| Band C (4,001–6,000 miles) | 81 | 83 | 85 | 162 | 166 | 170 | 332 | 340 |
| Band D (over 6,000 miles) | 92 | 94 | 97 | 184 | 188 | 194 | 376 | 388 |

**Notes**
[1] From 1 April 2013, APD has applied to all flights aboard aircraft 5.7 tonnes and above.
[2] From 1 January 2013, the rates for direct long-haul flights from NI were devolved to the Northern Ireland Executive, and set at £0. Direct long haul journeys from NI are those where the first part of the journey is to a destination outside Band A.
[3] If any class of travel provides a seat pitch in excess of 1.016 metres (40 inches), the standard rate is the minimum rate that applies.
[4] The higher rate applies to flights aboard aircraft of 20 tonnes and above with fewer than 19 seats.

## [¶24-100]  Destinations by band

(FA 1994, Sch. 5A)

| Band A | | | |
|---|---|---|---|
| **Country/Territory** | **Capital City** | **Country/Territory** | **Capital City** |
| Albania | Tirana | Malta | Valletta |
| Algeria | Algiers | Moldova | Chisinau |
| Andorra | Andorra la Vella | Monaco | Monaco |
| Austria | Vienna | Montenegro | Podgorica |
| Belarus | Minsk | Morocco | Rabat |
| Belgium | Brussels | Netherlands | Amsterdam |
| Bosnia & Herzegovina | Sarajevo | Norway | Oslo |
| Bulgaria | Sofia | Poland | Warsaw |
| Corsica | Ajaccio | Portugal | Lisbon |
| Croatia | Zagreb | Romania | Bucharest |
| Cyprus | Nicosia | Russian Federation (West of the Urals) | Moscow |
| Czech Republic | Prague | | |
| Denmark | Copenhagen | San Marino | San Marino |
| Estonia | Tallinn | Sardinia | Cagliari |
| Faroe Islands | Torshavn | Serbia | Belgrade |
| Finland | Helsinki | Sicily | Palermo |
| France | Paris | Slovakia | Bratislava |
| Germany | Berlin | Slovenia | Ljubljana |
| Gibraltar | Gibraltar | Spain | Madrid |
| Greece | Athens | Svalbard | Longyearbyen |
| Greenland | Nuuk | Sweden | Stockholm |
| Hungary | Budapest | Switzerland | Bern |
| Iceland | Reykjavik | The Azores | Ponta Delgada |
| Ireland | Dublin | The Balearic Islands | Palma |
| Isle of Man | Douglas | The Canary Islands | Santa Cruz de Tenerife |
| Italy | Rome | The Channel Islands | Encompassing the Bailiwick of Guernsey and the Bailiwick of Jersey |
| Kosovo | Pristina | | |
| Latvia | Riga | | |
| Libya | Tripoli | | |
| Liechtenstein | Vaduz | Tunisia | Tunis |
| Lithuania | Vilnius | Turkey | Ankara |
| Luxembourg | Luxembourg | Ukraine | Kiev |
| Macedonia | Skopje | United Kingdom | London |
| Madeira | Funchal | Vatican City | Vatican City |

Air Passenger Duty

| Band B: From 1 April 2015 destinations from bands B, C and D were merged into a single band B ||||
|---|---|---|---|
| Country/Territory | Capital City | Country/Territory | Capital City |
| Afghanistan | Kabul | Kazakhstan | Astana |
| Armenia | Yerevan | Kuwait | Kuwait City |
| Azerbaijan | Baku | Kyrgyzstan | Bishkek |
| Bahrain | Manama | Lebanon | Beirut |
| Benin | Porto-Novo | Liberia | Monrovia |
| Bermuda | Hamilton | Mali | Mali |
| Burkina Faso | Ouagadougou | Mauritania | Nouakchott |
| Cameroon | Yaounde | Niger | Niamey |
| Canada | Ottawa | Nigeria | Abuja |
| Cape Verde | Praia | Oman | Muscat |
| Central African Republic | Bangui | Pakistan | Islamabad |
| Chad | N'Djamena | Qatar | Doha |
| Congo, Democratic Republic of | Kinshasa | Russian Federation (East of the Urals) | |
| Congo, Republic of | Brazzaville | | |
| Djibouti | Djibouti | Saint Pierre & Miquelon | Saint-Pierre |
| Egypt | Cairo | Sao Tome and Principe | Sao Tome |
| Equatorial Guinea | Malabo | Saudi Arabia | Riyadh |
| Eritrea | Asmara | Senegal | Dakar |
| Ethiopia | Addis Ababa | Sierra Leone | Freetown |
| Gabon | Libreville | Republic of South Sudan | Juba |
| Gambia | Banjul | Sudan | Khartoum |
| Georgia | Tblisi | Syria | Damascus |
| Ghana | Accra | Tajikistan | Dushanbe |
| Guinea | Conakry | Togo | Lome |
| Guinea-Bissau | Bissau | Turkmenistan | Ashgabat |
| Iran | Tehran | Uganda | Kampala |
| Iraq | Baghdad | United Arab Emirates | Abu Dhabi |
| Israel | Jerusalem | United States | Washington D.C. |
| Ivory Coast | Yamoussoukro | Uzbekistan | Tashkent |
| Jordan | Amman | Yemen | Sanaa |

| Band B (former band C): From 1 April 2015 destinations from bands B, C and D were merged into a single band B | | | |
|---|---|---|---|
| Country/Territory | Capital City | Country/Territory | Capital City |
| Angola | Luanda | Lesotho | Maseru |
| Anguilla | The Valley | Macao SAR | – |
| Antigua & Barbuda | Saint John's | Madagascar | Antananarivo |
| Aruba | Oranjestad | Malawi | Lilongwe |
| Bahamas | Nassau | Maldives | Male |
| Bangladesh | Dhaka | Martinique | Fort de France |
| Barbados | Bridgetown | Mauritius | Port Louis |
| Belize | Belmopan | Mayotte | Mamoudzou |
| Bhutan | Thimphu | Mexico | Mexico City |
| Bonaire | Kralendijk | Mongolia | Ulaanbaatar |
| Botswana | Gabarone | Montserrat | Plymouth |
| Brazil | Brasilia | Mozambique | Maputo |
| British Indian Ocean Territories | | Namibia | Windhoek |
| | | Nepal | Kathmandu |
| British Virgin Islands | Road Town | Nicaragua | Managua |
| Burma | Rangoon | Panama | Panama City |
| Burundi | Bujumbura | Puerto Rico | San Juan |
| Cayman Islands | George Town | Reunion | Saint Denis |
| China | Beijing | Rwanda | Kigali |
| Colombia | Bogota | Saba | The Bottom |
| Comoros | Moroni | Saint Barthelemy | Gustavia |
| Costa Rica | San Jose | Saint Helena, Ascension and Tristan da Cunha | Jamestown |
| Cuba | Havana | Saint Kitts & Nevis | Basseterre |
| Curacao | Willemstad | Saint Lucia | Castries |
| Dominica | Roseau | Saint Martin | Marigot |
| Dominican Republic | Santo Domingo | Saint Vincent Grenadines | Kingstown |
| Ecuador | Quito | Seychelles | Victoria |
| El Salvador | San Salvador | Sint Eustatius | Oranjestad |
| French Guiana | Cayenne | Sint Maarten | Philipsburg |
| Grenada | Saint George's | Somalia | Mogadishu |
| Guadeloupe | Basse Terre | South Africa | Pretoria |

| Band B (former band C): From 1 April 2015 destinations from bands B, C and D were merged into a single band B | | | |
|---|---|---|---|
| Country/Territory | Capital City | Country/Territory | Capital City |
| Guatemala | Guatemala | Sri Lanka | Colombo |
| Guyana | Georgetown | Suriname | Paramaribo |
| Haiti | Port-au-Prince | Swaziland | Mbabane |
| Honduras | Tegucigalpa | Tanzania | Dar es Salaam |
| Hong Kong SAR | – | Thailand | Bangkok |
| India | New Delhi | Trinidad & Tobago | Port of Spain |
| Jamaica | Kingston | Turks & Caicos Islands | Grand Turk |
| Japan | Tokyo | Venezuela | Caracas |
| Kenya | Nairobi | Vietnam | Hanoi |
| Korea, North | Pyongyang | Virgin Islands | Charlotte Amalie |
| Korea, South | Seoul | Zambia | Lusaka |
| Laos | Vientiane | Zimbabwe | Harare |

# VEHICLE EXCISE DUTY

## [¶25-000]   Rates: general
(VERA 1994, Sch. 1, Pt. I)

| VED bands and rates for cars and vans registered before 1 March 2001 (pre-graduated VED) | | | | | |
|---|---|---|---|---|---|
| Engine size | 2017–18[1] £ | 2016–17 £ | 2015–16 £ | 2014–15 £ | 2013–14 £ |
| 1549cc and below | 150 | 145 | 145 | 145 | 140 |
| Above 1549cc | 245 | 235 | 230 | 230 | 225 |

**Note**
[1]  Rates announced at Spring Budget 2017.

## [¶25-050]   Rates: light passenger vehicles registered on or after 1 April 2017
(VERA 1994, Sch. 1, Pt. 1AA)

| VED bands and rates for cars first registered on or after 1 April 2017 | | |
|---|---|---|
| $CO_2$ emissions (g/km) | First year rate £ | Standard rate[1] £ |
| 0 | 0 | 0 |
| 1–50 | 10 | 140 |
| 51–75 | 25 | 140 |
| 76–90 | 100 | 140 |
| 91–100 | 120 | 140 |
| 101–110 | 140 | 140 |
| 111–130 | 160 | 140 |
| 131–150 | 200 | 140 |
| 151–170 | 500 | 140 |
| 171–190 | 800 | 140 |
| 191–225 | 1,200 | 140 |
| 226–255 | 1,700 | 140 |
| Over 255 | 2,000 | 140 |

**Note**
[1]  Cars with a list price of over £40,000 when new pay a supplement of £310 per year on top of the standard rate, for five years (VERA 1994, Sch. 1, para. 1GE).

## [¶25-100] Rates: light passenger vehicles: graduated rates of duty

(VERA 1994, Sch. 1, Pt. IA)

**VED bands and rates for cars registered on or after 1 March 2001 but before 1 April 2017 (graduated VED)**

| VED band | CO₂ emissions (g/km) | 2017–18 Std rate[1][3] £ | 2016–17 Std rate[1] £ | 2016–17 First year rate[1] £ | 2015–16 Std rate[1] £ | 2015–16 First year rate[1] £ | 2014–15 Std rate[1] £ | 2014–15 First year rate[1] £ | 2013–14 Std rate[1] £ | 2013–14 First year rate[1] £ |
|---|---|---|---|---|---|---|---|---|---|---|
| A | Up to 100 | 0 | 0 | 0 | 0 | 0 | 0 | 0 | 0 | 0 |
| B | 101–110 | 20 | 20 | 0 | 20 | 0 | 20 | 0 | 20 | 0 |
| C | 111–120 | 30 | 30 | 0 | 30 | 0 | 30 | 0 | 30 | 0 |
| D | 121–130 | 115 | 110 | 0 | 110 | 0 | 110 | 0 | 105 | 0 |
| E | 131–140 | 135 | 130 | 130 | 130 | 130 | 130 | 130 | 125 | 125 |
| F | 141–150 | 150 | 145 | 145 | 145 | 145 | 145 | 145 | 140 | 140 |
| G | 151–165 | 190 | 185 | 185 | 180 | 180 | 180 | 180 | 175 | 175 |
| H | 166–175 | 220 | 210 | 300 | 205 | 295 | 205 | 290 | 200 | 285 |
| I | 176–185 | 240 | 230 | 355 | 225 | 350 | 225 | 345 | 220 | 335 |
| J | 186–200 | 280 | 270 | 500 | 265 | 490 | 265 | 485 | 260 | 475 |
| K[2] | 201–225 | 305 | 295 | 650 | 290 | 640 | 285 | 635 | 280 | 620 |
| L | 226–255 | 520 | 500 | 885 | 490 | 870 | 485 | 860 | 475 | 840 |
| M | Over 255 | 535 | 515 | 1,120 | 505 | 1,100 | 500 | 1,090 | 490 | 1,065 |

**Notes**
[1] Alternative fuel discount 2010–11 onwards: £10 for all cars.
[2] Includes cars emitting over 225g/km registered before 23 March 2006.
[3] Rates announced at Spring Budget 2017. From 2017–18, there is no first year rate under the current graduated VED system because the new VED system is coming into effect (see ¶25-050).

## [¶25-200] Rates: light goods vehicles

(VERA 1994, Sch. 1, Pt. IB)

**VED bands and rates for vans registered on or after 1 March 2001**

| Vehicle registration date | 2017–18[1] £ | 2016–17 £ | 2015–16 £ | 2014–15 £ | 2013–14 £ |
|---|---|---|---|---|---|
| Early Euro 4 and Euro 5 compliant vans | 140 | 140 | 140 | 140 | 140 |
| All other vans | 240 | 230 | 225 | 225 | 220 |

**Note**
[1] Rates announced at Spring Budget 2017.

## [¶25-300] Rates: motorcycles
(VERA 1994, Sch. 1, Pt. II)

| VED bands and rates for motorcycles | | | | | |
|---|---|---|---|---|---|
| Engine size | 2017–18[1] £ | 2016–17 £ | 2015–16 £ | 2014–15 £ | 2013–14 £ |
| Not over 150cc | 18 | 17 | 17 | 17 | 17 |
| 151cc and 400cc | 41 | 39 | 38 | 38 | 37 |
| 401cc to 600c | 62 | 60 | 59 | 58 | 57 |
| Over 600cc | 85 | 82 | 81 | 80 | 78 |

| VED bands and rates for motor tricycles | | | | | |
|---|---|---|---|---|---|
| Engine size | 2017–18[1] £ | 2016–17 £ | 2015–16 £ | 2014–15 £ | 2013–14 £ |
| Not over 150cc | 18 | 17 | 17 | 17 | 17 |
| All other tricycles | 85 | 82 | 81 | 80 | 78 |

**Note**
[1] Rates announced at Spring Budget 2017.

## [¶25-400] Rates: trade licences
(VERA 1994, s. 13)

| VED bands and rates for trade licences | | | | | |
|---|---|---|---|---|---|
| Vehicle type | 2017–18[1] £ | 2016–17 £ | 2015–16 £ | 2014–15 £ | 2013–14 £ |
| Available for all vehicles | 165 | 165 | 165 | 165 | 165 |
| Available only for bicycles and tricycles (weighing no more than 450kg without a sidecar) | 85 | 82 | 81 | 80 | 78 |

**Note**
[1] Rates announced at Spring Budget 2017.

## [¶25-500] Rates: haulage and goods vehicles
(VERA 1994, Sch. 1, Pt. VII and VIII)

| 2014–15 to 2017–18[1] | | | | | | | |
|---|---|---|---|---|---|---|---|
| VED and levy bands and rates for articulated vehicles and rigid vehicles without trailers | | | | | | | |
| VED band (letter) and rate (number) | Total VED and levy | | VED rates | | Levy rates | | |
| | 12 months | 6 months | 12 months | 6 months | Levy bands | 12 months | 6 months |
| | £ | £ | £ | £ | £ | £ | £ |
| A0 | 165.00 | 90.75 | 165.00 | 90.75 | n/a | 0 | 0 |
| B0 | 200.00 | 110.00 | 200.00 | 110.00 | | | |

Vehicle Excise Duty

| VED band (letter) and rate (number) | Total VED and levy | | VED rates | | Levy bands | Levy rates | |
|---|---|---|---|---|---|---|---|
| | 12 months | 6 months | 12 months | 6 months | | 12 months | 6 months |
| | £ | £ | £ | £ | £ | £ | £ |
| A1 | 165.00 | 91.00 | 80.00 | 40.00 | A | 85 | 51 |
| A2 | 169.00 | 93.00 | 84.00 | 42.00 | | | |
| A3 | 185.00 | 101.00 | 100.00 | 50.00 | | | |
| A4 | 231.00 | 124.00 | 146.00 | 73.00 | | | |
| A5 | 236.00 | 126.50 | 151.00 | 75.50 | | | |
| B1 | 200.00 | 110.50 | 95.00 | 47.50 | B | 105 | 63 |
| B2 | 210.00 | 115.50 | 105.00 | 52.50 | | | |
| B3 | 230.00 | 125.50 | 125.00 | 62.50 | | | |
| C1 | 450.00 | 249.00 | 210.00 | 105.00 | C | 240 | 144 |
| C2 | 505.00 | 276.50 | 265.00 | 132.50 | | | |
| C3 | 529.00 | 288.50 | 289.00 | 144.50 | | | |
| D1 | 650.00 | 360.00 | 300.00 | 150.00 | D | 350 | 210 |
| E1 | 1,200.00 | 664.00 | 560.00 | 280.00 | E | 640 | 384 |
| E2 | 1,249.00 | 688.50 | 609.00 | 304.50 | | | |
| F | 1,500.00 | 831.00 | 690.00 | 345.00 | F | 810 | 486 |
| G | 1,850.00 | 1,025.00 | 850.00 | 425.00 | G | 1000 | 600 |

**Note**
[1] At Spring Budget 2017, it was announced that HGV, VED and Road User Levy will be frozen from April 2017, continuing the freeze that has been in place since 1 April 2015.

## 2014–15 to 2017–18[1]

### VED and levy amounts payable for rigid vehicles with trailers (vehicles WITH Road Friendly Suspension)

| HGV axles | Levy band | Trailer weight category | Total weight of HGV and trailer, not over | VED band (letter) and rate (number) | VED rates | | Levy rates | |
|---|---|---|---|---|---|---|---|---|
| | | | | | 12 months | 6 months | 12 months | 6 months |
| | | | | | £ | £ | £ | £ |
| Two | B(T) | 4,001–12,000kg | 27,000kg | B(T)1 | 230.00 | 115.00 | 135 | 81 |
| | | Over 12,000kg | 33,000kg | B(T)3 | 295.00 | 147.50 | | |
| | | | 36,000kg | B(T)6 | 401.00 | 200.50 | | |
| | | | 38,000kg | B(T)4 | 319.00 | 159.50 | | |
| | | | — | B(T)7 | 444.00 | 222.00 | | |
| | D(T) | 4,001–12,000kg | 30,000kg | D(T)1 | 365.00 | 182.50 | 450 | 270 |
| | | Over 12,000kg | 38,000kg | D(T)4 | 430.00 | 215.00 | | |
| | | | — | D(T)5 | 444.00 | 222.00 | | |
| Three | B(T) | 4,001–12,000kg | 33,000kg | B(T)1 | 230.00 | 115.00 | 135 | 81 |
| | | Over 12,000kg | 38,000kg | B(T)3 | 295.00 | 147.50 | | |
| | | | 40,000kg | B(T)5 | 392.00 | 196.00 | | |
| | | | — | B(T)3 | 295.00 | 147.50 | | |

| HGV axles | Levy band | Trailer weight category | Total weight of HGV and trailer, not over | VED band (letter) and rate (number) | VED rates 12 months £ | VED rates 6 months £ | Levy rates 12 months £ | Levy rates 6 months £ |
|---|---|---|---|---|---|---|---|---|
| | C(T) | 4,001–12,000kg | 35,000kg | C(T)1 | 305.00 | 152.50 | 310 | 186 |
| | | Over 12,000kg | 38,000kg | C(T)2 | 370.00 | 185.00 | | |
| | | | 40,000kg | C(T)3 | 392.00 | 196.00 | | |
| | | | – | C(T)2 | 370.00 | 185.00 | | |
| | D(T) | 4,001–10,000kg | 33,000kg | D(T)1 | 365.00 | 182.50 | 450 | 270 |
| | | | 36,000kg | D(T)3 | 401.00 | 200.50 | | |
| | | 10,001–12,000kg | 38,000kg | D(T)1 | 365.00 | 182.50 | | |
| | | Over 12,000kg | – | D(T)4 | 430.00 | 215.00 | | |
| Four | B(T) | 4,001–12,000kg | 35,000kg | B(T)1 | 230.00 | 115.00 | 135 | 81 |
| | | Over 12,000kg | – | B(T)3 | 295.00 | 147.50 | | |
| | C(T) | 4,001–12,000kg | 37,000kg | C(T)1 | 305.00 | 152.50 | 310 | 186 |
| | | Over 12,000kg | – | C(T)2 | 370.00 | 185.00 | | |
| | D(T) | 4,001–12,000kg | 39,000kg | D(T)1 | 365.00 | 182.50 | 450 | 270 |
| | | Over 12,000kg | – | D(T)4 | 430.00 | 215.00 | | |
| | E(T) | 4,001–12,000kg | 44,000kg | E(T)1 | 535.00 | 267.50 | 830 | 498 |
| | | Over 12,000kg | – | E(T)2 | 600.00 | 300.00 | | |

**Note**
[1] At Spring Budget 2017, it was announced that HGV, VED and Road User Levy will be frozen from April 2017, continuing the freeze that has been in place since 1 April 2015.

## 2014–15 to 2017–18[1]

### VED and levy amounts payable for rigid vehicles with trailers (vehicles WITHOUT Road Friendly Suspension)

| HGV axles | Levy band | Trailer weight category | Total weight of HGV and trailer, not over | VED band (letter) and rate (number) | VED rates 12 months £ | VED rates 6 months £ | Levy rates 12 months £ | Levy rates 6 months £ |
|---|---|---|---|---|---|---|---|---|
| Two | B(T) | 4,001–12,000kg | 27,000kg | B(T)1 | 230.00 | 115.00 | 135 | 81 |
| | | Over 12,000kg | 31,000kg | B(T)3 | 295.00 | 147.50 | | |
| | | | 33,000kg | B(T)6 | 401.00 | 200.50 | | |
| | | | 36,000kg | B(T)10 | 609.00 | 304.50 | | |
| | | | 38,000kg | B(T)7 | 444.00 | 222.00 | | |
| | | | – | B(T)9 | 604.00 | 302.00 | | |
| | D(T) | 4,001–12,000kg | 30,000kg | D(T)1 | 365.00 | 182.50 | 450 | 270 |
| | | Over 12,000kg | 33,000kg | D(T)4 | 430.00 | 215.00 | | |
| | | | 36,000kg | D(T)8 | 609.00 | 304.50 | | |
| | | | 38,000kg | D(T)5 | 444.00 | 222.00 | | |
| | | | – | D(T)7 | 604.00 | 302.00 | | |

| HGV axles | Levy band | Trailer weight category | Total weight of HGV and trailer, not over | VED band (letter) and rate (number) | VED rates | | Levy rates | |
|---|---|---|---|---|---|---|---|---|
| | | | | | 12 months £ | 6 months £ | 12 months £ | 6 months £ |
| Three | B(T) | 4,001–10,000kg | 29,000kg | B(T)1 | 230.00 | 115.00 | 135 | 81 |
| | | | 31,000kg | B(T)2 | 289.00 | 144.50 | | |
| | | 10,001–12,000kg | 33,000kg | B(T)1 | 230.00 | 115.00 | | |
| | | Over 12,000kg | 36,000kg | B(T)3 | 295.00 | 147.50 | | |
| | | | 38,000kg | B(T)5 | 392.00 | 196.00 | | |
| | | | — | B(T)8 | 542.00 | 271.00 | | |
| | C(T) | 4,001–10,000kg | 31,000kg | C(T)1 | 305.00 | 152.50 | 310 | 186 |
| | | | 33,000kg | C(T)4 | 401.00 | 200.50 | | |
| | | 10,001–12,000kg | 35,000kg | C(T)1 | 305.00 | 152.50 | | |
| | | Over 12,000kg | 36,000kg | C(T)2 | 370.00 | 185.00 | | |
| | | | 38,000kg | C(T)3 | 392.00 | 196.00 | | |
| | | | — | C(T)5 | 542.00 | 271.00 | | |
| | D(T) | 4,001–10,000kg | 31,000kg | D(T)1 | 365.00 | 182.50 | 450 | 270 |
| | | | 33,000kg | D(T)3 | 401.00 | 200.50 | | |
| | | | 35,000kg | D(T)8 | 609.00 | 304.50 | | |
| | | 10,001–12,000kg | 36,000kg | D(T)1 | 365.00 | 182.50 | | |
| | | | 37,000kg | D(T)2 | 392.00 | 196.00 | | |
| | | Over 12,000kg | 38,000kg | D(T)4 | 430.00 | 215.00 | | |
| | | | — | D(T)6 | 542.00 | 271.00 | | |
| Four | B(T) | 4,001–12,000kg | 35,000kg | B(T)1 | 230.00 | 115.00 | 135 | 81 |
| | | Over 12,000kg | — | B(T)3 | 295.00 | 147.50 | | |
| | C(T) | 4,001–12,000kg | 37,000kg | C(T)1 | 305.00 | 152.50 | 310 | 186 |
| | | Over 12,000kg | — | C(T)2 | 370.00 | 185.00 | | |
| | D(T) | 4,001–10,000kg | 36,000kg | D(T)1 | 365.00 | 182.50 | 450 | 270 |
| | | | 37,000kg | D(T)5 | 444.00 | 222.00 | | |
| | | 10,001–12,000kg | 39,000kg | D(T)1 | 365.00 | 182.50 | | |
| | | Over 12,000kg | — | D(T)4 | 430.00 | 215.00 | | |
| | E(T) | 4,001–10,000kg | 38,000kg | E(T)1 | 535.00 | 267.50 | 830 | 498 |
| | | | — | E(T)3 | 604.00 | 302.00 | | |
| | | 10,001–12,000kg | — | E(T)1 | 535.00 | 267.50 | | |

**Note**
[1] At Spring Budget 2017, it was announced that HGV, VED and Road User Levy will be frozen from April 2017, continuing the freeze that has been in place since 1 April 2015.

**2014–15 to 2017–18[1]**

**Rigid goods vehicle – WITHOUT trailer**

| Revenue weight of vehicle, kg | | 2 axles | 3 axles | 4 or more axles |
|---|---|---|---|---|
| Over | Not over | | | |
| 3,500 | 7,500 | A0 | A0 | A0 |
| 7,500 | 11,999 | B0 | B0 | B0 |
| 11,999 | 14,000 | B1 | B1 | B1 |
| 14,000 | 15,000 | B2 | | |
| 15,000 | 19,000 | D1 | | |
| 19,000 | 21,000 | | B3 | |
| 21,000 | 23,000 | | C1 | |
| 23,000 | 25,000 | | D1 | C1 |
| 25,000 | 27,000 | | | D1 |
| 27,000 | 44,000 | | | E1 |

**Note**

[1] At Spring Budget 2017, it was announced that HGV, VED and Road User Levy will be frozen from April 2017, continuing the freeze that has been in place since 1 April 2015.

**2014–15 to 2017–18[1]**

**Rigid vehicles – WITH trailer**

| Weight of rigid (not trailer), kg | | Two-axled rigid | Three-axled rigid | Four-axled rigid |
|---|---|---|---|---|
| Over | Not over | | | |
| 11,999 | 15,000 | B(T) | B(T) | B(T) |
| 15,000 | 21,000 | D(T) | | |
| 21,000 | 23,000 | E(T) | C(T) | |
| 23,000 | 25,000 | | D(T) | C(T) |
| 25,000 | 27,000 | | | D(T) |
| 27,000 | 44,000 | | E(T) | E(T) |

**Note**

[1] At Spring Budget 2017, it was announced that HGV, VED and Road User Levy will be frozen from April 2017, continuing the freeze that has been in place since 1 April 2015.

Vehicle Excise Duty

**2014–15 to 2017–18[1]**

**Articulated vehicles – tractive unit with three or more axles**

| Revenue weight of vehicle, kg | | One or more semi-trailer axles | Two or more semi-trailer axles | Three or more semi-trailer axles |
|---|---|---|---|---|
| Over | Not over | | | |
| 3,500 | 11,999 | A0 | A0 | A0 |
| 11,999 | 25,000 | A1 | A1 | A1 |
| 25,000 | 26,000 | A3 | | |
| 26,000 | 28,000 | A4 | | |
| 28,000 | 29,000 | C1 | | |
| 29,000 | 31,000 | C3 | | |
| 31,000 | 33,000 | E1 | C1 | |
| 33,000 | 34,000 | E2 | D1 | |
| 34,000 | 36,000 | | | C1 |
| 36,000 | 38,000 | F | E1 | D1 |
| 38,000 | 44,000 | G | G | E1 |

**Note**
[1] At Spring Budget 2017, it was announced that HGV, VED and Road User Levy will be frozen from April 2017, continuing the freeze that has been in place since 1 April 2015.

**2014–15 to 2017–18[1]**

**Articulated vehicles – tractive unit with two axles**

| Revenue weight of vehicle, kg | | One or more semi-trailer axles | Two or more semi-trailer axles | Three or more semi-trailer axles |
|---|---|---|---|---|
| Over | Not over | | | |
| 3,500 | 11,999 | A0 | A0 | A0 |
| 11,999 | 22,000 | A1 | A1 | A1 |
| 22,000 | 23,000 | A2 | | |
| 23,000 | 25,000 | A5 | | |
| 25,000 | 26,000 | C2 | A3 | |
| 26,000 | 28,000 | | A4 | |
| 28,000 | 31,000 | D1 | D1 | |
| 31,000 | 33,000 | E1 | E1 | C1 |
| 33,000 | 34,000 | | E2 | |
| 34,000 | 38,000 | F | F | E1 |
| 38,000 | 44,000 | G | G | G |

**Note**
[1] At Spring Budget 2017, it was announced that HGV, VED and Road User Levy will be frozen from April 2017, continuing the freeze that has been in place since 1 April 2015.

# SCOTTISH TAXES

## [¶26-000]   Scottish taxes

(*Scotland Act* 1998; *Scotland Act* 2012)

(Tax Reporter: ¶102-930)

The establishment of the Scottish Parliament and the Scottish Government was provided for in the *Scotland Act* 1998 (as amended by the *Scotland Act* 2012). The Scottish Parliament was officially convened on 1 July 1999.

The *Scotland Act* 1998 does not specify which matters are devolved to the Scottish Parliament, rather it specifies those matters that are reserved to the UK Parliament and those matters not reserved are devolved to the Scottish Parliament. Schedule 5 to the Act (as amended) sets out those matters which are reserved to the UK Parliament and all other issues are deemed to be devolved. The Scottish Parliament has primary legislative powers, i.e. the power to pass Acts.

The *Scotland Act* 1998, Pt. IV also introduced a tax-varying power, with effect from 6 May 1999 (SI 1998/3178), to enable the Scottish parliament to vary the rate of income tax levied on the income of Scottish taxpayers by up to 3%. However, this power has never been used and is replaced with a new power to set a Scottish rate of income tax (SRIT) (see below) by the *Scotland Act* 2012.

The *Scotland Act* 2012 also amended the *Scotland Act* 1998 to fully devolve the power to raise taxes on land transactions and on waste disposal to landfill which took effect from 1 April 2015 and since then, the existing stamp duty land tax and landfill tax do not apply in Scotland. The Act also provides powers for new taxes to be created in Scotland and for additional taxes to be devolved.

### Further devolution

Further powers were promised to Scotland by the three main UK political parties in the run-up to the Scottish independence referendum held on 18 September 2014 and following the 'No' vote by Scotland, the 'Smith Commission' (led by Lord Smith of Kelvin) was set up to convene cross-party talks and facilitate an inclusive engagement process across Scotland and produce Heads of Agreement with recommendations for further devolution of powers to the Scottish Parliament. The Smith Commission report was published on 27 November 2014 detailing Heads of Agreement on further devolution of powers to the Scottish Parliament which are delivered in the *Scotland Act* 2016.

The *Scotland Act* 2016 received Royal Assent on 23 March 2016 and is an enabling Act setting out the powers that are being transferred to the Scottish Parliament and or the Scottish Ministers. In particular, the *Scotland Act* 2016 amends sections of the *Scotland Act* 1998 and rebalances the devolved and reserved responsibilities between the administrations. The Act also includes provisions which set out the constitutional relationship of the Scottish Parliament and Scottish Government within the United Kingdom's constitutional arrangements. It does not amend this relationship. The Act also provides the structure within which the Scottish Parliament may legislate to set the rates of income tax and the limits at which these are paid for the non-savings and non-dividend income of Scottish taxpayers, replacing the power of the Scottish Parliament to set, by resolution, a single Scottish rate of income tax, enabling it to instead set a basic rate and any other rates of income tax; makes provision for Scotland to control the first ten percentage points of the standard rate of VAT receipts and first two and a half percentage points of the reduced rate of VAT receipts; and provides that air passenger duty and aggregates levy will be fully devolved taxes.

### Administration of devolved taxes

The devolved taxes are collected by Revenue Scotland, Scotland's new tax authority which started accepting returns and collecting taxes from 1 April 2015. Revenue Scotland was established by the *Revenue Scotland and Tax Powers Act* 2014 which received Royal Assent on 24 September 2014 and came into force on 1 April 2015 (to the extent not already in force). The RSTPA 2014:

- establishes Revenue Scotland and provides for its general functions and responsibilities (Pt. 2);
- makes provision about the use and protection of taxpayer and other information (Pt. 3);
- establishes the Scottish Tax Tribunals (the First-tier Tribunal for Scotland and the Upper Tribunal for Scotland) to exercise functions in relation to devolved taxes (Pt. 4);
- puts in place a general anti-avoidance rule (Pt. 5);
- contains provisions on the self-assessment system, the checking of tax returns by Revenue Scotland and claims for repayment of tax (Pt. 6);
- makes provision for Revenue Scotland's investigatory powers (Pt. 7);
- sets out the matters in relation to which penalties may be imposed (Pt. 8);
- makes provision about the interest payable on unpaid tax, on penalties and on tax repayments (Pt. 9);
- contains provisions on debt enforcement by Revenue Scotland (Pt. 10); and
- sets out the system for the review, mediation and appeal of Revenue Scotland decisions (Pt. 11).

### Scottish Tribunals

The *Tribunals (Scotland) Act* 2014, which received Royal Assent on 15 April 2014 (and came into force on 1 April 2015 (so far as not already in force), establishes the First-tier Tribunal for Scotland and the Upper Tribunal for Scotland. The Scottish Tribunals were constituted on 1 April 2015 and will operate in parallel with the existing tribunals exercising functions in relation to devolved taxes.

### Opinions

In order to allow taxpayers to file with certainty, Revenue Scotland will, in certain circumstances, provide its opinion on the tax consequences of specific transactions.

Applications should be sent to:

Revenue Scotland Opinions

PO Box 24068

Victoria Quay

Edinburgh

EH6 9BR

For further information, see www.revenue.scot/help/revenue-scotland-opinions.

## [¶26-100]   Scottish income tax

(*Scotland Act* 1998; ITA 2007, s. 6A and 11A)

(Tax Reporter: ¶148-160)

### Scottish income tax: 2017–18

| Scottish rates | Rate[(1)] % | Taxable income band[(1)] £ | Tax on band £ |
|---|---|---|---|
| Scottish basic rate | 20 | 1–31,500 | 6,300 |
| Scottish higher rate | 40 | 31,501–150,000 | 47,400 |
| Scottish additional rate | 45 | Over 150,000 | |

**Note**

[(1)] On 21 February 2017, the Scottish Parliament voted to freeze the basic rate of income tax of 20%, also freeze the higher and additional rates at 40% and 45% respectively, and maintain the higher rate of income tax threshold at £43,000 in 2017–18.

### Scottish income tax: 2016–17

| UK rate for England, Wales and Northern Ireland | Taxable income band £ | UK rate paid in Scotland % | Scottish rate[(1)] % | Total rate for Scottish taxpayers % |
|---|---|---|---|---|
| Basic rate 20% | 1–32,000 | 10 | 10 | 20 |
| Higher rate 40% | 32,001–150,000 | 30 | 10 | 40 |
| Additional rate 45% | Over £150,000 | 35 | 10 | 45 |

**Note**

[(1)] Rate proposed by draft Scottish Budget 2016–17 delivered to Parliament on 16 December 2015 and agreed by the Scottish Parliament on 11 February 2016.

SCA 1998, s. 80C, as introduced, enables the Scottish Parliament to levy the Scottish rate of income tax to be used for the purpose of calculating the rates of income tax to be paid by Scottish taxpayers. The *Scotland Act* 2016, however, amends this power to enable the Scottish Parliament to set instead a Scottish basic rate, and any other rates for the purposes of ITA 2007, s. 11A (which provides for the income of Scottish taxpayers which is charged at those rates).

Under the *Scotland Act* 2016 provisions, where the Scottish Parliament sets more than one rate of income tax, it must, by resolution, set out the limits at which those rates apply or make provision to determine which rates apply in relation to a Scottish taxpayer, however, a Scottish rate resolution may not provide for different rates to apply in relation to different types of income.

The Scottish basic, higher and additional rates of income tax will only apply to non-savings, non-dividend income of those defined as 'Scottish taxpayers' (ITA 2007, s. 11A, 13).

A 'Scottish taxpayer' is defined as an individual who in any tax year is treated as resident in the UK for income tax purposes for that year and who either:

*   has a close connection with Scotland;
*   does not have a close connection with England, Wales or Northern Ireland, and spends more days of that year in Scotland than in any other part of the UK; or
*   is a member of Parliament for a constituency in Scotland, a member of the European Parliament for Scotland, or a member of the Scottish Parliament.

A close connection is defined by reference to where the individual has their only or main residence. If an individual has one residence and it is in Scotland, they are a Scottish taxpayer. Where an individual has more than one residence, they will need to determine which has been their main residence for the longest period in the tax year and if this is in Scotland, they are a Scottish taxpayer. Individuals who cannot identify a main place of residence will need to count the days spent in Scotland and elsewhere in the UK and if they spend more days in Scotland, they are a Scottish taxpayer. Scottish taxpayer status applies for a whole year and split year treatment is not available (it is not possible to be a Scottish taxpayer for part of a tax year). HMRC's detailed technical guidance on who, from 6 April 2016, will be a Scottish taxpayer was published on 27 October 2015 and is available at www.gov.uk/government/publications/scottish-taxpayer-technical-guidance.

### Income tax devolution

*Finance Act* 2016 legislates to separate the income tax rates that apply to savings income (the savings rates), from those that apply to non-savings, non-dividends income (the main rates). The former will apply across the UK and the latter will be devolved to Scotland. The measure will take effect from the tax year 2017–18 (as the first tax year for which the Scottish Government can set Scottish rates of income tax (SI 2016/1161, reg. 3)) (FA 2016, s. 6).

### Administration

The Scottish rate of income tax will be administered by HMRC as part of the UK income tax system.

For employees and pensioners, the income tax change will be applied through PAYE. Scottish taxpayers have an 'S' prefix to their PAYE tax code.

For further guidance, see Employer Bulletin 54 (June 2015) at www.gov.uk/government/uploads/system/uploads/attachment_data/file/439968/Employer_Bulletin_June_2015.pdf.

# DEVOLVED TAXES

## Land and Buildings Transaction Tax (LBTT)

### [¶26-200]   LBTT rates from 1 April 2015

(*Land and Buildings Transaction Tax (Scotland) Act* 2013; SSI 2015/126)

(SLDT Reporter: ¶200-000ff.)

Scottish LBTT applies to transactions consisting of or including interests in land situated in Scotland from 1 April 2015, replacing stamp duty land tax which no longer applies in Scotland. The Scottish LBTT has a progressive rate structure, which means that the rates shown in the table below are marginal rates, payable on the portion of the total value which falls within each band. Tax bands and percentage tax rates are set by order of the Scottish Ministers.

| Residential transactions | | Non-residential transactions | | Non-residential leases | |
|---|---|---|---|---|---|
| | Rate % | | Rate % | | Rate % |
| Up to £145,000 | nil | Up to £150,000 | nil | Up to £150,000 | nil |
| £145,001 to £250,000 | 2.0 | £150,001 to £350,000 | 3.0 | Over £150,000 | 1.0 |
| £250,001 to £325,000 | 5.0 | Over £350,000 | 4.5 | | |
| £325,001 to £750,000 | 10.0 | | | | |
| Over £750,000 | 12.0 | | | | |

**Note**

As part of the Scottish Government's 2016–17 Draft Budget delivered to Parliament on 16 December 2015, the Finance Secretary proposed that LBTT rates would remain the same for 2016–17 but additional residential properties, such as buy to let or second homes where the relevant consideration exceeds £40,000, will be subject to a new LBTT supplement of 3% from 1 April 2016.

## Scottish Landfill Tax

## [¶26-300]  SLT rates from 1 April 2015

(*Landfill Tax (Scotland) Act* 2014; SSI 2016/93 and SSI 2016/94)

Rates are specified by order of the Scottish Ministers.

| | Standard rate (per tonne) £ | Lower rate (per tonne) £ | Scottish Landfill Communities Fund Credit rate % |
|---|---|---|---|
| From 1 April 2016 | 84.40 | 2.65 | 5.6 |
| From 1 April 2015 | 82.60 | 2.60 | 5.6 |

# SCOTTISH LAW

## [¶26-500]  Succession Scotland

**Prior rights of surviving spouse, on intestacy, in dwelling house and furniture**

(*Succession (Scotland) Act* 1964, s. 8–9; SSI 2011/436)

Prior rights apply where the deceased dies intestate leaving a spouse or civil partner. The surviving spouse or civil partner takes as follows:

Scottish Taxes

| Period | House £ | Furniture £ | Cash (children survive) £ | Cash (no children) £ |
|---|---|---|---|---|
| From 1/2/2012 | 473,000 | 29,000 | 50,000 | 89,000 |
| 1/6/2005–31/1/2012 | 300,000 | 24,000 | 42,000 | 75,000 |
| 1/4/1999–31/5/2005 | 130,000 | 22,000 | 35,000 | 58,000 |

## Legal rights

(HMRC manuals: IHTM12221)

Legal rights vest in beneficiaries by force of law and apply whether the deceased dies testate or intestate. Accordingly, rights by any provision in the deceased's will or rules of intestacy can only take effect once legal rights have been met. Prior rights may reduce or extinguish the estate that would otherwise be available to settle legal rights. Legal rights apply to the deceased's moveable estate only (which includes money, shares, cars, furniture, jewellery but excludes heritable property (land and buildings)).

| Surviving family | Right of surviving spouse or civil partner | Right of children | Deceased's part[1] |
|---|---|---|---|
| Spouse or civil partner and children | One-third | One-third | One-third |
| Spouse or civil partner but no children | One-half | N/A | One-half |
| Children but no spouse or civil partner | N/A | One-half | One-half |
| Neither spouse, civil partner or children | N/A | N/A | Whole moveable estate |

**Note**
[1] The balance of the estate is the part which the deceased was free to dispose of by will, or which passes under the rules of intestacy.

## Distributions under intestacy

(*Succession (Scotland) Act* 1964, s. 2)

After prior and legal rights have been satisfied, the remainder of the estate, both heritable and moveable devolves in the following order:

| Surviving family | Beneficiaries take: |
|---|---|
| **Children** | Whole estate |
| **Parents and brothers/sisters** Either of, or both, parents and also by brothers or sisters, but not by any prior relative | Surviving parent(s) take half; Surviving brothers and sisters take half |
| **Brother and sisters** Brothers or sisters, but not any prior relative | Surviving brothers and sisters take whole estate |
| **Parents** Either of, or both, parents, but not survived by any prior relative | Surviving parent(s) take whole estate |

| Surviving family | Beneficiaries take: |
|---|---|
| **Spouse**<br>Husband or a wife, but not any prior relative | Spouse takes whole estate |
| **Uncles or aunts**<br>Uncles or aunts (being brothers or sisters of either parent of the intestate), but not any prior relative | Surviving uncles and aunts take whole estate |
| **Grandparents**<br>A grandparent or grandparents (being a parent or parents of either parent of the intestate), but not any prior relative | Surviving grandparent(s) take whole estate |
| **Great uncles or aunts**<br>Brothers or sisters of any of his grandparents (being a parent or parents of either parent of the intestate), but not by any prior relative | Surviving brothers and sisters (or grandparents) take whole estate |
| **Other ancestors**<br>Where not survived by any prior relative, the ancestors of the intestate (being remoter than grandparents) generation by generation successively, without distinction between the paternal and maternal lines, shall have right to the whole of the intestate estate; so however that, failing ancestors of any generation, the brothers and sisters of any of those ancestors shall have right thereto before ancestors of the next more remote generation. | |

# WELSH TAXES

## [¶27-000]   Welsh taxes

(GoWA 2006, Pt. 4A; WA 2014, Pt. 2)

(Tax Reporter: ¶102-950)

The *Government of Wales Act* 1998 provided for the establishment of the National Assembly for Wales and for the transfer of all the powers of the Secretary of State for Wales to the new Assembly. The Assembly was established in 1999.

The *Government of Wales Act* (GoWA) 2006 led to the creation of a separate legislature (the National Assembly for Wales) and executive (the Welsh Government). The Assembly's enhanced legislative competence is set out in GoWA 2006, Sch. 7, Pt. 4 collectively known as the 'Assembly Act provisions'. These provisions enable the Assembly to legislate in relation to the subjects listed under the 20 headings in Sch. 7, as qualified by the exceptions and restrictions in that Schedule and in GoWA, s. 108.

The independent Commission on Devolution in Wales (the 'Silk Commission') was established in October 2011 to examine the financial and constitutional arrangements in Wales, and recommend ways in which they might be improved. The Commission reported in November 2012 making 33 recommendations to improve the financial accountability of the Assembly and the Welsh Government.

The *Wales Act* 2014, which received Royal Assent on 19 December 2014, implements almost all of the recommendations from the Silk Commission's first report on the devolution of tax and borrowing powers to the National Assembly for Wales and the Welsh Government.

The Act makes provision about the devolution of taxation powers to the Assembly and, in particular, makes provision about:

*   elections to and membership of the National Assembly for Wales;
*   the Welsh Assembly Government;
*   the setting by the Assembly of rates of income tax to be paid by Welsh taxpayer; and
*   borrowing by the Welsh Ministers.

The Act also provides for the Assembly to decide to trigger a referendum so that people in Wales can decide whether some of their income tax should be devolved; specifies taxes on land transactions and on disposals of waste to landfill as devolved taxes and makes provisions allowing the Assembly to bring in its own land transaction tax and its own tax on disposals of waste to landfill, as well as providing for additional taxes to be devolved to the Assembly by Order in council. Autumn Statement 2015, however, announced that the Government will legislate to remove the requirement for the Welsh Assembly to hold a referendum in order to implement the Welsh rates of income tax.

On 10 February 2015, the Welsh Government published a consultation document on the structure and rates for a new land transaction tax (LTT) to replace stamp duty in Wales in April 2018.

On 27 February 2015, new devolved powers for Wales were announced under the St David's Day Agreement and a command paper published setting out, in particular, a new model of devolution for Wales. A reserved powers model (as for Scotland) where the default position is that everything is devolved except those things that are reserved by Westminster will replace the existing model which specifies which matters are devolved.

The *Wales Act* 2017 received Royal Assent on 31 January 2017 and implements those elements of the St David's Day agreement which require legislative changes. The Act is an enabling Act and the majority of provisions set out the powers that are being transferred to the National Assembly for Wales and or the Welsh Ministers. In particular, the Act:

- amends the *Government of Wales Act* 2006 by moving to a reserved powers model for Wales (the same model as underpins the devolution settlement in Scotland);

- includes a declaration that the Assembly and the Welsh Ministers are considered permanent parts of the UK's constitutional arrangements and will not be abolished without a decision of the people of Wales, and that the UK Parliament will not normally legislate in devolved areas without the consent of the Assembly, whilst retaining sovereignty to do so.

- devolves further powers to the Assembly and in areas where there was a political consensus in support of devolution, including greater responsibility to run its own affairs (including deciding its name), responsibility for ports policy, speed limits, bus registration, taxi regulation, local government elections, sewerage and energy consenting (up to 350MW), marine licensing and conservation and energy consents in the Welsh offshore region, building regulations (including excepted energy building), power over all elements of Assembly elections and powers of the licensing of onshore oil and gas extraction.

## Administration of devolved taxes

On 25 April 2016, the *Tax Collection and Management (Wales) Act* 2016 received Royal Assent. The purpose of this Act is to put in place the legal framework necessary for the future collection and management of devolved taxes in Wales. In particular, the Act:

- establishes the Welsh Revenue Authority and makes provision about its organisation and main functions (which will be the collection and management of devolved taxes) (Pt. 2);

- makes provision about the assessment of devolved taxes (Pt. 3);

- makes provision about the Welsh Revenue Authority's investigatory powers, including provision about notices requiring information and the inspection of premises (Pt. 4);

- makes provision for and in connection with the imposition of penalties in relation to devolved taxes (Pt. 5);

- makes provision for interest to be payable on late payments to the Welsh Revenue Authority and on repayments by the Welsh Revenue Authority (Pt. 6);

- makes provision about payments to the Welsh Revenue Authority and the recovery of unpaid amounts (Pt. 7);

- makes provision for and in connection with reviews of and appeals against decisions of the Welsh Revenue Authority (Pt. 8);

- confers powers to make subordinate legislation about the investigation of criminal offences relating to devolved taxes (Pt. 9);

- contains provision that applies generally for the purposes of the Act (Pt. 10).

## [¶27-100]   Welsh rates of income tax

(WA 2014, s. 8–10; ITA 2007, s. 6B, 11B)

(Tax Reporter: ¶148-165)

Welsh Taxes

The *Wales Act* 2014, which received Royal Assent on 17 December 2014, legislates for new Welsh rates of income tax by conferring on the Assembly a power to set, by resolution, a Welsh basic, higher and additional rate of income tax, for 'Welsh taxpayers'. The new income tax provisions will be brought into force by HM Treasury Order, only if the majority of voters in a referendum vote in favour. The *Wales Act* 2014 provides for the Assembly to decide (by at least two-thirds majority) to trigger such a referendum so that people in Wales can decide whether some of their income tax should be devolved.

The Welsh basic rate, the Welsh higher rate and the Welsh additional rate for a tax year will be calculated under ITA 2007, s. 6B, as follows:

Step 1:

Take the basic rate, higher rate or additional rate.

Step 2:

Deduct ten percentage points.

Step 3:

Add the Welsh rate (if any) set by the National Assembly for Wales for that year for the purpose of calculating the Welsh basic rate, the Welsh higher rate or the Welsh additional rate (as the case may be).

The Welsh tax rates will only apply to non-saving, non-dividend income and applies for one tax year only, for the whole of that year.

A Welsh taxpayer is defined as an individual who is UK resident for income tax purposes for the tax year and who either:

* has a close connection with Wales;

* does not have a close connection with England, Scotland or Northern Ireland, and spends more days of that year in Wales than in any other part of the UK; or

* for the whole or any part of the year, is a member of Parliament for a constituency in Wales, a member of the European Parliament for Wales, or an Assembly member.

(GoWA 2006, s. 116E, as inserted by WA 2014, s. 8)

The system is similar in many respects to that currently in place in Scotland (see ¶26-100) and as with Scotland, the overall administration of Welsh income tax will remain with HMRC.

# NORTHERN IRISH TAXES

## [¶28-000]   Northern Irish taxes

(*Northern Ireland Act* 1998)

(Tax Reporter: ¶102-910)

The Agreement reached on Good Friday 1998, often referred to as the Belfast or Good Friday Agreement, and the subsequent *Northern Ireland Act* 1998 (as amended a number of times since 1998, particularly following the 2006 St Andrews Agreement) continue to form the basis of the constitutional structure in Northern Ireland with the devolved institutions in Northern Ireland being constituted under the *Northern Ireland Act* 1998.

The Northern Ireland devolution settlement gives legislative control over certain matters (known as 'transferred matters') to the Northern Ireland Assembly. In the main, these are in the economic and social field. The NI Assembly may also, in principle, legislate in respect of 'reserved' category matters subject to various consents, but has not yet done so to any significant degree.

Matters of national importance which, in the normal course of events, it is expected will remain the responsibility of HM Government and Westminster, are known as 'excepted matters', and the NI Assembly does not have competence to legislate on these. The *Northern Ireland Act* 1998, Sch. 2 sets out these areas.

Many UK-wide issues such as broadcasting and genetic research are known as 'reserved matters'. This category originally included policing and criminal justice, but those matters were devolved and, therefore, moved into the transferred field on 12 April 2010. The *Northern Ireland Act* 1998, Sch. 3 sets out which matters fall into the 'reserved' category.

Anything that is not explicitly reserved or excepted in Sch. 2 or 3 is deemed to be devolved and the Assembly has full legislative competence. It does not require consent from Westminster or HM Government to legislate.

Further details on devolution, including a full list of transferred, excepted and reserved matters can be found at www.gov.uk/devolution-settlement-northern-ireland.

## [¶28-100]   Northern Irish corporation tax

(*Corporation Tax (Northern Ireland) Act* 2015)

On 26 March 2015, the *Corporation Tax (Northern Ireland) Act* 2015 received Royal Assent. The Act makes provision for devolution of tax powers to the NI Assembly which should allow Northern Ireland to set its own rate of corporation tax for certain trading profits only from April 2017.

The Northern Ireland Assembly has the power to set the rate (including a nil rate) for one or more future financial years by way of a resolution. Corporation tax will then be charged at the Northern Ireland rate on Northern Ireland profits as distinct from mainstream profits. Once set, the Northern Ireland Assembly may cancel that rate by resolution, which will have effect provided the cancelling resolution is passed before the beginning of the financial year to which the rate applies. If a rate is not set by resolution for a financial year, the rate for that year will be the rate set for the previous financial year. Until the Northern Ireland Assembly exercises the power to set a rate for the first time, the Northern Ireland rate will be the UK main rate.

The rate, in general, will apply to all of the trading profits of a company if that company is a micro, small or medium-sized enterprise (SME), and the company's employee time and costs fall largely in Northern Ireland. It will also apply to a corporate partner's share of the profits of a partnership trade if that company and partnership are both SMEs and the partnership's employee time and costs fall largely in Northern Ireland. The rate will also apply to the profits of large companies, and (in the case of a corporate partner not covered by the SME rules referred to above) to a corporate partner's share of the profits of a partnership that are attributable to a Northern Ireland trading presence, that presence being termed as a 'Northern Ireland regional establishment' (NIRE).

A Memorandum of Understanding (MoU) has been signed between HMRC and the Northern Ireland Executive's Department of Finance and Personnel, Northern Ireland (DFPNI) setting out arrangements for implementing a devolved corporation tax rate. The MoU includes provisions on developing IT and administrative systems and on recharging to DFPNI costs incurred by HMRC on implementation and is available at www.gov.uk/government/uploads/system/uploads/attachment_data/file/485924/NICT_MoU_FINAL_signed.pdf.

HMRC's draft guidance on the operation of the Northern Ireland corporation tax legislation is available at www.gov.uk/government/uploads/system/uploads/attachment_data/file/554921/160922_Draft_guidance_Northern_Ireland_rate_of_Corporation_Tax.pdf.

**Rate from 2018**

The Northern Ireland parties have indicated that they wish to pursue the implementation of a new Northern Ireland rate of corporation tax of 12.5% in April 2018 (Autumn Statement 2015).

# INDEX

*References are to paragraph numbers.*

Index

Index

Index

Index

Index

Index

Index